THE PRACTITIONER'S GUIDE TO DEFENSE OF EPL CLAIMS

THIRD EDITION

AMY S. WILSON
EDITOR

AMERICAN BAR ASSOCIATION
Defending Liberty
Pursuing Justice

Cover design by Anthony Nuccio/ABA Publishing.

Printed in the United States of America.

17 16 15 14 13 5 4 3 2 1

Library of Congress Cataloging-in-Publication Data is on file.

ISBN: 978-1-62722-016-3

Contents

FOREWORD

Employment Practices Liability (EPL) insurance is a growing phenomenon in the insurance industry. The Practitioner's Guide to Defense of EPL Claims is provided by the Tort Trial and Insurance Practice Section of the American Bar Association and covers, in part, the fundamentals of an EPL policy, investigating EPL-covered claims, and litigation of EPL claims.

This book is a unique and invaluable tool for the employment law practitioner and others interested in EPL insurance. The contributing authors are all experts in their fields, and the compilation, expansive in scope, is reader-friendly and a valuable resource.

About the Editor

Amy S. Wilson is a member in the Indianapolis, Indiana, office of Frost Brown Todd LLC and practices in the firm's Labor and Employment Practice Group. She concentrates her practice in employment litigation and employer counseling, which includes the frequent handling of EPL Claims. Ms. Wilson defends employers against claims arising under Title VII, the ADEA, the ADAAA, the FMLA, the FLSA, and state law claims. In addition, Ms. Wilson counsels employers on all aspects of the employer-employee relationship, provides management and employee training, and drafts agreements, policies, and procedures. Ms. Wilson also speaks frequently on employment law topics for a variety of business and professional organizations. Ms. Wilson is Co-Chair of the Employment Law and Litigation Committee of the ABA Tort Trial and Insurance Practice Section. Ms. Wilson received her JD degree, summa cum laude, from the Indiana University Robert H. McKinney School of Law and a BA from Hanover College.

About the Authors

John Richard Carrigan Sr. litigates employment matters in Alabama and Florida, including two forty-day trials that involved statistical evidence. He received his BA and MBA from Florida State University, and his JD from Harvard Law School. He is a shareholder in the Birmingham, Alabama, office of Ogletree Deakins.

Roxella T. Cavazos is a labor and employment lawyer who represents employers and management in litigation and administrative agency claims and counsels employers on legal compliance and every aspect of the employer-employee relationship. Ms. Cavazos is board certified in labor and employment law by the Texas Board of Legal Specialization. She has served in ABA leadership positions and contributed to ABA books, including *Employee Benefits Law*, published by the ABA Labor and Employment Section, and *Litigating the Employment Discrimination Case*, published by the ABA Tort Trial and Insurance Practice Section. Ms. Cavazos currently practices with Atlas Hall & Rodriguez, LLP, in McAllen, Texas.

Michael Corey is a member of the health care practice group at Bricker & Eckler in Columbus, Ohio. A 2012 graduate of the Moritz College of Law at Ohio State University, Mr. Corey has a bachelor's degree from Duke University and a master's degree from the Ohio State University School of Education Policy and Leadership. Prior to becoming a lawyer, Mr. Corey worked as a consultant for the Ohio Board of Regents and as a legal fellow to U.S. senator Sherrod Brown.

Matthew Effland, a shareholder with Ogletree Deakins, represents business owners and managers nationwide in nearly every aspect of employment law. In addition to defending clients in state and federal court, Mr. Effland enjoys an active counseling and training practice that focuses on many of the more administratively complex areas of the law, including FMLA compliance, ADA accommodation, and employee privacy. In addition to providing in-depth client counseling, Mr. Effland is a regular speaker at state and national events, including the Annual Conference for the Society for Human Resource Management (SHRM). He is licensed and has practiced in California, Indiana, and Florida.

Frederick B. Finberg, shareholder and director of the Bennett Law Firm, P.A., represents management clients throughout the Northeast (and occasionally beyond) in both state and federal court as well as before administrative agencies, including human-rights commissions, EEOC, OSHA, state and federal wage and hour divisions, and the National Labor Relations Board. Mr. Finberg has a near-perfect record over the last twenty-two years defeating union organizing efforts. He also advises employers on discharge and discipline, FMLA, ADA, internal investigations, and all other aspects of the employer-employee relationship. Mr. Finberg served on the faculty of the University of Southern Maine, Department of Continuing Education for Business, teaching personnel law for almost twenty years. He received his BA degree, cum laude, from Brandeis University and his JD degree, cum laude, from the Boston University School of Law. He is ranked by Chambers USA as a leading lawyer in labor and employment law and has been selected by his peers to be included in *The Best Lawyers in America*. He is a member of the Cumberland County, Maine State, and American Bar associations as well as the Defense Research Institute. He is a former member of the board of directors and a current corporator of the Boys and Girls Clubs of Southern Maine, a former president of the Board of Trustees of the Portland Public Library, and a past president of Temple Beth El.

Kenneth M. Gorenberg is a partner in the Chicago office of Barnes & Thornburg LLP, where he is a member of the Litigation Department and the Policyholder Recovery, Toxic Tort, Construction, and Commercial Litigation Practice Groups. Mr. Gorenberg has practiced insurance coverage law across the country for more than twenty years. He also runs a robust national practice defending asbestos bodily injury cases. He is Co-Chair of the Asbestos Subcommittee of the Insurance Coverage Litigation Committee of the ABA Section of Litigation.

Margaret J. Grover is a trained and experienced mediator who enjoys resolving litigated cases and workplace disputes. She received her primary mediation training at Straus Institute for Dispute Resolution. She has fifteen years of dispute-resolution experience and nearly thirty years representing and advising employers on all aspects of employment law. Her areas of emphasis, in addition to dispute resolution, include personnel policies and procedures, human resources and employment consulting, workplace training and investigations, and employment litigation. Ms. Grover also speaks frequently on employment-related issues for a variety of business and professional organizations. She practices with the California-based law firm of Kronick, Moskovitz, Tiedemann & Girard, where she heads the San Francisco Bay area office.

Adam Hanley is an associate in the Columbus, Ohio, office of Frost Brown Todd LLC. He is a member of the Labor and Employment Practice Group. He has defended employers in state and federal court against claims brought under Title VII of the Civil Rights Act, the Family and Medical Leave Act, the Fair Labor Standards Act, and the Ohio Workers' Compensation Act. Mr. Hanley also regularly advises clients on a range of employment matters, including conducting proper investigations, drafting and enforcing workplace policies, and all other aspects of the employment relationship.

Todd J. Kaiser, a shareholder with Ogletree Deakins, concentrates his practice on state and federal court litigation and general labor and employment law. He has represented clients in lawsuits and administrative proceedings involving employment contracts, noncompetition / trade-secret disputes, commercial disputes, class action litigation, EEO claims, ERISA claims, wrongful discharge, labor arbitrations, and wage and hour disputes.

Catherine F. Lacho is a managing associate in the Columbus, Ohio, office of Frost Brown Todd LLC and practices in the firm's Labor and

Employment Practice Group. Ms. Lacho represents employers and insurance companies in both state and federal court as well as before numerous administrative agencies, including the Equal Employment Opportunity Commission and the National Labor Relations Board. Ms. Lacho holds a JD and an MBA from the College of William and Mary and a BA from Denison University.

Sandra R. McCandless, a Partner in the San Francisco office of the global law firm Dentons, represents California, national, and international employers in all types of employment litigation and disputes and counseling matters. Sandra is a member of the American Bar Association Board of Governors and the former Chair of its Tort Trial and Insurance Practice Section, the Chair of the Employment and Immigration Committee of the Inter-Pacific Bar Association, and a Member of the College of Labor and Employment. She also serves as a neutral arbitrator for the American Arbitration Association. Sandra is a graduate of Harvard College and the Georgetown University Law Center.

Gregory V. Mersol is chair of BakerHostetler's Cleveland Labor and Employment Law Practice Group. He received his BA and JD degrees from Case Western Reserve University, where he was the research editor of the law review. Mr. Mersol has represented employers in employment disputes since 1985 and is the editor and contributor to BakerHostetler's employment class action blog, located at www.employmentclassactionreport.com.

Kerry E. Notestine is a shareholder in the Houston office of Littler Mendelson and has represented management for thirty years in all aspects of employment matters, including litigation under federal, state, and local antidiscrimination statutes, as well as the common law; administrative proceedings before various federal and state government agencies; and counseling employers regarding employment issues, particularly leaves and reductions in force. Mr. Notestine's book, *Employment Law Trials: A Practical Guide*, published in 2005 by LexisNexis Publishing, is a leading work on the trials of employment cases. A graduate of the University of Virginia Law School, Mr. Notestine is board certified in employment and labor law by the Texas Board of Legal Specialization and was named Lawyer of the Year, Litigation, Labor & Employment, Houston, for 2013 by the publication *Best Lawyers in America.*

Christine Robek is Labor Counsel for AK Steel Corporation, where she manages employment litigation and advises the company on a wide variety of day-to-day labor and employment matters.

Benjamin W. Tull is a staff lawyer in the Chicago office of Barnes & Thornburg LLP, where he is a member of the Litigation Department. He holds a JD from IIT Chicago-Kent College of Law and a BA from Sarah Lawrence College.

Carolyn M. Wendel is an associate in the Chicago office of Barnes & Thornburg LLP, where she is a member of the Litigation Department and Commercial Litigation and Product Liability Practice Groups. Ms. Wendel earned her JD from the University of Notre Dame Law School, and earned her BA from Saint Louis University.

Acknowledgments

The editor would like to thank Beau Zoeller, Rachel Moore Schafer, and Janeen Feinberg, attorneys with the Indianapolis, Indiana office of Frost Brown Todd, LLC, for their assistance in editing this book. The editor would also like to thank the Chubb Group of Insurance Companies for their lending of a sample policy and endorsements to include in Chapter 1.

CHAPTER 1
Employment Practices Liability Insurance

Amy Wilson and Catherine Lacho

I. Origins and Evolution of Employment Practices Liability Insurance

Employment practices liability insurance (EPL) is a relatively recent phenomenon in the property-casualty insurance industry, tracing its origins only to the late 1980s. Indeed, the first policies offered were limited in scope and amounted to a cautious testing of the waters by the insurance industry. The policies offered coverage only for the costs of defense, for a limited period (typically for four years), and were subject to a monetary limit of liability. To the extent these policy forms are still available today, the demand for them would be minimal, given the expansion of the coverage since the 1980s. And the coverage has expanded. In 1991, there were approximately five carriers for EPL

The editor and authors would like to thank Joseph P. Monteleone for his significant contributions to chapter 1 in the second edition of this book.

insurance.[1] Now, there are more than fifty carriers with a volume of business of $1.6 billion just in the United States.[2]

In the 1990s, three major insurers began offering traditional liability policies covering not only defense expenses, but also "indemnity" amounts such as settlements and judgments coverage. The now-defunct Reliance Insurance Company was perhaps the first of the three to market a product that was designed for and limited to claims alleging a wrongful discharge from employment. Lexington Insurance Company, a member of the American International Group (AIG), and Federal Insurance Company, one of the Chubb Group of Insurance Companies, soon followed suit with policies covering not only wrongful terminations but also events of discrimination and sexual harassment, regardless of whether an employment termination had occurred.

Two seminal events occurred shortly thereafter that caused sales of the EPL product to increase dramatically and continue to sell with increasing frequency to the present. First, the Civil Rights Act of 1991 was enacted, and, for the first time, plaintiffs were able to recover significant compensatory and punitive damages for violations of Title VII of the Civil Rights Act of 1964. From a practical point of view, this energized plaintiffs' lawyers to bring more of these suits, because the damages caps could be as high as $300,000, in the case of the largest employers, and would be available in addition to back-pay awards and other nonmonetary and injunctive relief.

The second event was more in the nature of atmospherics, but one that certainly put the issue of workplace sexual harassment in the forefront of the business, legal, and general news media. In October 1991, the nation became fixated on the televised hearings for the nomination of Clarence Thomas to the U.S. Supreme Court. Regardless of the

1. Richard S. Betterley, The Betterley Report: Employment Practices Liability Insurance Market Survey 2011: Rates Begin to Firm, but Plenty of Competition Remains 3–4 (2011), *available at* http://betterley.com/samples/EPLI11_nt.pdf.

2. *Id.*

political overtones and ramifications of Justice Thomas's nomination, sexual harassment as a workplace phenomenon became widely known. As sexual harassment was actionable as a form of Title VII discrimination, the hearings, coupled with the newly available damages for these claims, caused the number of charges of discrimination involving sexual harassment filed before the Equal Employment Opportunity Commission (EEOC) to soar beginning in 1992. There was a concomitant rise in other discrimination claims as well, the amount of which continued to increase throughout the decade and has now leveled off at an amount far above the number of claims filed in 1991 and earlier years. Various state agencies having jurisdiction parallel to the EEOC, such as the California Department of Fair Employment and Housing, saw a similar rise in allegations of harassment and discrimination. As neither the EEOC nor the various state agencies directly precluded a claimant's ultimate right to sue, the number of matters in litigation also increased dramatically.

Sales of the EPL insurance product grew with claims and litigation until the insurance expanded in scope to the form discussed throughout the remainder of this chapter. A specimen policy form, including application, declarations, and endorsements, of Chubb Insurance are included as Appendices to this chapter. Although forms and endorsements can and do vary from one insurer to another, the Chubb form is fairly typical of the core product on the market today.

II. Fundamentals of the EPL Policy

The following is an overview of a typical EPL policy form, focusing on certain claim triggers and features that differentiate the EPL form from coverages that the practitioner outside the insurance arena may find more familiar, such as commercial general liability or a homeowner's or automobile policy.

The EPL policy is typically written on a claims-made basis. This means that the coverage is triggered when a claim is first made against an insured under and during the term of the policy. This differs from the typical automobile liability policy, which is triggered by the date of an accident, even though the actual claim may be made after the policy has expired.

In addition to this claims-made trigger, the claim itself must also be reported to the insurer within a certain time period. The most open ended of these reporting requirements simply states that the claim must be reported to the insurer as soon as practicable. A number of courts have held that an insurer can only deny coverage for late reporting under the "as soon as practicable" language if it can establish that the insured's late reporting of the claim prejudiced the insurer.[3] Prejudice is often difficult to establish because the test is generally whether the insurer would have done anything differently had it received more timely notice of the claim.[4]

An alternative reporting requirement, and one at the opposite end of the spectrum from "as soon as practicable," mandates that claims be made and reported during the policy period. Under a strict interpretation, this would require an insured to report a claim first made in the waning hours of the last day of the policy period to the insurer before the clock literally struck midnight on that day. Once commonplace, these harsh provisions are much less prevalent in EPL and other claims-made policy forms today.

The most typical reporting requirement requires reporting as soon as practicable, but in no event later than a fixed date after the policy has expired. The most common fixed date provision is a "bright line" drawn sixty days after policy expiration. Courts have routinely enforced

3. *See, e.g., Aetna Cas. & Sur. Co v. Dow Chem. Co.*, 10 F. Supp. 2d 800, 815 (E.D. Mich. 1998). But, many states have held that these so-called notice-prejudice rules do not apply to claims-made policies. *See, e.g., MGIC Indem. Corp. v. Cent. Bank of Monroe, La.*, 838 F.2d 1382, 1385–86 (5th Cir. 1988) (Louisiana); *Burns v. Int'l Ins. Co.*, 929 F.2d 1422, 1425 (9th Cir. 1991) (California); *Am. Home Assurance Co. v. Int'l Ins. Co.*, 684 N.E.2d 14, 16 (N.Y. 1997) (New York).

4. *See, e.g., Guardian Trust Co. v. Am. States Ins. Co.*, No. 95-4073-SAC, 1996 WL 509638, at *6 (D. Kan. July 30, 1996) (insurer must show it would have handled claim differently if it had had timely notice and the different handling would have reduced the loss exposure).

such provisions, and most jurisdictions will not require the insurer to establish that it has been prejudiced in the event there is noncompliance with the reporting requirement.[5]

It is important to note that, where there is both a "claims made" and "claims reported" trigger to be satisfied, compliance with one and not the other will result in an absence of coverage under the policy in which the claim is first reported, as well as under the policy in which the claim was first made.

In addition to reporting requirements, another prominent feature of EPL policies is that coverage for defense expenses is part of the limit of liability. This is contrasted with a general or automobile liability policy in which the insurer has an unlimited duty to defend despite settlement and judgment amounts often being capped by the contract. As such, the EPL buyer must be prudent in obtaining sufficient policy limits to cover the combined indemnity and defense exposures it faces. Further, as EPL policies are typically written with an annual aggregate limit of liability, the purchasing decision must be made with both expected frequency and severity of claims in mind.

Also, unlike the general liability arena, defense expenses under an EPL policy are typically subject to a deductible or retention amount. Setting this amount is typically a matter of negotiation between the insurer and the policyholder, but many insurers will set minimum retention amounts to avoid exposure to relatively routine and nonsevere claims. Likewise, the buyer who seeks only protection from the more catastrophic claims will seek a higher retention to keep premium costs down. Retentions of $25,000 or less per claim will generally require the insurer's focused involvement in all such claims, whereas a minimum retention of $250,000 will likely result in the vast majority of employment claims being resolved solely at the policyholder's expense, even when defense expenses are added to indemnity amounts.

5. *See, e.g., Burns*, 929 F.2d at 1425; *see also Heydar v. Westport Ins. Corp.*, 158 F. App'x 774 (9th Cir. 2005), *T.H.E. Ins. Co. v. P.T.P., Inc.*, 628 A.2d 223 (Md. 1993).

As is the case with most claims-made forms in other product lines, EPL policies contain an "awareness provision" that allows an insured to "report" potential claims during the policy period. Awareness reporting is not mandatory on the part of the insured, but it affords the insured an opportunity to "lock in" coverage for actual claims that may arise later. Awareness provisions require a certain amount of specificity to support the possibility of a claim before coverage being locked in. For example, a list of all workers terminated in a recent reduction in force will be insufficient to secure coverage for a future claim by any of the terminated employees after the EPL policy has expired.[6] If the insured can produce evidence that a particular employee threatened suit on the basis of age discrimination, however, that may well trigger the awareness provision and lock in later coverage.

It is important to understand the benefit of reporting potential claims to the incumbent EPL insurer, particularly if that policy is not going to be renewed. In applying for a replacement EPL policy, the applicant will be asked if it is aware of any act, error, omission, or circumstance that might give rise to a claim. If such acts, errors, omissions, or circumstances exist, any claim arising therefrom will be excluded from coverage under the new policy. Thus, if the insured has not locked in coverage, the insured would be left without coverage entirely.

For similar reasons, under certain conditions EPL policies also offer "discovery" or "extended reporting" periods. Essentially, in exchange for an additional premium, the insured can extend the policy for a fixed period (typically one year at a percentage of the actual policy premium), during which it can report claims that arise from acts that took place while, or in some cases even before, the policy was in force. Purchasing an extended reporting period is beneficial when the insured may be

6. *See FDIC v. Mijalis*, 15 F.3d 1314, 1332 (5th Cir. 1994) (general demand for regulatory compliance does not qualify as notice of a specific wrongful act); *see also Sapp v. Greif*, 961 F. Supp. 243, 247 (D. Kan. 1997), *aff'd*, No. 97-3200, 1998 WL 165116 (10th Cir. 1998) (insured must provide details concerning circumstances and reasons for anticipating a future claim).

moving coverage to another insurer who is unwilling to grant coverage for wrongful acts committed prior to the inception of its policy period.

Similarly, many carriers now offer prior-acts coverage. Prior-acts coverage is a valuable protection that used to be difficult to obtain because underwriters were reluctant to insure the prior activities of an employer. As carriers competed for business, however, prior-acts coverage became an attractive coverage for insureds. As carriers became more comfortable with the coverage, it became easier to offer the coverage even to new insureds. For many carriers, there is now no additional cost for prior-acts coverage.[7]

III. Defense Issues

The areas in which EPL policy forms vary greatly, both among different insurers and even among alternative forms and endorsements offered by the same insurer, regard who has the duty to defend and the concomitant right to select defense counsel.

The selection of defense counsel has been a source of controversy. Insurers generally prefer to appoint counsel on their regular defense panels because of that counsel's familiarity with the insurers' practices and procedures and because of the counsel's willingness to handle employment-related cases at a set hourly rate. Insureds, on the other hand, often prefer to have claims against them handled by their regular employment law counsel because of their familiarity with the law and with the insureds' operations.

Generally, if the policy provides that the insurer has the right and duty to defend, it will also expressly, or by implication of law, also provide that the insurer has the right to select defense counsel on behalf of its insureds. This is no different from most other business and personal liability forms available on the market today. If there is a conflict in interest between insured and insurer, state law may require the insurer to relinquish its right to select counsel and to allow the insured to select

7. BETTERLEY, *supra* note 1, at 12.

its own counsel to be paid by the insurer pursuant to the terms and conditions of the policy.[8]

The other major variation in this area is a policy form that permits the insured to select its own defense counsel, subject to prior notice to and consent by the insurer, "which shall not be unreasonably withheld." This is similar to the language in most directors' and officers' (D&O) liability policies. Though this latter variation appears to be, *prima facie*, the more attractive, the insured should bear in mind the following:

- Under duty to defend policies, many jurisdictions will require the insurer to defend the entire matter, even though only a small number of counts or allegations may be within the scope of coverage.[9] Under the non-duty to defend variation, however, the insurer will more likely be able to secure an allocation of defense costs as between covered and noncovered claims.[10]
- The ability to choose one's counsel does not come with an unfettered license. The insurer can legitimately refuse to consent to counsel who is not sufficiently experienced or otherwise qualified, and the insurer will typically only be required to pay the rates in place for its own approved employment litigators in that jurisdiction.[11] This could mean that the insured may find itself bearing a significant portion of the defense expenses if its chosen counsel will not adjust rates.
- Responsible EPL insurers use pre-approved counsel with employment litigation experience and qualifications. Thus, an insured's

---

8. *See, e.g.*, *Gafcon, Inc. v. Ponsor & Assocs.*, 120 Cal. Rptr. 2d 392, 406 (Cal. Ct. App. 2002); *see also* CAL. CIV. CODE § 2860.

9. *See Fulton Bellows, LLC v. Fed. Ins. Co.*, 662 F. Supp. 2d 976, 985 (E.D. Tenn. 2009).

10. *See Fed. Realty Inv. Trust v. Pac. Ins. Co.*, 760 F. Supp. 533, 537 (D. Md. 1991); *Cont'l Cas. Co. v. Bd. of Educ.*, 489 A.2d 536, 544 (Md. 1985).

11. *See, e.g.*, *Ctr. Found. v. Chicago Ins. Co.*, 278 Cal. Rptr. 13, 20–21(Cal. Ct. App. 1991).

fear of being provided with less-qualified representation is often unfounded.

- The ability to select counsel does not necessarily mean that the insurer will consent to multiple counsel, where individual or multiple defendants are named, if there is no demonstrable conflict of interest between or among insured defendants.

When the insured insists on using its own counsel and a negotiated rate cannot be agreed upon, one approach is to permit the insured to use its own counsel if the insured agrees to pay the difference between the highest rate the insurer is willing to pay and the lowest rate the insured's counsel is willing to accept.

In a duty to defend situation, the insurer typically also retains the right and obligation to settle the claim in appropriate circumstances. In forms in which the settlement obligation may be reserved to the insured along with the duty to defend, there may be a "consent to settle" provision, which is sometimes referenced pejoratively as a "hammer clause."

A hammer clause typically provides that if the insurer obtains an opportunity to settle—an offer that the plaintiff has stated he or she would accept—then, if the insured refuses to consent to the insurer settling the claim, the insurer's liability under the policy will be capped at the amount of the foregone settlement plus defense expenses incurred through that point. In effect, the insurer would have no further financial liability should the insured elect to continue with litigation.

Hammer clauses have been criticized as giving undue leverage to the EPL insurer,[12] although they create a situation that is no different from other liability policies in which the insurer can always elect to

12. The primary criticism is that the insured is arguably penalized if they "bet wrong" and insist the case not be settled. There is no concomitant penalty on the insurer for insisting that the case be settled at too high a price because the fact of that can never be objectively established. Of course, an insurer always faces the specter of potential exposure beyond its policy limits whenever it can reasonably be established that it refused to settle within its policy limits.

settle regardless of the wishes of its insured. Nonetheless, in the current EPL market, this provision is often removed or significantly limited by endorsement.

Because hammer clauses are criticized, some policies now contain a so-called "soft" hammer clause. A soft hammer clause calls for the insurer and insured to share any costs exceeding the amount for which the case could have been settled if not for the insured's refusal. This clause addresses the fact that, at times and for a multitude of reasons, it is in the mutual interest of the insurer and insured to continue to litigate a case that could have been settled at a favorable cost, and that they should both share the risk of an unfavorable outcome.

Most EPL policies also provide that the insureds have a duty to cooperate with the insurer in the defense of a claim. This is usually not problematic in the case of a duty to defend form, but, in other variations, securing the cooperation of defense counsel not selected by the insurer is often an issue. This may occur for a number of the following reasons, not all of which may be legitimate as a matter of the policy and applicable law:

- Counsel is unfamiliar with insurance defense work, and the insurer needs to receive frequent reporting to maintain adequate case reserves and to assess litigation continuously, including settlement strategy.
- Counsel is concerned that factual information developed in the course of investigating and defending the claim may be used adversely by the insurer with regard to coverage issues.[13] It should be noted that most jurisdictions would impose the same ethical constraints on both counsel selected by the insurer and independent counsel selected by the insured.[14]

13. *See infra* chapter 12.

14. *Newcomb v. Meiss*, 116 N.W.2d 593, 598 (Minn. 1962) (the lawyer who represents an insured owes him "undeviating and single allegiance" whether the lawyer is compensated by the insurer or the insured).

- Counsel and the insured do not want to alarm the insurer regarding the severity of the claim because the policy is due for renewal.
- Counsel believes it has no obligation to report to the insurer because it is not its client. Jurisdictions differ on this issue, but the practical bottom line is that the insurer needs to make an *informed* decision about whether to settle, including when and for what amount, or make other litigation-related tactical and strategic decisions.

IV. What Constitutes a Covered Claim?

The earliest EPL policy forms somewhat simplistically limited their coverage solely to matters in suit. Over the years, EPL insurers came to realize that their early intervention in the dispute process ensured more control and better results from the resolution process. Particularly after the enactment of the Civil Rights Act of 1991, insurers thought it better to provide coverage for EEOC and state agency proceedings and, thus, to become involved in the selection of counsel and possible opportunities to settle at an early, prelitigation stage.

Today, the typical EPL form deems a covered claim to be first made when any of the following first takes place:

- The insured receives a written demand for relief that is within the scope of the policy's coverage. This can be from the claimant or someone on behalf of the claimant, but most policies will not recognize oral demands because of issues of proof as to content and timing of receipt.
- A written demand or request for mediation or arbitration.
- Receipt by the insured of a Notice of a Charge of Discrimination from the EEOC or similar notice from another federal, state, or local agency.
- A civil proceeding commences by service of a complaint or similar pleading. It is important that the claim is only deemed to be first made upon receipt of a summons or similar filing. The mere filing of a complaint can have legal effects, such as tolling of a statute of

> limitation, but it would be unfair to encumber the insured with a duty to report something about which it does not know or reasonably should not know. Of course, if an insured receives a "courtesy copy" of a filed, but not served, complaint, the courtesy copy serves as a written demand.

As a general rule, the broader the definition of the term *claim* in this respect, the more advantageous it is to the insured. One caveat is that once a claim is made, the time frame within which to report it to the insurer begins to run. This can have ramifications for which, if any, an EPL insurer must cover an "event" that may or may not be a claim under all possibly applicable policies.

V. What Constitutes a Covered Loss?

EPL policies are generally worded broadly to cover all amounts that must be paid as defined "Loss." Although each policy must be carefully reviewed in its entirety, generally speaking, Loss will include the following:

- Judgment amounts;
- Settlement amounts;
- Amounts in the nature of back or front pay;
- Pre- and post-judgment interest awards;
- Awards of plaintiff fees and costs; and
- Defense expenses.

Though the above items constitute a basic inventory of what is covered under most EPL policy forms, scrutinizing the actual policy definitions, exclusions, and conditions is critical to determining what may not be covered in the first instance or otherwise carved out from the broad coverage grant described above.

Among the items typically not covered as Loss are the following:

- Wages, salaries, benefits, or expenses of any individual or entity insured under the policy.
- Punitive, exemplary, or multiplied damages. Many forms allow for such coverage if permitted by the most favorable and applicable law. Many states prohibit coverage for punitive damages, however, so most carriers offer separate coverage, either through a most favorable venue provision or with an offshore wraparound in a jurisdiction that does not frown on the coverage.
- Fines, penalties, or taxes.
- Amounts due under an express employment contract.
- Stock options, deferred compensation, and other items constituting compensation or benefits.
- Wage awards under the Fair Labor Standards Act (FLSA) or state law in this area. Disputes remain, however, as to whether wage awards under the FLSA or state law constitute covered loss.[15] Though often requested by insureds, wage and hour coverage continues to be rare because carriers are unwilling to cover what many see as a business risk under the control of the employer.[16]
- Injunctive relief, including the cost of complying with an award of or settlement in the nature of injunctive relief.

VI. What Are the Covered Perils?

Although not denominated specifically as such in the policy language, it is helpful to view the policy in terms of what "perils" are being insured. Many early policy forms were limited to coverage for employment

15. *Compare Cal. Dairies, Inc. v. RSUI Indem. Co.*, 617 F. Supp. 2d 1023 (E.D. Cal. 2009) (denying coverage for FLSA claims under directors' and officers' insurance policy), and *Payless Shoesource, Inc. v. Travelers Cos., Inc.*, 585 F.3d 1366 (10th Cir. 2009) (denying coverage for FLSA claims under employment practices liability insurance policy), *with Lincoln Cnty. Ambulance Dist. v. Pac. Emp'rs Ins. Co.*, 15 S.W.3d 739 (Mo. Ct. App. 1998) (finding coverage for FLSA claims under errors and omissions insurance policy), and *BLaST Intermediate Unit 17 v. CNA Ins. Cos.*, 674 A.2d 687 (Pa. 1996) (finding coverage for FLSA claims under board of education liability insurance policy).

16. Betterley, *supra* note 1, at 8.

terminations only. The forms have evolved to include a range of perils, limited only by the definitions, exclusions, other provisions of the policy, and applicable insurance law and public policy on the insurability of certain hazards.

Wrongful termination remains among the principal covered perils, and most forms include it in covered termination events such as constructive discharge or retaliatory discharge from employment.

Discrimination is another major covered peril. Though many forms detail the types of discrimination covered, this may be more of a limitation than an enhancement to the policyholder because the law in this area continues to expand, and certain acts of discrimination may be actionable in some jurisdictions but not others. Where discrimination types are listed as covered, it is always in the policyholder's interest to have included an omnibus clause such as "or other protected class or characteristic established under applicable federal, state, or local law."

Another principal peril is harassment. Of course, under Title VII and many state laws, sexual harassment is actionable as a form of prohibited sex discrimination. Nonetheless, it should be listed separately as an insured peril and expanded to include quid pro quo sexual harassment,[17] hostile work environment harassment, and harassment based on race or other classes and characteristics set forth in the applicable federal, state, and local laws.

Though many EPL insurers have backed away from coverage for "all other workplace torts" or similar language, EPL policies will generally respond to the following perils:

- Refusal to hire.
- Refusal to promote or grant tenure.

---

17. Quid pro quo harassment occurs when (1) job benefits, including employment, promotion, salary increases, shift or work assignments, performance expectations, and other conditions of employment are made contingent on the provision of sexual favors, or (2) the rejection of a sexual advance or request for sexual favors results in a tangible employment detriment. *Burlington Indus., Inc. v. Ellerth*, 524 U.S. 742 (1998).

- Wrongful discipline or demotion.
- Employment-related defamation or invasion of privacy. It should be noted that this might overlap with coverage provided by a commercial general liability policy.
- Violations of the Family and Medical Leave Act (FMLA).

It is rare that an employment-related claim does not involve one or more of the three major perils or the lesser perils discussed above. Nonetheless, insurers may be willing to entertain an endorsement to the policy to provide coverage for a particular peril specific to an industry or jurisdiction and not otherwise adequately addressed in the policy form.

For instance, one optional coverage that has become increasingly popular with insureds is third-party coverage. Third-party coverage essentially provides coverage for claims of discrimination, including harassment, brought by a company's vendors or customers, or employees of those customers or vendors. An example of such a claim would be the servers at Texas Roadhouse suing their employer for permitting patrons of the restaurant to refuse to be served by African Americans.[18] The rise in this type of coverage follows the concomitant rise in third-party claims.[19] Coverage initially applied only to discrimination, but due to the rise in third-party claims, it now applies to both discrimination and harassment.[20] All but one of the major carriers offer third-party coverage as part of their EPL form.[21]

In addition to concerns about the increase in third-party claims, there has been a great deal of discussion about social networking and bullying and their relationship to EPL coverage. Generally, though both social

---

18. *Mutua v. Tex. Roadhouse Mgmt. Corp.*, 753 F. Supp. 2d 954 (D.S.D. 2010) (holding that an employer could be liable when permitting patrons to refuse to be served by minority waitstaff).

19. *See, e.g.*, *Beckford v. Dep't. of Corr.*, 605 F.3d 951 (11th Cir. 2010).

20. BETTERLEY, *supra* note 1, at 8–9.

21. *Id.*

networking and bullying represent new avenues for exposure, little needs to be changed in terms of policy drafting to cover these claims.[22]

VII. Key Policy Exclusions

As with all liability insurance policies, the typical EPL form contains a number of important exclusions. The most common exclusions are discussed below.

An important caveat to bear in mind is that not all exclusions are contained in the "Exclusions" section of the policy. This is not to suggest attempts on the part of insurers to obfuscate or trick, but rather it is an evolution of customary practice and usage in the business.

Most policies will use the definition of the term *Loss* to set forth an exclusion for items such as penalties, fines, and taxes. Punitive and exemplary (including other multiplied) damages are also addressed here, as well as matters uninsurable under the applicable law. This latter provision is often subject to some debate as to what is the applicable law. Furthermore, it could be argued that the insurer will be precluded from covering uninsurable conduct, regardless of what the insurance policy does or does not say. For example, Section 533 of the California Insurance Code has been interpreted to "read into" every liability insurance policy an exclusion for intentional or willful wrongdoing.

In the exclusions section, most policies exclude claims for bodily injury, property damage, and certain personal injury claims to avoid, among other things, duplicate coverage already provided under a general liability policy. The EPL insurer, however, will typically not seek to apply this exclusion to allegations of emotional distress or mental anguish in connection with a covered wrongful act. In cases in which there are allegations of rape or physical assault, the insurer may insist upon an allocation between covered and noncovered aspects of the claim, such that the EPL insurer may be unwilling to fund the entire

22. *Id.* at 4.

amount of any judgment or settlement. The insurer could also seek an allocation of defense expenses.

The EPL form is not intended to provide coverage for claims for benefits that arise under a number of statutory claims, and these are evidenced under exclusions that pertain to unemployment compensation, disability, pension and other welfare benefits, workplace safety, and plant closings.

Further, it is against the public policy of most states to provide coverage for intentionally caused injuries.[23] In line with this public policy, some EPL policies contain exclusions eliminating coverage for dishonest, fraudulent, criminal, or malicious acts. A few, however, also exclude coverage for intentional acts. Because most employment-related claims involve intentional (as opposed to negligent) conduct, "intentional act" exclusions in EPL policies will likely be construed to bar coverage only when the injury (not the act that produced it) is intended. Otherwise, a risk exists that the policies will be held to provide illusory coverage.

Also, the exclusion is typically applied severally to each insured. Thus, it may be applied to exclude coverage for a supervisor who sexually assaults a subordinate[24] but may not necessarily be applicable to the liability of the employer that may be based solely on negligent hiring or negligent retention of that supervisor.

Claims for nonmonetary and other relief not in the nature of compensatory damages are typically excluded, and these may include claims seeking job reinstatement, physical accommodation pursuant to the Americans with Disabilities Act (ADA), and disgorgement of ill-gotten gain. Most policies provide that the EPL insurer will cover defense expenses in such situations.

Finally, EPL forms typically exclude claims for amounts allegedly due under an express and written employment contract. Typically, this

---

23. 1–5 New Appleman Insurance Law Practice Guide § 5.05 (2010).

24. *See Golf Course Superintendents Ass'n of Am. v. Underwriters at Lloyd's, London*, 761 F. Supp. 1485, 1489 (D. Kan. 1991).

will not include claims in which the employee seeks to defeat his or her "at will" status by alleging that an employment handbook constitutes a contract of employment.[25] The intent of most EPL insurers is to avoid often contentious and expensive disputes involving highly paid executives working under an employment contract.

VIII. "Other Insurance" Clause

The application of insurance policies other than EPL to employment-related claims is discussed in depth in Chapter 2, but the interplay between those policies and the EPL is largely dependent on the other insurance provisions in the respective policies.

Generally, other insurance clauses can be one of three major types. The first, and perhaps least common, is a provision that provides that no coverage exists under the policy when other insurance exists. Commonly referenced as an exclusionary or escape clause, the courts have not favored its enforceability.[26] If it is enforced, the insured is, essentially, being told that it cannot obtain the benefit of obtaining the coverage for which it paid premium because of the fortuity of the existence of another policy (such as a commercial general liability) for which it also paid premium.

A second variation, and perhaps the most common among EPL insurers, is one that provides that the EPL policy will be excess over other available insurance.[27] This version does not give the EPL insurer the "escape" that the version above would but simply provides that both policies will apply with the EPL not applying until the other policy's

25. Many EPL policies limit their contractual liability exclusion, which often is incorporated into the policy's definition of loss, to contracts that are both written and express. Though an employees' handbook likely meets the written qualification, few employment lawyers would consider it an express contract. At best, assuming there is no disclaimer to the contrary, a plaintiff's lawyer may argue that the handbook constitutes an implied contract.

26. *See, e.g., Auto. Underwriters, Inc. v. Fireman's Fund Ins. Cos.*, 874 F.2d 188, 191 (3d Cir. 1989).

27. *See, e.g., Fireman's Ins. Co. of Washington, D.C. v. Fed. Ins. Co.*, 649 N.Y.S.2d 700, 700 (N.Y. App. Div. 1996).

limits are exhausted. Thus, the insured gains the full benefit of the policies for which it paid. Two important and practical benefits in having a policy such as a general liability might apply on a "primary" basis in these cases:

- A general liability policy typically has an unlimited duty to defend that does not erode the available limits of liability. Therefore, the insured can enjoy the defense under the general liability policy, knowing that the limits of that policy *and* the EPL will be available to fund any covered judgment or settlement.
- A general liability policy often provides a duty to defend without any applicable deductible amount. The significance of this benefit can be enormous, particularly as six-figure deductibles or retentions are becoming commonplace in the EPL arena. Although the insured will ultimately have to bear the EPL deductible or retention if it wants to apply that policy to a settlement or judgment amount, there is a good chance that the general liability policy may cover the loss, including defense expenses, in its entirety.

The final variation specifically states that the policy is intended to be primary and will prorate with other applicable primary policies. For example, where two policies have this provision and one has a $2M limit and the other $5M, they will share the loss on a 2/7 and 5/7 basis. If one policy has this provision and the other is of the "excess" version discussed immediately above, the former will apply without any contribution from the latter unless the former's limits of liability become exhausted.

Problems in the area of other insurance typically occur when there are "mutually repugnant" clauses. The most common example is when each policy states it is excess over other available insurance. In most jurisdictions, the courts will require the insurers in those cases to prorate their liability according to their policies' respective limits.[28]

IX. Application Issues

In a claims-made policy situation, the insurer wants to assure itself that it is not writing insurance for a ship that is already sinking. Thus, as stated, there will be a question in most application forms as to whether the applicant is aware of any act, error, omission, fact, or circumstance that could give rise to a claim. If such act, error, omission, fact, or circumstance exists—regardless of whether it is disclosed in response to this question—the insurer will typically provide that it is entitled to one or both of the following remedies:

- It can deny coverage for any claim arising from what the applicant failed to disclose. In this case, the policy remains in force and the insured loses coverage only for the subject claim.
- It can rescind the policy or, in other words, hold it to be void *ab initio*. In such cases, the insurer will typically be required to return any premium that has been paid, perhaps with an added interest factor. The insured, however, loses coverage for all claims, regardless of whether they arose from application misrepresentation or omission.

Rescission, and even denials of coverage, can be harsh remedies. To afford a degree of protection to "innocent insureds," many EPL policy forms offer a limited form of severability protection with regard to representations made in or in connection with the application for insurance.

Each severability provision must be carefully examined because there is no standard approach in this area. There may be pertinent

---

28. *Ins. Co. of Tex. v. Emp'rs Liab. Assurance Corp.*, 163 F. Supp. 143, 147 (S.D. Cal. 1958).

language in both the policy form and the application itself, as well as in the case law.

Typically, the employer will not enjoy the benefit of severability if one of its executive-level officers knew of the pre-existing situation that gave rise to the claim. There may be, however, a grant of severability in which prior knowledge is possessed solely at a lower level in the organization. Insured individuals will generally enjoy severability as long as they personally were not aware of the situation that gave rise to the claim at issue.

X. *Future of EPL Insurance*

After little more than a twenty-year history of broad-based EPL insurance, most industry experts have concluded that this product is here for the long term. An increasing number of buyers, including small to mid-sized employers, appear to be emerging yearly with the insurance becoming less of a "discretionary" purchase.

As with any insurance product, the breadth of coverage offered tends to ebb and flow with the cycles of the market. In soft markets, rates fall and terms and conditions broaden as insurers become more competitive for business. In a soft market, one can look for features such as third-party coverage to be offered with increasing frequency. Further, premiums will continue to be largely stagnant, perhaps increasing only 5 to 10 percent for some of the larger carriers. A soft market, combined with a higher than expected claims frequency, however, is costly for insurers. This effect, when coupled with increasing defense costs and the need to keep premiums low, results in some carriers instituting mandatory higher deductibles. As markets harden, rates increase and the coverage constricts. During a hard market, underwriting gets more stringent. In addition, there is less competition among insurance carriers and employers see higher insurance premiums.

Carriers are also struggling with mass, or multiple plaintiff, claims. Mass claims are claims in which well-known, large businesses are targeted by multiple plaintiffs who threaten litigation unless the defendant settles quickly. Carriers have incurred large settlements for claims the insured was reluctant to fight, fearing damage to the insured's reputation. Mass claims make it difficult for insurance companies to price EPL insurance at a rate attractive for these large companies.[29] Alternatives include large mandatory deductibles, co-insurance, or single-claim deductibles. Most carriers require large retentions for mass claims.

Similarly, the United States Supreme Court's decision in *Wal-Mart Stores, Inc. v. Dukes*, 131 S. Ct. 2541 (2011), arguably making it more difficult for employee plaintiffs to bring class action lawsuits against their multinational, multi-organizational employers, raises questions about EPL coverage of class action claims.

Notwithstanding the Supreme Court's decision that the employee/plaintiffs in *Dukes* were not able to join together to bring a class action because they lacked "commonality" and because, in part, the employer's human resources function was decentralized,[30] EPL insurers remain concerned about the potential exposures in class-action lawsuits: defense costs and settlement costs in class actions can be exorbitant. Insurers, therefore, will likely focus on the overall risk associated with each company while simultaneously closely scrutinizing those companies in which human resources policies, procedures, and decisions are decentralized. Certainly, insurers will pay close attention to the level of discretion given to local managers and supervisors within multinational organizations. In the past, underwriters placed value on centralized human resources and legal functions, but this may change given the Supreme Court's decision. The court's decision may also cause insurers to focus on several terms and conditions of EPL policies such as the prior acts coverage and the definition of a claim.

Finally, as EPL insurance becomes more prevalent, plaintiffs' counsel will gain greater familiarity with EPL insurer claims professionals and other representatives. The insurers' long- and short-term interests

---

29. Betterley, *supra* note 1, at 5–6.

30. *Wal-Mart Stores, Inc. v. Dukes*, 131 S. Ct. 2541 (2011).

will become more closely aligned with those of their insureds as the insurers repeatedly see the same plaintiffs' lawyers and develop long-standing EPL insurance relationships with certain insureds. In such situations, there is less chance of a disconnect between settlement and trial strategic decisions.

APPENDIX 1A
Specimen Employment Practices Liability Policy

ABA Employers Edge℠

An Employment Practices Liability Insurance Policy for Law Firms

Endorsed by the American Bar Association

Executive Risk Indemnity Inc.
Home Office:
2711 Centerville Road, Suite 400
Wilmington, Delaware 19808

Administrative Offices/Mailing Address:
82 Hopmeadow Street
Simsbury, Connecticut 06070-7683
Phone: 860.408.2000
Fax: 860.408.2002
Email: info@chubb.com
Web Site: www.chubb.com

THIS IS A CLAIMS MADE POLICY
WITH DEFENSE EXPENSES INCLUDED IN THE LIMIT OF LIABILITY.
PLEASE READ THE ENTIRE POLICY CAREFULLY.

EXECUTIVE RISK INDEMNITY INC.

ABA EMPLOYERS EDGE[SM]
An Employment Practices Liability Insurance Policy for Law Firms
Endorsed by the American Bar Association

Executive Risk Indemnity Inc. (the "Underwriter") and the Insureds, subject to all of the terms, conditions, and limitations of this Policy, agree as follows:

I. INSURING AGREEMENT

The Underwriter will pay on behalf of the **Insureds Defense Expenses** and **Loss** in excess of the applicable retention set forth in ITEM 4 of the Declarations resulting from **Claims** first made against any **Insured** during the **Policy Period** or, if applicable, the Extended Reporting Period, for **Employment Practices Wrongful Acts** occurring subsequent to the Retroactive Date stated in ITEM 5 of the Declarations and before the expiration of the **Policy Period**.

II. DEFINITIONS

(A) "**Application**" means the application attached to and forming part of this Policy, including any materials submitted in connection with such application, all of which are on file with the Underwriter and are a part of this Policy, as if physically attached.

(B) "**Claim**" means:

(1) any written notice received by any **Insured** that any person or entity intends to hold an **Insured** responsible for an **Employment Practices Wrongful Act**;

(2) any judicial, administrative or other proceeding against any **Insured** for an **Employment Practices Wrongful Act**; or

(3) any written request to toll or waive a statute of limitations relating to a potential judicial, administrative or other proceeding against any **Insured** for an **Employment Practices Wrongful Act**;

provided, that **Claim** does not include any labor or grievance arbitration or other proceeding pursuant to a collective bargaining agreement, or any criminal proceeding against an **Insured**.

(C) "**Defense Expenses**" means reasonable legal fees and expenses incurred in the investigation, defense or appeal of any **Claim**; provided, that **Defense Expenses** does not include remuneration, salaries, wages, fees, expenses, overhead or benefit expenses of any **Insured**.

(D) "**Discrimination**" means any failure or refusal to hire any person, any failure or refusal to promote any person, any failure or refusal to offer any person a partnership or shareholder interest or to name any person as a partner or shareholder, the demotion or discharge of any person, employment-related defamation, wrongful failure to grant tenure, or any limitation, segregation or classification of **Employees** or applicants for employment in any way that would deprive or tend to deprive any person of employment opportunities or otherwise adversely affect his or her status as an **Employee** because of such person's race, color, religion, age, sex, national origin, disability, pregnancy, sexual orientation or preference or other status that is protected pursuant to any applicable federal, state or local statute or ordinance.

(E) "**Employee**" means any individual whose labor or service is engaged by and directed by the **Firm**. This includes part-time, seasonal and temporary **Employees** as well as any individual employed in a supervisory or managerial position. **Employee** also includes any partner, principal, director, officer, or shareholder of the **Firm**. In addition, **Employee** includes any volunteer working for the **Firm**, but solely for conduct within the scope of his or her duties as a volunteer for the **Firm**; any independent contractor working solely for the **Firm**, but solely for conduct within the scope of his or her duties as an independent contractor for the **Firm**; and any leased employee working solely for the **Firm**, but solely for conduct within the scope of his or her duties as a leased employee for the **Firm**.

(F) "**Employment Practices Wrongful Act**" means any actual or alleged: (1) **Wrongful Termination**; (2) **Discrimination**; (3) **Harassment**; (4) **Retaliation**; (5) **Third Party Discrimination**; (6) **Third Party Harassment**; or (7) **Workplace Tort**.

(G) "**Firm**" means the organization(s) engaged in the practice of law under the name first set forth in ITEM 1 of the Declarations whether as a partnership, professional corporation or association or otherwise, and also will include its predecessors as set forth in ITEM 1 of the Declarations.

(H) "**Harassment**" means:

(1) unwelcome sexual advances, requests for sexual favors, or other verbal, visual or physical conduct of a sexual nature that is made a condition of employment at the **Firm**, is used as a basis for employment decisions at the **Firm**, creates a work environment at the **Firm** that interferes with performance, or creates an intimidating, hostile, or offensive working environment; or

(2) workplace harassment (i.e., harassment of a non-sexual nature) which creates a work environment at the **Firm** that interferes with performance or creates an intimidating, hostile, or offensive working environment.

(I) "**Insured**" means the **Firm** and each person who was, is or becomes:

(1) a partner, a principal, a director, an officer, or a shareholder of the **Firm**;

(2) a full-time or part-time salaried **Employee** of the **Firm** or of an incorporated partner of the **Firm**; or

(3) "counsel" or "of counsel" to the **Firm**;

solely with respect to conduct or actions within the scope of their employment at the **Firm**.

(J) "**Loss**" means any damages (including back pay awards, front pay awards, compensatory damages and punitive damages if insurable under the law pursuant to which this policy is construed), pre-judgment interest, post-judgment interest, and settlements which an **Insured** is legally obligated to pay as a result of a **Claim**; provided, that **Loss** does not include:

(1) civil or criminal fines, sanctions, liquidated damages, taxes or penalties, the multiplied portion of any multiplied damage award (except for multiplied damages awarded pursuant to the Age Discrimination in Employment Act), or matters which are uninsurable under the law pursuant to which this Policy is construed;

(2) any costs associated with the modification of any building or property in order to provide any reasonable accommodations required by, made as a result of, or to conform with the requirements of the Americans With Disabilities Act and any amendments thereto or any similar federal, state or local statute, regulation, or common law;

(3) any other non-monetary relief awarded against any **Insured**, including without limitation any costs associated with compliance with any injunctive relief of any kind or nature;

(4) severance pay or damages determined to be owing under an express written contract of employment or an express written obligation to make payments in the event of the termination of employment;

(5) payment of insurance plan benefits; and

(6) amounts awarded pursuant to a labor or grievance arbitration or other proceeding pursuant to a collective bargaining agreement.

(K) "**Policy Period**" means the period from the Inception Date to the Expiration Date in ITEM 2 of the Declarations or to any earlier cancelation date.

(L) "**Potential Claim**" means any person or entity alleging an **Employment Practices Wrongful Act** by an **Insured**. "Alleging" as used in this paragraph means lodging a complaint or charge that does not constitute a **Claim**, but which may subsequently give rise to a **Claim**, with a **Supervisory Employee**, the **Firm's** human resources department, or the **Firm's** department that provides a similar function to a human resources department.

(M) "**Related Claims**" means all **Claims** based on, arising out of, directly or indirectly resulting from, in consequence of, or in any way involving the same or related facts, circumstances, situations, transactions, events, or **Employment Practices Wrongful Acts** or the same or related series of facts, circumstances, situations, transactions, events, or **Employment Practices Wrongful Acts**.

(N) "**Retaliation**" means retaliatory treatment against an **Employee** of the **Firm** on account of such **Employee's** exercise or attempted exercise of his or her rights under law.

(O) "**Supervisory Employee**" means a partner, a principal, a director, an officer, or a shareholder of the **Firm** or the personnel director or any other **Employee** of the **Firm** having management-level responsibility for personnel matters.

(P) "**Third Party Discrimination**" means any disparate treatment or classification of clients or other individuals based on race, color, religion, age, sex, national origin, disability, pregnancy, sexual orientation or preference, or other status that is protected pursuant to any applicable federal, state or local statute or ordinance.

(Q) "**Third Party Harassment**" means:

(1) unwelcome sexual advances, requests for sexual favors, or other verbal, visual or physical conduct of a sexual nature that is made by an **Employee** to a client or other individual; or

(2) any other harassment of a client or other individual, by an **Employee**, that creates an intimidating, hostile, or offensive environment.

(R) "**Workplace Tort**" means employment-related misrepresentation, negligent evaluation, wrongful discipline, or wrongful deprivation of career opportunity.

(S) "**Wrongful Termination**" means the actual or constructive termination of the employment of, or demotion of, failure or refusal to promote, failure or refusal to offer a partnership or shareholder interest to, or to name as a partner or shareholder, any **Employee** at the **Firm**, which is in violation of law or is against public policy, or is in breach of an implied agreement to continue employment or, subject to EXCLUSION (B)(4), is in breach of an express written agreement to continue employment.

III. EXCLUSIONS

(A) The Underwriter will not pay **Defense Expenses** or **Loss** for any **Claim**:

(1) arising out of any actual or alleged violation of the Employee Retirement Income Security Act of 1974 and any amendments thereto or any similar provisions of any federal, state or local statutes, ordinances, regulations, or common law;

(2) arising out of any actual or alleged bodily injury to, or sickness, loss of consortium, disease or death of, any person, or damage to or destruction of property, including the loss of use thereof; provided, that this EXCLUSION (A)(2) does not apply to **Claims** for emotional distress, mental anguish or humiliation actually or allegedly resulting from an **Employment Practices Wrongful Act**;

(3) arising out of:

(a) any fact, circumstance, situation, transaction or event of **Employment Practices Wrongful Acts** about which any **Supervisory Employee** had knowledge prior to the inception date of the first Employment Practices Liability Insurance Policy issued to the **Firm** by the Underwriter and continuously renewed by the Underwriter; or

(b) any **Claim** or fact, circumstance, situation, transaction, or event, of **Employment Practices Wrongful Acts** which, before the

Inception Date of this Policy as set forth in ITEM 2 of the Declarations, was the subject of any notice given under any other insurance policy, including but not limited to any policy of which this Policy is a renewal or replacement, or which was identified in any summary or statement of claims or circumstances which could give rise to a claim submitted in connection with the **Application** or an application for any policy of which this Policy is a renewal or replacement;

provided, however, that if EXCLUSION (A)(3)(a) is applicable because of any **Employment Practices Wrongful Acts** committed by a **Supervisory Employee**, and if no other **Supervisory Employee** had knowledge thereof prior to the inception date of the first Employment Practices Liability Insurance Policy issued to the **Firm** and continuously renewed by the Underwriter, EXCLUSION (A)(3)(a) shall apply only to the **Supervisory Employee** who committed such **Employment Practices Wrongful Acts** and shall not bar coverage for any other **Insured**;

(4) resulting in **Loss** that an **Insured** is obligated to pay by reason of the assumption of another person's liability for an **Employment Practices Wrongful Act** in a contract or an agreement; provided, that this EXCLUSION (A)(4) will not apply to **Loss** resulting from an **Employment Practices Wrongful Act** that would have been sustained even in the absence of such contract or agreement;

(5) arising out of a lockout, strike, picket line, hiring of replacement workers or other similar actions in connection with labor disputes or labor negotiations;

(6) by or on behalf of, in the name or right of or for the benefit of any partner, principal, director, officer, or shareholder of the **Firm** arising out of a partnership agreement, allocation of shares, ownership interests in the **Firm**, distribution of profits or capital, or any other similar financial relationship among **Insureds**; and

(7) by any person or entity arising out of, directly or indirectly resulting from, in consequence of, or in any way involving any actual or alleged act, error, omission, misstatement, misleading statement or breach of duty by any **Insured** under this Policy in connection with the rendering of, or actual or alleged failure to render, services to others as an attorney or a notary public or as an administrator, conservator, executor, guardian or committee or in any similar fiduciary capacity incidental to the practice of law.

(B) Subject to all of its other applicable terms, conditions, limitations and endorsements, this Policy will provide coverage for **Defense Expenses** only (but not for **Loss**) for **Claims**:

(1) arising out of any actual or alleged violation of the Workers' Adjustment and Retraining Notification Act and any amendments thereto, or any similar provisions of any federal, state or local statutes, ordinances, regulations, or common law;

(2) seeking only injunctive or non-monetary relief, regardless of whether a prevailing claimant may be entitled to recover attorneys' fees and costs;

(3) arising out of any actual or alleged violation of any workers' compensation law, any unemployment compensation law, any social security law, the Consolidated Omnibus Budget Reconciliation Act of 1985 and any amendments thereto, any disability benefits law, or any similar provisions of any federal, state or local statutes, ordinances, regulations, or common law; and

(4) for actual or constructive termination of the employment of, or demotion of, or failure or refusal to promote any **Employee** at the **Firm** which is in breach of an express written employment agreement.

IV. EXTENSIONS OF COVERAGE

(A) Extended Reporting Period:

(1) In the event that the Underwriter fails or refuses to renew this Policy, or in the event the **Firm** cancels or declines to renew this Policy, the **Firm** may purchase for an additional premium an Extended Reporting Period for a period of either:

(a) one (1) year following the expiration of the **Policy Period** or termination, for a premium equal to seventy-five percent (75%) of the then current annual premium for this Policy; or

(b) two (2) years following the expiration of the **Policy Period** or termination, for a premium equal to one hundred fifty percent (150%) of the then current annual premium for this Policy.

The coverage otherwise afforded under this Policy will be extended to apply for the Extended Reporting Period, subject to all of this Policy's terms, conditions, limitations and endorsements, to **Defense Expenses** and **Loss** from **Claims** first made against any **Insured** during the Extended Reporting Period for **Employment Practices Wrongful Acts** occurring subsequent to the Retroactive Date set forth in ITEM 5 of the Declarations and before the expiration of the **Policy Period** or termination. The **Firm** must notify the Underwriter in writing by certified mail at the address set forth in the Declarations of its decision to purchase such an

Extended Reporting Period and must pay the applicable additional premium for the length of the Extended Reporting Period selected by the **Firm** within thirty (30) days after the expiration of the **Policy Period** or termination. Payment of the full additional premium by the due date is a strict condition precedent to the right to purchase an Extended Reporting Period. The **Firm** may not change its election regarding the length of the Extended Reporting Period purchased once that election has been made by tendering the applicable premium.

(2) The maximum aggregate Limit of Liability set forth in ITEM 3(b) of the Declarations shall be the maximum aggregate Limit of Liability for the **Policy Period** and, if applicable, the Extended Reporting Period. The Policy's maximum aggregate Limit of Liability is not increased, reinstated or renewed by virtue of the applicability of any Extended Reporting Period.

(B) **Changes in Risk**:

(1) If, during the Policy Period, the total number of **Employees** in the **Firm** increases by more than twenty percent (20%) or twenty-five (25), whichever is less, as the result of the **Firm's** merger with or acquisition of any other law firm or any group of employees who practiced together at another law firm, the **Firm** must promptly give the Underwriter written notice thereof, together with such information as the Underwriter may require, and the Underwriter will be entitled to impose such additional coverage terms and charge such additional premium in connection therewith as the Underwriter, in its sole discretion, may require.

(2) In the event of the death, incapacity or bankruptcy of an **Insured**, a **Claim** against the estate, heirs, legal representatives, or assigns of such **Insured** will be deemed to be a **Claim** against such **Insured**.

(3) Bankruptcy or insolvency of an **Insured** or an **Insured's** estate will not relieve the Underwriter of any of its obligations hereunder.

V. CONDITIONS

(A) **Territory**:

This Policy applies to any **Employment Practices Wrongful Act** occurring and any **Claim** made anywhere in the world.

(B) **Reporting of Claims and Potential Claims**:

(1) If a **Claim** is made against any **Insured**, the **Insured** or the **Firm** shall give written notice thereof to the Underwriter as soon as practicable and in no event later than sixty (60) days after such **Claim** is first made as determined pursuant to CONDITION (C)(1) and shall immediately forward to the Underwriter every demand, notice, summons, complaint or other process received by any **Insured** or his/her/its representatives. Compliance with this notice requirement is a strict condition precedent to coverage under this Policy.

(2) If during the **Policy Period**, an **Insured** becomes aware of a **Potential Claim** and the **Insured** during the **Policy Period**:

(a) gives the Underwriter written notice of such **Potential Claim**, including a description of the **Potential Claim** in question, the identities of the potential claimants, the consequences which have resulted or may result from such **Potential Claim**, the damages which may result from such **Potential Claim**, and the circumstances by which the **Insured** first became aware of such **Potential Claim**; and

(b) requests coverage under this Policy for any **Claim** subsequently resulting from such **Potential Claim**;

then the Underwriter will treat any such subsequently resulting **Claim** as if it had been made against the **Insured** during the **Policy Period**. Notice of any such subsequently resulting **Claim** must be given in accordance with CONDITION (B)(1).

(3) All notices of **Claims** required under CONDITION (B)(1) and all notices of **Potential Claims** permitted under CONDITION (B)(2) must be sent by certified mail to the address set forth in the Declarations.

(C) **Timing and Interrelationship of Claims**:

(1) A **Claim** as defined in DEFINITIONS (B)(1) and (B)(3) is first made when the **Firm's** management committee (or similar committee or board), any partner, principal, director, officer or shareholder of the **Firm**, the **Firm's** human resources director, the **Firm's** administrator, or anyone designated by the **Firm** to receive employment related complaints receives a written notice or request as set forth therein; and a **Claim** as defined in DEFINITION (B)(2) is first made when the **Firm's** management committee (or similar committee or board), any partner, principal, director, officer or shareholder of the **Firm**, the **Firm's** human resources director, the **Firm's** administrator, or anyone designated by the **Firm** to receive employment related complaints first becomes aware, through service of process or otherwise, of the filing of a complaint, motion for judgment or similar document or pleading commencing a judicial, administrative or other proceeding against an **Insured**.

(2) All **Related Claims** will be treated as a single **Claim** made at the time the first of such **Related Claims** was made in accordance with CONDITION (C)(1), or when the first of such **Related Claims** is treated as having been made in accordance with CONDITION (B)(2), whichever is earlier.

(D) **Defense and Settlement of Claims**:

(1) The **Insureds** will have the right and duty to retain qualified counsel of their choosing to represent them in the defense or appeal of **Claims**, but no **Defense Expenses** may be incurred without the Underwriter's consent, such consent not to be unreasonably withheld. It shall not be unreasonable, if more than one **Insured** is involved in a **Claim**, for the Underwriter to withhold its consent to separate counsel for one or more of such **Insureds** unless there is a material actual or potential conflict of interest among such **Insureds**.

(2) The Underwriter will, upon written request, pay **Defense Expenses** owed under this Policy on a current basis. As a condition of any payment of **Defense Expenses** before the final disposition of a **Claim**, the Underwriter may require a written undertaking on terms and conditions satisfactory to it guaranteeing the repayment of any **Defense Expenses** paid on behalf of any **Insured** if it is finally determined that this Policy would not cover **Loss** incurred by such **Insured** in connection with such **Claim**. Except for **Defense Expenses** paid in accordance with this CONDITION (D)(2), the Underwriter will have no obligation to pay any **Loss** before the final disposition of a **Claim**.

(3) No **Insured** may admit any liability for any **Claim** or settle any **Claim** without the Underwriter's consent; provided, however, that the **Insureds**

may settle any **Claim** without the Underwriter's consent where **Defense Expenses** and the settlement amount in respect of such **Claim**, in the aggregate, do not exceed fifty percent (50%) of the applicable retention. The Underwriter will have the right to make investigations and conduct negotiations and, with the consent of the **Insureds**, enter into such settlement of any **Claim** as the Underwriter deems appropriate. If the **Insureds** refuse to consent to a settlement acceptable to the claimant in accordance with the Underwriter's recommendation, then the Underwriter's liability for such **Claim** will not exceed (i) the amount for which the **Claim** could have been settled plus any **Defense Expenses** incurred with the Underwriter's consent up to the date the **Insureds** refuse to settle such **Claim**, plus (ii) fifty percent (50%) of any amounts (including **Loss** and **Defense Expenses**) in excess of the amount set forth in clause (i) above, incurred in connection with such **Claim**; subject, in all events, to the applicable retention and the maximum aggregate Limit of Liability. The remaining fifty percent (50%) of all amounts in excess of the amount for which the **Claim** could have been settled will be carried by the **Insureds** at their own risk and will be uninsured.

(4) The Underwriter may, in its sole discretion and without any obligation to do so, undertake investigations and conduct negotiations with respect to any **Potential Claim** and, with the consent of the **Insureds**, enter into such settlement of any **Potential Claim** as the Underwriter deems appropriate. Any such settlement of a **Potential Claim** shall be treated as the settlement of a **Claim** made during the **Policy Period** in which the **Potential Claim** was reported to the Underwriter. If the **Insureds** refuse to consent to a settlement acceptable to the potential claimant in accordance with the Underwriter's recommendation, then the Underwriter's liability for any **Claim** resulting from such **Potential Claim** will not exceed (i) the amount for which the **Potential Claim** could have been settled, plus (ii) fifty percent (50%) of any amounts (including **Loss** and **Defense Expenses**) in excess of the amount set forth in clause (i) above, subject, in all events, to the applicable retention and the maximum aggregate Limit of Liability. The remaining fifty percent (50%) of all amounts in excess of the amount for which the **Potential Claim** could have been settled will be carried by the **Insureds** at their own risk and will be uninsured.

(E) **Limits of Liability; Retention**:

(1) The amount stated in ITEM 3(a) of the Declarations will be the maximum Limit of Liability of the Underwriter under this Policy for all **Defense Expenses** and **Loss** from any **Claim** or **Related Claims** for which this Policy provides coverage, regardless of the number of **Related Claims**, the number of persons or entities included within the definition of "**Insured**," the number of claimants who make **Claims** against the **Insureds**, or the number of **Insureds** named as defendants in any **Claim**.

(2) The amount stated in ITEM 3(b) of the Declarations will be the maximum Limit of Liability of the Underwriter under this Policy for all **Defense Expenses** and **Loss** from all **Claims** for which this Policy provides coverage, regardless of the number of **Claims**, the number of persons or entities included within the definition of "**Insured**," the number of claimants who make **Claims** against the **Insureds**, or the number of **Insureds** named as defendants in any **Claim**.

(3) **Defense Expenses** will be part of and not in addition to such Limit of Liability, and payment of **Defense Expenses** by the Underwriter will reduce, and may exhaust, the Limit of Liability.

(4) The obligation of the Underwriter to pay **Defense Expenses** and **Loss** in connection with any **Claim** will only be in excess of the retention. The **Insureds** must bear the amount of the retention. The Underwriter will have no obligation whatsoever, either to the **Insureds** or to any other person or entity, to pay all or any portion of the retention amount on behalf of any **Insured**. The Underwriter will, however, at its sole discretion, have the right and option to do so, in which event the **Insureds** must repay the Underwriter any such amounts promptly upon demand.

(F) **Cancelation**:

(1) The Underwriter may not cancel this Policy except for failure to pay a premium when due, in which case twenty (20) days' written notice will be given.

(2) The **Firm** may cancel this Policy by surrendering this Policy or by mailing or delivering to the Underwriter written notice stating when thereafter such cancelation will be effective. If this Policy is canceled by the **Firm**, the earned premium will be computed in accordance with the customary short rate table and procedure. Premium adjustment may be made either at the time cancelation is effective or as soon as practicable after cancelation becomes effective.

(3) The Underwriter will not be required to renew this Policy upon its

expiration. If the Underwriter elects not to renew this Policy, the Underwriter will deliver or mail to the **Firm** written notice to that effect at least sixty (60) days before the Expiration Date set forth in ITEM 2(b) of the Declarations.

(G) **Exhaustion**:

If the Limit of Liability is exhausted by the payment of **Defense Expenses** and/or **Loss**, all obligations of the Underwriter under this Policy will be completely fulfilled and exhausted, and the Underwriter will have no further obligations of any kind or nature whatsoever under this Policy, and the premium will be fully earned.

(H) **Cooperation and Subrogation**:

(1) In the event of a **Claim**, or after giving the Underwriter notice of a **Potential Claim**, the **Insureds** must provide the Underwriter with all information, assistance and cooperation as the Underwriter may reasonably request.

(2) The **Insureds** may do nothing to prejudice the Underwriter's position or the Underwriter's potential or actual rights of recovery in the event of a **Claim**.

(3) In the event of payment under this Policy, the Underwriter will be subrogated to, and entitled to an assignment of, all of the rights of recovery therefor of the **Insureds**. The **Insureds** shall execute all papers and do everything that may be necessary to secure such rights, including the execution of such documents as may be necessary to enable the Underwriter effectively to pursue and enforce such rights and to bring suit in the name of the **Insureds**.

(4) The obligations of the **Insureds** under this CONDITION (H) will survive the Policy.

(I) **Representations**:

The **Insureds** represent that the particulars and statements contained in the **Application** are true, accurate and complete, and agree that this Policy is issued in reliance on the truth of that representation and that such particulars and statements, which are deemed to be incorporated into and to constitute a part of this Policy, are the basis of this Policy and are material to the Underwriter's acceptance of this risk. This Policy shall not, however, be avoided as to any **Insured** on account of the untruth of the particulars and statements contained in the **Application** unless:

(1) such **Insured** knew of the untruth of such particular or statement, in which event such knowledge shall be imputed only to such **Insured**; or

(2) the person providing such particular or making such statement in the **Application** knew of its untruth, in which event such knowledge shall be imputed to all **Insureds**.

(J) **No Action against the Underwriter**:

(1) No action may be taken against the Underwriter unless, as a condition precedent thereto, there has been full compliance with all of the terms of this Policy and the amount of the obligation of the **Insureds** to pay has been finally determined either by judgment against the **Insureds** after adjudicatory proceedings or by written agreement of the **Insureds**, the claimant and the Underwriter.

(2) No person or entity will have any right under this Policy to join the Underwriter as a party to any **Claim** against any **Insured** to determine the liability of such **Insured**; nor may the Underwriter be impleaded by any **Insured** or any **Insured's** legal representative in any such **Claim**.

(K) **Arbitration of Coverage Disputes**:

Notwithstanding CONDITION (J), any coverage dispute or other controversy regarding the rights or obligations of the Underwriter and the **Insureds** under this Policy shall be submitted to binding arbitration in accordance with the Commercial Arbitration Rules of the American Arbitration Association ("AAA"). The Underwriter or the **Insureds** may invoke this arbitration procedure by giving written notice to that effect by certified mail to the other party. The Underwriter and the **Insureds** will attempt to agree upon a single arbitrator. If agreement regarding selection of a single arbitrator is not reached within thirty (30) days after the initial demand for arbitration, each party shall, within thirty (30) days thereafter, name an arbitrator. Those two arbitrators shall, within thirty (30) days after they both have been named, select a third arbitrator, who shall serve as the Chair of the arbitration panel. If the two party-selected arbitrators are unable to agree upon a third arbitrator, then the AAA shall appoint a person who is neutral to the parties to act as the Chair of the arbitration panel. None of the arbitrators may be former or current partners, principals, directors, officers, shareholders or employees of the Underwriter or of any **Insured**.

The Underwriter and the **Insureds** each shall file a written submission with supporting documents to the single arbitrator or, if applicable, to the arbitration panel (hereinafter, references to "arbitration panel" shall include a single arbitrator agreed upon by the parties) within ninety (90) days after appointment of the last member of the arbitration panel, which period may be extended by the arbitration panel. The arbitration hearing shall be held in the city where the **Firm** has its principal office, at a site and at a time designated by the arbitration panel, at which time the arbitration panel will receive oral evidence. The parties shall have at their disposal the same pre-trial discovery rights available under the Federal Rules of Civil Procedure and the Local Rules of the United States District Court for the District in which the arbitration hearing will be held; provided, that the arbitration panel may shorten the time permitted by those Rules for any discovery procedure in light of the ninety (90) day timetable for the parties' submissions specified above, and provided further that any dispute regarding discovery shall be submitted for decision to the arbitration panel. The arbitration panel shall be relieved of judicial formality and need not adhere to formal rules of evidence. The majority of the arbitration panel will issue a written decision resolving the controversy within thirty (30) days after the close of the hearing, which decision will state the facts reviewed, conclusions reached and reasons for the conclusions. The decision will be binding upon the Underwriter and the **Insureds** in any court of competent jurisdiction and will not be subject to appeal. The arbitration panel also shall allocate the fees and expenses of the arbitration panel between the Underwriter and the **Insureds**. Any finding of liability by the arbitration panel against the Underwriter shall not exceed the Policy's applicable remaining Limit of Liability after deduction of all **Defense Expenses** and **Loss** that the Underwriter has paid or is obligated to pay, plus the fees and expenses of the arbitration panel to the extent allocated solely to the Underwriter by the arbitration panel.

(L) **Authorization and Notices**:

(1) The person or entity first named in ITEM 1 of the Declarations will act on behalf of the **Insureds** with respect to all matters under this Policy, including but not limited to giving and receiving notices and other communications, effecting or accepting any endorsements to or cancelation of this Policy, the payment of premium and the receipt of any return premiums, and the purchase of any Extended Reporting Period.

(2) Unless otherwise specified, all notices permitted or required by this Policy shall be given in writing and shall be sent by first class or certified mail to the respective addresses of the person or entity first named in ITEM 1 of

the Declarations, if to the **Insureds**, or of the Underwriter, if to the Underwriter, as set forth in the Declarations.

(M) **Changes**:

Notice to any agent or knowledge possessed by any agent or other person acting on behalf of the Underwriter will not effect a waiver or change in any part of this Policy or estop the Underwriter from asserting any right under its terms, conditions and limitations.

(N) **No Transfer or Assignment of Insured Interest**:

No transfer or assignment of interest under this Policy or of any cause of action against the Underwriter arising out of its performance of, or alleged failure to perform in accordance with, the terms and conditions of this Policy will be effective without the Underwriter's written consent.

(O) **Headings**:

The descriptions in the headings and sub-headings of this Policy are solely for convenience, and form no part of the terms, conditions and limitations of the Policy.

(P) **Entire Agreement**:

The **Insureds** agree that this Policy, including the **Application** and any endorsements, constitutes the entire agreement existing between the **Insureds** and the Underwriter or any of its agents relating to this insurance and that the terms, conditions, limitations and endorsements of this Policy may not be waived or changed except by written endorsement issued to form a part of this Policy.

(Q) **Underwriter's Signature**:

In witness whereof the Underwriter has caused this Policy to be executed by its authorized officers, but this Policy will not be valid unless countersigned on the Declarations Page by a duly authorized representative of the Underwriter.

Secretary *President*

APPENDIX 1B

Application

Executive Risk Indemnity Inc.
Home Office
Wilmington, Delaware 19808

Administrative Offices Mailing
82 Hopmeadow
Simsbury, Connecticut 06070-7683

AMERICAN BAR ASSOCIATION

APPLICATION FOR ABA EMPLOYERS EDGE[SM]
AN EMPLOYMENT PRACTICES LIABILITY INSURANCE POLICY FOR LAW FIRMS
ENDORSED BY THE AMERICAN BAR ASSOCIATION

NOTICE: THE POLICY FOR WHICH APPLICATION IS MADE APPLIES, SUBJECT TO ITS TERMS, ONLY TO "CLAIMS" FIRST MADE DURING THE "POLICY PERIOD" OR, IF PURCHASED, ANY EXTENDED REPORTING PERIOD. THE LIMIT OF LIABILITY AVAILABLE TO PAY DAMAGES OR SETTLEMENTS WILL BE REDUCED BY "DEFENSE EXPENSES," AND "DEFENSE EXPENSES" WILL BE APPLIED AGAINST THE RETENTION. THE UNDERWRITER WILL HAVE NO DUTY TO DEFEND ANY "CLAIM." PLEASE READ THE ENTIRE APPLICATION CAREFULLY BEFORE SIGNING.

1. GENERAL INFORMATION

A. **Applicant's** name: ______________________________
Applicant's address: ______________________________
City: ______________________ State: _____ ZIP: __________

B. Date of organization: ______________________________

C. List all locations or branch offices by city and state (include approximate number of employees at each location). Please use a separate addendum if necessary.

Locations or Branch Offices	Approximate Number of Employees

D. List prior employment practices liability insurance for the past three (3) years (either stand-alone policies or supplemental coverage provided under some other type of insurance). Please use a separate addendum if necessary.

Period	Insurer	Limit	Retention	Coinsurance	Premium

E. **MISSOURI APPLICANTS/AGENTS - DO NOT ANSWER THIS QUESTION.**
Has a previous insurer ever canceled or non-renewed the **Applicant** for employment practices liability insurance (either on a stand-alone basis or as supplemental coverage provided under some other type of insurance)? ☐ Yes ☐ No

If "Yes," provide details of the circumstances of cancelation or non-renewal.

____
____
____

F. Desired coverage: Limit of liability: ____________ Retention: ____________

2. EMPLOYEES

A. Current number of
Partners: ________
All other attorneys: ________
All other full-time employees: ________
Part-time employees (including seasonal and temporary): ________

B. What was the annual employee (including all attorneys) turnover rate for the last four (4) years?
19____: ____% 19____: ____% 19____: ____% 19____: ____%

C. How many involuntary terminations have occurred in the past two (2) years?
Employees: ______ All attorneys: ______

D. Percentage of employees (including all attorneys) with salaries (including bonuses):
Less than $50,000: ______%
$50,000 - $100,000: ______%
$100,000 - $250,000: ______%
Greater than $250,000: ______%

E. Current number of dedicated independent contractors (i.e., independent contractors working exclusively for the **Applicant** on the **Applicant's** premises): ____________

F. Please describe the nature of the work done by the independent contractors included above. Please use a separate addendum if necessary. ______________________________
____
____

3. LOSS HISTORY

A. Please provide a listing of all employment practices claims by employees or applicants for employment over the past three (3) years, including information regarding the type of claim, the parties involved, and any settlement or final determination of the claim. If none, so state. Please use a separate addendum if necessary.

____
____
____

B. Please provide a listing of any facts or circumstances which may result in employment practices claims being made against the **Applicant**. If none, so state. Please use a separate addendum if necessary.

____
____
____

C. Has the **Applicant** ever been involved in any grievance or administrative hearing before the following agencies or under any of the following Acts:

1. National Labor Relations Board ☐ Yes ☐ No
2. Equal Employment Opportunity Commission ☐ Yes ☐ No
3. Civil Rights Act of 1991 ☐ Yes ☐ No
4. Age Discrimination in Employment Act ☐ Yes ☐ No
5. Americans With Disabilities Act ☐ Yes ☐ No
6. Any other Governmental Agency or Act ☐ Yes ☐ No

If "Yes," please provide details. Please use a separate addendum if necessary.

D. Does the **Applicant** utilize any form of alternative dispute resolution in connection with employment practices claims? ☐ Yes ☐ No
If "Yes," please describe on a separate addendum.

E. Please provide a listing of all third party lawsuits (i.e., suits by entities or individuals who are not employees nor applicants for employment) for discrimination, sexual harassment and related claims over the past three (3) years, including information regarding the type of claim, the parties involved, and any settlement or final determination of the lawsuit. If none, so state. Please use a separate addendum if necessary. ____________

____

____

F. Please provide a listing of any facts or circumstances which may result in claims of the type described in 3. E. above being brought against the **Applicant**. If none, so state. Please use a separate addendum if necessary.

____

____

____

Without prejudice to any other rights and remedies of the Underwriter, any claim based on or directly or indirectly arising out of or resulting from any claim, suit, circumstance, allegation, or contention required to be disclosed in response to Question 3. A., B., C., E., and F is excluded from the proposed insurance.

4. HUMAN RESOURCES

A. Does the **Applicant** have a human resources department? ☐ Yes ☐ No

B. Provide the name of the head of this department and the total number of employees therein.
Name: ______________________________________ Total number of employees: __________

C. How are human resources matters handled in branch offices? Please use a separate addendum if necessary.

____

____

____

D. Does the **Applicant** have written procedures in place with regard to the following:

1. Termination ☐ Yes ☐ No
2. Hiring ☐ Yes ☐ No
3. Discipline ☐ Yes ☐ No

E. Is there an employee handbook? ☐ Yes ☐ No
If "Yes": 1. Is it distributed to all new employees (including all attorneys)? ☐ Yes ☐ No
2. Does it contain a comprehensive "employment at will" statement? ☐ Yes ☐ No

F. Is there a written procedure for handling employee complaints of harassment and/or discrimination? ☐ Yes ☐ No

G. Have anti-sexual harassment policies and procedures been implemented by the **Applicant**? ☐ Yes ☐ No
If "Yes," has the **Applicant** informed employees that incidents of sexual harassment may be reported without fear of retaliation by the **Applicant**?

H. Does the **Applicant's** sexual harassment and/or discrimination policy encompass third parties in addition to employees? ☐ Yes ☐ No

I. Does the **Applicant** use any tests to screen applicants either for hire or promotion? ☐ Yes ☐ No
If "Yes," please provide details. Please use a separate addendum if necessary.

____
____
____

J. Are all prospective employees required to complete an employment application prior to hire? ☐ Yes ☐ No

K. Is there a formal orientation program for new employees? ☐ Yes ☐ No

L. Are regular, written performance evaluations completed for and provided to all employees? ☐ Yes ☐ No

M. Does the **Applicant** anticipate any branch/location closings, consolidations, or layoffs? ☐ Yes ☐ No
If "Yes," please provide details including the year, anticipated number of layoffs, and the circumstances surrounding those layoffs. Please use a separate addendum if necessary.

____
____
____

N. Does the **Applicant** have a formal out-placement program which assists former employees in obtaining alternate employment? ☐ Yes ☐ No

O. Does the **Applicant** require terminations to be reviewed by outside counsel in addition to its human resources department? ☐ Yes ☐ No

P. Is there a policy concerning assistance provided to employees with AIDS or any other life-threatening or communicable diseases? ☐ Yes ☐ No

Q. Does the **Applicant** provide employees with client relations training designed to avoid third party discrimination and harassment claims? ☐ Yes ☐ No

5. FIRM HISTORY

If the **Applicant** answers "Yes" to any of the following questions, please provide further details on a separate addendum.

A. Has the **Applicant** acquired any other partnerships, firms, or limited liability companies in the last ten (10) years? ☐ Yes ☐ No

B. If "Yes" to question 5. A., did the acquisition include the assumption of liabilities? ☐ Yes ☐ No

C. With respect to any acquisitions, were any employees, partners, or other attorneys terminated, or does the **Applicant** plan in the next eighteen (18) months to terminate any employees, partners, or other attorneys? ☐ Yes ☐ No
If "Yes," please explain on a separate addendum.

6. PLEASE PROVIDE COPIES OF THE FOLLOWING:

A. Firm Financial Information Supplement (Attachment)
B. Employee handbook
C. Procedure for handling employee complaints of discrimination or sexual harassment

NOTICE TO APPLICANT — PLEASE READ CAREFULLY.

FOR THE PURPOSES OF THIS APPLICATION, THE UNDERSIGNED AUTHORIZED AGENT OF THE PERSON(S) AND ENTITY(IES) PROPOSED FOR THIS INSURANCE DECLARES THAT TO THE BEST OF HIS/HER KNOWLEDGE AND BELIEF, AFTER REASONABLE INQUIRY, THE STATEMENTS HEREIN ARE TRUE AND COMPLETE. THE UNDERWRITER IS AUTHORIZED TO MAKE INQUIRY IN CONNECTION WITH THIS APPLICATION. SIGNING THIS APPLICATION DOES NOT BIND THE UNDERWRITER TO COMPLETE, OR THE APPLICANT TO PURCHASE, THE INSURANCE.

THE INFORMATION CONTAINED IN AND SUBMITTED WITH THIS APPLICATION IS ON FILE WITH THE UNDERWRITER AND ALONG WITH THE APPLICATION IS CONSIDERED PHYSICALLY ATTACHED TO THE POLICY AND WILL BECOME A PART OF IT. THE UNDERWRITER WILL HAVE RELIED UPON THIS APPLICATION AND ATTACHMENTS IN ISSUING ANY POLICY. THE APPLICATION WILL BECOME A PART OF SUCH POLICY IF ISSUED.

IF THE INFORMATION IN THIS APPLICATION MATERIALLY CHANGES BETWEEN THE DATE OF THIS APPLICATION AND THE POLICY EFFECTIVE DATE, THE APPLICANT WILL NOTIFY THE UNDERWRITER, WHO MAY MODIFY OR WITHDRAW ANY OUTSTANDING QUOTATION.

THE UNDERSIGNED DECLARES THAT THE PERSON(S) AND ENTITY(IES) PROPOSED FOR THIS INSURANCE UNDERSTAND THAT

(I) THE POLICY SHALL APPLY ONLY TO "CLAIMS" MADE (OR DEEMED MADE) TO THE UNDERWRITER DURING THE "POLICY PERIOD" OR TO "CLAIMS" MADE TO THE UNDERWRITER DURING ANY APPLICABLE "EXTENDED REPORTING PERIOD";

(II) THE LIMIT OF LIABILITY CONTAINED IN THE POLICY SHALL BE REDUCED, AND MAY BE COMPLETELY EXHAUSTED, BY "DEFENSE EXPENSES" AND, IN SUCH EVENT, THE UNDERWRITER SHALL NOT BE LIABLE FOR "DEFENSE EXPENSES" OR FOR THE AMOUNT OF ANY JUDGMENT OR SETTLEMENT TO THE EXTENT THAT SUCH COST OR LIMIT EXCEEDS THE LIMIT OF LIABILITY IN THE POLICY; AND

(III) "DEFENSE EXPENSES" THAT ARE INCURRED SHALL BE APPLIED AGAINST THE RETENTION AMOUNT.

NOTICE TO ARKANSAS, MINNESOTA, AND OHIO APPLICANTS: ANY PERSON WHO, WITH INTENT TO DEFRAUD OR KNOWING THAT HE/SHE IS FACILITATING A FRAUD AGAINST AN INSURER, SUBMITS AN APPLICATION OR FILES A CLAIM CONTAINING A FALSE OR DECEPTIVE STATEMENT IS GUILTY OF INSURANCE FRAUD, WHICH IS A CRIME.

NOTICE TO COLORADO APPLICANTS: IT IS UNLAWFUL TO KNOWINGLY PROVIDE FALSE, INCOMPLETE, OR MISLEADING FACTS OR INFORMATION TO AN INSURANCE COMPANY FOR THE PURPOSE OF DEFRAUDING OR ATTEMPTING TO DEFRAUD THE COMPANY. PENALTIES MAY INCLUDE IMPRISONMENT, FINES, DENIAL OF INSURANCE, AND CIVIL DAMAGES. ANY INSURANCE COMPANY OR AGENT OF AN INSURANCE COMPANY WHO KNOWINGLY PROVIDES FALSE, INCOMPLETE, OR MISLEADING FACTS OR INFORMATION TO A POLICY HOLDER OR CLAIMANT FOR THE PURPOSE OF DEFRAUDING OR ATTEMPTING TO DEFRAUD THE POLICY HOLDER OR CLAIMANT WITH REGARD TO A SETTLEMENT OR AWARD PAYABLE FROM INSURANCE PROCEEDS SHALL BE REPORTED TO THE COLORADO DIVISION OF INSURANCE WITHIN THE DEPARTMENT OF REGULATORY AGENCIES.

NOTICE TO DISTRICT OF COLUMBIA, MAINE AND VIRGINIA APPLICANTS: IT IS A CRIME TO KNOWINGLY PROVIDE FALSE, INCOMPLETE OR MISLEADING INFORMATION TO AN INSURANCE COMPANY FOR THE PURPOSE OF DEFRAUDING THE COMPANY. PENALTIES MAY INCLUDE IMPRISONMENT, FINES, OR A DENIAL OF INSURANCE BENEFITS.

NOTICE TO FLORIDA APPLICANTS: ANY PERSON WHO, KNOWINGLY AND WITH INTENT TO INJURE, DEFRAUD, OR DECEIVE ANY EMPLOYER OR EMPLOYEE, INSURANCE COMPANY, OR SELF-INSURED PROGRAM, FILES A STATEMENT OF CLAIM OR AN APPLICATION CONTAINING ANY FALSE OR MISLEADING INFORMATION IS GUILTY OF A FELONY OF THE THIRD DEGREE.

NOTICE TO KENTUCKY APPLICANTS: ANY PERSON WHO KNOWINGLY AND WITH INTENT TO DEFRAUD ANY INSURANCE COMPANY OR OTHER PERSON FILES AN APPLICATION FOR INSURANCE CONTAINING ANY FALSE INFORMATION, OR CONCEALS FOR THE PURPOSE OF MISLEADING, INFORMATION CONCERNING ANY FACT MATERIAL THERETO, COMMITS A FRAUDULENT INSURANCE ACT, WHICH IS A CRIME.

NOTICE TO LOUISIANA AND NEW MEXICO APPLICANTS: ANY PERSON WHO KNOWINGLY PRESENTS A FALSE OR FRAUDULENT CLAIM FOR PAYMENT OF A LOSS OR BENEFIT OR KNOWINGLY PRESENTS FALSE INFORMATION IN AN APPLICATION FOR INSURANCE IS GUILTY OF A CRIME AND MAY BE SUBJECT TO CIVIL FINES AND CRIMINAL PENALTIES.

NOTICE TO MARYLAND APPLICANTS: ANY PERSON WHO, WITH INTENT TO DEFRAUD OR KNOWING THAT HE/SHE IS FACILITATING A FRAUD AGAINST AN INSURER, SUBMITS AN APPLICATION OR FILES A CLAIM CONTAINING A FALSE OR DECEPTIVE STATEMENT MAY BE GUILTY OF INSURANCE FRAUD.

NOTICE TO NEW JERSEY APPLICANTS: ANY PERSON WHO INCLUDES ANY FALSE OR MISLEADING INFORMATION ON AN APPLICATION FOR AN INSURANCE POLICY IS SUBJECT TO CRIMINAL AND CIVIL PENALTIES.

NOTICE TO NEW YORK APPLICANTS: ANY PERSON WHO KNOWINGLY AND WITH INTENT TO DEFRAUD ANY INSURANCE COMPANY OR OTHER PERSON FILES AN APPLICATION FOR INSURANCE OR STATEMENT OF CLAIM CONTAINING ANY MATERIALLY FALSE INFORMATION, OR CONCEALS FOR THE PURPOSE OF MISLEADING, INFORMATION CONCERNING ANY FACT MATERIAL THERETO, COMMITS A FRAUDULENT INSURANCE ACT, WHICH IS A CRIME AND SHALL ALSO BE SUBJECT TO A CIVIL PENALTY NOT TO EXCEED FIVE THOUSAND DOLLARS AND THE STATED VALUE OF THE CLAIM FOR EACH SUCH VIOLATION.

NOTICE TO OKLAHOMA APPLICANTS: ANY PERSON WHO KNOWINGLY AND WITH INTENT TO INJURE, DEFRAUD OR DECEIVE ANY INSURER, MAKES ANY CLAIM FOR THE PROCEEDS OF AN INSURANCE POLICY CONTAINING ANY FALSE, INCOMPLETE OR MISLEADING INFORMATION IS GUILTY OF A FELONY.

NOTICE TO OREGON AND TEXAS APPLICANTS: ANY PERSON WHO MAKES AN INTENTIONAL MISSTATEMENT THAT IS MATERIAL TO THE RISK MAY BE FOUND GUILTY OF INSURANCE FRAUD BY A COURT OF LAW.

NOTICE TO PENNSYLVANIA APPLICANTS: ANY PERSON WHO KNOWINGLY AND WITH INTENT TO DEFRAUD ANY INSURANCE COMPANY OR OTHER PERSON FILES AN APPLICATION FOR INSURANCE OR STATEMENT OF CLAIM CONTAINING ANY MATERIALLY FALSE INFORMATION, OR CONCEALS FOR THE PURPOSE OF MISLEADING, INFORMATION CONCERNING ANY FACT MATERIAL THERETO, COMMITS A FRAUDULENT INSURANCE ACT, WHICH IS A CRIME AND SUBJECTS SUCH PERSON TO CRIMINAL AND CIVIL PENALTIES.

APPLICANT		
BY *(Principal, Partner, or Shareholder)*	TITLE	DATE

NOTE: This Application is signed by the undersigned authorized agent of the **Applicant** on behalf of the **Applicant** and all of its partners, owners, shareholders, officers, and employees.

REQUIRED INFORMATION

PRODUCED BY *(Insurance Agent)* Please print and sign name ____________________ ____________________	
INSURANCE AGENCY	
INSURANCE AGENCY TAXPAYER ID OR SOCIAL SECURITY NO.	AGENT LICENSE NO.
ADDRESS *(No., Street, City, State, and ZIP)*	
EMAIL ADDRESS	

SUBMITTED BY *(Insurance Agency)*	INSURANCE AGENCY TAXPAYER ID OR SOCIAL SECURITY NO.	AGENT LICENSE NO.
ADDRESS *(No., Street, City, State, and ZIP)*		

EXECUTIVE RISK INDEMNITY INC. APPLICATION FOR ABA EMPLOYERS EDGE℠
AN EMPLOYMENT PRACTICES LIABILITY INSURANCE POLICY FOR LAW FIRMS
ENDORSED BY THE AMERICAN BAR ASSOCIATION
FIRM FINANCIAL INFORMATION SUPPLEMENT

Name of **Applicant**: ____________________

This supplement is part of the Application for ABA Employers Edge℠, An Employment Practices Liability Insurance Policy for Law Firms.

Please supply the following information and the source financial documents listed below. For items 1, 2, and 3, supply information for your latest completed fiscal year and the prior two fiscal years. For items 4, 5, and 6, please supply the amount at year end.

	Latest Fiscal Year (ending __/__/__)	**1st Prior Fiscal Year (ending __/__/__)**	**2nd Prior Fiscal Year (ending __/__/__)**
1. Gross Revenues: Cash receipts from professional services, excluding expense reimbursements.			
2. Net Income: Total net income for distribution to active equity partners or shareholders.			
3. Total Debt (Net present value): The sum of long- and short-term debt to all creditors. Please indicate the discount rate used to compute net present value. (If net present value estimate is not available, list each obligation and its maturity date.)			
4. Lease Obligations (Net present value): Please include all leases — e.g., for real estate, furnishings, office equipment, etc. Please indicate the discount rate used to compute net present value. (If net present value estimate is not available, list all leases and show payment due by year for each.)			
5. Obligations to Former Partners/Shareholders (Net present value): Total of all payments due to retired partners/shareholders or former partners/shareholders, for whatever reasons. Please indicate the discount rate used to compute net present value. (If net present value estimate is not available, please list obligations per year for each individual.)			
6. Partner or Shareholder Equity: Total partner or shareholder equity.			

Please provide latest fiscal year financial statements (income statement and balance sheet), audited if available, with this supplement.

I understand that information submitted herein becomes part of the Applicant's Application for ABA Employers Edge℠, An Employment Practices Liability Insurance Policy for Law Firms, and is subject to all of the representations and conditions set forth therein.

____________________ ____________________
Authorized Signature of **Applicant** (Principal, Partner, or Shareholder) Date

____________________ ____________________
Print Name Date

Form C26025 (4/98 ed.) 7 Catalog No. ABAa-I
Form 14-03-0229

APPENDIX 1C
DECLARATIONS

Executive Risk Specialty Insurance Company

Home Office:
82 Hopmeadow Street
Simsbury, Connecticut 06070-7683

ABA EMPLOYERS EDGE℠
AN EMPLOYMENT PRACTICES LIABILITY INSURANCE POLICY FOR LAW FIRMS ENDORSED BY THE AMERICAN BAR ASSOCIATION

DECLARATIONS

THIS IS A CLAIMS MADE POLICY WITH DEFENSE EXPENSES INCLUDED IN THE LIMIT OF LIABILITY. PLEASE READ THE ENTIRE POLICY CAREFULLY.

RENEWAL OF	POLICY NUMBER
[Prior Years policy number]	[Formatted Policy Number]

NOTICE: THIS IS A CLAIMS MADE POLICY WHICH APPLIES, SUBJECT TO ITS TERMS, ONLY TO "CLAIMS" FIRST MADE DURING THE "POLICY PERIOD," OR, IF PURCHASED, ANY EXTENDED REPORTING PERIOD. THE LIMIT OF LIABILITY AVAILABLE TO PAY DAMAGES OR SETTLEMENTS WILL BE REDUCED BY "DEFENSE EXPENSES," AND "DEFENSE EXPENSES" WILL BE APPLIED AGAINST THE RETENTION. THE UNDERWRITER WILL HAVE NO DUTY TO DEFEND ANY "CLAIM."

ITEM 1. **INSURED FIRM** - NAME AND PRINCIPAL ADDRESS:
[Account Name]
[Account Address including address1 and address2]
[Account City Name], [Account Domicile State] [Account Zip Code]
Predecessor Firm(s):[Predecessor Firm(s)]
Address(es): [Address(es) for Predecessor Firms(s)]

ITEM 2. **POLICY PERIOD**:
(a) Inception Date: [Effective Date]
(b) Expiration Date: [Expiration Date of the Policy]
at 12:01 a.m. both dates at the Principal Address in ITEM 1.

ITEM 3. **LIMIT OF LIABILITY** (Inclusive of **Defense Expenses**):
(a) $[Individual Limit] maximum Limit of Liability for each **Claim**.
(b) $[Aggregate Limit] maximum aggregate Limit of Liability for all **Claims**.

ITEM 4. **RETENTIONS**:
(a) $[Individual retention] each and every **Claim**.
(b) [EPLI Aggregate Retention] aggregate.

ITEM 5. **RETROACTIVE DATE**:
[Retro date for DEC page]

ITEM 6. **PREMIUM**:
$[Total Premium] premium.
[Premium Due Date - get default wording]

ITEM 7. **EXTENDED REPORTING PERIOD**:
[Discovery Period] Extended Reporting Period.
$<DISCPRM> additional premium for Extended Reporting Period.

ITEM 8. **ENDORSEMENTS ATTACHED AT ISSUANCE**:

[Endorsement Code on Dec Page]	[Endorsement Code on Dec Page]	[Endorsement Code on Dec Page]	[Endorsement Code on Dec Page]	[Endorsement Code on Dec Page]
[Endorsement Code on Dec Page]	[Endorsement Code on Dec Page]	[Endorsement Code on Dec Page]	[Endorsement Code on Dec Page]	[Endorsement Code on Dec Page]
[Endorsement Code on Dec Page]	[Endorsement Code on Dec Page]	[Endorsement Code on Dec Page]	[Endorsement Code on Dec Page]	[Endorsement Code on Dec Page]
[Endorsement Code on Dec Page]	[Endorsement Code on Dec Page]	[Endorsement Code on Dec Page]	[Endorsement Code on Dec Page]	[Endorsement Code on Dec Page]
[Endorsement Code on Dec Page]	[Endorsement Code on Dec Page]	[Endorsement Code on Dec Page]	[Endorsement Code on Dec Page]	[Endorsement Code on Dec Page]
[Endorsement Code on Dec Page]	[Endorsement Code on Dec Page]	[Endorsement Code on Dec Page]	[Endorsement Code on Dec Page]	[Endorsement Code on Dec Page]

These Declarations, the completed signed Application and the Policy with Endorsements shall constitute the contract between the Underwriter and the Insureds.

EXECUTIVE RISK SPECIALTY INSURANCE COMPANY by (Authorized Company Representative):

Form B26028 (4/98 ed.) Catalog No. ABAd-S

May 13, 1998

[CURRENCYTYPE]

APPENDIX 1D
Specimen Duty to Defend Endorsement with Coverage Enhancements

ENDORSEMENT/RIDER

[Print Coverage Section description on Endorsements]

Effective date of
this endorsement/rider: [Transaction Effective Date]

[Carrier name]

Endorsement/Rider No. [Endorsement number that is calculated when form fill-ins are entered]

To be attached to and
form a part of Policy No. [Formatted Policy Number]

Issued to: [Account Name]

DUTY TO DEFEND ENDORSEMENT WITH COVERAGE ENHANCEMENTS

In consideration of the premium charged, it is agreed that:

(1) Section I., Insuring Agreement, of the Policy is deleted and replaced with the following:

I. **INSURING AGREEMENTS**

(A) The Underwriter will pay on behalf of the **Insureds Defense Expenses** and **Loss** in excess of the applicable retention set forth in ITEM 4 of the Declarations resulting from **Claims** first made against any **Insured** during the **Policy Period** or, if applicable, the Extended Reporting Period, for **Employment Practices Wrongful Acts** occurring subsequent to the Retroactive Date stated in ITEM 5 of the Declarations and before the expiration of the **Policy Period**.

(B) The Underwriter will have the right and duty to defend any covered **Claim**, even if the allegations thereof are groundless, false, or fraudulent; provided, that the Underwriter's obligation to defend is subject to the applicable retention and Limit of Liability provisions as set forth in CONDITION (E) below."

(2) Subparagraph (2) of the definition of "**Claim**" as set forth in Section II., Definitions, paragraph (B) of the Policy, is deleted and replaced with the following:

(2) any judicial, administrative or other proceeding, include any criminal proceeding, against any **Insured** for an **Employment Practices Wrongful Acts**; or"

(3) The term "**Defense Expenses**" as defined in Section II., Definitions, paragraph (C) of the Policy, is deleted and replaced with the following:

(C) "**Defense Expenses**" means reasonable legal fees and expenses incurred through counsel of the Underwriter's choice in the investigation, defense or appeal of any **Claim** (including, with the consent of the Underwriter, fees for appeal bonds and expert witnesses); provided, that **Defense Expenses** does not include remuneration, salaries, wages, fees, expenses, overhead or benefit expenses of any **Insured**.

(4) The term "**Loss**" as defined in Section II., Definitions, paragraph (J) of the Policy, is deleted and replaced with the following:

D28571 (03/2007) rev Page 1
<NYFTZFOOTER><NYFTZNOTICE>

(J) "**Loss**" means any damages (including back pay awards, front pay awards, compensatory damages and punitive or exemplary damages if insurable under the law pursuant to which this policy is construed), pre-judgment interest, post-judgment interest, and settlements which an **Insured** is legally obligated to pay as a result of a **Claim**; provided, that **Loss** does not include:

(1) civil or criminal fines, sanctions, liquidated damages, taxes or penalties, the multiplied portion of any multiplied damage award (except for multiplied damages awarded pursuant to the Age Discrimination in Employment Act and the Equal Pay Act), or matters which are uninsurable under the law pursuant to which this Policy is construed;

(2) any costs associated with the modification of any building or property in order to provide any reasonable accommodations required by, made as a result of, or to conform with the requirements of the Americans With Disabilities Act and any amendments thereto or any similar federal, state or local statute, regulation, or common law;

(3) any other non-monetary relief awarded against any **Insured**, including without limitation any costs associated with compliance with any injunctive relief of any kind or nature;

(4) severance pay or damages determined to be owing under an express written contract of employment or an express written obligation to make payments in the event of the termination of employment;

(5) payment of insurance plan benefits; and

(6) amounts awarded pursuant to a labor or grievance arbitration or other proceeding pursuant to a collective bargaining agreement."

(5) The term "**Workplace Tort**" as defined in Section II., Definitions, paragraph (R) of the Policy is deleted and replaced with the following:

(R) "**Workplace Tort**" means employment-related: misrepresentation, defamation (including libel and slander), invasion of privacy, false imprisonment, negligent evaluation, wrongful discipline, or wrongful deprivation of career opportunity."

(6) Section V., Conditions, paragraph (B), Reporting of Claims and Potential Claims, subparagraph (1) of the Policy is deleted and replaced with the following:

(1) If a **Claim** is made against any **Insured**, the **Insured** or the Firm shall give written notice thereof to the Underwriter as soon as practicable after such **Claim** is first made as determined pursuant to CONDITION (C)(1) and shall immediately forward to the Underwriter every demand, notice, summons, complaint or other process received by any Insured or his/her/its representatives. Compliance with this notice requirement is a strict condition precedent to coverage under this Policy."

(7) Section V., Conditions, paragraph (D), Defense and Settlement of Claims, of the Policy is deleted and replaced with the following:

(D) **Defense and Settlement of Claims**:

(1) No **Insured** may admit any liability for any **Claim** or settle any **Claim** without the Underwriter's consent; provided, however, that the **Insureds** may settle any **Claim** without the Underwriter's consent where **Defense Expenses** and the settlement amount in respect of such **Claim**, in the

aggregate, do not exceed fifty percent (50%) of the applicable retention. The Underwriter will have the right to make investigations and conduct negotiations and, with the consent of the **Insureds**, enter into such settlement of any **Claim** as the Underwriter deems appropriate. If the **Insureds** refuse to consent to a settlement acceptable to the claimant in accordance with the Underwriter's recommendation, then the Underwriter's liability for such **Claim** will not exceed:

(a) the amount for which the **Claim** could have been settled plus any **Defense Expenses** incurred up to the date the **Insureds** refuse to settle such **Claim**, plus

(b) eighty percent (80%) of any amounts (including **Loss** and **Defense Expenses**) in excess of the amount set forth in clause (a) above, incurred in connection with such **Claim**; subject, in all events, to the applicable retention and the maximum aggregate Limit of Liability. The remaining twenty percent (20%) of all amounts in excess of the amount for which the **Claim** could have been settled will be carried by the Insureds at their own risk and will be uninsured.

(2) The Underwriter may, in its sole discretion and without any obligation to do so, undertake investigations and conduct negotiations with respect to any **Potential Claim** and, with the consent of the **Insureds**, enter into such settlement of any **Potential Claim** as the Underwriter deems appropriate. Any such settlement of a **Potential Claim** shall be treated as the settlement of a **Claim** made during the **Policy Period** in which the **Potential Claim** was reported to the Underwriter. If the **Insureds** refuse to consent to a settlement acceptable to the potential claimant in accordance with the Underwriter's recommendation, then the Underwriter's liability for any **Claim** resulting from such **Potential Claim** will not exceed:

(a) the amount for which the **Potential Claim** could have been settled, plus

(b) eighty percent (80%) of any amounts (including **Loss** and **Defense Expenses**) in excess of the amount set forth in clause (a) above, subject, in all events, to the applicable retention and the maximum aggregate Limit of Liability. The remaining twenty percent (20%) of all amounts in excess of the amount for which the **Potential Claim** could have been settled will be carried by the **Insureds** at their own risk and will be uninsured."

(8) Section V., Conditions, paragraph (E), Limits of Liability; Retention, subparagraph (3) of the Policy is deleted and replaced with the following:

(3) **Defenses Expenses** will be part of and not in addition to such Limit of Liability, and payment of **Defense Expenses** by the Underwriter will reduce, and may exhaust, the Limit of Liability. If the Limit of Liability is exhausted prior to the conclusion of any **Claim**, the Underwriter shall have the right to withdraw from the defense of the **Claim** by tendering control of the defense to the **Insureds** against whom the **Claim** is made and in that event the Underwriter will have no further obligations of any kind or nature whatsoever under this Policy.

The title and any headings in this endorsement/rider are solely for convenience and form no part of the terms and conditions of coverage.

All other terms, conditions and limitations of this Policy shall remain unchanged.

____
Authorized Representative

APPENDIX 1E
Specimen Amended Reporting Provision Endorsement

ENDORSEMENT/RIDER

[Print Coverage Section description on Endorsements]

Effective date of
this endorsement/rider: [Transaction Effective Date]

[Carrier name]

Endorsement/Rider No. [Endorsement number that is calculated when form fill-ins are entered]

To be attached to and
form a part of Policy No. [Formatted Policy Number]

Issued to: [Account Name]

AMENDED REPORTING PROVISION ENDORSEMENT

In consideration of the premium charged, it is agreed that:

(1) Subparagraph (B)(1), Reporting of Claims and Potential Claims, of Section V, Conditions, is amended to include the following:

Notwithstanding the foregoing and solely with respect to any **Claim** that is brought as a formal administrative or regulatory proceeding commenced by the filing of a notice of charges against any **Insured**, the **Insured** or **the Firm**, shall, as a condition precedent to exercising any right to coverage under this Policy, give written notice thereof to the Underwriter during the **Policy Period**, or, if applicable, in no event later than the earliest of the following dates:

(i) if this Policy is renewed, 180 days after the end of the **Policy Period**,

(ii) if this Policy expires (or is otherwise terminated) without being renewed and if no Extended Reporting Period is purchased, sixty (60) days after the effective date of such expiration or termination; or

(iii) the expiration date of the Extended Reporting Period, if purchased.

With respect to the reporting of any **Claim** under this Policy, it is agreed that in determining whether the reporting of such **Claim** has been timely made, the Underwriter shall make such determination by applying the law of any jurisdiction which has a substantial relationship to the **Insureds**, the Underwriter, this Policy or the **Claim** and which is most favorable to such determination of timeliness.

(2) Nothing in this Endorsement is intended nor shall it be construed to violate the applicable laws of any state and therefore, notwithstanding the provisions of any "Amendatory Endorsement" attached to this Policy (the "Amendatory"), the terms of this Endorsement shall supersede and take precedence over the provisions, if any, of the Amendatory applicable to the reporting and notice of claims.

The title and any headings in this endorsement/rider are solely for convenience and form no part of the terms and conditions of coverage.

All other terms, conditions and limitations of this Policy shall remain unchanged.

____
Authorized Representative

APPENDIX 1F
Specimen Violation of Employee Privacy Endorsement (Defense Costs Only with Sublimit)

ENDORSEMENT/RIDER

[Print Coverage Section description on Endorsements]

Effective date of
this endorsement/rider: [Transaction Effective Date]

[Carrier name]

Endorsement/Rider No. [Endorsement number that is calculated when form fill-ins are entered]

To be attached to and
form a part of Policy No. [Formatted Policy Number]

Issued to: [Account Name]

VIOLATION OF EMPLOYEE PRIVACY ENDORSEMENT
(DEFENSE COSTS ONLY WITH SUBLIMIT)

In consideration of the premium charged, it is agreed that the following shall apply:

(1) The Underwriter's maximum aggregate liability for all **Defense Expenses** on account of all **Claims** for a "Violation of Employee Privacy" (as defined below) shall be [Sub-Limit], which amount is part of, and not in addition to, the Underwriter's maximum aggregate Limit of Liability as set forth in Item 3 of the Declarations.

(2) No coverage will be available under this Policy for **Loss**, other than **Defense Expenses**, on account of any **Claim** for a Violation of Employee Privacy.

(3) The definition of **Employment Practices Wrongful Act**, as set forth in Section II, Definitions, is amended to include the following:

> **Employment Practices Wrongful Act** shall also mean any actual or alleged Violation of Employee Privacy.

(4) For the purposes of this endorsement, the following terms shall have the meanings set forth below:

"Violation of Employee Privacy" means a **Firm's** failure to:

(i) secure an **Employee's** "Record" (as defined below) from actual or potential unauthorized access by another person or by an organization which results in injury to such **Employee**; or

(ii) provide notice as required by any state, federal or local statutory law or common law anywhere in the world to an **Employee** whose Record was accessed or may have been accessed by an unauthorized person.

"Record" means an **Employee's** first name or first initial, and last name, in combination with:

(i) their social security number, driver's license number or other personal identification number (including an employee identification number or student identification number);

(ii) their financial account number (including a bank account number, retirement account number, or healthcare spending account number);

(iii) their credit, debit or other payment card number; or

(iv) any individually identifiable health information, pursuant to the Health Insurance Portability and Accountability Act of 1996 ("HIPAA"), held by the **Firm**,

when any such information in (i) through (iv) above is intended by the **Firm** to be accessible only by persons or organizations specifically authorized by the **Firm** to have access to such information.

(5) For the purposes of this endorsement, the following provision is added to this Policy:

Coordination of Coverage

Any **Loss** otherwise covered both pursuant to the terms of this endorsement and the *CyberSecurity by Chubb*^{SM} policy, if purchased, shall be first covered under this Policy, subject to its terms, conditions, and limitations.

The title and any headings in this endorsement/rider are solely for convenience and form no part of the terms and conditions of coverage.

All other terms, conditions and limitations of this Policy shall remain unchanged.

____
Authorized Representative

APPENDIX 1G
Specimen Spousal and Domestic Partner Extension Endorsement

ENDORSEMENT NO. [Endorsement number that is calculated when form fill-ins are entered]
SPOUSAL AND DOMESTIC PARTNER EXTENSION ENDORSEMENT

This Endorsement, effective at 12:01 a.m. on [Transaction Effective Date], forms part of

Policy No. [Formatted Policy Number]
Issued to [Account Name]
Issued by [Carrier name]

In consideration of the premium charged:

(1) The term **Insured**, as defined in Section II Definitions (I) of this Policy, is amended to include the lawful spouse or **Domestic Partner** of a natural person **Insured** against whom a **Claim** is made solely by reason of:

(a) such spouse or **Domestic Partner's** legal status as a spouse or **Domestic Partner** of such **Insured**; or

(b) such spouse or **Domestic Partner's** ownership interest in property which the claimant seeks as recovery for an alleged **Employment Practices Wrongful Act** by such **Insured**;

provided such **Insured** and his or her spouse or **Domestic Partner** are represented by the same counsel in connection with such **Claim**.

(2) No spouse or **Domestic Partner** of a natural person **Insured** will, by reason of this endorsement, have any greater right to coverage under this Policy than such **Insured**.

(3) The Underwriter will not be liable under this endorsement to make any payment of **Defense Expenses** or **Loss** in connection with any **Claim** against a spouse or **Domestic Partner** of a natural person **Insured** for any actual or alleged **Employment Practices Wrongful Act** by such spouse or **Domestic Partner**.

(4) For the purposes of this endorsement, the term **Domestic Partner** means any natural person qualifying as a domestic partner under the provisions of any applicable federal, state or local law or under the provisions of any formal program established by the **Firm**.

All other terms, conditions and limitations of this Policy shall remain unchanged.

____
Authorized Representative

CHAPTER 2
Coverage for Employment Claims Under Other Insurance Policies

Kenneth M. Gorenberg, Carolyn M. Wendel, Benjamin W. Tull

I. Introduction

This chapter addresses the circumstances under which claims typically thought of as employment claims—claims brought under Title VII, the Age Discrimination in Employment Act (ADEA), the Americans with Disabilities Act (ADA), as well as wrongful discharge and retaliatory discharge claims—may be covered under insurance other than employment practices liability (EPL) insurance. Even before the widespread availability of EPL policies, employers sought insurance coverage for employment-related claims. When individuals first began filing employment discrimination claims, employment liabilities were not specifically addressed in insurance policies. Employers began seeking coverage under commercial general liability (CGL) policies because nearly every employer purchases a CGL policy. Eventually, insurers reacted to the employment claims by creating employment exclusions under CGL (and other policies) and providing separate EPL policies.

Recent developments over the past few years have increased the need for employers to be concerned with coverage for employment-related claims. The economic crisis facing our country has led many employers to reduce their workforces, exposing employers to potential claims. Additionally, recent legislative changes have made it easier for certain employment-related claims to be brought against employers.[1] In 2011, the EEOC received just shy of 100,000 charges, the most filings in its history.[2] Now more than ever, employers must be concerned with whether they have coverage for potential claims.

Whether a particular employment claim brought by a particular employee (or former employee) is potentially covered by a particular insurance policy depends on the allegations in the complaint and the terms of the policy at issue. Given the rise of EPL insurance policies and exclusions for employment-related practices, establishing that a non-EPL insurance policy covers employment claims against the insured can be a challenge. However, employers should not assume that coverage is or is not available under a particular policy; every complaint and every insurance policy is unique.

This chapter provides guidance on the types of language in various insurance policies that, if present, can be used to establish that employment claims are covered by a policy. First, the chapter covers basic presumptions courts apply when assessing whether an insurance policy requires the insurer to defend or indemnify an employer for employment-related claims. Second, the chapter discusses coverage

---

1. The Lilly Ledbetter Fair Pay Act of 2009 provides that each discriminatory paycheck is deemed an unlawful employment practice and will start the 180-day statute of limitations anew. Lilly Ledbetter Fair Pay Act of 2009, Pub. L. No. 111-2, § 181, 123 Stat. 5 (2009). The ADA Amendments of 2008 revised the definition of *disability* and, in doing so, broadened the class of employees who can qualify as disabled. ADA Amendments Act of 2008, Pub L. No. 110-325, 122 Stat. 3553 (2008).

2. EEOC Charge Statistics FY 1997 Through FY 2011, *available at* http://eeoc.gov/eeoc/statistics/enforcement/charges.cfm (in 2011, there were 99,947 charges).

for employment claims under CGL policies, the insurance (other than EPL) most often used by employers to obtain coverage for employment claims. Third, the chapter discusses coverage for employment claims under Directors and Officers, Errors and Omissions, and Workers' Compensation and Employer's Liability policies.

II. Background Information

The following is a brief explanation of an insurer's general duties to its insured under an insurance policy. This discussion is applicable to almost any liability insurance policy. We include it as a useful guide for understanding a court's consideration of whether particular employment claims are covered by a particular insurance policy.

A. Legal Framework for Determining Duty to Defend and Indemnification

Liability policies typically include two separate duties for the insurer: (1) indemnification of the policyholder for judgments or settlements paid by the policyholder and (2) defense of the policyholder while a claim is pending. The duty to indemnify arises when the insured pays a judgment or settlement for a claim that actually falls within the coverage terms of the policy. The duty to defend (that is, to provide or pay for lawyers to represent the insured defendant) is broader than the duty to indemnify because it is determined without regard to the merits of the claims.[3] Rather, the duty to defend is triggered by mere

3. *Agric. Ins. Co. v. Focus Homes, Inc.*, 212 F.3d 407, 410 (8th Cir. 2000) (Minnesota); *Adams v. Pro Sources, Inc.*, 231 F. Supp. 2d 499, 505 (M.D. La. 2002) (Louisiana); *ARC Water Treatment Co. of Pa., Inc. v. Hartford Cas. Ins. Co.*, No. 98-CV-6358, 2002 WL 32392683, at *2 (E.D. Pa. Mar. 27, 2002) (Pennsylvania); *Sidney Frank Importing Co. v. Farmington Cas. Co.*, No. 97 CIV 9324 LAP, 1999 WL 173263, at *3 (S.D. N.Y. March 26, 1999), *aff'd*, 199 F.3d 1323 (2d Cir. 1999) (New York); *N. Am. Bldg. Maint., Inc. v. Fireman's Fund Ins. Co.*, 40 Cal. Rptr. 3d 468, 475 (Cal. Ct. App. 2006) (California); *Springdale Donuts, Inc. v. Aetna Cas. & Sur. Co.*, 724 A.2d 1117, 1120 (Conn. 1999) (Connecticut) ("an insurer's duty to defend, being much broader in scope and application than its duty to indemnify, is determined by reference to the allegations contained in the underlying complaint"); *Pekin Ins. Co. v. Wilson*, 930 N.E.2d 1011,

allegations that potentially come within the policy's indemnity terms.[4] To determine whether the policy covers the claims at issue, the court compares the allegations in the complaint with the terms of the policy. In some states, the insurer must defend unless the complaint "unambiguously excludes coverage."[5] The duty to defend may also arise by looking to facts beyond the complaint that are known to the insurer,[6] though the insurer typically has no duty to investigate facts beyond the complaint.[7] Some courts have held that the court may look not only to the complaint but also to other pleadings to determine whether the case as a whole gives rise to a situation that an insurer must defend.[8]

1017 (Ill. 2010) (Illinois); *John's Cocktail Lounge, Inc. v. N. River Ins. Co.*, 563 A.2d 473, 476 (N.J. Sup. Ct. App. Div. 1989) (New Jersey); *Sch. Dist. No. 1 v. Mission Ins. Co.*, 650 P.2d 929, 933 (Or. Ct. App. 1982) (Oregon).

4. *Focus Homes*, 212 F.3d at 410 (Minnesota); *Old Republic Ins. v. Comprehensive Health Care Assocs., Inc.*, 2 F.3d 105, 107 (5th Cir. 1993) (Texas) ("In Texas, an insurer's duty to defend is based solely on the allegations of the state or federal court petition."); *Hawkeye-Security Ins. Co. v. Bob Propheter Constr., L.L.C.*, No. 01 C 3278, 2002 WL 31176183, at *8 (N.D. Ill. Sept. 30, 2002) (Illinois); *ARC Water*, 2002 WL 32392683, at *2 (Pennsylvania); *Mut. Serv. Cas. Ins. Co. v. Co-op Supply, Inc.*, 699 F. Supp. 1438, 1439 (D. Mont. 1988) (Montana); *St. Paul Fire & Marine Ins. Co. v. Superior Court*, 208 Cal. Rptr. 5, 7 (Cal. Ct. App. 1984) (California); *Presidential Hotel v. Canal Ins. Co.*, 373 S.E.2d 671, 672 (Ga. Ct. App. 1988) (Georgia); *Smithway Motor Xpress, Inc. v. Liberty Mut. Ins. Co.*, 484 N.W.2d 192, 194 (Iowa 1992) ("an insurer has a duty to defend whenever there is potential or possible liability to indemnify the insured based on the facts appearing at the outset of the case") (quoting *First Newton Nat'l Bank v. General Cas. Co.*, 426 N.W.2d 618, 623 (Iowa 1988)); *John's Cocktail Lounge*, 563 A.2d at 475 (New Jersey); *Sch. Dist. No. 1*, 650 P.2d at 933 (Oregon).

5. *E.g.*, *Adams*, 231 F. Supp. 2d at 502; *see also Dixon Distrib. Co. v. Hanover Ins. Co.*, 641 N.E.2d 395, 398 (Ill. 1994) ("Refusal to defend is unjustifiable unless it is clear from the face of the underlying complaint that the allegations fail to state facts that bring the case within, or potentially within, the policy's coverage"); *Int'l Ins. Co. v. Allied Van Lines, Inc.*, 688 N.E.2d 680, 681 (Ill. App. Ct. 1997) ("[insurer] has a duty to defend [insured] unless it is clear from the face of the underlying complaint that the allegations fail to state facts that bring the case within, or potentially within, the policy's coverage") (emphasis and internal quotations removed).

6. *N. Am. Bldg. Maint.*, 40 Cal. Rptr. 3d at 475; *SL Indus., Inc. v. Am. Motorists Ins. Co.*, 607 A.2d 1266, 1272 (N.J. 1992).

7. *SL Indus.*, 607 A.2d at 1272.

8. *Nat'l Fire Ins. Co. of Hartford v. NWM-Oklahoma, LLC, Inc.*, 546 F. Supp. 2d 1238, 1244 (W.D. Okla. 2008) ("The insurer's defense duty is determined on the basis of information gleaned from the petition (and other pleadings)"); *Pekin Ins. Co. v. Wilson*,

Typically, if even one claim of a complaint is potentially covered by the policy, the insurer has a duty to defend the entire suit.[9] This can be very important for insured employers because if the employer can establish that one of the underlying plaintiff's claims is potentially covered by the policy, then its insurer will be obligated to defend the entire suit. On the other hand, once the covered claims drop out of the suit, the insurer is no longer obligated to defend the insured in that lawsuit.[10] Of course, the insurer will be required to indemnify the employer only with respect to the covered claims. Accordingly, if the insurer's defense of a lawsuit results in a liability determination or settlement with respect to only the claims that are not covered by the insurance policy, the employer will not be indemnified for the amount it pays in damages. Similarly, if the employer is found liable or settles both covered and uncovered claims, the insurer most likely will be required to indemnify only for the covered portions of the judgment or settlement. Nevertheless, because defense costs for employment liabilities are often one of the primary concerns for the employer, the breadth of the duty to defend underscores the importance of carefully examining all policies, not just EPL policies. This subchapter discusses both the duty to indemnify and the duty to defend, but focuses on the duty to defend.

---

930 N.E.2d 1011, 1022 (Ill. 2010) (where policy contained a self-defense exception to the intentional act exclusion, it was necessary to look beyond the complaint because it was unlikely the complaint would set forth evidence of the insured's self-defense).

9. *Sidney Frank Importing Co. v. Farmington Cas. Co.*, No. 97 CIV 9324 LAP, 1999 WL 173263, at *3 (S.D. N.Y. March 26, 1999) ("An insurer must defend [if the] complaint against the insured asserts alternate grounds for recovery and at least one such theory is within the protection of the policy"), *aff'd*, 199 F.3d 1323 (2d Cir. 1999); *Golden Eagle Ins. Corp. v. Rocky Cola Cafe, Inc.*, 114 Cal. Rptr. 2d 16, 19, 23 (Cal. Ct. App. 2001) (insurer had to defend suit involving claims of sexual harassment, retaliation, intentional infliction of emotional distress, wrongful termination and defamation where defamation claim was covered by policy); *W. Bend Mut. Ins. Co. v. Rosemont Exposition Servs., Inc.*, 880 N.E.2d 640, 649 n.1 (Ill. App. Ct. 2007); *Cardiothoracic & Vascular Surgical Specialists, Inc. v. Travelers Indem. Co.*, No. 05AP-1355, 2006 WL 3805675, at *5 (Ohio Ct. App. Dec. 28, 2006).

10. *See Conway Chevrolet-Buick, Inc. v. Travelers Indem. Co.*, 136 F.3d 210, 214 (1st Cir. 1998).

B. Presumptions Courts Use When Interpreting Insurance Contracts

Courts construe insurance contracts by using the same principles they apply to other contracts.[11] In construing the terms of an insurance policy, "the court must ascertain the intent of the parties to the contract by construing the policy as a whole while giving due regard to the risk undertaken."[12] Thus, courts will enforce the clear and unambiguous language of an insurance contract.[13] Similarly, plainly worded, conspicuous exclusions are given effect.[14] But ambiguities in insurance contracts are construed in favor of the insured.[15]

---

11. *N. Am. Bldg. Maint., Inc. v. Fireman's Fund Ins. Co.*, 40 Cal. Rptr. 3d 468, 479 (Cal. Ct. App. 2006); *Truck Ins. Exch. v. Gagnon*, 33 P.3d 901, 903 (N.M. Ct. App. 2001).

12. *Hawkeye-Security Ins. Co. v. Bob Propheter Constr., L.L.C.*, No. 01 C 3278, 2002 WL 31176183, at *5 (N.D. Ill. Sept. 30, 2002); *see also Foster v. Kentucky Hous. Corp.*, 850 F. Supp. 558, 561 (E.D. Ky. 1994); *St. Paul Fire & Marine Ins. Co. v. Superior Court*, 208 Cal. Rptr. 5, 7 (Cal. Ct. App. 1984) ("When the language is clear, a court should not give it a strained construction to impose on the insurer a liability it has not assumed") (citation omitted); *Springdale Donuts, Inc. v. Aetna Cas. & Sur. Co.*, 724 A.2d 1117, 1120 (Conn. 1999) ("a contract of insurance must be viewed in its entirety, and the intent of the parties for entering it derived from the four corners of the policy") (citation omitted); *City of Muncie v. United Nat'l Ins. Co.*, 564 N.E.2d 979, 982 (Ind. Ct. App. 1991) ("[I]f the language in an insurance policy is clear and unambiguous, it should be given its plain and ordinary meaning"); *Northeast Battery & Alternator Co. v. Seaco Ins. Co.*, No. 97-00208A, 2002 WL 1009913, at *2 (Mass. Sup. Ct. May 17, 2002) ("Where the wording of a contract is unambiguous, the agreement must be enforced according to its terms"); *Sch. Dist. No. 1 v. Mission Ins. Co.*, 650 P.2d 929, 933 (Or. Ct. App. 1982) ("The primary objective [in construing insurance policies] is to give effect to the intent of the parties"); *E-Z Loader Boat Trailers, Inc. v. Travelers Indem. Co.*, 726 P.2d 439, 443 (Wash. 1986) ("In construing the language of an insurance contract, the entire contract is to be construed together for the purpose of giving force and effect to each clause").

13. *ARC Water Treatment Co. of Penn., Inc. v. Hartford Cas. Ins. Co.*, No. 98-CV-6358, 2002 WL 32392683, at *2 (E.D. Penn. March 27, 2002); *E-Z Loader*, 726 P.2d at 443 (Washington) ("If the policy language is clear and unambiguous, the court may not modify the contract or create an ambiguity where none exists").

14. *See ARC Water*, 2002 WL 32392683, at *2; *Foster*, 850 F. Supp. at 561 ("exceptions and exclusions should be strictly construed to make insurance effective").

15. *Old Republic Ins. v. Comprehensive Health Care Assoc.*, 2 F.3d 105, 107 (5th Cir. 1993) ("An ambiguous policy, susceptible to more than one reasonable interpretation, must be construed in favor of the insured") (Texas); *Foster*, 850 F. Supp. at

III. Commercial General Liability Insurance

A. Description of Insurance and Typical Terms

Nearly all companies purchase commercial general liability insurance to protect themselves against liability. Because many companies have no other liability coverage, the CGL policy should be evaluated whenever the company faces any sort of claim.

The basic insuring language of a CGL policy typically provides that

> The Company will pay on behalf of the insured all sums which the insured shall become legally obligated to pay as damages *because of bodily injury or property damage to which this insurance applies, caused by an occurrence* . . . and the company shall have the right and duty to defend any suit against the insured seeking damages on account of such bodily injury or property damage, even if any of the allegations of the suit are groundless, false or fraudulent.[16]

CGL policies generally define *bodily injury* as "bodily injury, sickness or disease sustained by any person which occurs during the policy period, including death at any time resulting therefrom."[17] CGL policies normally define *property damage* as "physical injury to tangible

---

561 ("contracts are to be liberally construed with all doubts resolved in favor of the insureds") (Kentucky); *see also Adams v. Pro Sources, Inc.*, 231 F. Supp. 2d 499, 502 (M.D. La. 2002) (Louisiana); *ARC Water*, 2002 WL 32392683, at *2 (Pennsylvania); *Sidney Frank Importing Co. v. Farmington Cas. Co.*, No. 97 CIV 9324 LAP, 1999 WL 173263, at *4 (S.D.N.Y. March 26, 1999), *aff'd*, 199 F.3d 1323 (2d Cir. 1999) (New York); *Springdale Donuts*, 724 A.2d at 1120 (Connecticut); *Truck Ins. Exch.*, 33 P.3d at 903 (New Mexico); *Sch. Dist. No. 1*, 650 P.2d at 933 (Oregon); *E-Z Loader*, 726 P.2d at 443 (Washington).

16. *Presidential Hotel v. Canal Ins. Co.*, 373 S.E.2d 671, 672 (Ga. Ct. App. 1988) (emphasis added); *see also Mut. Serv. Cas. Ins. Co. v. Co-op Supply, Inc.*, 699 F. Supp. 1438, 1439 (D. Mont. 1988); *John's Cocktail Lounge, Inc. v. N. River Ins. Co.*, 563 A.2d 473, 475 (N.J. Super. Ct. App. Div. 1989).

17. *Presidential Hotel*, 373 S.E.2d at 672; *see also SL Indus., Inc. v. Am. Motorists Ins. Co.*, 607 A.2d 1266, 1269–70 (N.J. 1992); *Mut. Serv. Cas. Ins. Co.*, 699 F. Supp. at 1440.

property or the loss of use of tangible property."[18] Property damage is discussed in Part B.3.

In addition to bodily injury and property damage, many policies also cover personal injury.[19] Typically, CGL policies define *personal injury* as some variation of the following:

(a) False arrest, detention, or imprisonment;
(b) Malicious prosecution;
(c) The wrongful eviction from, wrongful entry into, or invasion of the right of private occupancy of a room, dwelling, or premises that a person occupies by or on behalf of its owner, landlord, or lessor;
(d) Oral or written publication of material that slanders or libels a person or organization or disparages a person's or organization's goods, products, or services; or
(e) Oral or written publication of material that violates a person's right of privacy.[20]

Whereas nearly all CGL policies cover bodily injury and property damage only if they result from an "occurrence," some CGL policies cover personal injury even when the personal injury is not caused by an "occurrence." Under the typical CGL policy, *occurrence* is defined as "an accident, including continuous or repeated exposure to conditions,

---

18. *See ARC Water*, 2002 WL 32392683, at *3; *see also Lamar Truck Plaza, Inc. v. Sentry Ins.*, 757 P.2d 1143, 1144 (Colo. App. 1988) (property damage defined as "a. Physical injury to or destruction of tangible property which occurs during the policy period, including the loss of use thereof at any time resulting therefrom, or b. *loss of use of tangible property* which has not been physically injured or destroyed, provided the loss or use is caused by an occurrence during the policy period") (emphasis in original).

19. *See Dixon Distrib. Co. v. Hanover Ins. Co.*, 641 N.E.2d 395, 398 (Ill. 1994) (CGL policy covered "(a) Bodily Injury Liability, (b) Personal Injury Liability, (c) Property Damage Liability, or (d) Advertising Liability, arising out of an occurrence").

20. *Am. States Ins. Co. v. M.G. Electronics & Equip. Co.*, No. CIV.A 98-1075, 1999 WL 212716, at *2 (E.D. La. April 12, 1999); *Emtech Machining & Grinding, Inc. v. Transcon. Ins. Co.*, 695 N.E.2d 545, 546 (Ill. App. Ct. 1998).

which results in bodily injury or property damage neither expected nor intended from the standpoint of the insured."[21] Other CGL policies require that the personal injury result from an occurrence.

B. Coverage for Bodily Injury, Personal Injury, or Property Damage

1. Bodily Injury

As explained above, whether a CGL insurer must defend a particular employment-related claim against the insured depends on the allegations of the particular employee's complaint. To establish that employment claims are covered under a CGL policy, employers sometimes argue that the complaint contains bodily injury allegations.

An employment claim that alleges physical harm may trigger the duty to defend a "bodily injury" claim under a CGL policy.[22] Accordingly, if the plaintiff in the underlying suit alleges physical harm in connection with at least one claim, the insurer may have the duty to defend the entire suit.

Employment discrimination plaintiffs sometimes include allegations of emotional distress. Several courts have concluded that emotional distress—even without any physical manifestation—can constitute "bodily injury."[23] Accordingly, where the court follows (or can be persuaded to

---

21. *Presidential Hotel*, 373 S.E.2d at 672.

22. *Agric. Ins. Co. v. Focus Homes, Inc.*, 212 F.3d 407, 410 (8th Cir. 2000) (finding existence of bodily injury where the underlying claim for sexual harassment included an alleged rape that resulted in a broken wrist); *see also Voorhees v. Preferred Mut. Ins. Co.*, 607 A.2d 1255, 1262 (N.J. 1992) (emotional distress injuries resulting in nausea and headaches were covered as "bodily injury").

23. *Washington v. Krahn*, 440 F. Supp. 2d 911, 913 (E.D. Wis. 2006), *citing Doyle v. Engelke*, 580 N.W.2d 245 (Wis. 1998); *Tortoso v. MetLife Auto & Home Ins. Co.*, 21 A.D.3d 276 (N.Y. App. Div. 2005); *York Ins. Group of Me. v. Lambert*, 740 A.2d 984, 986 (Me. 1999); *Pekin Ins. Co. v. Hugh*, 501 N.W.2d 508, 512 (Iowa 1993); *see also Lavanant v. Gen. Accident Ins. Co. of Am.*, 79 N.Y.2d 623, 630 (1992) (holding that emotional distress constitutes "bodily injury" under a CGL policy, recognizing "that emotional trauma may be as disabling as physical injury, and that whether a person suffers one form of injury or the other may be a fortuity determined solely by the particular vulnerability of an individual").

follow) this developing position, the insurer may have a duty to defend the entire suit if the employee in the underlying suit alleges emotional distress with respect to at least one of his or her claims.

Other courts, however, have concluded that mere emotional distress without a physical component does not constitute bodily injury and, hence, is not covered under a CGL policy as a bodily injury.[24] Where this narrow interpretation of "bodily injury" applies, an insurer will not be required to defend a claim alleging emotional distress without a physical component.[25]

Courts have also concluded that allegations of lost salary or benefits, without more, do not constitute "bodily injury." Typically, when alleging unlawful termination due to race, sex, age, or disability status (among others), a plaintiff will allege that the discharge caused lost

24. *Evanston Ins. Co. v. Legacy of Life, Inc.*, 370 S.W.3d 377, 381–82 (Tex. 2012) (rejecting argument that the term *personal injury* was broader than *bodily injury*, and holding that under Texas law insurance policy did not cover "purely emotional injuries"); *ARC Water Treatment Co. of Penn., Inc. v. Hartford Cas. Ins. Co.*, No. 98-CV-6358, 2002 WL 32392683, at *3 (E.D. Penn. March 27, 2002) (concluding that plaintiff's allegations that discrimination and harassment caused him "extensive emotional distress" were not allegations of physical harm and, hence, were not allegations of "bodily injury" under the policy); *Smith v. Animal Urgent Care, Inc.*, 542 S.E.2d 827, 831 (W. Va. 2000) (concluding that the "purely mental or emotional harm that arises from a claim of sexual harassment and lacks physical manifestation does not fall within a definition of 'bodily injury'").

25. *Nat'l Fire Ins. Co. of Hartford v. NWM-Oklahoma, LLC, Inc.*, 546 F. Supp. 2d 1238, 1246 (W.D. Okla. 2008) (applying Oklahoma law and concluding that if faced with the situation, Oklahoma courts would follow the majority of courts that "hold that a claim for emotional distress, absent any physical injury, does not constitute 'bodily injury' in the insurance context"); *Batter-Up, Inc. v. Commercial Union Ins. Co.*, No. 97 C 4032, 1997 WL 545348, at *4, *5 (N.D. Ill. Aug. 29, 1997) (no coverage for plaintiff's sexual harassment claim because "bodily injury" required more than emotional pain and suffering, and the fact that plaintiff took medication for panic and anxiety did not mean she suffered physical injury); *SL Indus., Inc. v. Am. Motorists Ins. Co.*, 607 A.2d 1266, 1275 (N.J. 1992) ("In sum, we conclude that in the context of purely emotional injuries, without physical manifestations, the phrase 'bodily injury' in not ambiguous. Its ordinary meaning connotes a physical problem."); *Presidential Hotel v. Canal Ins. Co.*, 373 S.E.2d 671, 673 (Ga. Ct. App. 1988) (finding no bodily injury where "[i]n asserting their sexual harassment, fraud and implied contract claims, plaintiffs seek monetary and 'mental damages' . . . . not . . . for actual physical harm").

earnings, the difference between the amount that would have been made if not terminated and the amount actually received. If the plaintiff alleges only lost earnings or other financial loss, the plaintiff has not alleged bodily injury, and the insurer will not be required to defend the employer.[26] Again, whether an insurer must defend a particular lawsuit depends on the allegations in the particular complaint. Some employment discrimination plaintiffs assert only lost earnings or other money damages. Accordingly, those claims do not allege bodily injury that an insurer must defend.

Where the underlying complaint or petition includes allegations of physical injury or emotional injury with physical manifestations, however, defense under the bodily injury portion of a CGL policy may be available. Furthermore, a minority of courts has concluded that emotional distress can be a bodily injury. In those courts, allegations of emotional distress—such as allegations of emotional distress caused by sexual harassment or disparate treatment—may be sufficient to trigger an insurer's duty to defend under a CGL policy.

2. *Personal Injury*

Insureds have also sought coverage under CGL policies for employment claims based on allegations of "personal injury." In addition to the five categories of personal injury listed above, some policies add that personal injury includes "discrimination."[27] Other policies include

26. *SL Indus.*, 607 A.2d at 1271 (explaining that the plaintiff's ADEA claims could not be covered by the policy because the statute allows recovery only of lost wages and liquidated damages, which are not "bodily injury"); *see also Int'l Ins. Co. v. Allied Van Lines, Inc.*, 688 N.E.2d 680, 682 (Ill. App. Ct. 1997) (policy did not cover the ADEA claim "[b]ecause the [ADEA discrimination] complaint alleges monetary loss rather than bodily injury"); *E-Z Loader Boat Trailers, Inc. v. Travelers Indem. Co.*, 726 P.2d 439, 443 (Wash. 1986) (sex and age discrimination claims seeking "loss of earnings and prospective earnings, humiliation, mental anguish and emotional distress" were not covered as bodily injury because they were not "covered by the express terms" of the policy).

27. *Globe Indem. Co. v. Mobenis Servs., Inc.*, No. CIV. A. 97-3849, 1998 WL 409026, at *12 (E.D. Penn. June 29, 1998) (policy defined "'personal injury' as 'injury . . . arising out of . . . (f) discrimination'").

"humiliation" in the definition. Employers have several ways to obtain coverage for employment claims under the personal injury language.

First, employers have successfully argued that employment discrimination claims are covered where the definition of personal injury includes discrimination.[28]

Second, as mentioned above, if the lawsuit contains at least one covered claim, an insurer generally must defend the entire suit. Thus, if the plaintiff includes a potentially covered claim such as defamation with his or her employment claims, the insurer must defend the entire lawsuit. Two cases illustrate the fact-specific nature of these claims.

The employer in *Springdale Donuts, Inc. v. Aetna Casualty & Surety Co. of Illinois*[29] had a CGL policy that defined *personal injury* as "injury . . . arising out of . . . oral . . . publication of material that slanders . . . a person . . . or oral . . . publication of material that violates a person's right of privacy." The insured asserted that the personal injury provision of its CGL policy should cover a former employee's sexual harassment claims, arguing that the allegations of "lewd and lascivious remarks" constituted slander.[30] The Connecticut Supreme Court rejected the argument, however, because "the underlying complaints did not allege 'publication' of material to a third party, but instead were based entirely on comments directly made only to the claimants."[31]

On the other hand, the court in *National Fire Insurance Co. of Hartford v. NWM-Oklahoma, LLC, Inc.*,[32] considered a CGL policy that contained a personal injury definition almost identical to that in *Springfield Donuts* and found there was a duty to defend. The underlying

28. *North Bank v. Cincinnati Ins. Co.*, 125 F.3d 983, 986, 987 (6th Cir. 1997) (concluding that because the employer's policy defined *personal injury* to include discrimination, the plaintiff's state law employment discrimination claims alleged a "personal injury").

29. *Springdale Donuts, Inc. v. Aetna Cas. & Sur. Co.*, 724 A.2d 1117, 1122 (Conn. 1999).

30. *Id.* at 1119.

31. *Id.* at 1122.

32. *National Fire Ins. Co. of Hartford v. NWM-Oklahoma, LLC, Inc.*, 546 F. Supp. 2d 1238, 1243 (W.D. Okla. 2008).

complaint alleged that a baby-monitoring system had been secretly set up to monitor employee conversations such that anyone near the monitor would have the ability to hear the conversations.[33] The *National Fire* court held that there was sufficient evidence that the underlying action would arguably constitute "publication" and fall within the personal injury coverage of the insurance policy.[34]

Third, employees (and former employees) filing employment claims sometimes include allegations that the allegedly unlawful conduct caused "humiliation." Some policies specifically enumerate humiliation as a "personal injury." Accordingly, under those policies, an employment claim may be covered.[35]

Generally, the "personal injury" definition and the allegations in the underlying complaint will determine whether employment claims sufficiently allege personal injury. Where an employment claim includes slander or libel allegations, the duty to defend may be triggered. Furthermore, if the definition of *personal injury* includes discrimination, many employment claims may be within the insurer's duty to defend. Importantly, if the employer can establish that at least one of the claims is potentially within the terms of the policy, the insurer has a duty to defend the entire suit.

Establishing that the insurer has a duty to indemnify is, of course, more difficult.

---

33. *Id.* at 1247.

34. *Id.*

35. Although not an employment case, the reasoning in *Lineberry v. State Farm Fire & Cas. Co.*, 885 F. Supp. 1095, 1097–99 (M.D. Tenn. 1995), would likely apply if the plaintiffs had been employees. There, the court held that the insurer had a duty to defend invasion-of-privacy suits by women who were secretly videotaped by the plaintiff; *see also SL Indus., Inc. v. Am. Motorists Ins. Co.*, 607 A.2d 1266, 1270, 1276 (N.J. 1992) (insurer had a duty to defend ADEA suit under policy that defined *personal injury* as "humiliation" because plaintiff in the underlying suit alleged that he suffered "loss of self esteem, humiliation and irritability" as a result of the insured's alleged violation of the ADEA).

3. Property Damage

Many CGL policies also cover claims for "property damage." The property damage language provides little assistance to employers faced with employment claims.

As mentioned above, employment claims tend to include allegations of lost earnings or benefits. Some employers have argued that employees have a property interest in their earnings such that their allegations of lost earnings would constitute allegations of "property damage" under a CGL policy. Courts have concluded, however, that lost earnings (such as back pay and front pay) do not constitute "property damage" or the loss of use of property, because money is not tangible property.[36] Several recent decisions, however, have determined that complaints alleging that the employer took hard currency from the employee can allege property damage. In *Hortica-Florists' Mutual Ins. Co. v. Pittman Nursery Corp.*,[37] the employer had been sued by a group of employees who alleged that the company president had extorted them for cash in order to keep their jobs. Though the court acknowledged that "loss of wages" did not constitute "property damage" under the CGL policy, the plaintiffs in the underlying employment case were alleging the loss of tangible property, and therefore the insurer had a duty to defend the entire suit.[38]

---

36. *Lamar Truck Plaza, Inc. v. Sentry Ins.*, 757 P.2d 1143, 1144 (Colo. Ct. App. 1988) (holding that the underlying employment claims did not allege property damage because the alleged damages for sex discrimination and sexual harassment "were purely economic, and . . . did not constitute damage to, or loss of use of, tangible property"); *see also ARC Water Treatment Co. of Penn. v. Hartford Cas. Ins. Co.*, No. 98-CV-6358, 2002 WL 32392683, at *2 (E.D. Penn. March 27, 2002) ("Although he sought back pay, lost earnings and fringe benefits, emotional distress damages, punitive damages, and attorney's fees as a result of his constructive discharge, such losses do not fall within the definition of 'property damage' in the insurance context").

37. 2010 U.S. Dist. LEXIS 18521, *14–16 (W.D. Ark. Mar. 2, 2010), *citing Capital Indem. Corp. v. Wright*, 341 F. Supp. 2d 1152, 1159 (D. Nev. 2004); *Security State Bank of Kansas City v. Aetna Cas. & Surety Co.*, 825 F. Supp. 944, 947 (D. Kan. 1993); *Mack v. Nationwide Mut. Fire Ins. Co.*, 517 S.E.2d 839, 840 (Ga. Ct. App. 1999).

38. *Id.* at *16.

Generally, then, the property damage provision of a CGL policy does not provide coverage to employers for employment claims.

C. The Occurrence Requirement

An *occurrence* is usually defined as "an accident, including continuous or repeated exposure to conditions, which results in bodily injury or property damage neither expected nor intended from the standpoint of the insured."[39] Not every CGL policy applies the occurrence requirement to personal injury as well as to bodily injury and property damage. Accordingly, an employer should check the language of the particular CGL policy to determine whether a personal injury must be caused by an occurrence to be covered under the policy.

Generally, courts conclude that employment claims based on harassment or discrimination are not caused by "occurrences," because they are not accidental. Rather, they are intentional.[40] For example, in

---

39. *Nat'l Union Fire Ins. v. Puget Plastics Corp.*, 532 F.3d 398, 401 (5th Cir. 2008); *Presidential Hotel v. Canal Ins. Co.*, 373 S.E.2d 671, 672 (Ga. Ct. App. 1988); *see also Mut. Serv. Cas. Ins. Co. v. Co-op Supply, Inc.*, 699 F. Supp. 1438, 1441 (D. Mont. 1988); *Commercial Union Ins. Co. v. Superior Ct. of Humboldt Cty.*, 242 Cal. Rptr. 454, (Cal. Ct. App. 1987); *Smithway Motor Xpress, Inc. v. Liberty Mut. Ins. Co.*, 484 N.W.2d 192, 194–195 (Iowa 1992); *SL Indus.*, 607 A.2d at 1269–70 (New Jersey); *John's Cocktail Lounge, Inc. v. N. River Ins. Co.*, 563 A.2d 473, 475 (N.J. Sup. Ct. App. Div. 1989); *E-Z Loader Boat Trailers, Inc. v. Travelers Indem. Co.*, 726 P.2d 439, 441 (Wash. 1986) (defining *occurrence* as "an accident, including continuous or repeated exposure to conditions, which results in bodily injury or property damage neither expected or intended from the standpoint of the Insured").

40. *Swan Consultants, Inc. v. Travelers Property Cas. Co.*, 360 F. Supp. 2d 582, 589–90 (S.D.N.Y. 2005) (doctor's alleged sexual harassment of female job applicant was not an accident and, therefore, could not be a covered "occurrence"); *ARC Water*, 2002 WL 32392683, at *3 (harassment and discrimination claims did not amount to occurrence—even though complaint did not include the word *intentional*—because the conduct alleged could not be thought to be accidental); *St. Paul Fire & Marine Ins. Co. v. Superior Ct. of Yuba Cty.*, 208 Cal. Rptr. 5, 7 (Cal. Ct. App. 1984) ("The termination of [the former employee's] employment was not an unintentional, unexpected, chance occurrence, and thus there is no potential liability under the insurance policy and [the insurer] owes no obligation to defend [the wrongful termination claim]"); *Soc'y of Mt. Carmel v. Nat'l Ben Franklin Ins. Co.*, 643 N.E.2d 1280, 1289 (Ill. App. Ct. 1994) (wrongful termination claim alleged intentional conduct and, hence, was not a covered "occurrence") (applying California law); *Presidential Hotel*, 373 S.E.2d at 673 (sexual

Rideout v. Crum & Forster Commercial Insurance,[41] the insured sought indemnity coverage of its liability for unlawful sex discrimination and retaliatory discharge. The plaintiffs in the underlying suit established that an insured's supervisor "denied the plaintiffs the opportunity to work overtime because of their sex, stating that men needed the overtime work to support their families."[42] The plaintiffs also established that the supervisor "failed to transfer the plaintiffs to higher paying positions because of their sex, stating that 'no woman has ever worked in this department and never will . . . I only hire men, and women would distract them.'"[43] Finally, the plaintiffs established that they were terminated in retaliation for their discrimination complaints. The court concluded that the conduct was clearly intentional and, hence, could not be considered an "occurrence" under the CGL policy.[44] Accordingly, the insurer was not required to indemnify the insured.

The conclusions in *Rideout* (disparate treatment and retaliation are intentional) are difficult (though not impossible, as explained below) to avoid. The Seventh Circuit has explained why a disparate treatment claim generally cannot be caused by an "occurrence":

> What emerges from an overview of the above burdens [of proof on disparate treatment claims] is that proof of discriminatory motive is critical in a disparate treatment action. . . . While the concepts of motive and intent are not identical, we think in the

---

harassment claims alleged intentional conduct and was not a covered "occurrence"); *John's Cocktail Lounge*, 563 A.2d at 476 (wrongful dismissal was "not an accident" and, hence, was not a covered "occurrence"); *E-Z Loader*, 726 P.2d at 442 (Wash. 1986) (sex and age discrimination claims were not a covered "occurrence" because "[t]he plaintiffs were discharged; an intentional, not an accidental, act of [the insured]"); *see also Northland Cas. Co. v. HBE Corp.*, 160 F. Supp. 2d 1348, 1361–62 (M.D. Fla. 2001) (where hotel chain was sued in multiple suits, some of which alleged corporate policy of discrimination against black patrons, insurance company had no duty to defend suits that only alleged purposeful discrimination).

41. 633 N.E.2d 376, 377 (Mass. 1994).
42. *Id.*
43. *Id.*
44. *Id.* at 379.

> narrow context of determining the scope of coverage under this insurance policy, there is a similarity. The policy definition of an insured occurrence would extend only to a liability incurred by reason of [the insured's] unintentionally exposing women to discriminatory conditions. The extent of coverage is therefore inconsistent with liability predicated on the disparate treatment theory since such a liability would necessarily involve a determination that [the insured] acted with a discriminatory motive or purpose.[45]

Nevertheless, a disparate treatment claim may contain allegations that an injury was caused by an occurrence. For example, some employers have successfully argued that injuries flowing from discrimination are unintended consequences of their conduct and, hence, are caused by an "occurrence." In *Mutual Service Casualty Insurance Co. v. Co-op Supply, Inc.*,[46] the plaintiff alleged discriminatory termination resulting in bodily injury and pain. Although the alleged discriminatory conduct was intentional, the court concluded that the injury was caused by an occurrence (and, hence, was potentially covered by the CGL policy).[47] The court explained it this way:

> [C]onstruing the definition of "occurrence" broadly, the court concludes that unintended bodily injury falls within the purview of the definition regardless of the fact that [the insured's] actions in terminating [the former employee] was intentional.[48]

45. *Solo Cup Co. v. Federal Ins. Co.*, 619 F.2d 1178, 1186 (7th Cir. 1980) (internal citations omitted).

46. 699 F. Supp. 1438 (D. Mont. 1988).

47. *Id.* at 1440.

48. *Id.* at 1441.

Similarly, in *SL Industries, Inc. v. American Motorists Insurance Co.*,[49] the court explained that the appropriate consideration is "on the insured's intent to cause the injury rather than on its intent to commit the act that resulted in the injury" because intent to cause the injury "cannot be presumed."[50] Though most courts have rejected this argument,[51] employers should not discount an unintentional consequences argument if the plaintiff in the underlying suit alleges potentially covered consequences such as bodily injury.

In addition to the unintended consequences argument, some employers have successfully argued that, where sexual harassment allegations against an employer are based on coworker harassment, the action is not intentional and, hence, can amount to an occurrence. In *General Accident Insurance Co. of America v. Gastineau*,[52] the court accepted this view. The court concluded that since liability for the sexual harassment claim was based on allegations of the employer's

49. 607 A.2d 1266 (N.J. 1992).

50. *Id.* at 1276.

51. *See Republic Indem. Co. v. The Superior Ct. of Los Angeles Cty.*, 273 Cal. Rptr. 331, 338 (Cal. Ct. App. 1990) ("Because the termination of an employee is no 'accident' under these policies, no coverage is afforded even though the termination caused unintended damages."); *Commercial Union Ins. Co. v. Superior Ct. of Humboldt Cty.*, 242 Cal. Rptr. 454, 455–56 (Cal. Ct. App. 1987) (wrongful discharge claim not an occurrence because issue is not whether the "consequences of the act" are intended but rather whether the "happening of the act itself" was intended); *Smithway Motor Xpress, Inc. v. Liberty Mut. Ins. Co.*, 484 N.W.2d 192, 195 (Iowa 1992) ("We conclude that intentional discharge of an employee is not an accident and any resulting damages claimed are intended and expected. Thus, we hold that a wrongful discharge claim is not an 'occurrence' covered by the insurance policy."); *Elliot v. Nat'l Fire Ins. Co.*, 922 S.W.2d 791, 793 (Mo. Ct. App. 1996) ("Here, [the insured] intentionally discharged plaintiff. Although he may not have intended the degree of injury which did occur, he was substantially certain that some injury to plaintiff would result. We therefore hold that because the plaintiff's injuries were caused by an intentional act of defendant's insured, they are not damages covered by the policy."); *John's Cocktail Lounge, Inc. v. N. River Ins. Co.*, 563 A.2d 473, 476 (N.J. Sup. Ct. App. Div. 1989) ("The fact that the [insured] may have discharged [the former employee] carelessly or that the discharge resulted in a claim of emotional bodily injury does not control. The accidental or non-accidental quality of the alleged occurrence controls.").

52. 990 F. Supp. 631, 638 (S.D. Ind. 1998).

mere negligence in failing to prevent coworker harassment, the alleged injury was caused by an occurrence.[53]

Other courts have rejected the argument, concluding that sexual harassment is inherently not accidental and, hence, cannot be caused by an occurrence.[54] Still, where the plaintiff in the underlying lawsuit alleges sexual harassment by a coworker, the insurer may have a duty to defend the entire suit.

Other employers have argued that disparate impact claims contain allegations of an occurrence. More specifically, they have successfully argued that because disparate impact claims do not require proof of intent, the acts giving rise to disparate impact claims can be covered occurrences under CGL policies.

In *Solo Cup v. Federal Insurance Co.*,[55] the plaintiffs in the underlying suit alleged that Solo Cup's policy of requiring sales experience of promotion candidates disqualified a disproportionate number of women. The court concluded:

> Since disparate impact liability does not require proof of discriminatory motive, and since [the insurer] has, moreover, conceded that the policy covers at least some types of disparate impact claims, we therefore hold that the disparate impact claim which could have been proved under the allegations of the underlying complaint was a claim potentially within the coverage of the

53. *Id.*; *see also Sphere Drake Ins., P.L.C. v. Shoney's, Inc.*, 923 F. Supp. 1481, 1492 (M.D. Ala. 1996) (because, under *Faragher v. City of Boca Ratan*, 524 U.S. 775 (1998), allegations of coworker harassment required showing of agency relationship rather than intent, insurer had duty to defend coworker sexual harassment claims).

54. *Sidney Frank Importing Co. v. Farmington Cas. Co.*, No. 97 CIV. 9324 LAP, 1999 WL 173263, at *6 (S.D.N.Y. March 26, 1999), *aff'd*, 199 F.3d 1323 (2d Cir. 1999) (even though plaintiff's sexual harassment claims were based on both negligent and intentional harassment theories, they were not caused by occurrences because "the operative acts giving rise to any recovery are the intentional sexual assaults") (applying New York law); *Smith v. Animal Urgent Care, Inc.*, 542 S.E.2d 827, 832 (W. Va. 2000) (holding negligence-based sexual harassment is not an "occurrence" and is not covered under the CGL policy).

55. 619 F.2d 1178 (7th Cir. 1980).

> policy. Consequently, under Illinois law, [the insurer] has breached its duty to defend its insured in the action.[56]

Other courts, however, have rejected the argument that disparate impact claims can be caused by occurrences. These courts emphasize that a facially neutral policy, even if it was not adopted with the intent to discriminate, was still intentionally adopted. For example, in *Loyola Marymount University v. Hartford Accident and Indemnity Co.*,[57] the court explained:

> Even assuming this policy could be cast as "facially neutral" in the manner theorized, [the insured] without question intentionally cast the policy, and intentionally applied it to [the former employee], in the form of revoking his employment. The conduct for which liability is asserted in [the former employee's] federal action clearly was intentional.[58]

Finally, courts sometimes are skeptical of negligence counts that allege only intentional conduct. For example, in *Society of Mount Carmel v. National Ben Franklin Insurance Co. of Illinois*,[59] the plaintiffs alleged not just wrongful discharge (which the court concluded was intentional and, hence, not a covered occurrence) but also negligent infliction of

---

56. *Id.* at 1187; *see also Save Mart Supermarkets v. Underwriters at Lloyd's London*, 843 F. Supp. 597, 606 (N.D. Cal. 1994) (rejecting insurer's argument that disparate impact claims cannot be occurrences); *Lapeka, Inc. v. Security Nat'l Ins. Co.*, 814 F. Supp. 1540, 1548 (D. Kan. 1993) (same). Ultimately, however, the disparate impact age discrimination claims in the *Lapeka* case were found not to be covered under the CGL policy because there were no allegations of bodily injury, property damage, or personal injury. 814 F. Supp. at 1549.

57. 271 Cal. Rptr. 528 (Cal. Ct. App. 1990).

58. *Id.* at 532; *see also Am. Guarantee & Liab. Ins. Co. v. Vista Med. Supply*, 699 F. Supp. 787, 792 (N.D. Cal. 1988) ("The act of setting an employment policy is intentional, and thus is not an 'occurrence.' Under a disparate impact theory a plaintiff does not need to prove that the employer intended to discriminate, but the possibility that the employer may not have intended the harm does not create coverage.").

59. 643 N.E.2d 1280 (Ill. App. Ct. 1994) (applying California law).

emotional distress. The court rejected the insured's argument that the negligence allegations could be covered:

> Here [the former employee's] complaint seeks recovery for negligent infliction of emotional distress. However, the complaint sets forth no negligent acts or any facts from which such negligence can be inferred. Rather, the acts upon which that count is based are the very same acts which underlie every other count of the [former employee's] complaint, the intentional discharge. Thus, the count alleging negligent infliction of emotional distress does not constitute an occurrence or accident under the terms of the comprehensive general liability policy, and the trial court was incorrect in so finding.[60]

Although many employment claims—particularly disparate treatment claims—require proof of intent, employers should not discount the possibility that a plaintiff's lawsuit contains allegations of an occurrence. Some employers have successfully argued that allegations of coworker harassment—which is subject to a negligence standard—can be an occurrence. Similarly, some courts have concluded that even intentional conduct can be an occurrence if the consequences are unintended. In addition, some courts have held that disparate treatment claims can be caused by occurrences. Given that an insurer generally has a duty to defend a lawsuit if at least one of the claims is potentially covered, even a complaint containing disparate impact allegations may contain allegations of a covered occurrence.

D. Exclusions

1. In General

Even where a complaint contains allegations of (a) bodily injury, personal injury, or property damage that was (b) caused by an occurrence,

60. *Id.* at 1289.

the CGL policy may not cover the claims due to one or more of the policy's exclusions. It is important, therefore, for the employer to consider the language of the particular policy upon receipt of a lawsuit. The employer's policy may not contain a particular exclusion, or the exclusion may not apply to all injuries, and in some policies there may even be exceptions to the exclusions.[61] Therefore, the following discussion of typical exclusions provides some guidance but does not address all exclusions that an insurer may invoke in an effort to defeat coverage under a CGL policy.

2. *Employment Practices*

As insurers have increased their marketing of EPL policies, they have added employment practices exclusions to other types of insurance policies (including some CGL policies). The typical employment practices exclusion excludes injuries to employees arising out of and in the course of employment.[62] These policies tend also to exclude injury

61. *Pekin Ins. Co. v. Wilson*, 930 N.E.2d 1011, 1013 (2010) (policy contained a self-defense exception to the intentional act exclusion).

62. *See Conway Chevrolet-Buick, Inc. v. Travelers Indem. Co.*, 136 F.3d 210, 214 (1st Cir. 1998) (policy excluded coverage for injury "arising out of any termination of employment or coercion, demotion, evaluation, reassignment, discipline, defamation, harassment, humiliation, discrimination or other employment-related practices, policies, acts or omissions" (internal quotation marks omitted)); *Hawkeye-Security Ins. Co. v. Propheter Constr., L.L.C.*, No. 01 C 3278, 2002 WL 31176183, at *7 (N.D. Ill. Sept. 27, 2002) (exclusion stated that "policy does not apply to 'bodily injury' or 'personal injury' arising out of employment practices of the Insured, including: (a) refusal to employ; (b) termination of employment; (c) . . . or other employment-related practices"); *Scottsdale Ins. Co. v. Scholl-Fassnacht*, No. Civ.A.00-CV-268(CRW), 2000 WL 875693, at *2 (E.D. Pa. June 26, 2000) (CGL policy excluded coverage for the injury of an employee "arising out of and in the course of his employment" with the insured); *Golden Eagle Ins. Corp. v. Rocky Cola Cafe, Inc.*, 114 Cal. Rptr. 2d 16, 20 (Cal. Ct. App. 2001) (CGL policy did not apply to personal injuries "arising out of any . . . [e]mployment-related practices, policies, acts or omissions, such as coercion, demotion, evaluation, reassignment, discipline, defamation, harassment, humiliation or discrimination directed at that person"); *W. Bend Mut. Ins. Co. v. Rosemont Exposition Servs.*, 880 N.E.2d 640, 649 (Ill. App. Ct. 2007); *Truck Ins. Exch. v. Gagnon*, 33 P.3d 901, 903 (N.M. Ct. App. 2001) (excluding coverage for "[i]njury to any employee of yours arising out of and in the course of employment"); *Cardiothoracic & Vascular Surgical Specialists, Inc. v. Travelers Indem. Co.*, No. 05AP-1355, 2006 WL 3805675, at *1 (Ohio Ct. App. 2006)

arising out of "employment practices" such that they would presumably exclude failure to hire claims that would not be excluded by "in the course of employment" language.[63]

Most claims that we think of as employment claims—sexual harassment, discrimination (whether based on race, sex, national origin, age, disability, or other protected status), wrongful termination, and retaliation clearly arise out of an employee's employment. Such claims require allegations that the plaintiff was treated differently with respect to the *terms and conditions of employment* or in the hiring process. Accordingly, those claims are generally (though not always) excluded from coverage under a CGL policy that contains an employment practices exclusion.[64]

(CGL policy excluded coverage for "[e]mployment-related practices, policies, acts or omissions, such as coercion, demotion, evaluation, reassignment, discipline, defamation, harassment, humiliation or discrimination").

63. *See Conway Chevrolet-Buick, Inc.*, 136 F.3d at 214; *Hawkeye-Security Ins. Co.*, 2002 WL 31176183, at *7; *Golden Eagle*, 114 Cal. Rptr. at 20; *Gagnon*, 33 P.3d at 903.

64. *See Agric. Ins. Co. v. Focus Homes, Inc.*, 212 F.3d 407, 4110 (8th Cir. 2000) (sexual harassment claims excluded by employment practices exclusion because "allegations in the complaint only addressed [insured] as an employer"); *Adams v. Pro Sources, Inc.*, 231 F. Supp. 2d 499, (M.D. La. 2002) ("claims under federal and state anti-discrimination laws based on the hostile work environment he was allegedly subjected to while employed at [insured], including the retaliation claims, are clearly excluded under the Employment-Related Practices Exclusion"); *Hawkeye-Security Ins. Co.*, 2002 WL 31176183, at *7 (plaintiff's Title VII discrimination and retaliation claims clearly excluded by employment practices exclusion); *ARC Water Treatment Co. of Penn. v. Hartford Cas. Ins. Co.*, No. Civ.A. 98-CV-6358, 2002 WL 32392683, at *4 (E.D. Penn. March 27, 2002) (claims for discrimination and harassment not covered by CGL policy, which excluded claims "arising out of employment"); *Gagnon*, 33 P.3d at 905 (former employee's sexual harassment claims arose out of his employment and, hence, were excluded by CGL policy's employment practices exclusion); *Collins Bldg. Serv., Inc. v. United Capitol Ins. Co.*, No. 98 CIV 3502(AGS), 1999 WL 259519, at *4 n.3 (S.D.N.Y. Apr. 30, 1999) (former employee's claims for sexual harassment, wrongful termination, and sex discrimination were excluded by the employment practices exclusion); *but see SCI Liquidating Corp. v. Hartford Ins. Co.*, 526 S.E.2d 555, 557 (Ga. 2000) (concluding that sexual harassment does not "arise out of employment" because sexual harassment causes an injury "due to the willful act of a third person for personal reasons rather than a work-related condition" (internal quotation marks omitted)). In *SCI Liquidating Corp.*, the Georgia Supreme Court relied on the definition of "arise out of employment"

For a claim to arise out of the plaintiff's employment, the alleged conduct need not have happened on the employer's premises or during the employee's work time. Rather, courts have enforced such employment practices exclusions in CGL policies when the alleged conduct arose out of the employment relationship.

For example, in *Collins Building Service, Inc. v. United Capitol Insurance Co.*,[65] the plaintiff in the underlying suit alleged sexual harassment, some of which occurred off of the employer's premises. The court rejected the insured's argument that the conduct did not arise out of employment, explaining that "the fact that some of the harassment occurred outside of the workplace is not dispositive of the issue of whether the harassment injury arose out of the course of [the former employee's] employment."[66]

Similarly, in *Scottsdale Insurance Co. v. Scholl-Fassnacht*,[67] the court concluded that the CGL policy's employment exclusion excluded a sexual harassment claim, even though the complaint alleged that the plaintiff was sexually assaulted on the employer's premises while she was off duty and checking her schedule.[68] The court explained that the claims were still based on her employment relationship with her employer. Some courts have even concluded that where some claims within a single complaint are excluded by an employment practices exclusion, non-employment claims—such as slander or negligence—that are based on the same facts are also excluded. For example, in *Old Republic Insurance Co. v. Comprehensive Health Care Associates, Inc.*, the CGL policy excluded "any claim arising from the employment relationship between the insured and any of its employees."[69] One of

---

that is used under the Georgia workers' compensation statute. 526 S.E.2d at 557.

65. 1999 WL 259519.

66. *Id.*, at *4 n.3; *see also Smith v. Animal Urgent Care, Inc.*, 542 S.E.2d 827, 834–35 (W. Va. 2000) ("Even where part of the alleged misconduct occurs away from the work premises, courts have nonetheless found that the employee exclusion is applicable").

67. No. Civ.A.00-CV-268 (CRW), 2000 WL 875693 (E.D. Penn. June 26, 2000).

68. *Id.* at *2.

69. 2 F.3d 105, 108 (5th Cir. 1993).

the insured's supervisors subjected two employees to sexual advances, innuendo, harassment, and requests for sexual favors. When the supervisor was rebuffed, he told the employees that they would not get pay raises, that he would not sign their paychecks, that working conditions and scheduling might be changed to something less than desirable, and that they would be unemployable in their chosen field either in this area or another.[70] The employees asserted claims for sex discrimination, sexual harassment, negligence, slander, and intentional infliction of emotional distress. Affirming summary judgment for the insurer, the Fifth Circuit concluded that the employment exclusion excluded not only the sex discrimination and harassment claims but also the slander, negligence, and emotional distress claims. The court explained that these non-employment claims were "inextricably intertwined with the underlying sexual harassment and discrimination claims."[71]

Even when a defamation claim is not accompanied by an employment claim, it may be excluded by an employment practices exclusion. For example, in *Adams v. Pro Sources, Inc.*, the court concluded that a defamation claim was excluded from coverage under the CGL policy because the allegedly defamatory statement was a comment regarding the former employee's performance on his last day of work.[72] However, in *Golden Eagle Insurance Corp. v. Rocky Cola Cafe, Inc.*, the court required the insurer to defend allegations that one of the insured's employees said the plaintiff was a "sexually promiscuous and calculating bitch."[73] The court explained that the comment "was not made in the context of [her] employment" and was not "directed to her performance during employment."[74] Thus, where the alleged defamatory

70. *Id.*

71. *Id.* at 109.

72. 231 F. Supp. 2d 499, 505 (M.D. La. 2002).

73. 114 Cal. Rptr. 2d 16, 21 (Cal. Ct. App. 2001).

74. *Id.* at 22; *but see Alexandra House, Inc. v. St. Paul Fire & Marine Ins. Co.*, 419 N.W.2d 506, 510 (Minn. Ct. App. 1988) (statement regarding former employee's sexual preferences was related to employment because it was related to her suitability as an advocate for women).

statement is unrelated to the employee's performance, courts tend to conclude that the statement does not "arise out of employment" and is not excluded by an employment practices exclusion.

3. Discrimination

Some CGL policies exclude "discrimination" claims. In *Dobb v. State Farm Fire and Casualty Co.*, the court concluded that the insurer did not need to defend a gender discrimination suit as a personal injury where the policy contained an endorsement that explicitly excluded coverage for discrimination.[75]

4. Actual Malice

Some policies exclude acts "committed with actual malice," but that can be a difficult standard for an insurer to meet. In *Dixon Distributing Co. v. Hanover Insurance Co.*,[76] the plaintiff in the underlying lawsuit alleged that she was discharged in retaliation for filing a workers' compensation claim. The court concluded that the workers' compensation retaliatory discharge claim was not excluded by the "actual malice" exclusion, because proof of retaliatory discharge required proof of only intent/causation, not malice.[77]

5. Intentional Injury Exclusion

As previously mentioned, not all CGL policies apply the occurrence requirement to personal injury, bodily injury, or property damage. For policies that do not impose an occurrence requirement, it would generally be possible that the intent-based claims, such as harassment or discrimination, could be covered under the policy. Some CGL policies,

---

75. 773 N.E.2d 1251, 1254 (Ill. App. Ct. 2002); *see also Town of South Whitley v. Cincinnati Ins. Co.*, 921 F.2d 104, 107, 108 (7th Cir. 1990) (ADEA intentional discrimination (failure to hire) claim was excluded by provision that excluded "discrimination . . . committed by or at your direction").

76. 641 N.E.2d 395 (Ill. 1994).

77. *Id.* at 400.

however, contain "intentional injury" exclusions that will relieve an insurer from the duty to defend where the injury was intentionally caused by the insured. In *Millers Mutual Insurance Co. v. Plastivax, Inc.*, the CGL policy at issue excluded coverage for "expected or intended" injuries.[78] The court held that in light of such an exclusion, the policy denied coverage where the employee had sued for an intentional tort.[79]

IV. Other Types of Insurance

A. Directors and Officers

Directors and officers (D&O) liability insurance policies warrant particularly close attention as possible sources of coverage for employment claims. There is no such thing as a "standard" D&O policy. Each insurer uses its own D&O policy forms, and many offer several markedly different D&O policies.

In recent years, many insurers have begun to include employment practices coverage in most of their D&O policies, although it will typically be narrower than stand-alone EPL insurance coverage. A threshold issue in many D&O policies is the definition of *wrongful act*, which is the insured conduct for which the policyholder is sued. Some D&O policies expressly state whether employment practices are included in the definition of *wrongful act* and, therefore, whether they may be covered. If the definition of *wrongful act* is silent on this issue, it probably does include employment practices. Other D&O policies expressly cover employment claims within a special section of the policy form or by way of an endorsement.

As always, policy exclusions must also be considered. Some D&O policies have specific exclusions for employment-related claims, much

78. 681 N.E.2d 1363, 1367 (Ohio Ct. App. 1996).

79. *Id.* at 1364; *see also Swan Consultants, Inc. v. Travelers Property Cas. Co.*, 360 F. Supp. 2d 582, 590 (S.D.N.Y. 2005) ("expected or intended" exclusion in CGL policy applied to claim alleging that doctor sexually harassed plaintiff and groped her during job interview); *Northland Cas. Co. v. HBE Corp.*, 160 F. Supp. 2d 1348, 1361–62 (M.D. Fla. 2001) (damages that flow from corporate policy of racial discrimination "cannot be viewed as unexpected or unintended").

like those in many CGL policies. Most policies have an "insured versus insured" exclusion, which requires especially careful review because the plaintiff in an employment claim often is a current or former employee who is also an insured under the D&O policy.[80] In *Biltmore Associates, LLC v. Twin City Fire Insurance Co.*, the Ninth Circuit explained the history and purpose of the insured-versus-insured exclusion.[81] The exclusion was designed to prevent collusion by company insiders at the expense of the insurance company, and it originated as a reaction to a number of lawsuits during the 1980s in which insured corporations sued their own directors to recoup operational losses caused by improvident or unauthorized actions.[82] Some versions of the insured-versus-insured exclusion, including the one at issue in *Biltmore Associates*, do not apply to wrongful termination claims, and thus the exclusion should be carefully scrutinized.[83]

Another complex question in a D&O policy is the extent to which it covers the employer entity as well as the directors and officers of the entity. Entity coverage—also known as coverage C or side C—is often optional in a D&O policy, and the declarations page may indicate whether the policyholder purchased that option. Moreover, entity coverage may be expressly limited to only certain types of claims, such as securities or antitrust claims. Such claims are likely to be filed against the entity and its directors and officers, and for the same reason, entity coverage may extend to employment claims. On the other hand, where a D&O policy provides no entity coverage, it is somewhat less likely to cover employment claims, which often cannot be filed against individual directors and officers. However, some employment claims, such

80. *Foster v. Kentucky Housing Corp.*, 850 F. Supp. 558, 561 (E.D. Ky. 1994) (former director brought a wrongful discharge claim against the other directors and officers. Because both the current directors and the former director were covered under the policy, the insurer had no duty to defend the suit.).

81. 572 F.3d 663, 668 (9th Cir. 2009) (explaining history and purpose of the insured-versus-insured exclusion as a tool for controlling collusion by company insiders).

82. *Id.*

83. *Id.* at 669.

as wrongful discharge claims in certain states or Fair Labor Standards Act claims, may be brought against individuals[84] and, hence, may be covered by D&O insurance.[85]

B. Errors and Omissions Insurance

Employers have also attempted to use their errors and omissions (E&O) policies to compel insurers to defend or indemnify them against employment claims. Generally, E&O insurance is designed to cover risks inherent in the insured's profession.[86] Many insurance companies now include the profession in the name of the policy and market it as specialized insurance for that profession. Some of these policies also include features of CGL policies. Accordingly, employers should analyze all of their insurance policies, regardless of their names.

A typical errors and omissions policy provides the following:

> The company will pay on behalf of the insured all sums which the insured shall become legally obligated to pay on account of any claim for breach of duty made against the insured *by reason of any negligent act, error or omission* of the insured . . . and the company shall have the right and duty to defend any suit against [the insured] seeking damages on account of such breach of duty even if any of the allegations of the suit are groundless, false or

---

84. *See Rasic v. City of Northlake*, 563 F. Supp. 2d 885, 889 (N.D. Ill. 2008) (explaining that individuals may sometimes be liable under the Fair Labor Standards Act).

85. *See Chicago Bd. of Options Exchange v. Harbor Ins. Co.*, 738 F. Supp. 1184, 1187–88 (N.D. Ill. 1990) (rejecting insurer's argument that wrongful discharge action brought against directors was not covered by D&O policy); *Philadelphia Indem. Ins. Co. v. Maryland Yacht Club, Inc.*, 742 A.2d 79, 92 (Md. Ct. Spec. App. 1999) (D&O policy covered claims for wrongful discharge because wrongful discharge did not fall within "bodily injury" exclusion).

86. *See Arthur J. Gallagher & Co. v. Bellamy-Baronowskus*, No. CV990588311, 2001 WL 285268, at *3 (Conn. Super. Ct. Mar. 12, 2001) ("Errors and omissions policies form the equivalent to malpractice insurance for occupations other than those in the legal and medical fields.") (citing reference omitted); *Sch. Dist. No. 1 v. Mission Ins. Co.*, 650 P.2d 929, 934 (Or. Ct. App. 1982).

> fraudulent, and may make such investigation and settlement of any claim or suit as it deems expedient . . . .[87]

E&O policies generally apply only to errors and omissions arising out of professional conduct. For example, the policy at issue in *International Surplus Lines Insurance Co. v. Seagrave House, Inc.* covered errors or omissions by:

> Any person who was, is now or hereafter becomes a partner, executive officer, director, stockholder or employee of any of the foregoing, whether named or not, but only while acting in the scope of their duties as such.[88]

Consequently, a potential obstacle to coverage for employment claims under E&O policies is that they tend to cover errors and omissions arising in the course of professional conduct. In *International Surplus Lines Insurance Co.*, the insured's profession was providing a therapeutic group home, and the policy at issue covered errors and omissions "in professional services."[89] When a former employee sued for wrongful discharge, the insured sought a declaratory judgment that its E&O carrier owed a duty to defend the suit. The court explained the problem with the insured's claim:

> Simply stated it is appellant's position that appellees are being sued for wrongful discharge from employment and not for professional malpractice. The trial court defined the issue as being "whether a duty to properly hire and fire employees is included within the 'professional services' category of the policy."

---

87. *Sch. Dist. No. 1*, 650 P.2d at 932 (emphasis added).
88. 572 So.2d 933, 934 (Fla. Ct. App. 1990).
89. *Id.* at 934, 935.

> It is our interpretation of the insurance contract that coverage is not for wrongful discharge from employment and other alleged torts but is only for injuries suffered by patients or clients of the insured as a result of improper or inadequate provision of professional services.[90]

Accordingly, the insurer was not obligated to defend the insured.

Notwithstanding the "professional services" obstacle, the employer in *Biborosch v. Transamerica Insurance Co.* successfully argued that the E&O policy should cover employment claims.[91] There, the insured individual was an insurance agency manager who was responsible for, among other things, recruiting, training, and supervising the agents working for the agency. After the insured discharged one of the agents who had worked for him, the agent filed a lawsuit alleging, among other things, wrongful discharge. The policy at issue covered errors and omissions "in the rendering or failing to render professional services for others in the conduct of the named insured's profession as . . . insurance general agent or manager."[92] The court concluded that the underlying claim for wrongful discharge was covered by the policy because the policy covered the insured "in his profession as general agency manager and that terminating [the plaintiff in the underlying suit] was done in furtherance of that profession."[93]

Furthermore, as is true of other types of insurance, employers have successfully argued that an E&O policy could cover employment claims based on a disparate impact theory. In *School District No. 1 v. Mission Insurance Co.*, the court explained:

> [C]laims of discrimination based on disparate impact, which do not require a showing of discriminatory intent, could encompass

90. *Id.* at 936–37.
91. 603 A.2d 1050, 1051 (Pa. Super. Ct. 1992).
92. *Id.* at 1055.
93. *Id.* at 1056.

> actions, judgments or decisions that might be considered negligent acts, errors or omissions under the policy. Discrimination claims containing allegations that *could be* interpreted as disparate impact claims, that is, that would allow the complainant to prove discrimination by disparate impact, are potentially within the coverage of the policy, and [the insurer] had a duty to defend such claims if other policy requirements were met.[94]

In addition, sometimes the language of the particular policy does not limit coverage to negligent acts. In *Independent School District No. 697 v. St. Paul Fire & Marine Insurance Co.*, the policy covered "wrongful act[s] based on: an error or omission, negligence, breach of duty, or misstatement or misleading statement" in connection with the administration of a school.[95] One of the teachers sued the school, alleging that the school reduced her salary and changed her job duties because of her age. The insurer refused to defend the suit, and the school sued for breach of the insurance contract. The court rejected the insurer's argument that the policy covered only negligent acts, not intentional discrimination. The court concluded that the words *wrongful act* could include intentional conduct and that the words *breach of duty* could cover intentional discrimination. Accordingly, the plaintiff's underlying suit was covered by the E&O policy.[96]

At the same time, other courts have concluded that the "negligent act, error, or omission" language in a typical E&O policy does not extend to intentional conduct. Accordingly, one obstacle to coverage for employment claims under an E&O policy is that some E&O policies do not cover intentional conduct.[97]

94. 650 P.2d 929, 936 (Or. Ct. App. 1982) (emphasis in original).

95. 515 N.W.2d 576, 579 (Minn. 1994).

96. *Id.*

97. *See City of Muncie v. United Nat'l Ins. Co.*, 564 N.E.2d 979, 983 (Ind. Ct. App. 1991) (claims under 42 U.S.C. § 1983 not covered by E&O policy because the claims required proof of intent); *Sch. Dist. No. 1 v. Mission Ins. Co.*, 650 P.2d 929, 935–36 (Or. Ct. App. 1982) (holding that claims of disparate treatment are not covered by E&O

Like other insurance policies, whether an E&O policy covers an employment claim depends on the terms of the policy and the allegations in the complaint. As with other types of insurance, the negligence language in an E&O policy may provide coverage for disparate impact claims but not disparate treatment claims. Furthermore, a unique obstacle to coverage for employment claims under an E&O policy is that E&O policies tend to cover errors and omissions in connection with professional services. If the professional service does not involve engaging in employment practices (such as hiring and firing), the E&O policy is unlikely to cover the employment claim.

C. Workers' Compensation and Employer's Liability Policies

Employers have also sought coverage for employment claims under their workers' compensation and employer's liability policies. These policies contain two types of coverage.

The workers' compensation provisions have generally been held not to cover employment claims. In *La Jolla Beach & Tennis Club, Inc. v. Industrial Indemnity Co.*, the insured sought coverage for a former employee's claim that he was discharged in retaliation for filing a workers' compensation claim.[98] The insured argued that the claim was potentially within the coverage of the workers' compensation policy. The court disagreed, noting that civil suits could not grant workers' compensation benefits, so the underlying civil suit had no potential for granting the benefits covered by the insurance. Accordingly, the court held that the former employee's claim was not covered.[99] Other courts have reached the same conclusion.[100]

---

policy because they are claims for intentional discrimination).

98. 884 P.2d 1048, 1057 (Cal. Super. 1994).

99. *Id.* at 1059. On appeal, the insured did not challenge the trial court's conclusion that the retaliatory discharge claim was not covered by the employer's liability portion of the workers' compensation policy. *Id.* at 1050.

100. *Tamrac, Inc. v. California Ins. Guarantee Ass'n.*, 74 Cal. Rptr. 2d 338, 344 (Cal. Ct. App. 1998) (insurer had no duty to defend age discrimination and wrongful

The second part of the policy, employer's liability insurance,[101] is meant to provide coverage for "common-law liabilities for injuries resulting to employees."[102] The employer's liability insurance typically covers "bodily injury by accident or bodily injury by disease."[103]

The bodily injury language is similar to language used in CGL policies, and some employers have successfully obtained coverage for employment claims under part two of a workers' compensation and employer's liability insurance policy. For example, in *NPS Corp. v. Insurance Co. of North America*, the plaintiff in the underlying suit alleged that she was sexually harassed, that her coworker offensively touched her, and that the conduct caused her to suffer "serious emotional distress and disruption of her personal life."[104] The court concluded that the plaintiff's claim was covered by the workers' compensation and employer's liability insurance policy, stating, "we are convinced that the term 'bodily injury,' as used in the policy, encompasses claims for emotional distress caused by an assault and battery."[105]

Similarly, in *Seminole Point Hospital Corp. v. Aetna Casualty & Surety Co.*, the plaintiff in the underlying suit alleged that she was

---

termination claims against insured); *Springdale Donuts, Inc. v. Aetna Cas. & Sur. Co.*, 724 A.2d 1117, 1121 (Conn. 1999) ("Viewed in its entirety, the policy language unequivocally indicates that the policy was intended to provide coverage only for claims for workers' compensation benefits. Because the underlying claims were filed in federal court, not with the workers' compensation commission, and did not state any claims for workers' compensation benefits, the underlying claims are not within the purview of the plaintiff's workers' compensation policy. We conclude, therefore, that the defendants had no duty under the plaintiff's workers' compensation policy to defend the plaintiff against the underlying claims.").

101. Employer's liability insurance should not be confused with employment practices liability insurance, which is the subject of chapter 1 of this book.

102. *Ottumwa Hous. Auth. v. State Farm Fire & Cas. Co.*, 495 N.W.2d 723, 729 (Iowa 1993).

103. *Aetna Cas. & Sur. Co. v. Wannamoisett Country Club, Inc.*, 706 A.2d 1329, 1329 (R.I. 1998); *see also Interface Group-Massachusetts, Inc. v. United States Fire Ins. Co.*, No. 93-12659-Z, 1994 WL 175022, at *1 (D. Mass. Apr. 21, 1994) (policy covered "bodily injury by accident or bodily injury by disease").

104. 517 A.2d 1211, 1212 (N.J. Super. Ct. App. Div. 1986).

105. *Id.* at 1214.

sexually harassed by her supervisor and that her employer negligently failed to investigate and prevent the harassment.[106] Although the policy at issue excluded intentional conduct, the court concluded that such allegations of negligence were covered by the employer's liability provisions.[107]

An obstacle to coverage under the employer's liability portion of a workers' compensation and employer's liability insurance policy, however, is that many such policies contain employment practices or discrimination exclusions. In *HDH Corp. v. Atlantic Charter Insurance Co.*, for example, the insured sought coverage for a sex discrimination lawsuit.[108] The court affirmed a grant of summary judgment to the insurer, concluding that the sex discrimination claim was not covered by part two of the policy because "the insurance policy expressly excluded coverage of 'damages arising out of the discharge of, coercion of, or discrimination against any employee in violation of law.'"[109] Exclusions for discrimination and harassment are common in employer's liability portions of workers' compensation and employer's liability insurance policies, and, hence, many employment claims are excluded from coverage under those policies.[110]

106. 675 F. Supp. 44, 47 (D.N.H. 1987).

107. *Id.*

108. 681 N.E.2d 847, 849 (Mass. 1997).

109. *Id.*

110. *See Employers Mut. Cas. Co. v. D.S. Wilson Enters., Inc.*, No. CIV. A. 00-0001-BH-C, 2000 WL 1196154 at *1, *2 (S.D. Ala. Aug. 10, 2000) (Workers' compensation and employer's liability policy that excluded "damages arising out of coercion, criticism, demotion, evaluation, reassignment, discipline, defamation, harassment, humiliation, discrimination against or termination of any employee, or any personnel policies, acts, or omissions" did not cover claim for retaliatory discharge); *TIG Ins. Co. v. Sweet Factory, Inc.*, 748 So.2d 337, 338, 339 (Fla. Ct. App. 1999) (sexual harassment claim was not covered by workers' compensation and employer's liability insurance policy, which excluded "damages arising out of coercion, criticism, demotion, evaluation, reassignment, discipline, defamation, harassment, humiliation, discrimination against or termination of any employee, or any personnel practices, policies, acts or omissions"); *Interface Group-Massachusetts, Inc. v. United States Fire Ins. Co.*, No. 93-12659-Z, 1994 WL 175022, at *1 (D. Mass. April 21, 1994) (claims of racial discrimination and retaliation were excluded from workers' compensation and employer's liability insurance by policy

V. Conclusion

Whether an insurer must defend an employment-related claim depends on the specific allegations in the plaintiff's complaint and on the language and exclusions in the policy at issue. Although not every employment claim is covered by every non-EPL policy, an employer should not discount the possibility that a lawsuit against it may be covered by a policy other than an EPL policy. In fact, if at least one of the claims in the underlying lawsuit is potentially covered by a policy, the insurer generally has a duty to defend the entire suit.

Of the types of insurance beyond EPL, employers have achieved the most coverage for employment claims under commercial general liability policies. Employment claims that include allegations of physical injury or physical manifestations of emotional distress may trigger the bodily injury coverage of CGL policies. Some courts even recognize emotional distress, which is often alleged in connection with employment claims, as "bodily injury." In addition, some employment claims may allege a personal injury, either because the particular policy at issue includes discrimination in the definition of *personal injury* or because the plaintiff in the underlying complaint alleged one of the other enumerated forms of personal injury, such as slander. Claims involving disparate impact or intentional acts with unintended consequences have the best chance of satisfying the "occurrence" requirement of a CGL policy. Accordingly, under certain circumstances, employment claims may be covered by CGL policies.

Other types of insurance offer some protection for employers facing employment claims. Many directors and officers liability policies cover some employment claims. Moreover, some employers have persuaded courts that errors and omissions policies may cover employment claims. Finally, workers' compensation and employer's liability insurance, like

---

language that excluded "damages arising out of personnel practices, policies, acts or omissions including coercion, criticism, demotion, evaluation, reassignment, discipline, defamation, harassment, humiliation or termination of, or discrimination against any employee").

CGL policies, cover certain types of "bodily injury," so some allegations of physical or emotional injury may bring an employment claim within the terms of a workers' compensation and employer's liability policy.

Because allegations vary among complaints and terms vary among policies, employers should not discount the possibility that the particular lawsuit is covered by a non-EFL policy until the allegations are carefully compared with the terms of the policy.

CHAPTER 3
Insurability of Intentional Conduct and Punitive Damages

Christine Robek and Adam Hanley

Most insurance contracts are premised on the understanding that insurance is intended to provide coverage for fortuitous events: unintended acts that have caused unexpected damages. In contrast, employment practices liability (EPL) insurance policies are designed to provide protection from damages caused by a course of intentional conduct. Indeed, a wrongful discharge motivated by gender discrimination is hardly a fortuitous accident, but it is precisely the sort of event that EPL policies are designed to cover.

The editor and authors would like to thank Jonathan H. Kurens for his significant contributions to chapter 3 in the second edition of this book.

EPL policies are also unique among most insurance products because they frequently insure against punitive damages unless prohibited by regulation or case law. Coverage of and restrictions to insuring both intentional conduct and punitive damages, as well as other issues, are discussed below.

I. Intentional Misconduct

A. Intentional Conduct

Historically, insurance contracts only insured unintentional or fortuitous conduct. Whether by limiting the definition of an "occurrence" to only accidental events, or by specifically excluding acts that are expected or intended to cause damages, traditional comprehensive general liability (CGL) policies have been drafted and interpreted to exclude any damages that arise from conduct either intended to cause harm or that a reasonable person would believe created a substantial certainty of harm.

B. Construing the Intentional Act Exclusion Under Non-EPL Policies

The exclusion of coverage for intentional acts is, at first blush, intuitive: one should not be able to insure against his or her own intentional conduct, because the availability of insurance may incentivize the insured to commit a wrongful act.[1] As the Fifth Circuit has explained, "Where a person is able to insure himself against punishment, he gains a freedom of misconduct inconsistent with the establishment of sanctions against such misconduct."[2]

Upon closer examination, however, the rationale for the intentional act exclusion becomes more complicated. Indeed, "intent" is a matter of degree, and virtually all conduct, even negligence, has at least some

1. *Ranger Ins. Co. v. Bal Harbour Club, Inc.*, 549 So.2d 1005, 1007 (Fla. 1989).
2. *Northwestern Nat'l Cas. Co. v. McNulty*, 307 F.2d 432, 440 (5th Cir. 1962) (punitive damages as potential violation of public policy superseded by statute as stated in *United Services Ass'n v. Webb*, 369 S.E.2d 196 (Va. 1988)).

modicum of intent.[3] For example, though reckless conduct is not purely accidental, it is also not malicious, and CGL policies are often drafted or interpreted to insure for such conduct.[4] Thus, courts faced with an intentional-act exclusion struggle to draw the line between intentional and unintentional conduct, with varying results.[5]

The distinction between "intentional" and "reckless" conduct is defined in the characterization of intent in the Restatement (Third) of Torts:

> A person acts with the intent to produce a consequence if:
> (a) the person has the purpose of producing that consequence; or
> (b) the person acts knowing that the consequence is substantially certain to result.
> A person acts recklessly in engaging in conduct if:
> (a) the person knows of the risk of harm created by the conduct or knows facts that make the risk obvious to another in the person's situation, and
> (b) the precaution that would eliminate or reduce that risk involves burdens that are so slight relative to the magnitude of the risk as to render the person's failure to adopt the precaution a demonstration of the person's indifference to the risk.[6]

The difference between the two concepts is slight. Intuitively, it would seem wrong to insure against either act, for "if a single insured is

3. *Pachucki v. Republic Ins. Co.*, 278 N.W.2d 898, 902 (Wis. 1979).

4. Anthony J. Sebok, *Purpose, Belief, and Recklessness: Pruning the* Restatement (Third)*'s Definition of Intent*, 54 Vand. L. Rev. 1165, 1181 (April 2001).

5. David A. Fischer & Robert H. Jerry, II, *Teaching Torts Without Insurance: A Second-Best Solution*, 45 St. Louis U. L.J. 857, 885 (2001).

6. Restatement (Third) of Torts: Liability for Physical and Emotional Harm §§ 1, 2 (2010).

allowed through intentional or reckless acts to consciously control risks covered by policy, the central concept of insurance is violated."[7]

Moreover, reconciling the tort definitions of *reckless* and *intentional* with insurance principles poses some difficulty. Under the "fortuity doctrine," insurance law begins with the premise that nonfortuitous losses are uninsurable,[8] and no insurance coverage exists for conduct intended or expected from the insured's standpoint. However, the meaning of *intended* and *expected* for purposes of applying the insurance policy exclusion is not necessarily the same as the meaning of *intentional* for tort law purposes.[9] Courts have been unable to reach a consensus as to the correct interpretation of these words when they appear in such an exclusionary clause.[10]

Three general rules have emerged with respect to the construction of intentional tort exclusions. Some courts focus on the classic tort doctrine of looking to the natural and probable consequences of the insured's act. Other courts focus on whether the insured had the specific intent to cause the type of injury suffered. The majority view, however, is that the insured must have intended the act and intended to have caused some sort of bodily injury.[11]

The majority position was explained further in *Butler v. Behaeghe*.[12] In order for an intentional-act exclusion to apply, it is necessary that the insured intend both the act as well as to cause bodily harm. This intent may be actual or inferred by the nature of the act and the accompanying reasonable foreseeability of harm. Once it is found that the

---

7. *Mut. Serv. Cas. Ins. Co. v. McGehee*, 711 P.2d 826, 828 (Mont. 1985) (quoting *Transamerica Ins. Group v. Meere*, 694 P.2d 181, 186 (Ariz. 1984) (quoting 7A APPLEMAN, INSURANCE LAW AND PRACTICE, § 4492.01 (1979))).

8. Fischer & Jerry, *supra* note 5, at 888.

9. *Id.*

10. *United Servs. Auto. Ass'n v. Elitzky*, 517 A.2d 982, 987 (Pa. Super. Ct. 1986).

11. *Pachucki v. Republic Ins. Co.*, 278 N.W.2d 898, 901 (Wis. 1979) (citing *Home Ins. Co. v. Neilsen*, 332 N.E.2d 240 (Ind. Ct. App. 1975)).

12. 548 P.2d 934, 938 (Colo. Ct. App. 1976).

harm was intended, it is immaterial that the actual harm is of a different character or magnitude than that intended.[13]

Courts have applied these principles in cases involving intentional-act exclusions and allegations of sexual misconduct, with varying results. In *K.A.G. by Carson v. Stanford*,[14] the Wisconsin Court of Appeals interpreted an intentional-injury exclusion clause in a child sexual molestation case to exclude coverage for the insured.[15] The court held that when faced with an intentional-injury exclusion clause, it would infer intent to injure only if: (1) the insured acts intentionally and (2) the injury is substantially certain to occur.[16] The court concluded that sexual molestation is an intentional act from which injury is substantially certain to result, and thus intent may be inferred.[17] Indeed, the majority of courts have supported the adoption of this inferred intent rule by noting that the state's proscription of sexual contact between an adult and a minor is a clear indication that such contact is inherently injurious to the child.[18]

The issue in *St. Paul Fire and Marine Insurance Co. v. Shernow* was whether professional liability (malpractice) insurance covers injuries sustained by a patient when a dentist, in the course of treatment, sexually assaulted her, having overcome her ability to resist through misuse of anesthesia.[19] The evidence seemingly disclosed an intentional, sexual attack. Not surprisingly, the insurer argued that coverage under the professional liability policy should depend upon the nature of the act and the intent of the actor and not the means used to accomplish the act.[20] Though this argument seems logical, the court rejected it, holding

13. *Id.*
14. 434 N.W.2d 790, 792 (Wis. Ct. App. 1988) (setting forth two-part test to determine when "inferred intent" is correct approach).
15. *Id.* at 793–94.
16. *Id.*
17. *Id.*
18. *Wiley v. State Farm Fire & Cas. Co.*, 995 F.2d 457, 464 (3d Cir. 1993).
19. 610 A.2d 1281, 1283 (Conn. 1992).
20. *Id.*

that "[w]hen the medically negligent procedure is so inextricably intertwined and inseparable from the intentional conduct that serves as the basis for the separate claim of sexual assault, we join those jurisdictions that conclude that professional liability policies must, in such instances, extend coverage."[21]

The court in *Lindheimer v. St. Paul Fire and Marine Insurance Co.* reached the opposite conclusion.[22] This case, like *Shernow*, involved allegations of sexual misconduct, where the injuries allegedly suffered by the patient arose from a battery and not from any medical diagnosis, treatment, or care.[23] The *Lindheimer* court, however, held that for coverage to extend, "[t]here must be some causal connection between an act and the nature of the doctor-patient relationship."[24] The *Lindheimer* court reasoned that, had the doctor assaulted the woman at a bar, said misconduct would not be considered medical malpractice; the result should not be any different simply because of the locality of the act.[25] When the doctor stopped providing dental treatment and began sexually assaulting the woman, his professional services ended; therefore the sexual assault was not covered under the terms of the professional liability policy.[26]

C. Intentional Acts and EPL Coverage

EPL policies generally do not contain an express exclusion for intentional conduct. But although the major EPL carriers do not have such an express exclusion, their policies do generally exclude any amount that is deemed uninsurable under the law selected to interpret the policy. Because several important jurisdictions, including New York,

---

21. *Id.* at 1285.
22. *Lindheimer v. St. Paul Fire and Marine Ins. Co.*, 643 So.2d 636 (Fla. App. 1994).
23. *Id.* at 638.
24. *Id.*
25. *Id.*
26. *Id.*

California, and Illinois, among others,[27] restrict the ability of insurance companies to indemnify for certain types of intentional conduct, all domestic insurers have restrictions on their ability to pay damages arising from intentional conduct, regardless of whether such restrictions are stated as express exclusions in the contract.

II. Punitive Damages

A. Attitude Toward Punitive Damages

"Punitive damages have long been a part of traditional state tort law."[28] In the United States, punitive damages are permitted in all but four states.[29] Though the amounts can be staggering, empirical evidence indicates that punitive damages are awarded rarely, and large punitive damages awards are very rare indeed.[30] The large majority of punitive damages are quite modest, and the mean size of punitive awards is reasonably predictable as a function of compensatory damages.[31]

Still, punitive damages awards continue to garner lots of media attention. Businesses are bombarded with anecdotal horror stories of multimillion-dollar punitive damages verdicts in product liability lawsuits. Similarly, businesses are all too familiar with the looming threat of massive verdicts associated with employment litigation. Indeed, employment litigation poses an ever-increasing threat to businesses, as the Equal Employment Opportunity Commission boasts year after

---

27. *See, e.g.*, Cal. Ins. Code § 533; *Beaver v. Country Mut. Ins. Co.*, 420 N.E.2d 1058, 1061 (Ill. App. Ct. 1981); *Home Ins. Co. v. Am. Home Prods. Corp.*, 550 N.E.2d 930 (N.Y. 1990).

28. *Silkwood v. Kerr-McGee Corp.*, 464 U.S. 238, 255 (1984).

29. *See Miller v. Kinglsey*, 230 N.W.2d 472 (Neb. 1975); *Spokane Truck & Dray Co. v. Hoefer*, 25 P.2d 1072 (Wash. 1891). New Hampshire and Michigan do not permit punitive damages per se, but do allow "enhanced" or "exemplary" compensatory damages in certain circumstances. *See Peisner v. Detroit Free Press*, 304 N.W.2d 814 (Mich. Ct. App. 1981); *Munson v. Raudonis*, 387 A.2d 1174 (N.H. 1978).

30. Thomas H. Cohen & Kyle Harbacek, Punitive Damages Awards in State Courts, 2005, *available at* http://bjs.ojp.usdoj.gov/index.cfm?ty=pbdetail&iid=2376.

31. *Id.*

year of record-breaking numbers in charges of discrimination filed and monetary relief obtained against employers.[32]

Moreover, the threshold for Title VII liability is low, and an employer's conduct need not be egregious to be subject to punitive damages.[33] Furthermore, plaintiffs can recover punitive damages even if the jury awards only nominal damages.[34] It is not surprising, then, that many businesses are relying on a variety of insurance policies, including EPL policies, to guard against the risk of punitive damages whenever possible.

Given the variances among the states as to the insurability of intentional acts, it follows that policies regarding the insurability of punitive damages vary among states.[35] Most states allow punitive damages to

32. Equal Employment Opportunity Commission, Fiscal Year 2011 Performance and Accountability Report, *available at* http://www.eeoc.gov/eeoc/plan/2011par_performance.cfm.

33. *Kolstad v. Am. Dental Ass'n*, 527 U.S. 526, 535 (1999).

34. *See, e.g.*, *Abner v. Kansas City*, 513 F.3d 154 (5th Cir. 2008) (holding that a punitive damages award, without an award of compensatory damages, did not violate due process); *Cush-Crawford v. Adchem Corp.*, 271 F.3d 352, 357 (2d Cir. 2001) (holding that a Title VII plaintiff may recover statutory punitive damages absent an award of either actual or nominal damages).

35. A. Mitchell Polinsky & Steven Shavell, *Punitive Damages: An Economic Analysis*, 111 Harv. L. Rev. 869, 930 (1998).

be covered by liability insurance in at least some circumstances,[36] but some, at least in the context of direct liability, do not.[37]

36. *See, e.g.*, *Meijer, Inc. v. General Star Indem. Co.*, 826 F. Supp. 241, 246 (W.D. Mich. 1993); ARK. CODE ANN. § 23-79-307(8); *State Farm Mut. Auto. Ins. Co. v. Lawrence*, 26 P.3d 1074 (Ala. 2001); *Am. Fidelity & Cas. v. Werfel*, 164 So. 383, 385 (Ala. 1935); *Aetna Cas. & Sur. Co. v. Marion Equip. Co.*, 894 P.2d 664, 671 (Alaska 1995); *Price v. Hartford Accident & Indem. Co.*, 502 P.2d 522, 525 (Ariz. 1972); *Southern Farm Bureau Cas. Ins. Co. v. Daniel*, 440 S.W.2d 582, 584 (Ark. 1969); *Whalen v. On-Deck, Inc.*, 514 A.2d 1072, 1074 (Del. 1986); *Greenwood Cemetery Inc. v. Travelers Indem. Co.*, 232 S.E.2d 910, 914 (Ga. 1977); GA. CODE ANN. § 56-408 (1); HAW. REV. STAT. § 431:10-240; *Abbie Uriguen Oldsmobile Buick, Inc. v. United States Fire Ins. Co.*, 511 P.2d 783, 789 (Idaho 1973); *Grinnell Mut. Reinsurance Co. v. Jungling*, 654 N.W.2d 530 (Iowa 2002); *Continental Ins. Cos. v. Hancock*, 507 S.W.2d 146, 151 (Ky. 1973); *Sharp v. Daigre*, 555 So.2d 1361, 1364 (La. 1990); *First Nat'l Bank v. Fid. & Deposit Co.*, 389 A.2d 359, 360 (Md. 1978); *James W. Sessums Timber Co., Inc. v. McDaniel*, 635 So.2d 875, 884 (Miss. 1994); MONT. CODE ANN. § 33-15-317; NEV. REV. STAT. § 681A.095; *Baker v. Armstrong*, 744 P.2d 170, 173–74 (N.M. 1987); *Mazza v. Med. Mut. Ins. Co.*, 319 S.E.2d 217, 219 (N.C. 1984); N.C. GEN. STAT. § 58-41-50; *Harrell v. Travelers Indem. Co.*, 567 P.2d 1013, 1017 (Or. 1977); *Cumberland v R.I. Interlocal Risk Mgmt. Trust Inc.*, 860 A.2d 1210, 1218–19 (R.I. 2004); *South Carolina State Budget & Control Bd. v. Prince*, 403 S.E.2d 643, 648 (S.C. 1991); *Lazenby v. Universal Underwriters Ins. Co.*, 383 S.W.2d 1, 5 (Tenn. 1964); *Dairyland County Mut. Ins. Co. v. Wallgren*, 477 S.W.2d 341, 342 (Tex. App. 1972); *Am. Protection Ins. Co. v. McMahan*, 562 A.2d 462, 466–67 (Vt. 1989); *Fluke Corp. v. Hartford Accident & Indem. Co.*, 34 P.3d 809, 815 (Wash. 2001); *Henlsey v. Erie Ins. Co.*, 283 S.E.2d 227, 233 (W. Va. 1981); *Brown v. Maxey*, 369 N.W.2d 677, 688 (Wis. 1985); *Sinclair Oil Corp. v. Columbia Cas. Co.*, 682 P.2d 975, 981 (Wyo. 1984).

37. *See, e.g.*, UTAH CODE ANN. § 31A-20-101; *Wausau Ins. Co. v. Valspar Corp.*, 594 F. Supp. 269, 273 (N.D. Ill. 1984); *Grant v. North River Ins. Co.*, 453 F. Supp. 1361, 1370 (N.D. Ind. 1978); *State Farm Fire & Cas. Co v. Superior Court*, 191 Cal. App. 3d 74, 77–78 (1987); *Bohrer v. Church Mut Ins. Co.*, 12 P.3d 854 (Colo. Ct. App. 2000); *Universal Indem. Ins. Co. v. Tenery*, 39 P.2d 776, 779 (Colo. 1934); *Bodner v. United States Auto. Ass'n*, 610 A.2d 1212, 1221–22 (Conn. 1992); *Morrison v. Hugger*, 369 So.2d 614, 615 (Fla. Dist. Ct. App. 1979); *St. Paul Surplus Lines Ins. Co. v. Int'l Playtex, Inc.*, 777 P.2d 1259, 1269 (Kan. 1989); *Santos v. Lumbermens Mut. Cas. Co.*, 556 N.E.2d 983, 990, 992 (Mass. 1990); *Rosenbloom v. Flygare*, 501 N.W.2d 597, 602 (Minn. 1993); *DeShong v. Mid-States Adjustment, Inc.*, 876 S.W.2d 5 (Mo. Ct. App. 1994); *Heartland Stores, Inc. v. Royal Ins. Co.*, 815 S.W.2d 39, 43 (Mo. Ct. App. 1991); *Johnson & Johnson v. Aetna Cas. & Sur. Co.*, 667 A.2d 1087, 1091 (N.J. Super. Ct. App. Div. 1995); *Home Ins. Co. v. Am. Home Prods. Corp.*, 550 N.E.2d 930, 932 (N.Y. 1990); *Carey v. Calhoun*, 531 N.E.2d 1348, 1348 (Ohio Ct. App. 1987); OHIO REV. CODE ANN. § 3937.182; S.D. CODIFIED LAWS § 53-9-3; *Allen v. Simmons*, 533 A.2d 541, 544 (R.I. 1987); *City of Ft. Pierre v. United Fire & Cas. Co.*, 463 N.W.2d 845, 848–49 (S.D. 1990).

B. Punitive Damages Coverage

1. Public Policy and the Insurability of Punitive Damages

Many courts have struggled with whether the insurability of punitive damages violates state public policy, and there is a sharp split of authority nationwide over whether insurance may validly cover liability for punitive damages.[38] The outcome of a court's public policy analysis will frequently turn on how the court characterizes punitive damages.[39] In determining whether the coverage of punitive damages contravenes public policy, courts look to two factors:[40] (1) the conduct of the insured (that is, will insurability of punitive damages encourage the insured's bad conduct?); and (2) the purpose served by the imposition of liability for that conduct (that is, are the punitive damages intended to deter wrongdoers or to compensate victims?).[41] Because "one should not be able to insure against one's own intentional misconduct," punitive damage insurance may be found to violate public policy if it has the effect of directly stimulating the commission of a wrongful act.[42] Likewise, if punitive damages are imposed in a given situation in order to punish the wrongdoer, their insurability may defeat this policy.[43]

The thrust of these arguments is that if the insurer, rather than the insured, bears the risk of paying punitive damages for the insured's misdeed, then the wrongdoer will not actually be punished for what he or she has done.[44] When punitive damages are shifted to the insurance company, they fail in their purpose to punish the bad actor and to

38. *City Prods. Corp. v. Globe Indemnity Co.*, 151 Cal. Rptr. 494, 499 (Cal. Ct. App. 1979).

39. *Northwestern Nat'l Cas. Co. v. McNulty*, 307 F.2d 432, 434 (5th Cir. 1962) (characterizing punitive damages as a penalty to deter rather than to compensate) (punitive damages as potential violation of public policy superseded by statute as stated in *United Services Ass'n v. Webb*, 369 S.E.2d 196 (Va. 1988)).

40. *Ranger Ins. Co. v. Bal Harbour Club, Inc.*, 549 So.2d 1005, 1007 (Fla. 1989).

41. *Id.*

42. *Id.*

43. *Id.*

44. *See Dahlen v. Landis*, 314 N.W.2d 63, 68 (N.D. 1981).

deter others from committing similar conduct in the future.[45] As Justice Cardozo stated, "no one shall be permitted to take advantage of his own wrong."[46] This view garnered some support in the early days of the public policy debate over insuring punitive damages but has since been rejected by the majority of courts in favor of the view that punitive damages may be covered by insurance.

a. The Minority View: Insuring Punitive Damages Violates Public Policy

The leading case on the minority view is *Northwestern National Casualty Co. v. McNulty*.[47] In rejecting the notion that punitive damages can be insured, the *McNulty* court referenced the vindictive nature of punitive damages, which has been described as a combination of personal and public revenge that may be justified as a means of discouraging self-help.[48] The court found that the insurance of punitive damages is inconsistent with public policy:

> The policy considerations in a state where, as in Florida and Virginia, punitive damages are awarded for punishment and deterrence, would seem to require that the damages rest ultimately as well nominally on the party actually responsible for the wrong. If that person were permitted to shift the burden to an insurance company, punitive damages would serve no useful purpose. Such damages do not compensate the plaintiff for his injury, since compensatory damages already have made the plaintiff whole. And there is no point in punishing the insurance company; it has done

45. *Id.*

46. *Messersmith v. Am. Fid. Co.*, 133 N.E. 432, 433 (N.Y. 1921).

47. 307 F.2d 432 (5th Cir. 1962). Notably, McNulty has since been superseded by statute, but its legal analysis and discussion of the purpose of punitive damages are still cited by courts today. *See, e.g., TIG Ins. Co. v. Premier Parks, Inc.*, No. Civ.A.02C04126JRS, 2004 WL 728858 (Del. Super. Ct. Mar. 10, 2004).

48. *Id.* at 434 n.3 (*citing Gostkowski v. Roman Catholic Church of the Sacred Hearts*, 262 N.Y. 320, 186 N.E. 798, 800 (1933)).

> nothing. In actual fact, of course, and considering the extent to which the public is insured, the burden would ultimately come to rest not on the insurance companies but on the public, since the added liability to the insurance companies would be passed along to the premium payers. Society would then be punishing itself for the wrong committed by the insured.[49]

McNulty suggests that if punitive damages are allowed to be insured, then the wrongdoer is effectively permitted to escape punishment. To that end, the deterrence effect of punitive damages becomes illusory when it is the insurance company, not the wrongdoer, who bears the risk of paying the penalty.

b. The Majority View: Insuring Punitive Damages Does Not Violate Public Policy

Though *McNulty* stands as the leading case against the insurability of punitive damages, as the minority view, it has come under serious attack. For instance, the courts in *Price v. Hartford Accident and Indemnity Co.*,[50] *Harrell v. Travelers Indemnity Co.*,[51] *Fairfield Insurance Co. v. Stevens Martin Paving, LP*,[52] and *Lazenby v. Universal Underwriters Insurance Co.*[53] rejected *McNulty*'s holding and required the insurers to pay the punitive damages assessed against their insureds.

After outlining *McNulty*'s logic, the Tennessee Supreme Court in *Lazenby* stated, "We, however, are not able to agree the closing of the insurance market, on the payment of punitive damages, to such drivers would necessarily accomplish the result of deterring them in their wrongful conduct."[54] That court further reasoned, "[t]he insurance

49. *Id.* at 440–41.
50. 502 P.2d 522 (Ariz. 1972).
51. 567 P.2d 1013 (Or. 1977).
52. 246 S.W.3d 653 (Tex. 2008).
53. 383 S.W.2d 1 (Tenn. 1964).
54. *Id.* at 5.

contract in the case at bar is a private contract between defendant and their assured . . . which when construed as written would be held to protect him against claims for both compensatory and punitive damages. Then, to hold the assured, as a matter of public policy, is not protected by the policy on a claim for punitive damages would, in effect, partially void the contract."[55]

Similarly, the *Price* court found that Arizona's public policy did not void an insurance contract insofar as it covered punitive damages.[56] Like *Lazenby*, the *Price* court poked a number of holes in *McNulty*'s logic. The court noted, for example, "even though a driver is insured for punitive damages, he cannot engage in wanton conduct with impunity. In the instant case, drag racing would subject him to criminal penalties. His insurance rates would soar."[57] And since "Hartford has voluntarily covered its insured's liability for punitive damages, and since its premiums were based on its exposure, it may be presumed that holding it liable for what it has promised to pay would not result in additional burdens on the driving public."[58] Furthermore, "there is no evidence that those states which deny coverage have accomplished any appreciable effect on the slaughter on their highways."[59]

In *Harrell*, the Supreme Court of Oregon's scathing critique of *McNulty* suggested that its logic "is naive at least, if not pure fiction."[60] The court stated that "[i]t has long been recognized that there is no empirical evidence that contracts of insurance to protect against liability for negligent conduct are invalid, as a matter of public policy, because of any 'evil tendency' to make negligent conduct 'more probable' or because there is any 'substantial relationship' between the fact of insurance and such negligent conduct."[61]

---

55. *Id.*
56. *Price*, 502 P.2d at 524.
57. *Id.*
58. *Id.*
59. *Id.*
60. *Harrell*, 567 P.2d at 1019.
61. *Id.* at 1017.

These public policy–based opinions reflect the majority view, which dismisses *McNulty*'s hypothesis that insurance coverage for punitive damages may corrupt individual responsibility and accountability in a civil society.

2. Jurisprudential Construction of Typical Policy Language

Courts have also required insurers to pay their insureds' punitive damages based on basic principles of contract interpretation.[62] In *Carroway v. Johnson*, for instance, the Supreme Court of South Carolina broadly construed the insurance policy's requirement that the insurer pay "all sums" assessed against the insured, and required the insurer to pay the punitive damages award assessed against the insured.[63] The court stated:

> The policy here is a voluntary policy and defendant agreed to pay "all sums" which the insured "shall become legally obligated to pay as damages" because of bodily injury. The punitive damage award is a sum, which the insured is legally obligated to pay as damages.[64]

The Arizona Supreme Court followed South Carolina's lead in *Price v. Hartford Accident & Indemnity Co.*[65] According to the *Price* court, an insurer that agrees to pay "all sums" is responsible for the payment of punitive damages:

> It is our holding that the premium has been paid and accepted and the protection has been tendered, and that under the

62. Tom Baker, *Liability Insurance Conflicts and Defense Lawyers: From Triangles to Tetrahedrons*, 4 Conn. Ins. L.J. 101, 103 (1997–98).

63. *Carroway v. Johnson*, 245 S.C. 200, 139 S.E.2d 908, 910 (1965).

64. *Id.*

65. 502 P.2d 522 (Ariz. 1972).

> circumstances public policy would be best served by requiring the insurance company to honor its obligation.[66]

In *American Home Assurance Co. v. Safeway Steel Products Co., Inc.*, the Texas Court of Appeals outlined the other most common contract law–based arguments used by courts to find coverage for punitive damages:

> (1) the average insured, in the absence of an express policy exclusion from liability from punitive damages, would assume that the term "damages" would include punitive damages, since they would become by judgment a "sum" that the insured would be legally obligated to pay; (2) because the insurer drafted the policy and could have made clear its intention to exclude coverage for punitive damages, the rules of construction require it to bear the burden of ambiguity; and (3) punitive damages are covered because they always "arise" out of the underlying action for injury.[67]

Not all states have fallen in line with South Carolina and Arizona, however. For instance, in *Caspersen v. Webber*, the Supreme Court of Minnesota court did not require the insurer to pay the punitive damages award assessed against its insured, even though the policy did not specifically exempt them:

> There were actual damages, which presumably compensated the plaintiff for any actual loss sustained. The punitive damages were awarded to plaintiff as punishment to the defendant and as a

66. *Id.* at 525.

67. 743 S.W.2d 693, 702 (Tex. App. 1987) (*citing* Burrell & Young, *Insurability of Punitive Damages*, 62 Marg. L. Rev. 1, 12 (1978); Ghiardi & Kircher, Punitive Damages: Law and Practice § 705 (1984); Schumaier & McKinsey, *The Insurability of Punitive Damages*, 72 Am. B.J. 68 (Mar. 1, 1986)).

deterrence to others. The punitive damages then were not awarded because of bodily injury, and the company's policy afforded no coverage for the punitive damages.[68]

3. Vicarious Liability

The trend toward the insurability of punitive damages is especially evident when the punitive damages are assessed against the insured vicariously, as in principal-agent situations.[69] The case *Ohio Casualty Insurance Co. v. Welfare Finance Co.* illustrates this proposition well.[70] The plaintiff sued the employer, alleging wrongful, wanton, and reckless operation of a truck on the part of an employee.[71] The court, in finding that punitive damages were cognizable under the employer's policy, stated:

> A different situation is present where the sole liability of the insured arises out of the relation of master and servant. If the master participates in, authorizes, or knows in advance that his servant will probably commit the unlawful injurious act, then the situation may be analogous to where the insured himself commits an intentional act with an intended injury and the same reasons for holding a protecting policy invalid as to such acts would exist. . . . [On the other hand,] where there was no direct or indirect volition upon the part of the master in the commission of the act, no public policy is violated by protecting him from the unauthorized and unnatural act of his servant.[72]

68. 213 N.W.2d 327, 331 (Minn. 1973).

69. *See, e.g., Commercial Union Ins. Co. v. Reichard*, 404 F.2d 868 (5th Cir. 1968); *Norfolk & W. Ry. Co. v. Hartford Accident & Indem. Co.*, 420 F. Supp. 92 (N.D. Ind. 1976); *Dayton-Hudson Corp. v. Am. Mut. Liability Ins. Co.*, 526 F. Supp. 730 (W.D. Okla. 1981).

70. 75 F.2d 58 (8th Cir. 1994).

71. *Id.* at 58.

72. *Id.* at 60.

Similarly, in *Sterling Insurance Co. v. Hughes*, a case in which the insured's beach boy was found guilty of committing an assault and battery upon the plaintiff,[73] the court stated:

> It is generally held that there is a distinction between the actual tortfeasor and one only vicariously liable and therefore public policy is not violated by construing a liability policy to include punitive damages recovered by an injured person where the insured did not participate in or authorize the act.[74]

These cases highlight the distinction between primary and vicarious liability in the context of punitive damages. Whether the punitive damages are borne by the insurer or the insured, they do not punish or deter the third-party wrongdoer. For this reason, the policy reasons against allowing insurance to cover the damages are simply not in play when the plaintiff obtains a punitive damages award against an insured who was not the actual wrongdoer.

---

73. *Sterling Ins. Co. v. Hughes*, 187 So.2d 898, 899 (Fla. Dist. Ct. App. 1966).
74. *Id.* at 900.

CHAPTER 4
Investigating EPLI-Covered Claims

Matthew S. Effland and Todd J. Kaiser

There are many ways to win an employment lawsuit—good facts, favorable court decisions, sympathetic witnesses, and strong strategic planning are keys to a successful defense and possible early resolution on summary judgment. Likewise, conflicting evidence, the appearance of deception, and built-in employee bias in juries can all contribute to an expensive and image-damaging loss. However, the core of any result, whether favorable or otherwise, can almost always be traced back to the investigations performed by the employer in anticipation of—or subsequent to—an employment claim being filed. The difference between a reasonable settlement and/or summary judgment on the one hand and a lengthy jury trial and expensive judgment on the other often hinges on the scope and thoroughness of pre- and post-claim investigations performed by (or on behalf of) the employer.

This chapter focuses on the three types of investigations in which employers will typically take part, as well as the preservation of privilege and confidentiality of internal records generated during the course of the different types of investigations. First, this chapter discusses pre-EPLI policy investigations and audits, in the context of what an employer may expect prior to receiving employment litigation coverage. Next, this chapter looks at the type of investigations performed following the filing of an Equal Employment Opportunity Commission charge of discrimination. Finally, this chapter addresses ongoing investigations conducted by employers and their counsel during the course of litigation.

I. Pre-Policy Investigations

A. The Need for EPLI Coverage and What to Expect Prior to Coverage

In the last decade of the twentieth century, the number of employment-related claims (that is, those claims based on federal employment law statutes, such as Title VII or the Americans with Disabilities Act) more than doubled, from 8,273 in 1990 to 21,032 in 2000.[1] The total number of employment-related claims decreased to 14,353 in 2006 but has been on an upward trend since 2008.[2] Additionally, the total number of discrimination charges filed with the Equal Employment Opportunity Commission has been steadily increasing since 2009, with nearly one million discrimination charges filed in 2011 alone.[3]

Accordingly, many companies have found that discrimination lawsuits, once treated as simply another "cost of doing business," are in reality a significant drain on business resources. In an effort to stanch the flow of increasing litigation costs, companies are turning to EPLI policies. What many companies do not realize, however, is that the protection offered by EPLI policies does not simply start with putting pen to the paper of the policy contract. To both evaluate the risk of

---

1. U.S. Courts Judicial Facts and Figures 2008, *Table 4.4: Civil Cases Filed by Nature of Suit*, *available at* http://www.uscourts.gov/Statistics/JudicialFactsAndFigures/JudicialFactsAndFigures2008.aspx.

2. *Id.*

3. U.S. Equal Employment Opportunity Commission, Charge Statistics FY 1997 through FY 2011, *available at* http://eeoc.gov/eeoc/statistics/enforcement/charges.cfm.

exposure to litigation and set policy limits and conditions, many—if not all—modern EPLI carriers at one time generally require an employment practices audit prior to policy issuance. The purpose of the audit is primarily to provide information to the insurer for purposes of assessing the relative risk associated with insuring a given company, thus enabling the carrier to set an appropriate premium for coverage. The insurer may also use the results of an audit to outline steps that an employer must take to obtain coverage or remain covered (conduct supervisor training, rewrite job descriptions, alter company policies, and so forth). Even if the EPLI carrier does not require the employer to amend its practices following the audit, it will at least provide a benchmark for the carrier when deciding whether to renew the policy the following year.[4]

Audits are usually conducted by the carrier based on information provided by the employer as part of the rigorous EPLI application process. The audit typically involves a review of the company's handbooks, written procedures for investigating harassment and discrimination claims, hiring and termination practices, and recent claims or lawsuits made against the company by its employees.[5] In some instances, an on-site investigation is conducted in which the auditors observe and evaluate the day-to-day running of the employer's business.

The price for these audits is usually passed along to the policyholder through increased premiums during the first year; however, if an employer is willing (or required) to alter policies, practices, or other aspects of its workplace in response to the results of the audit,

4. Glenn Kramer, *Reasonableness for Free: Why Buy Employment Practices Liability Insurance When EEOC.GOV Gives Protection Away?*, 3 CARDOZO PUB. L. POL'Y & ETHICS J. 459, 468–469 (2005).

5. Joan Gabel et al., *Evolving Conflict between Standards for Employment Discrimination Liability and the Delegation of That Liability: Does Employment Practices Liability Insurance Offer Appropriate Risk Transference?*, 4 U. PA. J. LAB. & EMP. L. 1, 34, n.239 (2001); Lorelie S. Masters, *Protection from the Storm: Insurance Coverage for Employment Liability*, 53 BUS. LAW. 1249, 1275–1276 (1998); Nancy H. Van der Veer, *Employment Practices Liability Insurance: Are EPLI Policies a License to Discriminate? Or Are They a Necessary Reality Check for Employers?*, 12 CONN. INS. L.J. 173, 195–200 (2005).

the policyholder might expect to see its premiums decline during the subsequent years of a multiyear EPLI contract, or upon renewal of a one-year contract.

Since the introduction of EPLI policies in the 1990s, the number of carriers offering EPLI coverage has dramatically increased, resulting in growing competition among those carriers for the opportunity to provide coverage to employers. Originally, this competition resulted in across-the-board price cuts for most EPLI policies as insurers fought for market share. It also allowed employers to negotiate over the scope and method of precoverage audits. Now, though most EPLI carriers require on-site audits only for very large companies or for companies with a significant past history of employment litigation issues, prices have started to increase once again.[6] Even though smaller companies can expect to receive some level of coverage simply by providing their written policies and procedures to a carrier, many may find that the affordable EPLI policies of the 1990s have doubled or even tripled in price.[7]

Because EPLI on-site audits are no longer mandatory for many companies, the overall process of applying for and receiving EPLI coverage has grown less expensive, even though premiums have continued to rise. To compensate for the higher risk associated with not performing a thorough on-site audit before awarding coverage, insurers have almost uniformly switched to a policy term of no more than one year.[8] In addition, despite increased cost-cutting pressures from employers, most EPLI carriers refuse to accept self-audits performed by the employers as a

---

6. Reed Abelson, *Surge in Bias Cases Punishes Insurers, and Premiums Rise*, N.Y. TIMES, January 9, 2002, *available at* http://www.nytimes.com/2002/01/09/business/09HARA.html?pagewanted=all (hereinafter "Abelson"); Marla Donovan, *The Rising Tide of EPLI*, AMERICAN AGENT & BROKER, May 5, 2010; Dave Willis, *The EPLI Market*, Rough Notes (July 1, 2009) (on file with author).

7. Abelson, *supra* note 6.

8. As competition continues to escalate between carriers, some companies have successfully negotiated policy terms of more than a year. However, the standard policy term for EPLI contracts remains one year.

basis upon which to determine coverage or premiums. In some situations, however, employers have successfully negotiated permission to use their own outside counsel to conduct the audits, particularly when that company has been pre-approved by the EPLI carrier.

B. Concerns about Confidentiality and Privilege

1. Introduction

Regardless of who does the audit, one of the primary concerns for employers is preventing the public disclosure of the investigation's results. Unfortunately, because most EPLI investigative audits are done prior to the start of legal proceedings, very little exists in the way of legal protection for audit results.

2. Attorney-Client Privilege at the Audit Stage

Attorney-client privilege is the most likely means of preventing disclosure of audit results, but only if it is performed in a very careful manner by a lawyer (that is, not a paralegal).[9] To qualify, a lawyer must be in charge of the audit (a condition that may be difficult to meet, depending on the policy of the EPLI carrier), and that lawyer must work closely with management so that legal advice can be requested and offered freely.[10] Because direct legal advice is protected, anyone interviewed should be told to keep the issues discussed confidential, and the results of the lawyer's audit should be disclosed only to senior management, because this will support a court's finding that the material is protected.[11]

---

9. S. Beville May & Kimberly Cozza, *Internal Investigations and Audits: Are They Privileged?*, 629 PLI/LIT 313, 338–340 (2000).

10. *Id.* (citing *Spectrum Sys. Int'l Corp. v. Chem. Bank*, 581 N.E.2d 1055, 1061 (N.Y. 1991); *Wellpoint Health Networks, Inc. v. Superior Court of Los Angeles County*, 59 Cal. App. 4th 110, 123 (1997)).

11. *Barfoot v. Boeing Co.*, 184 F.R.D. 642, 645 (N.D. Ala. 1999).

3. *Work-Product Doctrine at the Audit Stage*

Unfortunately, the other time-honored method of protecting information from disclosure, the "work-product doctrine," simply does not apply to prelitigation audits. The desire to obtain insurance coverage will usually be seen as a business decision, rather than a legal directive, and any investigation with such a basis will be treated as a management tool rather than as the result of any specific directive.[12]

4. *The Self-Critical Analysis Privilege*

The self-critical analysis privilege (SCAP) has existed, in one form or another, since the early 1970s.[13] The underlying premise of the SCAP is that a company that conducts a "candid and conscientious evaluation" of internal procedures and practices is entitled to a qualified privilege for information gained on the basis of public policy.[14] The application of the SCAP to employment-related actions has varied, with a majority rejecting its use.[15] Its only real application would be in situations in which neither the attorney-client privilege nor the work-products doctrine would apply (that is, when the audit is performed by the carrier or by the company itself without reliance upon legal counsel or assistance). Nevertheless, because the SCAP is accepted in so few

---

12. *In Re Grand Jury Subpoena*, 599 F.2d 504, 511 (2d Cir. 1979).

13. *Johnson v. United Parcel Serv., Inc.*, 206 F.R.D. 686, 688 (M.D. Fla. 2002) (citing *Bredice v. Doctors Hosps., Inc.*, 50 F.R.D. 249 (D.D.C. 1970), *aff'd*, 479 F.2d 920 (D.C. Cir. 1973)).

14. *Id.*

15. *Id.* at 689–90 (citing *Reid v. Lockheed Martin Aeronautics Co.*, 199 F.R.D. 379 (N.D. Ga. 2001); *see also Univ. of Penn. v. E.E.O.C.*, 493 U.S. 182, 189 (1990) (declining to expand federal privilege law to protect peer-reviewed documents in Title VII discrimination action); *Dowling v. Am. Haw. Cruises, Inc.*, 971 F.2d 423, 426 (9th Cir. 1992); *Troupin v. Metro. Life Ins. Co.*, 169 F.R.D. 546, 550 (S.D.N.Y. 1996); *Gatewood v. Stone Container Corp.*, 170 F.R.D. 455, 459 (S.D. Iowa 1996); *Brem v. DeCarlo, Lyon Heron & Pazourek P.A.*, 162 F.R.D. 94, 102 (D. Md. 1995) (declining to recognize or apply the privilege); *Etienne v. Mitre Corp.*, 146 F.R.D. 145, 148–49 (E.D. Va. 1993); James E. Scheuerman, *Employment Practices Liability Insurance: Navigating the Hazards when Exploring the Market*, 29 THE BRIEF 64, 65 n.8 (Fall 1999) (recognizing the privilege).

jurisdictions (particularly with regard to employment-related actions[16]), a company should be extremely wary of relying upon it to prevent audit information from being disclosed during discovery.

C. Practical Considerations When Considering an EPLI Policy

Since almost every EPLI carrier requires some degree of precoverage audit, that alone should not be the determining factor when a company is deciding whether such coverage is appropriate. However, because of the current high level of competition within the EPLI market, employers that are interested in securing coverage should not be afraid to quiz prospective carriers on the scope, cost, and method of conducting such precoverage audits.

For example, a business may be able to negotiate a lower overall premium in exchange for a single, one-time cost of a thorough precoverage audit. Likewise, a company may be successful in negotiating a more limited audit in exchange for higher deductibles and/or a shorter policy term. Employers can also negotiate who will perform the audit. In some cases, insurance carriers have been willing to allow an employer to choose the firm or organization to perform the precoverage audit, pay for the audit itself, and then receive a credit toward its policy payments to compensate for the out-of-pocket expense of the audit.

Furthermore, because so much is at stake in protecting the results of an internal investigation and/or audit (which may reveal significant deficiencies in areas ripe for litigation), a company seeking EPLI coverage—or a lawyer advising his client to secure such coverage—should make every effort to maintain as much control over the process as possible. With the increased competition between EPLI carriers, a savvy employer should try to incorporate into any EPLI policy the option of providing a self-audit for coverage purposes, even if it means following the guidelines set forth by the carrier. Also, the use of outside counsel

16. *See, e.g., Univ. of Penn. v. E.E.O.C.*, 493 U.S. at 189.

with experience in limiting the creation of discoverable material can dramatically lower the likelihood of being forced to turn over the results of internal audits and investigations during the course of litigation.

If a company can find an EPLI carrier that already has its preferred outside counsel on an "approved" list, it will likely be much easier to convince the carrier to allow that lawyer to participate in the policy-mandated audit. For management lawyers, it is in their best interest to get onto the approved list of as many EPLI carriers as possible, to ensure that a client will never have to choose between coverage and representation.

II. The Post-Charge Investigation

A. Introduction

Once a covered employer receives notice from the EEOC that a charge of discrimination has been filed (or, in the case of statutes that do not have a charge requirement, is served with the lawsuit[17]), EPLI insurance contracts almost uniformly require immediate notification to be supplied to the carrier of the claim. An investigation into the allegations must be conducted quickly, whether to assist the company in drafting a response to the EEOC or to help counsel evaluate the case and prepare for its defense. Additionally, a prompt and effective investigation is a necessary part of the affirmative defense available to employers to sever vicarious liability for sexual harassment under federal employment discrimination law.[18] Conversely, failure to conduct an investigation—or worse, conducting a sham investigation merely for the sake of appearances—may result in strict liability for the company (and possible exclusion from coverage under some EPLI contracts).

17. For example, suits brought under the Family and Medical Leave Act of 1993, 29 U.S.C. § 2601 *et seq*., have no administrative prerequisites to filing suit. The first notice a company may have that litigation is imminent is the point when the process server arrives to serve the complaint.

18. *Faragher v. City of Boca Raton*, 524 U.S. 775, 804 (1998); *Burlington Industries v. Ellerth*, 524 U.S. 742, 765 (1998).

The least expensive and most convenient form of post-charge investigation is one that is performed by the employer itself. It is crucial to fully document the investigation, because both the company's EPLI carrier and defense counsel will wish to review the results (albeit for different reasons). Furthermore, disciplinary action may be necessary for one or more employees. Before taking any disciplinary action, however, supervisors and managers should understand that there are certain procedures that should be followed to help justify the disciplinary decision. The investigation may be conducted by the company's own Human Resources / Legal Department, by outside independent counsel, or (depending on the language of the EPLI contract) by agents of the carrier itself.

B. Self-Investigation

1. Conducting the Investigation

It is important to have proper documentation to support the basis for the disciplinary action. This is particularly true because supervisors or managers may be called upon months or even years later to testify concerning the basis for the disciplinary action. Moreover, the company's EPLI carrier will usually demand the results of any investigation to verify coverage is available and/or appropriate. A few basic rules should be kept in mind in obtaining the information:

a. The Hearsay or No-Gossip Rule

Most nonlawyers have heard of the "hearsay" rule. It might also be called the no-gossip rule, because this explains exactly what the hearsay rule provides. An employer *should not rely* on second- or third-hand reports about an employee's conduct, but should go directly to the employee or employees involved or those who actually witnessed the behavior or incident. Hearsay is typically unreliable, and it is not difficult to go beyond a hearsay report in an effort to confirm it.

b. Avoid Opinions

Like hearsay, opinions of other people as reported to supervisors are frequently unreliable. Therefore, rather than relying on opinions, supervisors should try to obtain facts. Other employees' opinions are often drawn from inferences based upon their own experience and may not be inferences that are reliable as applied to other employees.

c. Support Subjective Conclusions

Some cases, particularly those involving discipline for poor work performance, necessarily involve judgment or opinion of an employee's work. In such cases, the facts on which the judgment or opinion is based should be documented. For example, if an employee is to be disciplined for poor work performance, the ways in which the employee's work has failed to meet established standards should be documented and specific examples given. If possible, samples of the defective or substandard work product should be preserved.

d. Get the Best Evidence

When an incident is being investigated, the best evidence of the incident should be preserved. For example, a photograph of a liquor bottle is not as good as the liquor bottle itself.

e. Interview the Employee

Always interview the employee whose conduct is under investigation and give that person the opportunity to tell his or her side of the story and explain his or her actions.

f. Get Witness Statements Promptly

Witnesses to any occurrence should be interviewed as promptly as possible, and statements should be obtained from those witnesses. This will permit them to give a better recollection because the occurrence will be fresh in their minds. The written statements should include as many details about the incident as the witnesses can recall. The statements should be signed and dated by the witnesses. It is important to interview witnesses as promptly as possible because:

- Many times a witness will be called upon to testify about an event that occurred years earlier. A written statement can be crucial for refreshing the witness's recollection.
- It will help prevent witnesses from changing their story at some later time.
- If a witness is unwilling to put his or her account in writing, there is a good chance he or she would be unwilling to testify at a later hearing should the employee challenge the disciplinary action before some agency or in court.

g. Supplemental Report

In addition to gathering the evidence and witness statements, the supervisor should keep a narrative record of the steps of the investigation. The employer's reason for its action will have more credence if based on a thorough, good-faith investigation, the steps of which can be traced by a supervisor-witness.

2. Remember Employee Rights

While conducting an internal investigation in the manner outlined above, an employer must be certain not to inadvertently violate the rights of those employees involved (voluntarily or otherwise) in the investigation. The National Labor Relations Board (NLRB) reversed prior case law and found that nonunionized employees may insist upon a coworker's presence as a witness at an employer's investigatory interview that the employee reasonably believes might result in disciplinary action against her or him.[19] As a result, disciplining or discharging an employee for

19. *Epilepsy Found. of Northeast Ohio v. N.L.R.B.*, 268 F.3d 1095, 1098–99 (D.C. Cir. 2001).

refusal to cooperate in such an interview without a witness is a violation of the National Labor Relations Act.[20]

Several important points should be made about these rights, which have come to be known as "*Weingarten* rights," named after the case establishing the legal principle, *National Labor Relations Board v. J. Weingarten, Inc.*:[21]

- They apply *whether* or not the employees are represented by a labor organization.
- The right exists *only* where there is a reasonable expectation by the employee that the interview may lead to his discipline.
- The employer does not have to offer representation to the employee. The employer must specifically request a representative.
- If the employee asks for a representative, the employer may exercise one of three options:
    a. Grant the request and halt the interview until the representative is present;
    b. Discontinue the interview; or
    c. Offer the employee the choice between continuing the interview unaccompanied by a representative or having no interview at all.
- The employer may not require that the representative remain silent during the interview but may limit his or her role to avoid disrupting the interview.

The NLRB also has held that an employer violates the law by refusing to inform the employee under investigation and his or her representative of the nature of the matter being investigated, as well as by refusing to allow the employee to consult with the representative before the

20. *Id.*
21. 420 U.S. 251 (1975).

interviews.[22] The NLRB reasons that the *Weingarten* right to representation is ineffective without the opportunity for prior consultation, because the representative would be precluded from performing his or her role as a "knowledgeable" representative. Keep in mind, however, that the investigators need not inform the employee-witness of the *Weingarten* right, because the right to a representative is required only if specifically requested.

3. Privilege Issues in Self-Investigations

a. Attorney-Client Privilege

Obviously, if the investigation is done internally without any assistance from a lawyer, there will be no attorney-client privilege. For investigations conducted by in-house lawyers, it is a bit more of a mixed bag. Courts generally agree that a company may invoke attorney-client privilege for work performed by in-house counsel.[23] However, the privilege is not absolute, particularly in situations where the in-house lawyer "wears other hats" (for example, business advisor, financial consultant).[24] A key area where this may come into play is when a company's in-house counsel is also its senior human resources (HR) manager. In such situations, there may be a question as to whether the lawyer is acting in his or her legal or HR role. To help support the application of the privilege in these situations, it is usually preferable to have an in-house lawyer act solely in a legal advisory role. One possible way to accomplish this goal is to have a clear policy outlining the role of each member of management involved in investigating and resolving discrimination claims.

---

22. *Pacific Telephone and Telegraph Co. v. N.L.R.B.*, 711 F.2d 134, 137 (9th Cir. 1983) (upholding NLRB decision that employer had committed an unfair labor practice by refusing to allow the employee to meet with his union representative on company time during a speedy investigation); *see also United States Postal Serv. v. N.L.R.B.*, 969 F.2d 1064, 1067-68 (D.C. Cir. 1992).

23. *In re Sealed Case*, 737 F.2d 94, 99 (D.C. Cir. 1984); *City of Springfield v. Rexnord Corp.*, 196 F.R.D. 7, 9 (D. Mass. 2000).

24. *City of Springfield*, 196 F.R.D. at 9.

b. Work-Product Doctrine

In the case of an investigation undertaken pursuant to company policy following a charge of an employment law violation, the work-product doctrine may offer some protection to the results of that investigation, but only if prompted by a lawyer for purposes of preparing for litigation defense.[25] Courts have been reluctant to extend the work-product doctrine too far beyond that which is prepared *directly* in anticipation of a known and discrete expectation of litigation, but have held the doctrine applies to documents prepared not only by a company's lawyer but also by any other representative working on behalf of the company.[26] Though opinion work-product (such as notes of discussions and strategy memoranda prepared by lawyers) is always protected from discovery, more general "fact" work product (such as witness statements and incident reports) is treated more like a qualified immunity than a privilege.[27] Therefore, a company must be cognizant of the fact that, should an opposing party show substantial need for the materials, it is possible that the results of any investigation *may* be discoverable, regardless of who prepared them.

c. Documents Used to Support or Defend a Company's Position

One final point to keep in mind when a self-investigation is being conducted is that any documents used in preparing a response to a charge of discrimination will lose their privileged status once they are turned over to the EEOC (or any other investigating agency). This is true whether the documents were prepared by counsel, organized in

---

25. *In re Grand Jury Subpoena*, 599 F.2d 504, 511–12 (2d Cir. 1979). Here, the company performed two investigations. The first was for an internal audit committee when litigation was suspected. The court held that this was not protected. The second, prompted by corporate counsel, was deemed to be protected. *See also Gingerich v. City of Elkhart Probation Dept.*, 273 F.R.D. 532, 544 (N.D. Ill. 2011) (finding that in-house counsel's investigation was a "fact finding mission to prepare [the employer's] defense," so investigation notes were therefore protected by work-product doctrine).

26. *Shipes v. BIC Corp.*, 154 F.R.D. 301, 305 (M.D. Ga. 1994).

27. 8 Charles Alan Wright & Arthur R. Miller, Federal Practice and Procedure § 2025 (3d ed. 1998).

anticipation of litigation, or held in some other capacity that would otherwise entitle the company to keep them secret. Though not technically public record at the time they are disclosed to the EEOC, once the agency closes its file on a charge of discrimination and a lawsuit is filed, *anyone*, including both the plaintiff and the general public, can obtain nearly everything filed with the EEOC through a Freedom of Information Act (FOIA) request. Therefore, any documents that might be privileged, or are not known of by a charging party, should only be disclosed as part of a position statement if (a) the document is crucial to a favorable decision by the investigating agency and (b) the document would likely be subject to discovery in the event of a lawsuit.

4. Practical Considerations for Self-Investigations

Following the basic rules set forth above will assist defense counsel in protecting the company's interests during litigation, as well as provide valuable information to the company's EPLI carrier in making coverage decisions. Furthermore, because the procedure is conducted in-house, a self-investigation has the inherent advantages of both lower cost and greater control over the process.

Unfortunately, it is also possible that the internal investigation may not be sufficiently detailed to satisfy an EPLI carrier, particularly if the carrier has specific guidelines that must be followed or requires some level of independent verification. In addition, the results of almost any internal investigation may be subject to at least partial disclosure through subsequent discovery and/or the EEOC investigation process, primarily because information gained in the investigation will often be used as the basis for raising one or more (affirmative) defenses. As a result, the courts disfavor restricting access to such information.[28] Therefore, it is crucial that any internally prepared investigative report limit information to that which is strictly relevant to the investigation at hand.

---

28. *Barfoot v. Boeing Co.*, 184 F.R.D. 642, 644–45 (N.D. Ala. 1999).

C. Investigation by Outside Counsel

1. Introduction

Outside independent counsel will likely conduct an investigation substantially similar in form to what was discussed above in the self-investigation section. However, the benefits of using outside counsel include both an inherent objectivity in conducting interviews and an expertise in extracting information relevant to a legal defense (while minimizing improper or unnecessary statements of opinion). Though certainly more expensive in terms of a per-hour cost when compared with internal self-investigations, the additional cost is often justified by virtue of the increased familiarity defense counsel will then have with the facts of the case.

2. Privilege Issues in Outside Counsel Investigations

One key advantage to bringing in outside counsel for the purpose of investigating charges of discrimination is that attorney-client privilege and the work-product doctrine will generally apply. Bringing in a lawyer for the purpose of "ascertaining the factual background and sifting through the facts with an eye to the legally relevant" is precisely the goal that the privilege laws are designed to promote.[29] Similarly, documents prepared by the company's employees/representatives specifically in response to outside counsel's request are much more likely to be deemed "prepared in anticipation of litigation" and therefore protected by the work-product doctrine.[30]

To ensure that the investigation conducted by outside defense counsel preserves these privileges, however, certain simple but necessary steps must be taken. First, all notes, memoranda, e-mails, and other forms of communication or information prepared by counsel should be clearly marked as confidential (for example, "This Memo Is Confidential and Is Protected by Attorney-Client Information" or "This

---

29. *Upjohn Co. v. United States*, 449 U.S. 383, 390–91 (1981).

30. *City of Springfield v. Rexnord Corp.*, 196 F.R.D. 7, 10 (D. Mass. 2000).

Document Is Prepared in Anticipation of Litigation and Is Subject to the Work-Product Doctrine").

Second, during the investigation, any employee-witnesses that are interviewed must be told that the lawyers conducting the interviews represent the *company*, not the employees. Failure to make this clear to the employees exposes the counsel to possible conflict of interest problems, should those employees later sue the company themselves.[31] Finally, employees who are interviewed should be told that their conversations with counsel are confidential.[32] This will show an intent on the part of the company to maintain privilege and the protections of work product.

3. Practical Considerations for Investigations by Outside Counsel

In many cases, and despite the advantages to using outside counsel to conduct post-charge investigations, the expense involved in using outside lawyers can be prohibitive. This is especially true for smaller companies that may not be able to afford the hourly rates of many experienced labor firms. In addition, if the outside lawyer is not on the company's EPLI insurer's "approved list," some or all of that expense may not be covered.

Finally, and most significantly, having outside counsel conduct the post-charge investigation, particularly when disciplinary action is ultimately required, can result in the lawyers retained to conduct the investigation (and, presumably, to litigate in the company's defense) finding themselves on the receiving end of a subpoena to testify.[33] To

31. *E.g., E. F. Hutton & Co. v. Brown*, 305 F. Supp. 371, 389 (S.D. Tex. 1969).

32. *Id.*

33. *E.g., Pray v. New York City Ballet Co.*, No. 96 Civ. 5723 RLC, 1998 WL 558796, at *1 (S.D.N.Y. Feb. 13, 1998); *Johnson v. Rauland-Borg Corp.*, 961 F. Supp. 208, 209, 211 (N.D. Ill. 1997); *Harding v. Dana Transp., Inc.*, 914 F. Supp. 1084, 1103 (D.N.J. 1996); *see also* Jeffrey A. Van Detta, *Lawyers as Investigators: How Ellerth and Faragher Reveal a Crisis of Ethics and Professionalism Through Trial Counsel Disqualification and Waivers of Privilege in Workplace Harassment Cases*, 24 J. Legal Prof. 261, 267–70 (2000).

the extent that the investigation reveals information relevant to the plaintiff's underlying employment claim and/or leads to disciplinary or remedial action being taken, outside lawyers can find themselves conflicted out of participating in the litigation as anything more than a witness.[34] Generally, this only happens when counsel is brought in to conduct pre-charge claims, rather than in the investigation of and response to EEOC charges of discrimination. Nevertheless, conflicts can occur, and therefore care is required by the company and outside counsel alike.

D. Investigation by EPLI Carrier

Regardless of whether a company is willing to investigate employment-related claims on its own, its EPLI carrier may decide to step in and coordinate the investigation itself. Many EPLI policies contain a provision similar to the following: "We may, at our discretion, investigate any wrongful employment practice which is alleged to have taken place. We may, with your written consent, settle any claim which may result."[35] Effectively, this clause allows the EPLI carrier to assume control over any investigation arising out of a potentially covered claim and offer to settle the claim should it decide to do so.

The advantage to an investigation run by the carrier is primarily the lower cost. Allowing the carrier to perform the investigation avoids the inherent cost of retaining outside counsel to conduct the investigation. It also limits the lost productivity that can result from lengthy investigations run by in-house counsel and/or human resources staff. Plus, a carrier-run investigation will provide the EPLI provider with the clearest picture of what risk a given claim may hold and give it the opportunity to resolve the issue quickly, with a minimum of conflict.

---

34. Van Detta, *supra* note 33, at 270–71.

35. John A. Ricca, *Employment Practices Liability Insurance: A Practical Analysis from the Trenches*, 592 PLI/LIT 937, 949 (1998).

Unfortunately, there are also disadvantages to investigations conducted by EPLI carriers. The most significant is that the carrier is investigating with the primary intent of assessing risk, rather than to prepare a litigation defense. Therefore, conflict may develop between the carrier—who is concerned primarily with costs—and a company's outside defense counsel—who is concerned primarily with limiting exposure and preparing a defense. Almost as important, the results of the investigation may well be discoverable in subsequent litigation, if a plaintiff employee rejects the offer of the EPLI carrier.

III. Post-Litigation Investigations

Once a lawsuit has been filed and outside defense counsel has been retained (whether by the EPLI carrier or the business itself), certain prelitigation concerns no longer exist. For example, documents generated through any additional investigation that is conducted for purposes of furthering the defense will likely be protected by the work-product doctrine, as long as counsel prompts the additional investigation.[36] This holds true whether the additional investigation is conducted directly by the company, its lawyers, or even the EPLI carrier. Similarly, discussions between employers and their lawyers related to the legal concerns of the company will be protected by the time-honored attorney-client privilege, provided those conversations involve management-level employees.[37] Therefore, concerns that were paramount in the audit and prelitigation stages virtually disappear once a lawsuit is filed.[38]

Investigations conducted during the course of litigation often arise from a need by defense lawyers to follow up on issues raised during earlier investigations. This typically involves a close look at potential

36. *Guzzino v. Felterman*, 174 F.R.D. 59, 62 (W.D. La. 1997); *see also Hickman v. Taylor*, 329 U.S. 495 (1947).

37. *United States v. El Paso Co.*, 682 F.2d 530, 538 (5th Cir. 1982).

38. Nevertheless, it is important that any additional investigation that occurs follows the same structure as a prelitigation investigation, if for no other reason than to minimize the risks of additional lawsuits by other employees.

fact witnesses, determining what evidence exists that must be turned over to opposing counsel during the course of discovery, or meeting with those employees who are expected to be called to give testimony during a deposition and/or at trial. These investigations tend to include significant document review, because employee records, company policies, and even information generated by internal (possibly EPLI-required) audits are reviewed to establish theories for defense.

For example, if the investigation turns up evidence that managers engaged in a good-faith effort to comply with applicable employment laws, those efforts can be presented at trial to limit or eliminate company liability for punitive damages (damages that are designed to punish an employer for particularly bad behavior).[39] Thus, evidence that the company required regular training on issues such as discrimination and harassment, comprehensive policies, and quick action to change inappropriate behavior can all demonstrate that punitive damages are not warranted even if illegal discrimination did take place.

Another key defensive argument that a post-litigation investigation may foster involves what is known as the "after-acquired evidence defense." Also known as the "*McKennon* rule" (taken from the U.S. Supreme Court case of *McKennon v. Nashville Banner Publishing Co.*[40]), the after-acquired evidence defense serves to limit the possible damages to be gained during the course of a discrimination lawsuit. Essentially, the rule stands for the following proposition:

- If the employer discovers information about the plaintiff during the course of litigation; and
- If that information would have resulted in the plaintiff's termination had the employer known about it prior to the plaintiff having filed suit; then

39. *Kolstad v. Am. Dental Ass'n*, 527 U.S. 526, 545-46 (1999).
40. 513 U.S. 352, 362–63 (1995).

- The plaintiff may not be reinstated and may not be awarded front pay past the date upon which the employer discovered the information, even if the plaintiff is successful at trial.[41]

Clearly, a thorough investigation, regardless of when it is conducted, can have serious consequences for issues of liability and possible damages. Discovering information damaging to the plaintiff may make pursuing litigation less attractive to his or her lawyer and may result in an early settlement or a greater chance of success at summary judgment.

IV. Final Thoughts

Ultimately, the goal of any investigation relating to EPLI policies is to minimize the risk to both the company and the insurer by identifying and altering potentially illegal practices and procedures. Similarly, investigations conducted both post-charge and post-lawsuit serve the purpose of limiting liability should illegal activity be found to exist. Such investigations may be time consuming, distracting, and expensive, but nevertheless represent the first line of defense in almost any legal action (not to mention being required for EPLI coverage). This makes them invaluable, and they should be regarded as a tool of effective business practice rather than as a burden on time and resources.

41. Some state and federal courts have held that the *McKennon* rule applies not only to discrimination claims but also to breach of contract claims. *See Johnson v. Honeywell Info. Sys., Inc.*, 955 F.2d 409, 412–14 (6th Cir. 1992); *Crawford Rehab. Servs., Inc. v. Weissman*, 938 P.2d 540, 549 (Colo. 1997); *Gassmann v. Evangelical Lutheran Good Samaritan Soc'y, Inc.*, 933 P.2d 743, 745 (Kan. 1997).

CHAPTER 5
Pleading Strategies, Affirmative Defenses, and Burdens of Proof

Gregory V. Mersol

I. Introduction

In all litigation, early decisions regarding the proper forum, defenses, and motion practice may dramatically impact the handling of the case. In employment litigation, these decisions are especially critical, and practitioners defending employment-related claims face a wide range of strategic and tactical decisions even before suit is filed.

In addition to a host of preliminary decisions to be made regarding removal, myriad issues may arise regarding the appropriate forum in employment litigation. Further, early dispositive motions can potentially whittle away a plaintiff's most valuable claims. In addition to the defenses that may be available with respect to state law tort claims, there may be a host of procedural defenses that will be available with respect to specific statutes alleged by the plaintiff, elections of remedies, and similar issues.

Employment litigation is also complicated by different and shifting burdens of proof. Indeed, depending on the case's procedural posture, both parties may bear burdens of proof or of production with respect to the very same fact.

This chapter is intended to provide an overview of the issues regarding affirmative defenses, pleading strategies, and burdens of proof in employment litigation.

II. Pleading Strategies

A. Introduction

Many critical decisions regarding employment litigation must be made before or as part of the answer. In many instances, decisions regarding the appropriate forum must be made immediately or else may be waived.

Challenges to venue may change the judge or jury pool that will ultimately hear the case. Such challenges may change the case from one of large exposure, great travel expense, and large publicity value to one that can be much more easily managed.

Even beyond the question of forum or venue, the lawyer defending an employment dispute must make a number of tactical decisions with respect to pleadings. Many defenses must be raised immediately. Others may be raised at a later time but, for tactical reasons, the timing of the defense may be critical. In some instances, defenses that might arguably be asserted at the outset of the litigation by way of a motion may be more beneficially raised later on, after some or all discovery has been completed. In many respects, the way in which the initial pleadings are framed and the employer's initial pleading strategies may change the course of handling for the entire case.

B. Forum

The choice of forum may have a great potential to change the outcome of an employment lawsuit. Most employers believe that federal courts are more favorable venues than state courts, if for no other reason than that the federal judiciary is more familiar with the resolution of employment disputes. Issues may also arise regarding the location of the litigation, particularly if the employee wishes to litigate in a remote location for the employer, or if a jury pool is more favorable to one side or the other. Counsel for the employer can challenge or seek to change the forum in the following ways.

1. *Jurisdictional Challenges*

Jurisdictional challenges are the most aggressive manner to challenge the forum. In some instances, the lack of subject-matter jurisdiction may prove to be the very death of a claim. At a minimum, a successful challenge to jurisdiction will cause the matter to be heard in a different court or in a different jurisdiction altogether.

a. Subject-Matter Jurisdiction

Subject-matter jurisdiction may prove to be inappropriate on any number of grounds. For example, claims under Section 510 of the Employee Retirement Income Security Act of 1974 (ERISA)[1] are subject to exclusive federal jurisdiction and may not be brought in state court. Further, a plaintiff may not avoid federal preemption by trying to recast such a claim as a state law "public policy claim."[2] Under Rule 12(b)(1) of the Federal Rules of Civil Procedure, challenges to subject-matter jurisdiction may be made in the initial response to the complaint, but a lack of subject-matter jurisdiction can be raised at any time, including at the Supreme Court level. Subject-matter jurisdiction may also be challenged if a state law claim for which there is no federal court jurisdiction has been filed in federal court, such as when there is no federal claim and diversity of citizenship is lacking.

---

1. 29 U.S.C. § 1140 (2012).

2. *Ingersoll-Rand Co. v. McClendon*, 498 U.S. 133, 140 (1990); *Kollman v. Hewitt Assocs., LLC*, 487 F.3d 139, 147–50 (3d Cir. 2007) (state law claim against an agent of an employer preempted by ERISA).

b. *Personal Jurisdiction*

Personal jurisdiction does not look whether the court has the power to determine the underlying merits of the case but, instead, looks to whether the court has the power to adjudicate claims involving the particular party.[3] Personal jurisdiction may become an issue when the defendant lacks sufficient contacts with the state to justify its exercise of jurisdiction. Personal jurisdiction issues may often arise when a plaintiff has sought to sue not only the employer but also supervisors or parents, subsidiaries, or affiliates. In many cases, the party sought to be named as a defendant has little or no contact with the jurisdiction at issue and is not properly a defendant before the court. Challenges to personal jurisdiction must be made as a part of the initial response to the complaint, frequently by way of a motion to dismiss or for summary judgment.[4]

c. *Arbitration*

The question of whether a particular claim is arbitrable may prove to be highly complex. Such challenges, however, should be made as early as possible in the proceeding. Notwithstanding their protestations to the contrary, many courts continue to view arbitration with suspicion and may be quick to find a waiver if it is not asserted at the outset of the case.[5] If the defendant engages in significant discovery or other efforts, the court may very well find that the right to arbitration has been waived. Motions to compel arbitration are frequently accompanied by motions to stay the proceedings pending the arbitration itself.

---

3. *Burger King Corp. v. Rudzewicz*, 471 U.S. 462, 476–77 (1985); *Int'l Shoe Co. v. Washington*, 326 U.S. 310, 320 (1945).

4. Fed. R. Civ. P. 12(b)(2) (2012).

5. *See, e.g.*, *McMullen v. Meijer, Inc.*, 335 F.3d 485, 494 (6th Cir. 2004) (employer's arguable limits on pool of arbitrators rendered agreement unenforceable); *Floss v. Ryan's Family of Steak Houses, Inc.*, 211 F.3d 306, 309 (6th Cir. 2000); *Hooters of Am. v. Phillips*, 173 F.3d 933, 941 (4th Cir. 1999) (enforcement denied on grounds of lopsided provisions favoring employer); *Champ v. Siegel Trading Co.*, 55 F.3d 269, 271 (7th Cir. 1995) (refusing to order arbitration of class actions claims).

2. Removal

Removal of the case must typically occur at the very outset of the matter. In most cases, the defendant or defendants must remove the case within thirty days after receiving the summons and complaint. If the case stated is not initially removable, it must be removed within thirty days of when it becomes apparent that it is removable, such as when the plaintiff asserts a federal claim or a nondiverse defendant is dismissed.[6]

3. Venue

Challenges to venue do not necessarily attack the existence of a cause of action but, instead, assert that it has been filed in an improper forum. In the federal court system, as well as many state court systems, the remedy may be one to transfer the case to the correct court. In others, the case should be dismissed on the doctrine of *forum non conveniens*.

a. Motions to Transfer

If an action has been filed in federal court and the court possesses both subject matter and personal jurisdiction but has a tenuous connection to the district, the court may transfer it pursuant to 28 U.S.C. § 1404. Motions for a change in venue should be addressed at the outset of the litigation. Courts will give deference to the plaintiff's choice of the forum in which he or she chooses to litigate and the decision to transfer lies within the court's discretion.[7] A motion to transfer may be the appropriate remedy, particularly if the plaintiff does not reside in the district and if a substantial part of the controversy has occurred in another district. The result of a transfer is simply moving the case from one district court to another, and not the dismissal of the matter.

---

6. In diversity cases, once a case has been pending in the state court for one year, it is no longer removable unless the plaintiff has acted in bad faith to prevent a defendant from removing the action. *See* 28 U.S.C. § 1446(c)(1) (2012).

7. *Gulf Oil Corp. v. Gilbert*, 330 U.S. 501, 508 (1947); *Moses v. Business Card Express, Inc.*, 929 F.2d 1131, 1137–38 (6th Cir. 1991), *cert. denied*, 502 U.S. 821 (1991).

b. Forum Non Conveniens

By contrast, *forum non conveniens* is a judicially developed doctrine that will actually result in the dismissal of a case. If, in fact, the case has no connection to the jurisdiction in which it has been filed, whether or not there is personal jurisdiction, the court may dismiss it on *forum non conveniens* grounds so that it may be refiled in a state that does have a significant connection with the dispute.[8] *Forum non conveniens* matters, like motions to transfer, lie within the court's discretion.[9]

C. When to Assert Potential Affirmative Defenses

Like challenges to venue, early dispositive motions may change a case's entire framework. Successful motions may pare down a case, change its complexion, or dispose of it entirely. On the other hand, prematurely filed motions bear the risk of simply educating opposing counsel. Employment defense counsel should carefully consider whether motions are appropriate at an early stage and, if so, when.

1. Strategic Considerations

Deciding which motion to file, if any, is virtually always a judgment call that requires consideration of a number of factors. The first factor is whether, of course, the motion is likely to be granted. Motions filed early in the case may be less likely to be granted than those filed after the close of discovery. The standard with respect to such motions is not only typically higher, but courts may be reluctant to dismiss a case before a plaintiff has had a chance to develop the necessary facts.

---

8. *Broderick v. Rosner*, 294 U.S. 629, 642–43 (1935); *Archibald v. Cinerama Hotels*, 544 P.2d 947, 950 (Cal. 1976); *Traveler's Casualty & Surety Co. v. Cincinnati Gas & Electric Co.*, 862 N.E.2d 201, 204 (Ohio Ct. App. 2006).

9. *Yousef v. Gen. Dynamics Corp.*, 16 A.3d 1040, 1048–49 (N.J. 2011) (holding that *forum non conveniens* is left to the sound discretion of the trial court); *Chambers v. Merrill-Dow Pharm., Inc.*, 519 N.E.2d 370, 374 (Ohio 1988); *Nezan v. Aries Technologies, Inc.*, 704 S.E.2d 631, 638 (W. Va. 2010) (holding that the standard of review for *forum non conveniens* is abuse of discretion).

Despite questions regarding whether a motion may be granted, there may be issues for which a motion is completely appropriate. For example, if an action is seriously time barred, it may be worthwhile to file a dispositive motion at an early stage. The same is true with respect to claims that may not be granted in the jurisdiction in which the case is pending.

In some instances, an early dispositive motion is essential. Under Rule 12(b) of the Federal Rules of Civil Procedure, a party is required to assert the defenses of lack of jurisdiction over the person, improper venue, or insufficiency of process or service of process in the initial response to the complaint, or else they are waived.[10] In those cases the motion should be raised, if at all, immediately.

Though some defenses are not waived, the employer must make a strategic decision about whether to move to dismiss.[11] Of course, counsel should also make a decision as to what exactly is being sought with respect to the initial pleadings. A motion to dismiss portions of the plaintiff's complaint may narrow or preclude discovery on difficult or potentially burdensome or expensive matters. In some instances, the claim that is most subject to a motion to dismiss may be the one that might ultimately cause the most trouble for the employer, leaving weaker claims that may be more easily disposed of at a later stage.

If the question is whether defense counsel truly does not understand what the plaintiff is seeking, a motion for a more definitive statement may be a more appropriate means of dealing with it.[12] Similarly, if the employer or counsel is disturbed by irrelevant or unnecessary derogatory allegations raised in the complaint and simply wants to have them

10. Fed. R. Civ. P. 12(b) (2012).

11. Rule 12(b)(6) would be the appropriate vehicle if the complaint fails to state a claim upon which relief may be granted. If an answer has already been filed, then the same defense may be assessed under Rule 12(c) as a motion for judgment on the pleadings.

12. Fed. R. Civ. P. 12(e).

removed, a motion to strike under Rule 12(f) is the more appropriate vehicle.[13]

The difficulty with early dispositive motions is the greater likelihood that a court will deny them and the risk that a plaintiff's lawyer may simply amend the complaint to avoid certain challenges. Or the plaintiff's lawyer may simply be able to reframe the case and discovery to address deficiencies raised by the employer early on. If, for example, the plaintiff has failed to plead an essential element of his or her claim, a motion filed by the employer may simply cause the plaintiff to amend the complaint and develop evidence in support of that missing element. Tactically, the employer may be better off not raising the defense at all and insuring that no evidence in support of that claim is developed during the discovery process. Another alternative is to obtain favorable testimony during the plaintiff's deposition and then raise the matter before it is too late for the plaintiff to correct the mistake.

One dramatic example of how early motions can shape a case is preemption under ERISA.[14] ERISA claims are not subject to the "well pleaded complaint rule" and, thus, if the plaintiff asserts a claim for recovery of plan benefits, the case may be removed to federal court even though no federal statute is cited.[15] Put another way, the suit is completely preempted. The same rule applies with respect to claims in which a plaintiff contends that he or she was discharged to avoid the payment of benefits. Even if the employee contends that he or she is seeking to recover under the state law public policy, and not under ERISA itself, the claim is still preempted.

Once an employee's claim is held preempted by ERISA, there are a host of other rules that apply that will significantly impact the litigation.

---

13. Fed. R. Civ. P. 12(f).

14. 29 U.S.C. § 1001 *et seq.* (2012).

15. *Metro. Life Ins. Co. v. Taylor*, 481 U.S. 58, 66–67 (1987); *Totten v. Hill*, 154 Cal. Rptr. 3d 357, 365 (Cal. Ct. App. 2007) (breach of contract claim against employee for reimbursement of amounts paid on her behalf preempted by ERISA); *Am. Mar. Officers Union v. Merriken*, 981 So.2d 544, 549 (Fla. Dist. Ct. App. 2008) (claim for wrongful discharge under Florida whistleblower statute preempted by ERISA).

For example, most courts have held that there is no jury trial under ERISA, nor is there any ability to recover compensatory or punitive damages.[16] For the most part, the case will also involve a very deferential standard of review and the introduction of very limited evidence.[17] The assertion of ERISA preemption at an early stage, therefore, may quickly narrow the scope of the litigation and may result in it being resolved at an early stage, either by settlement or by dispositive motion. In each case, counsel for the employer should consider the strategic impact of the contemplated defense.

2. Motion to Dismiss

A motion to dismiss is filed in lieu of an answer and may address either technical defects in the complaint or causes of action that, as a law, cannot be maintained. Such motions may prove worthwhile when the plaintiff has failed to plead an essential element of a particular cause of action, especially when, based upon its initial investigation, counsel for the employer believes that the element could never be established. Motions to dismiss may also be useful when the plaintiff has asserted a cause of action that cannot, as a matter of law, be maintained. Common examples would include a cause of action for "wrongful discharge" in a state that adheres to the employment at will doctrine, or a claim that relates to an employee benefit plan that would be entirely preempted by ERISA.

As a tactical matter, motions to dismiss should be considered carefully. On the one hand, they may quickly winnow out legally insufficient

---

16. *See, e.g., Massachusetts Mut. Life Ins. Co. v. Russell*, 473 U.S. 134, 145 (1985) (no punitive damages for fiduciary duty claims); *Graham v. Hartford Life & Accident Ins. Co.*, 589 F.3d 1345, 1355 n.5 (10th Cir. 2009) (listing the circuit courts that have found no right to a jury trial in ERISA cases); *Bair v. General Motors Corp.*, 895 F.2d 1094, 1097 (6th Cir. 1990) (no jury trial).

17. *Firestone Tire & Rubber Co. v. Bruch*, 489 U.S. 101, 111 (1989) (deferential standard of review); *Yeager v. Reliance Std. Life Ins. Co.*, 88 F.3d 376, 381 (6th Cir. 1996) (limited evidence); *Eppley v. Provident Life & Accident Ins. Co.*, 789 F. Supp. 2d 546, 565 (E.D. Pa. 2011) (reviewing court limited to facts known to plan administrator at the time the decision was made).

claims. On the other, however, such a motion may cause the plaintiff to amend the complaint to assert stronger causes of action.

Recent Supreme Court authority has bolstered early challenges to pleadings that lack specific detail. In *Bell Atlantic Corp. v. Twombly*[18] and *Ashcroft v. Iqbal*,[19] the Supreme Court set forth minimum requirements for a complaint to survive a motion to dismiss under Rule 12(b)(6) in all civil actions. In each case, the court analyzed the meaning of "a short and plain statement of the claim showing that the pleader is entitled to relief" within the context of Rule 8(a)(2).

In *Twombly*, the court held that the "threshold requirement [of Rule 8(a)(2) is] that the 'plain statement' possesses enough heft to 'sho[w] that the pleader is entitled to relief.'"[20] Accordingly, a complaint must state "enough facts to state a claim to relief that is plausible on its face."[21] The court clarified *Twombly*'s reach in *Iqbal*, holding that the "plausibility" standard applies in all civil actions, not just antitrust cases. The court then set forth a two-step approach to examining the sufficiency of a complaint. First, a district court is to disregard statements that are "[t]hreadbare recitals of the elements of a cause of action, supported by mere conclusory statements."[22] These conclusions "can provide the framework of a complaint" but, due to the absence of factual support, they "are not entitled to the assumption of truth."[23] Second, a district court should "assume [the] veracity" of "well-pleaded factual allegations" and "determine whether they plausibly give rise to an entitlement to relief."[24] The *Twombly/Iqbal* standard may make it easier to challenge a complaint for failure to plead claims with sufficient specificity.

Balanced against this new favorable pleading standard are the 2009 changes to Rule 15(a)(1) of the Federal Rules of Civil Procedure, which

18. 550 U.S. 544 (2007).
19. 556 U.S. 662 (2009).
20. 550 U.S. at 557.
21. *Id.* at 570.
22. 556 U.S. at 678.
23. *Id.* at 679.
24. *Id.*

now give a plaintiff leave to amend once as a matter of course when presented with a motion to dismiss. Thus, a plaintiff can relatively easily correct flaws in the initial complaint, at least once, without seeking leave of court. Still, however, a motion to dismiss may be worthwhile to obtain sufficient detail to respond, to force the plaintiff to disclose the facts supporting its claims, or to crystallize the issues for a second motion.

3. Motion for Judgment on the Pleadings

A motion for judgment on the pleadings is judged by the same standard as a motion to dismiss.[25] The primary difference between the two motions is that a motion for judgment on the pleadings may be filed after the defendant has already answered the complaint. Such motions may be viable when, for example, there is a change in the law while the action is pending that renders one or more causes of action unsustainable, or when it becomes apparent during discovery that a claim should be challenged for practical reasons. Like motions to dismiss, motions for judgment on the pleadings should be considered carefully to prevent the plaintiff from simply amending the complaint to assert stronger causes of action.

4. Motion to Strike

Motions to strike under Rule 12(f) typically are not directed toward causes of action but, instead, toward inappropriate material included in a complaint. Such a motion might, for example, be directed toward unnecessary insulting or irrelevant libelous contentions contained in the complaint.[26] They may also be addressed to matters such as trade-secret

25. Historically, to prevail, the moving party must establish that the plaintiff "can prove no set of facts in support of his claim which would entitle him to relief." *Conley v. Gibson*, 355 U.S. 41, 45–46 (1957). Such motions are authorized by FED. R. CIV. P. 12(c). *Twombly* and *Iqbal* have altered this historic pleading standard. Now, a complaint "must contain sufficient factual matter, accepted as true, to 'state a claim to relief that is plausible on its face.'" *Iqbal*, 556 U.S. at 678 (quoting *Twombly*, 550 U.S. at 570).

26. *See* FED. R. CIV. P. 12(f) (2012).

information or other material that does not belong in the pleading itself. In some instances, a motion to strike may be directed toward a particular part of the complaint, such as a prayer for relief. For instance, if a plaintiff has asserted a claim that is governed by ERISA, it may be appropriate to strike the prayers for compensatory and punitive damages, as well as the jury demand, as none are available under the ERISA statute.

5. Motion for a More Definite Statement

In some instances, particularly in *pro se* matters, it may be difficult to discern exactly what claim or claims are being asserted in the complaint. In others, a complaint may be so poorly phrased that a defendant cannot determine what, if any, motions might be appropriately directed to one or more causes of action. An appropriate motion in such a case may be a motion for a more definite statement under Rule 12(e).[27] Though such a motion will almost inevitably lead to an amendment to the complaint, it may also help frame the issues and assist the employer in focusing on the issues that demonstrate its entitlement to a dismissal, particularly under the plausibility standard of *Iqbal* and *Twombly*.

6. Motion for Summary Judgment

A large number of employment claims are disposed of by way of a motion for summary judgment.[28] The advantage of a motion for summary judgment is that it typically takes place after there has been some or all of the discovery in the case. In most instances, the employer has already taken the plaintiff's deposition, and the depositions of other key witnesses have already been concluded. At that point, because the parties are locked into their respective positions, there is less likelihood that the plaintiff can simply change his or her story to avoid summary disposition.

27. FED. R. CIV. P. 12(e).
28. *See* FED. R. CIV. P. 56.

As a tactical matter, it may sometimes be worthwhile to forgo filing a motion to dismiss knowing that a summary judgment motion can be filed later.[29] Because a court ruling on a motion for summary judgment can look beyond the pleadings, and because motions for summary judgment are viewed under a more lenient standard than a motion to dismiss, it is more likely that such a motion will be granted.

7. Trial and Beyond

If summary judgment is denied, the employer should still assert its affirmative defenses at trial. Indeed, unless the employer asserts and introduces evidence with respect to its affirmative defenses, they will likely be deemed to have been waived,[30] or dismissed by way of motion.

D. Answer

The answer to the complaint is the foundation of the employer's defense. Careful crafting of an answer may not only help frame the litigation but may be essential to preserve the employer's affirmative defenses. Answers themselves also create practical issues with respect to admitting to defensive matter contained in the complaint, distinguishing between co-defendants whose interests may not necessarily be aligned, and educating the court and opposing counsel of fatal weaknesses contained in the plaintiff's claims.

1. Denials

The employer should obviously deny any allegation of the complaint that is not true. If the employer lacks sufficient knowledge to admit or deny an allegation, it should state that it lacks knowledge or information

29. Summary dismissal is authorized "if the movant shows that there is no genuine dispute as to any material fact and that the moving party is entitled to a judgment as a matter of law." FED. R. CIV. P. 56(a). The movant may support this assertion by depositions, documents, electronically stored information, affidavits or declarations, stipulations, admissions, interrogatory answers, or other materials. FED. R. CIV. P. 56(c).

30. *See* FED. R. CIV. P. 50(a); *cf.* FED. R. CIV. P. 15(b).

sufficient to form a belief as to the truth of the allegation. By operation of Rule 8 such a statement acts as a denial of the allegation.

2. *Defenses*

The answer should obviously also identify the affirmative defenses the employer seeks to assert. In fact, they may be waived if not asserted.[31] Those defenses are discussed in § III (below).

E. Jury Demand

The conventional wisdom is that juries are more prone to rule in favor of employees than are judges. Historically, of course, when Title VII[32] was initially enacted, Congress provided only for equitable relief, so cases were to be tried to the court and not to a jury. The concern at that time was that juries would refuse to rule in favor of plaintiffs in race discrimination cases. In twenty-five years, however, that experience did not prove true, and Title VII was amended to provide for trial by jury, by this time reflecting the realization that jurors were, in fact, far more plaintiff oriented than the judiciary.[33]

Although many attorneys representing employers will therefore not include a jury demand in a pleading, a jury demand should still be considered in every case. At the outset, though jury verdict research does show that jurors generally are more inclined to find for the employees, that is not always the case. Indeed, in many cases, a judge may be more prone to find for a plaintiff, particularly if the plaintiff may be bringing an unpopular type of claim or may not appeal to the typical juror pool.

Moreover, some plaintiffs may not have jury appeal based upon, for example, their personality, earnings,[34] and other factors. Likewise, the

---

31. Fed. R. Civ. P. 8(c).

32. 42 U.S.C. § 2000e *et seq.* (2012).

33. Civil Rights Act of 1991, 42 U.S.C. § 1981a (2012).

34. Plaintiffs whose earnings greatly exceed those of the average juror may not engender as much sympathy, particularly in nondischarge cases.

representatives of some defendants may make such good witnesses that selection of a jury is prudent.

Even if the judge assigned the case is not believed to have such a bias, such biases may become apparent during the course of the handling of the case. Furthermore, cases can be and frequently are transferred from one judge to another. In a worst-case scenario, the employer may find itself in front of a judge with a strong pro-plaintiff or pro-employee bias, or who may have some other bias that would affect the outcome of the case.

If the employer has no jury demand and the plaintiff waives his or her demand, the case will be tried to the court. If, however, the employer has included a jury demand, it may attempt to waive it but will need the consent of all parties.[35]

F. Amendment

It is often the case that the employer learns of additional facts or defenses during the course of discovery. For example, facts that may not have been evident when the answer was filed may become apparent during the employer's investigation or in the taking of depositions themselves. Furthermore, in some cases the plaintiff's lawyer will reveal strategies that may present additional defenses for the employer. In some cases, given the dynamic nature of the body of case law governing employment disputes, a case may make a defense available that the employer was not aware of at the time the initial defense was filed. Rule 15(a) promotes a liberal policy in favor of amendment, and absent factors such as bad faith, undue delay, prejudice to the opposing party, futility of amendment, or multiple prior amendments, leave should be freely granted.[36] Of these factors, undue prejudice to the opponent is considered the most important,[37] but as a practical matter

35. Fed. R. Civ. P. 38(d).

36. *Forman v. Davis*, 371 U.S. 178, 182 (1962).

37. *Barnes v. AT&T Pension Benefit Plan—Nonbargained Program*, 273 F.R.D. 562, 566 (N.D. Cal. 2011).

an employer seeking to amend a pleading should review whether to include additional defenses at the same time to avoid repeat amendments. Practitioners should also beware of specific pretrial court orders on local rules that may fix the time to seek amendment.[38]

G. Counterclaims

Counterclaims are technically not defenses but may play an important strategic role in employment litigation, particularly if the employee is involved in egregious misconduct. Counterclaims, however, should be asserted very carefully. If the employer fails to establish the counterclaim, or a jury believes that it is petty, insubstantial, or even frivolous, there may be a tremendous backlash against the employer.[39] Further, a court may view a counterclaim as evidence of retaliation against the employee.[40] If, however, the employer has substantial proof that the employee has engaged in misconduct such as fraud, stealing, or theft of trade secrets, it may be worthwhile to include a counterclaim. In some instances, in which it may not be clear whether a claim is properly a counterclaim or an affirmative defense, the better practice may be to include it in both contexts, because the court always has the ability to correct a misdesignation.[41]

---

38. *See, e.g.*, *Lurie v. Mid-Atlantic Permanente Med. Group, P.C.*, 589 F. Supp. 2d 21, 23–24 (D.D.C. 2008).

39. *See, e.g.*, *Jacques v. DiMarzio*, 200 F. Supp. 2d 151, 162–63 (E.D.N.Y. 2002) (finding counterclaim to be "in bad faith" and "*in terrorem* tactics"; ordering employer to show why sanctions should not be imposed).

40. *Burlington Northern & Santa Fe Ry. Co. v. White*, 548 U.S. 53, 64 (2006) (anti-retaliation provision of Title VII not limited to workplace-related or employment-related retaliatory acts). As lower courts have interpreted *White*, an employer counterclaim can be a non-workplace-related act constituting retaliation. *See Kendel v. Local 17-A United Food & Commercial Workers*, 835 F. Supp. 2d 421, 429 (N.D. Ohio 2011); *Mohamed v. Sanofi-Aventis Pharmaceuticals*, No. 06 Civ. 1504, 2009 WL 4975260, at *22 (S.D.N.Y. Dec. 22, 2009).

41. Fed. R. Civ. P. 8(c) (2012).

III. Affirmative Defenses

A. Introduction

The issue of affirmative defense may be more difficult in employment actions than in any other type of case. A typical wrongful discharge complaint contains numerous causes of action, many of which may still be in their infancy and for which all the elements have not yet been developed. Further, even a garden-variety discrimination case presents issue of different burdens of proof and production depending upon the stage of the case.

In some instances, the employer bears a burden of proof or production on certain issues. In others, that burden rests with the employee. In still other instances, however, a clear consensus has not arisen as to which party bears the burden of proof and, if so, whether a particular matter must be pleaded. Finally, given the nature of many employment disputes, many affirmative defenses may not become immediately apparent to the employer. Though neither the Supreme Court nor any courts of appeals have addressed the issue, some district courts have held that the *Twombly/Iqbal* heightened pleading standard applies to affirmative defenses.[42] Some district courts have gone so far as to suggest that extending the *Twombly/Iqbal* pleading standard to affirmative defenses is the majority approach.[43] Courts extending *Twombly* and *Iqbal* to Rule 8(c) affirmative defenses have appealed both to the

42. *See, e.g.*, *Microsoft Corp. v. Lutian*, No. 1:10 CV 1373, 2011 WL 4496531, at *2 (N.D. Ohio Sept. 27, 2011); *Nixson v. The Health Alliance*, No. 1:10-CV-00338, 2010 WL 5230867, at *2 (S.D. Ohio Dec. 16, 2010); *HCRI TRS Acquirer, LLC v. Iwer*, 708 F. Supp. 2d 687, 691 (N.D. Ohio 2010); *Bradshaw v. Hilco Receivables, LLC*, 725 F. Supp. 2d 532, 534 (D. Md. 2010); *Palmer v. Oakland Farms, Inc.*, No. 5:10cv00029, 2010 WL 2605179, at *5–6 (W.D. Va. June 24, 2010); *Barnes v. AT&T Pension Benefit Plan—Nonbargained Program*, 718 F. Supp. 2d 1167, 1171 (N.D. Cal. 2010); *Burns v. Dodeka, LLC*, No. 4:09-CV-19-BJ, 2010 WL 1903987, at *1 (N.D. Tex. May 11, 2010); *On Command Video Corp. v. Roti*, No. 09 C 3130, 2010 WL 1752350, at *4 (N.D. Ill. Apr. 30, 2010).

43. *See, e.g.*, *Shaw v. Prudential Ins. Co. of Am.*, No. 10-03355-CV-W-DGK, 2011 WL 1050004, at *2 (W.D. Mo. Mar. 21, 2011); *Lane v. Page*, 272 F.R.D. 581, 589 (D.N.M. 2011); *Bradshaw*, 725 F. Supp. 2d at 536; *Hayne v. Green Ford Sales, Inc.*, 263 F.R.D. 647, 649–50 (D. Kan. 2009).

language of Rule 8(c) and the underlying rationale and policies to justify their holdings.

Yet, others have rejected the application of *Twombly* and *Iqbal* to pleading affirmative defenses.[44] Courts that have declined to extend *Twombly* and *Iqbal* to affirmative defenses have chiefly relied "on the fact that neither Rule 8(b)(1)(A) nor Rule 8(c) require defendants to 'show' their affirmative defenses, in contrast to Rule 8(a)(2)'s requirement that pleaders 'show' that they are entitled to relief."[45] Some courts have relied directly on the language of *Twombly* and *Iqbal* to limit their holdings to complaints.[46]

Even if courts extending *Twombly* and *Iqbal* are in the numerical majority, such a designation carries little persuasive weight. Decisions on either side of the issue continue to be published monthly, and many judges have spurned prior holdings within their districts when ruling on whether the heightened pleading standard applies to affirmative defenses. Thus, until the issue has been definitively resolved within a particular circuit, the prudent approach is to follow the requirements of *Twombly* and *Iqbal* in pleading affirmative defenses or risk an order striking those defenses.

---

44. *See, e.g.*, *Chiancone v. City of Akron*, No. 5:11-CV-337, 2011 WL 4436587, at *3 (N.D. Ohio Sept. 23, 2011); *Microsoft Corp. v. Delta Computers, Inc.*, No. 1:10-CV-1161, 2010 LEXIS 143933, at *4 (N.D. Ohio Aug. 11, 2010); *Lane*, 272 F.R.D. at 590; *Ameristar Fence Prods., Inc. v. Phoenix Fence Co.*, No. CV-10-299-PHX-DGC, 2010 WL 2803907, at *1 (D. Ariz. July 15, 2010); *McLemore v. Regions Bank*, Nos. 3:08-cv-0021, 3:08-cv-1003, 2010 WL 1010092, at *13 (M.D. Tenn. Mar. 18, 2010); *Holdbrook v. SAIA Motor Freight Line, LLC*, No. 09-cv-02870-LTB-BNB, 2010 WL 865380, at *2 (D. Colo. Mar. 8, 2010); *Charleswell v. Chase Manhattan Bank, N.A.*, No. 01-119, 2009 WL 4981730, at *4 (D.V.I. Dec. 8, 2009); *Romantine v. CH2M Hill Eng'rs, Inc.*, No. 09-973, 2009 WL 3417469, at *1 (W.D. Pa. Oct. 23, 2009); *First Nat'l Ins. Co. of Am. v. Camps Servs., Ltd.*, No. 08-cv-12805, 2009 WL 22861, at *2 (E.D. Mich. Jan. 5, 2009).

45. *Tiscareno v. Frasier*, No. 2:07-CV-336, 2012 WL 1377886, at *14 (D. Utah Apr. 19, 2012); *see also Falley v. Friends Univ.*, 787 F. Supp. 2d 1255, 1257–58 (D. Kan. 2011).

46. *See, e.g.*, *McLemore*, 2010 WL 1010092, at *13.

Care must be taken with respect to pleading affirmative defenses in the employer's answer.

B. The Rule 8(c) Defenses

1. Generally

The starting point for the consideration of affirmative defenses is Rule 8(c) of the Federal Rules of Civil Procedure, or the equivalent rule under state law. Rule 8(c) requires that the employer affirmatively plead a number of defenses, including:

- Accord and satisfaction;
- Arbitration and award;
- Assumption of risk;
- Contributory negligence;
- Duress;
- Estoppel;
- Failure of consideration;
- Fraud;
- Illegality;
- Injury by fellow servant;
- Laches;
- License;
- Payment;
- Release;
- Res judicata;
- Statute of frauds;
- Statute of limitations; and
- Waiver.

Though in some instances a failure to allege a defense will not be construed as a waiver,[47] in most cases the employer should assert its

47. See *Matthews v. Wisconsin Energy Corp.*, 642 F.3d 565, 569–70 (7th Cir.

affirmative defenses early in the litigation to avoid waiver arguments. The first step, therefore, in framing an answer is to insure that any Rule 8(c) defenses have been asserted.

2. *Arbitration and Award*

Rule 8(c) of the Federal Rules of Civil Procedure requires a defense to raise the defense of arbitration and award in its answer. The defense of arbitration and award is different from the defense that an action should be stayed in order to compel arbitration. The defense of arbitration and award applies in the limited situation in which a dispute has already been litigated and an arbitration award has been obtained.[48] If the employer has previously arbitrated the case, this defense should be pleaded. A previous arbitral award may also be good grounds to assert an early dispositive motion.

3. *Fraud*

Rule 8(c) also requires a defendant to raise the defense of fraud in its answer, although such defenses are rare in employment actions.[49] The general elements of a claim of fraud are: (1) misrepresentation, including false representation, concealment, or nondisclosure, of a material fact; (2) knowledge of falsity or lack of reasonable ground for belief in the truth of the representation; (3) intent to induce reliance; (4) actual and justifiable reliance; and (5) damage.[50]

2011) (permitting assertion of arguably late defense in employment case due to lack of prejudice).

48. *Lee v. Grandcor Med. Sys., Inc.*, 702 F. Supp. 252, 254 (D. Colo. 1988); *Thyssen, Inc. v. Calypso Shipping Corp., S.A.*, 310 F.3d 102, 106 (2d Cir. 2002).

49. *Illinois Conference of Teamsters and Employers Welfare Fund v. Steve Gilbert Trucking*, 71 F.3d 1361, 1365 (7th Cir. 1995); *but see Trustees of ALA-Lithographic Pension Plan v. Crestwood Printing Corp.*, 127 F. Supp. 2d 475, 478–79 (S.D.N.Y. 2001) (using Rule 15(a) discretion to allow fraud defense despite its omission from defendant's answer and motion for summary judgment).

50. California Torts § 40.02 (Matthew Bender & Co., Inc. 2002); Florida Torts § 26.01 (Matthew Bender & Co., Inc. 2002).

Most fraud-related defenses concern an employee's misrepresentation of background education or employment, a defense that is better characterized as part of the "after-acquired evidence" doctrine.[51] Fraud defenses should be considered carefully because of the likely negative impact they may have on a jury, particularly if the claim of fraud is found to be unsubstantiated.

Fraud claims may appropriately be subject to a motion to dismiss, especially if the complaint does not allege many details. Rule 9(b) of the Federal Rules of Civil Procedure requires that though intent may be alleged generally, fraud must otherwise be alleged with specificity. Most courts attribute this requirement to the need to give the defendant notice of the claim against it.[52]

4. Illegality

If an employer is sued for breach of contract, it must raise the defense of illegality of the contract or the defense will be waived.[53] This defense, if raised, has important ramifications for the burden of proof in a breach of contract action. If the defense is not raised, the plaintiff need only show the existence and execution of the contract, and that it was supported by consideration.[54] If, however, the defendant alleges the illegality of the contract, the plaintiff must bear the burden of proving the contract's validity.[55]

---

51. *McKennan v. Nashville Banner Publishing Co.*, 513 U.S. 352, 359 (1995). After-acquired evidence may not bar employees from all recovery. In *McKennon*, the court concluded that employees may be entitled to back pay from the date of the unlawful discharge until the date the new information was discovered. *Id.* at 362; *see also Quinn-Hunt v. Bennett Enters., Inc.*, 122 Fed. Appx. 205, 207–08 (6th Cir. 2005) (reversing granting of summary judgment when trial court did not balance employee's misappropriation of confidential documents against harm caused by employer's racial discrimination).

52. *E.g., Brinkmeier v. Graco Children's Prods., Inc.*, 767 F. Supp. 2d 488, 492 (D. Del. 2011).

53. *Dev. Fin. Corp. v. Alpha Hous. & Health Care*, 54 F.3d 156, 163 n.3 (3d Cir. 1995); *United States v. Krieger*, 773 F. Supp. 580, 582–83 (S.D.N.Y. 1991).

54. *Krieger*, 773 F. Supp. at 583.

55. *Id.*

5. *Injury by Fellow Servant*

When an employee alleges that he or she was harmed by a negligent employer, the employer may defend itself by alleging that the harm was in fact caused by another employee, rather than the employer itself. Although listed as a defense under Rule 8(c), it is rarely applicable in employment actions outside of the context of certain workers' compensation claims.[56]

6. *Release*

Generally, if a plaintiff signs a waiver or release of its claims against the defendant, the defendant will obviously seek to assert it as a defense in subsequent litigation. If such a release exists, it must be pleaded as an affirmative defense.[57]

In employment cases, releases are subject to numerous limitations. Courts will uphold such waivers only if they are knowing and voluntary, and only if they release *past* claims.[58] Two different tests exist to determine whether a waiver is knowing and voluntary—the "ordinary contract principles" test and the "totality of the circumstances" test.[59] The "ordinary contract principles" test looks at the circumstances surrounding the execution of the waiver, the clarity of the waiver, and whether counsel represented the complainant.[60] The "totality of the circumstances" test examines in detail the plaintiff, the agreement, and whether counsel represented the plaintiff.[61]

---

56. *See Am. Smelting & Ref. Co. v. Sutyak*, 175 F.2d 123, 127 (10th Cir. 1949).

57. FED. R. CIV. P. 8(c) (2012).

58. BARBARA LINDEMANN & PAUL GROSSMAN, EMPLOYMENT DISCRIMINATION LAW 1916 (3d ed. 1996).

59. *Id.* at 1917; *see also Melanson v. Browning-Ferris Indus., Inc.*, 281 F.3d 272, 276 (1st Cir. 2002).

60. LINDEMANN & GROSSMAN, *supra* note 58, at 1917. Even the circuits that have adopted the "ordinary contract principles" test frequently cite to and use the "totality of the circumstances" test. *See* Daniel P. O'Gorman, *A State of Disarray: The "Knowing and Voluntary" Standard for Releasing Claims under Title VII of the Civil Rights Act of 1964*, 8 U. PA. J. LAB. & EMP. L. 73, 78 (2005).

61. LINDEMANN & GROSSMAN, *supra* note 58, at 1918; *see also Howell v. Motorola, Inc.*, 633 F.3d 552, 559 (7th Cir. 2011) (using eight factors to determine the totality of

Waivers of claims made under the Age Discrimination in Employment Act of 1967 (ADEA) are subject to even greater strictures.[62] Under the Older Workers Benefit Protection Act, any release of ADEA claims must satisfy seven requirements, a handful of which applied at common law as well. The release must be written in language calculated to be understood by the recipient. The employer must furnish consideration and cannot bar future claims. The employee must be advised in writing to consult with a lawyer, and the release must specifically identify the ADEA. Unless the employee has asserted a claim under the ADEA or its state law equivalent, the employee must be given at least twenty-one days to consider the release before signing it, and seven days to revoke it afterward.[63]

If the release is part of a plan or program that affects two or more employees, yet another set of requirements applies if it is to cover ADEA claims. In addition to the requirements listed above, the employer must provide the employee with statistical information about the numbers and job titles both of the employees offered the release and those who are not, as well as forty-five days to consider the release.[64]

As a practical matter, it is ordinarily best to assert the validity of the release at the outset of the matter. Later challenges will likely require the employer to engage in otherwise unnecessary discovery that will increase costs and prolong the litigation. Further, a court may limit or defer discovery if it appears that early resolution of a defense may resolve the case entirely.

7. Res Judicata

The defense of *res judicata* can be used to bar subsequent litigation on the same subject. To assert *res judicata*, there must be a final judgment

---

the circumstances); *Melanson*, 281 F.3d at 276 (using six factors to determine the totality of the circumstances).

62. 29 U.S.C. § 626(f) (2012).
63. *See* 29 U.S.C. § 626(f)(1)–(2); 29 C.F.R. § 1625.22 (2012).
64. 29 U.S.C. § 626(f)(1)(H); 29 C.F.R. § 1625.22(f).

on the merits that was obtained without fraud or collusion by a court of competent jurisdiction.[65] This defense serves to bar *all* actions arising out of a transaction or occurrence that was the subject of a previous action, whether the claims were actually asserted in the first action or not. This prohibition on subsequent litigation applies even when the original disposition was administrative or quasi-judicial in nature. *Res judicata* must be asserted as an affirmative defense or else it is waived.[66]

8. Statute of Frauds

The defense of statute of frauds applies when an employee alleges an action for breach of an employment contract against the employer. A typical statute of frauds requires that any agreement that is not to be performed within one year of its making must be in writing, contain the essential terms of the agreement, and be signed by the party to be charged.[67] For example, in *Buck v. Dayton Heidelberg Distributing Co., Inc.*, the plaintiff and the defendant had a written employment contract for a two-year term.[68] The agreement provided that it was renewable for five years upon the mutual consent or renegotiation of the parties. Upon the expiration of his original contract, the plaintiff continued to work for three years, without signing a new employment contract. The court held that the employment contract was enforceable for a two-year term only, and that any renewal or renegotiation for an additional five-year term must be in writing.[69] A similar result was reached in *DeCavitch v. Thomas Steel Strip Corp.*, in which the

65. *See Kremer v. Chem. Constr. Corp.*, 456 U.S. 461, 467 n.6 (1982); *Montana v. United States*, 440 U.S. 147, 153 (1979). *Res judicata* also applies between state and federal courts. 28 U.S.C. § 1738; *Grava v. Parkman Twp.*, 653 N.E.2d 226, 227 (Ohio 1995).

66. *See* FED. R. CIV. P. 8(c) (2012).

67. *See, e.g.*, OHIO REV. CODE ANN. § 1335.05 (2012); TEX. BUS. & COM. CODE ANN. § 26.01 (2012).

68. No. 8067, 1983 WL 2555, at *1 (Ohio Ct. App. Nov. 29, 1983).

69. *Id.* at *3.

court held that an oral employment contract for a two-year term was not enforceable.[70]

On the other hand, in *Sullivan v. Leor Energy*, an employee with a draft employment contract for two-and-a-half years providing for termination without cause argued that his contract created at-will employment for an indefinite term and was not subject to the Texas statute of frauds.[71] The court ruled that the Texas statute of frauds applied to employment contracts with a possibility of termination within one year, so long as the contract stated a term longer than a year.[72]

9. Statute of Limitations

The statute of limitations defense is waived unless it is raised in the answer. This can be a complicated defense in employment cases due to the administrative requirements of some statutes. Plaintiffs seeking redress under the ADEA, EPA, ADA, or Title VII generally have 180 days from the alleged discriminatory act to file a charge with the Equal Employment Opportunity Commission (EEOC), or 300 days in so-called deferral states.[73] The EEOC will investigate the charge and in some instances issue a notice of right to sue. Plaintiffs pursuing claims under the ADA, ADEA, or Title VII have only 90 days from receipt of the Notice of Right to Sue to file a lawsuit.[74] Questions may also arise regarding the date on which the statute of limitations begins to run, such as when an employee is advised in advance of his or her termination date, or when a personnel action is taken against an employee whose effects are not felt until months or even years later.[75]

---

70. 585 N.E.2d 879, 882 (Ohio Ct. App. 1990).
71. 600 F.3d 542, 548 (5th Cir. 2010).
72. *Id.* at 547.
73. *See EEOC v. North Gibson School Corp.*, 266 F.3d 607, 617 (7th Cir. 2001).
74. *See* 29 U.S.C. § 626(e); 42 U.S.C. § 12117; 42 U.S.C. § 2000e-5(f)(1).
75. *See Delaware State College v. Ricks*, 449 U.S. 250, 258 (1980); *see also Alleyne v. Am. Airlines, Inc.*, 548 F.3d 219, 222 (2d Cir. 2008) (upholding dismissal of employee's complaint when employee failed to file EEOC charge after loss of seniority but waited until discharge to file, when statute of limitations had already run).

10. Other

In many cases, the employer may wish to reserve the right to amend its answer to assert additional affirmative defenses. This may occur, for example, if the employer is unsure of the employee's claims or if they have not been artfully pleaded. It may also apply in situations in which the employer is not in possession of the information and wishes to preserve the right to amend.

Though it may be a good practice to reserve the right to amend an answer, care must be taken that the employers actually do so. If the employer realizes that an additional defense applies, yet fails to assert it, it may be held to have waived that defense. Leave should still be sought to amend the answer pursuant to Rule 15(a) of the Federal Rules of Civil Procedure, and courts should liberally allow amendment.[76]

C. Additional Potential Defenses

1. Failure to Exhaust Administrative Remedies

a. Federal Law

A plaintiff filing a lawsuit pursuant to the ADEA, EPA, ADA, or Title VII must first file a charge with the EEOC. Because filing a charge with the EEOC is a clear prerequisite to judicial determination, a plaintiff's failure to do so will likely bar his or her claim.[77] Further, questions may arise as to whether the plaintiff has asserted the correct claim or named the appropriate party in the charge. In many cases, such errors will prove fatal to the plaintiff's claim.[78]

---

76. *See Hartley v. Pocono Mountain Reg'l Police Dep't*, 417 Fed. Appx. 153, 157 (3d Cir. 2011) (allowing amendment at trial for issues that had been litigated throughout the case).

77. *See, e.g.*, 29 U.S.C. § 626(e), 42 U.S.C. § 12117; 42 U.S.C. § 2000e-5(e)(1).

78. *See, e.g.*, *Barzanty v. Verizon PA, Inc.*, 361 Fed. Appx. 411, 414 (3d Cir. 2010) (upholding dismissal of hostile work environment claim as outside the scope of employee's EEOC charge that alleged only one discrete instance of discrimination); *Davis v. Sodexho, Cumberland College Cafeteria*, 157 F.3d 460, 462 (6th Cir. 1998); *Marshall v. Fed. Express Corp.*, 130 F.3d 1095, 1098 (D.C. Cir. 1997).

b. State Law

State laws prohibiting employment discrimination often overlap with federal statutes. For instance, in Iowa it is an unfair employment practice to refuse to hire, accept, refer for employment, or discharge from employment anyone on the basis of age, race, creed, color, sex, sexual orientation, gender identity, national origin, religion, or disability.[79] A claimant must file a charge and receive a release from the Iowa Commission on Civil Rights as a prerequisite to filing suit.[80] Some states permit direct civil actions, whether or not the plaintiff has filed a charge.[81] In others, the filing of a charge may constitute an election of remedies.[82] Any procedural defect should be asserted in the answer or by way of a motion to dismiss.

c. ERISA

ERISA claims arise in many contexts in employment litigation, whether the plaintiff is seeking unpaid benefits or claiming retaliation for exercising benefit rights. Under ERISA, a plaintiff seeking benefits must first exhaust the appeal procedures under the plan.[83] Even if the plan language makes exhaustion permissive, courts have required exhaustion prior to judicial determination.[84] By making exhaustion mandatory, the congressional goal to "minimize the number of frivolous ERISA lawsuits; promote the consistent treatment of benefit claims; provide a nonadversarial dispute resolution process; and decrease the cost and time of claims settlement"[85] is met. Only if the resort to administrative

---

79. Iowa Code § 216.6 (2012).

80. Iowa Code § 216.15.

81. *See, e.g.*, *Elek v. Huntington Nat'l Bank*, 573 N.E.2d 1056, 1057 (Ohio 1991).

82. *See, e.g.*, Ohio Rev. Code Ann. § 4112.08 (2012) (election of remedies for age claims only).

83. *See, e.g.*, *Weiner v. Klais & Co.*, 108 F.3d 86, 90–91 (6th Cir. 1997); *Baxter v. C.A. Muer Corp.*, 941 F.2d 451, 453–54 (6th Cir. 1991).

84. *Baxter*, 941 F.2d at 454.

85. *Makar v. Health Care Corp. of Mid-Atlantic*, 872 F.2d 80, 83 (4th Cir. 1989).

process would be futile is the exhaustion requirement waived, and this exception is narrowly construed.[86]

2. *Arbitration Agreements*

In *Circuit City Stores, Inc. v. Adams*, the Supreme Court specifically endorsed the use of arbitration agreements in the employment context.[87] In that case, the plaintiff signed an agreement to arbitrate all claims arising out of his employment with his employer. In contravention of that agreement, the plaintiff brought suit for discrimination.[88] The employer sought to enjoin the state court action and compel arbitration of plaintiff's claims. The Supreme Court held that arbitration agreements in the employment context are fully enforceable. In fact, the court cited several benefits to arbitration of employment claims in lieu of litigation, including avoiding the large costs of litigation and avoiding the sticky choice of law questions that often arise in employment cases.[89] It is a particular benefit to plaintiffs to avoid the costs of litigation because the sums of money recovered in litigation are much smaller than traditional commercial disputes.[90]

Though plaintiffs have raised numerous types of challenges to arbitration agreements, the employer must be sure to raise the existence of one immediately if a lawsuit is filed in contravention of a signed arbitration agreement. The employer should seek to compel enforcement of an arbitration agreement at the earliest possible stage. The failure to raise the existence of the agreement in an answer and to file a motion to stay judicial proceedings and compel arbitration, coupled

---

86. *Harrow v. Prudential Ins. Co. of Am.*, 279 F.3d 244, 250 (3d Cir. 2002) (listing factors court should consider when excusing exhaustion on futility grounds). To use the futility exception, the plaintiff must clearly and positively show that its claim will be denied on appeal. *Laird v. Norton Healthcare, Inc.*, 442 Fed. Appx. 194, 200 (6th Cir. 2011).

87. 532 U.S. 105, 113 (2001).

88. *Id.* at 110.

89. *Id.* at 123.

90. *Id.*

with significant use of litigation procedures, may provide the plaintiff with an argument that the employer has waived its right to arbitrate.

3. Defamation Defenses

Defamation claims are among the most complex in the workplace. To establish a defamation claim, the plaintiff must prove that the employer made a false and defamatory statement of fact, that the statement was "published" to others, and that the plaintiff suffered damages.[91] If a plaintiff establishes a prima facie case, numerous affirmative defenses may become available to the employer.

a. Truth

Truth is an absolute defense to a defamation action. Though courts in the past have demanded that a statement be completely true for the defense to be applicable, modern courts have been more expansive.[92]

For instance, in *Campanelli v. Regents of the University of California*, the school's athletic director publicly stated that the coach was fired because the pressure he placed on players made them physically ill, and that his tirades after losses had beaten the players down psychologically.[93] The coach admitted in his complaint that he had leveled sharp criticism at players and had fits of anger.[94] The court found that to establish the defense of truth, the defendant need not prove the literal truth of the statements, so long as the "imputation is substantially true so as to justify the 'gist or sting' of the remark."[95] Because the plaintiff essentially admitted the accuracy of the statements made to the media, no liability resulted.[96]

---

91. Restatement (Second) of Torts § 558 (1977).

92. See John B. Lewis et al., *Defamation and the Workplace: A Survey of the Law and Proposals for Reform*, 54 Mo. L. Rev. 797, 822 (1989).

93. 44 Cal. App. 4th 572, 576 (Cal. Ct. App. 1996).

94. *Id.* at 581.

95. *Id.* at 582.

96. The New York courts take a substantially similar view, allowing the truth defense when, "[e]ven if a publication is not literally or technically true in all respects,

b. Consent

Consent is another defense that employers can use to limit or, in some instances, completely bar any recovery by the plaintiff. Thus, if an employee signs a release or consent form to allow prior employers to release personnel, disciplinary, or other employment-related information to a prospective employer, the employee will have a hard time establishing a defamation if the information provided by the previous employer is within the scope of the release.

In *Cox v. Nasch*, that is precisely what happened.[97] The plaintiff applied for a job with the Federal Aviation Administration and signed a broad release allowing his prior employer to release information about his employment.[98] When the employer released unflattering statements about the employee's job performance, he sued for defamation. The Ninth Circuit, interpreting Alaska law, held that the statements made were within the scope of the release, and that the signed release constitutes consent to the statements made.[99]

---

the absolute defense applies as long as the publication is 'substantially true.'" *Carter v. Visconti*, 233 A.D.2d 473, 474 (N.Y. App. Div. 1996). Missouri, likewise, allows the truth defense even when the allegedly defamatory statement contains slight inaccuracies but is substantially true. *Nigro v. St. Joseph Med. Ctr.*, No. WD 73810, 2012 WL 1499898, at *7 (Mo. Ct. App. May 1, 2012). In *Nigro*, an employee filed a defamation claim based on a letter recounting the facts of the employee's disciplinary hearing. According to the employee, the letter's averment that the employee had requested adjournment of the disciplinary hearing was false and defamatory because both sides mutually agreed to terminate the disciplinary hearing. The court found the statement to be substantially true, reasoning that it carried the same "sting" as the employee's version of the events. *Id.* at *9.

97. 70 F.3d 1030, 1031 (9th Cir. 1995).

98. *Id.* at 1030–31.

99. *Id.* at 1032; *see also Conlay v. Baylor College of Med.*, 688 F. Supp. 2d 586, 590 (S.D. Tex. 2010) (granting summary judgment to employer when employee assured publication of an otherwise private negative performance letter by contacting the human resources department); *Carroll v. City of Westminster*, 52 F. Supp. 2d 546, 566 (D. Md. 1999); *Charles v. State Dep't of Children & Families Dist. Nine*, 914 So.2d 1, 4 (Fla. Ct. App. 2005) (when employee repeatedly requested an explanation for his termination, employee consented to the resulting remarks); *Baker v. Bhajan*, 871 P.2d 374, 377 (N.M. 1994).

Though a written consent is binding, courts may also imply consent based upon the facts and circumstances, such as when the plaintiff demands that the employer repeat an accusation in front of others.[100] Consent is widely recognized as a complete defense to a defamation claim, but some states provide only a limitation, rather than a complete bar, to recovery.

c. Privileges

Privileges, whether absolute or qualified, are among the most important defamation defenses and must be asserted in the answer. A privilege may either bar a claim altogether or substantially increase the plaintiff's burden of proof.

An absolute privilege provides a complete defense to a defamation claim.[101] Such a privilege applies only in those instances in which public policy requires that a statement be totally protected. The most common examples are statements made during judicial or quasi-judicial proceedings, such as at a trial or hearing.[102] If a statement is absolutely privileged, it is not actionable even if knowingly falsely made.

A qualified privilege is more common but provides lesser protection. Such a privilege typically applies when the speaker and listener share a legitimate common interest.[103] Employment references, for example, are generally held to be qualifiedly privileged.[104] Although the privilege

---

100. *See Georgia Power Co. v. Busbin*, 289 S.E.2d 514, 515 (Ga. 1982). Some courts have also found union membership to constitute consent to giving of notice to the union. *Baker v. Lafayette College*, 504 A.2d 247 (1986), *aff'd*, 516 Pa. 291, 532 A.2d 399 (1987); *Rouch v. Continental Airlines*, 70 S.W.3d 170, 173 (Tex. App. 2001) (employee who challenged her termination and requested reinstatement through employer's appeal procedure consented to remarks).

101. *E.g.*, W. Keeton et al., Prosser and Keeton on the Law of Torts § 114, at 815–16 (5th ed. 1984).

102. Restatement (Second) of Torts §§ 585–591 (1977).

103. Restatement (Second) of Torts § 596.

104. *Alford v. George-Pacific Corp.*, 331 So.2d 558, 561–62 (La. Ct. App. 1976), *cert. denied*, 334 So.2d 247 (1976); *see also Miron v. Univ. of New Haven Police*, 931 A.2d 847, 853–54 (Conn. 2007) (listing states that have recognized a qualified privilege for employment references and recognizing the privilege under Connecticut law).

will not completely bar a claim, it will require that the plaintiff establish that the statement was made with "actual malice."[105] "Actual malice" is generally defined to mean that the statement was made with knowledge of its falsity or reckless disregard for the truth.[106]

d. Opinion

The law concerning the defense of opinion in the workplace remains very much unsettled. The Supreme Court has largely rejected the existence of a Constitutional defense of "opinion" per se, but a number of courts continue to apply an opinion analysis when analyzing various types of defamation claims.[107] A number of courts have recognized that an employer is not liable for libel or slander for statements of its pure subjective intent, or in situations in which the comments are laced with rhetorical hyperbole.[108]

4. Discrimination Claim Defenses

a. Timeliness

Under Title VII and the ADA, a complainant must first file a charge with the EEOC within 180 days of the discriminatory act or within 300 days in so-called deferral status.[109] Courts may and frequently will dismiss a case for lack of a timely charge.[110] This rule applies if the charge was

---

105. *See, e.g.*, *Frakes v. Crete Carrier Corp.*, 579 F.3d 426, 430 (5th Cir. 2009); *Babb v. Minder*, 806 F.2d 749, 754 (7th Cir. 1986).

106. *See Snodgrass v. Headco Indus., Inc.*, 640 S.W.2d 147, 153 (Mo. Ct. App. 1982); RESTATEMENT (SECOND) OF TORTS § 600 (1977); *see also Bahr v. Boise Cascade Corp.*, 766 N.W.2d 910, 922 (Minn. 2009) (no actual malice when employer republished co-worker's defamatory statements in a bona fide investigation into co-worker's allegations).

107. *Milkovich v. Lorain Journal Co.*, 497 U.S. 1, 10 (1990).

108. *See generally* John B. Lewis & Gregory V. Mersol, *Opinion and Rhetorical Hyperbole in Workplace Defamation Actions: The Continuing Quest for Meaningful Standards*, 52 DEPAUL L. REV. 19 (2002).

109. 42 U.S.C. § 2000e-5 (2012).

110. *Miles v. New York City Transit Auth.*, 182 F.3d 900, 900 (2d Cir. 1999) (plaintiff's Title VII and ADEA action dismissed for failure to timely file an EEOC charge); *Santa Maria v. Pacific Bell*, 202 F.3d 1170, 1176 (9th Cir. 2000) (failure to file EEOC

filed late or not at all. In one instance, a plaintiff in a race and sex discrimination case filed a charge with the EEOC alleging discriminatory acts by her employer occurring nearly two years beforehand.[111] After she filed this charge, she experienced two more incidents of alleged discrimination. The court held that any incidents occurring more than 300 days prior to filing the EEOC charge were time barred, and that it lacked jurisdiction to hear the uncharged incidents.[112]

b. Damage Caps

Besides providing for make-whole relief, the Civil Rights Act of 1991 affords plaintiffs the right to recover compensatory and punitive damages for intentional discrimination under Title VII or the ADA.[113] These amounts are subject to damage caps.

Compensatory damages do not include back pay or other equitable relief, but do include "future pecuniary losses, emotional pain, suffering, inconvenience, mental anguish, loss of enjoyment of life, and other nonpecuniary losses,"[114] and punitive damages are available only if the plaintiff proves that the employer acted "with malice or with reckless indifference."[115] Because the burden of proof for punitive damages under federal law may be different than that under state law, it may be worthwhile to include the correct standard as a defense.

Compensatory damages are capped at $50,000 for employers of 15 to 100; $100,000 for employers of 101 to 200; $200,000 for employers of 201 to 500; and $300,000 for employers of more than 500.[116]

---

charge in Title VII action is treated as statute of limitations violation); *Cobb v. XSport Fitness, Inc.*, No. 09 CV 3553, 2010 WL 2245531, at *2 (E.D.N.Y. May 28, 2010) (Title VII action dismissed for failure to timely file EEOC charge).

111. *Butts v. City of New York Dep't of Hous. Pres. & Dev.*, 990 F.2d 1397, 1402 (2d Cir. 1993).

112. *Id.*

113. *Kolstad v. Am. Dental Ass'n*, 527 U.S. 526, 533 (1999); 42 U.S.C. § 1981a(b).

114. 42 U.S.C. § 1981a(b)(3).

115. 42 U.S.C. § 1981a(b)(1).

116. 42 U.S.C. § 1981a(b)(3).

These caps do not apply to front pay, however.[117] Further, there may be no damage caps under state law.[118] If caps are available,[119] they should be asserted in the answer.

c. BFOQ

Under Title VII and the ADEA, an employer may in some instances defend against a claim of discrimination by asserting the "bona fide occupational qualification defense" (BFOQ). Thus, for example, an employer defending an ADEA case must prove that the age limit is reasonably necessary to the essence of the business; and either that all or substantially all of the individuals excluded are in fact disqualified for the job; or that some of the excluded individuals possess a disqualifying trait that cannot be ascertained but for the reference to age.[120] For instance, under federal law, air cargo operators regulated by the Federal Aviation Administration are prohibited from employing pilots sixty years of age or older.[121] Courts have upheld this requirement as valid due to the safety concerns posed by aging pilots and the inability of medical or other tests to determine whether a given pilot poses a safety risk due to infirmity or unreliability.[122]

In Title VII gender discrimination cases, an employer must prove that the gender-based discrimination is reasonably necessary to the

---

117. *Pollard v. E.I. Du Pont de Nemours Co.*, 532 U.S. 843, 848 (2001).

118. Indeed, some courts will apportion damages between federal and state statutes to avoid reducing damages awards. The Third Circuit attributed the maximum amount of damages possible to the capped federal statute and then allocated the remainder of the jury award to the uncapped state statute. *Gagliardo v. Connaught Labs., Inc.*, 311 F.3d 565, 572 (3d Cir. 2002).

119. Ohio imposes damage caps on tort claims. *See* Ohio Rev. Code Ann. § 2315.18 (2012) (compensatory damage cap for noneconomic loss in a tort action); Ohio Rev. Code Ann. § 2315.21 (punitive damage cap). These damage caps apply to state law employment discrimination claims. *See Luri v. Republic Servs., Inc.*, 953 N.E.2d 859, 864 (Ohio Ct. App. 2011).

120. *Coupe v. Fed. Express Corp.*, 121 F.3d 1022, 1024 (6th Cir. 1997).

121. *Id.* at 1023. Federal regulations now restrict air cargo operators from employing pilots sixty-five years of age or older. *See* 14 C.F.R. § 121.383(d)(1) (2012).

122. *Coupe*, 21 F.3d at 1025–26.

operation of particular business or enterprise. The employer must also have a "basis in fact" for the belief that no members of one sex could perform the job in question.[123] The exception is a narrow one, and the employer bears the burden of establishing a BFOQ.[124]

In *Healy v. Southwood Psychiatric Hospital*, a hospital for emotionally disturbed or abused youths assigned the plaintiff to the night shift because it needed a female childcare specialist on that shift.[125] The plaintiff challenged the gender-based policy as discriminatory under Title VII. The court upheld the hospital's decision due to the need to have specialists of both sexes available for all shifts due to the therapeutic and privacy concerns of the patients.[126] A BFOQ, if it exists, should be pleaded as an affirmative defense.

d. Legitimate, Nondiscriminatory Reasons

In *McDonnell Douglas Corp. v. Green*, the Supreme Court set forth a test to be applied in Title VII race discrimination cases.[127] This test has been widely adopted by many courts and now generally applies to all kinds of discrimination cases.

First, the plaintiff bears the burden of proving that he belongs to a protected class; he was meeting his employer's expectations; he suffered an adverse employement action; and similarly situated employees outside the protected class were treated more favorably.[128] The burden

---

123. *Healy v. Southwood Psychiatric Hosp.*, 78 F.3d 128, 132 (3d Cir. 1996).

124. *Henry v. Milwaukee County*, 539 F.3d 573, 579, 580 (7th Cir. 2008).

125. 78 F.3d at 130.

126. *Id.* at 134; *see also Reed v. County of Casey*, 184 F.3d 597, 599 (6th Cir. 1999) (female jailor transferred to third shift to comply with state law requiring female jailor on duty when female inmate is housed in the jail was justified as BFOQ); *but see Henry*, 539 F.3d at 585 (juvenile detention center did not show it was reasonably necessary to staff third shift solely with juvenile corrections officers of same sex as the juveniles in the cells the officers were monitoring).

127. 411 U.S. 792, 802 (1973). The Supreme Court has reiterated this test on numerous occasions and it has been cited countless times by both district and circuit courts. *See, e.g.*, *Raytheon Co. v. Hernandez*, 540 U.S. 44, 49–50 (2003). This framework applies to other employment actions, such as discipline or promotion.

128. *McDonnell Douglas Corp.*, 411 U.S. at 802.

then shifts to the defendant to articulate a legitimate, nondiscriminatory reason for the adverse employement action.[129] Finally, the plaintiff has an opportunity to show that the defendant's stated reason was a pretext, and in fact the decision was motivated by discriminatory intent instead.[130]

The existence of a legitimate, nondiscriminatory reason is not truly an affirmative defense because the burden of proving discrimination always remains with the plaintiff. The defendant merely has the burden of articulating a legitimate, nondiscriminatory reason for its decision. Though the test sets forth an evidentiary framework, it does not require the specific assertion of affirmative defenses, although in practice, many employers do so.

e. Election of Remedies

In some instances, a plaintiff may waive his right to litigate claims when he files discrimination charges with the EEOC and state civil rights commissions. Under Ohio law, for instance, age discrimination plaintiffs may seek to enforce the prohibition against age discrimination either by filing a charge in an administrative forum *or* by filing a lawsuit in a judicial forum.[131] If the plaintiff did file an administrative charge, any subsequent state age lawsuit may be barred due to the election of remedies.[132]

5. Negligence Defenses

a. Contributory Negligence

Although negligence is a less common cause of action in employment law, it remains important for employers to know what defenses are

---

129. *Id.*

130. *Id.* at 804.

131. OHIO REV. CODE ANN. § 4112.08 (2012). According to the Supreme Court, election of remedies occurs when a plaintiff pursues remedies that are legally or factually inconsistent with each other. *14 Penn Plaza LLC v. Pyett*, 556 U.S. 247, 262 (2009).

132. *Smith v. Friendship Village of Dublin, Ohio, Inc.*, 751 N.E.2d 1010, 1014 (Ohio 2001).

available if such a case arises. Negligent hiring or retention claims are frequently brought when, for example, an individual has been harmed by a coworker acting outside of the course and scope of his or her employment, but the employer is alleged to have known or should have known the conduct might occur.[133]

Contributory negligence, or its counterpart comparative negligence, vary in their application among the states. In some states, contributory negligence will completely bar any plaintiff's recovery.[134] In others, the plaintiff's negligence will merely reduce his or her recovery.[135] Plaintiff's conduct must contribute to his or her injury.[136] The standard is an objective one—what a reasonable person of ordinary prudence would do under similar circumstances.[137]

To successfully assert this defense, the defendant must show that plaintiff's conduct was unreasonable in a given situation. That is, the plaintiff's conduct must fall below the standard to which plaintiff should conform to protect him- or herself.[138] Also, the plaintiff's unreasonable conduct must contribute to his or her injury.[139]

b. Acts or Omissions of Others

A defendant can use the acts or omissions of a third party, if a contributing factor to plaintiff's injuries, as a defense. In the employment context, the defense may be available when the employee has been harmed by a customer or stranger to the employer. The defense applies

---

133. *Dorsey v. Morris*, 611 N.E.2d 509, 512 (Ohio Ct. App. 1992); *Pittard v. Four Seasons Motor Inn, Inc.*, 688 P.2d 333, 341 (N.M. Ct. App. 1984).

134. *See Andrews v. Wilkins*, 934 F.2d 1267, 1272 (D.C. Cir. 1991).

135. *See Hunnings v. Texaco, Inc.*, 29 F.3d 1480, 1487 (11th Cir. 1994); *Olson v. Shumaker Trucking & Excavating Contractors, Inc.*, 196 P.3d 1265, 1277 (Mont. 2008) (fact finder should apportion liability when plaintiff is contributorily negligent).

136. *Hunnings*, 29 F.3d at 1487.

137. *Id.*; *see also Jones v. Owens-Corning Fiberglass Corp.*, 69 F.3d 712, 719 (4th Cir. 1995) (claimant failed to use reasonable care under the circumstances and his failure was a proximate cause of his injury).

138. *Piedmont Resolution, L.L.C. v. Johnston, Rivlin & Foley*, 999 F. Supp. 34, 55 (D.D.C. 1998).

139. *Id.*

even if the responsible third party is not a party to the lawsuit, or is in fact immune from suit.[140]

c. Assumption of the Risk

Assumption of the risk is a defense that should be considered carefully in the employment context. It may be available if the employee has knowingly exposed him- or herself to harm, such as engaging a dangerous customer, but also implies that the employer concedes that the danger, in fact, existed and could be recognized.

In some states, assumption of the risk completely bars any recovery by the plaintiff, whereas in others the defense merely limits the plaintiff's potential recovery. For instance, in Rhode Island, assumption of the risk acts as a complete bar to plaintiff's recovery.[141] To establish the defense, the defendant must show that plaintiff subjectively knew of the existence of a danger, appreciated the danger's unreasonable character, and voluntarily exposed him- or herself to the danger.[142] In Colorado, however, assumption of the risk acts only to limit, not preclude, a plaintiff's recovery.[143] Under Colorado law, when danger is readily apparent and plaintiff chooses to engage in the activity, assumption of the risk is only a partial bar to recovery.[144]

6. Harassment Claim Defenses

Harassment claims are among the most dangerous for employers and have been the source of many astronomical verdicts. Harassment claims are divided into two categories: quid pro quo and hostile environment.[145]

Quid pro quo claims arise when a supervisor conditions job benefits or employment on the employee's participation in conduct of a sexual

---

140. *Laney v. Celotex Corp.*, 901 F.2d 1319, 1320 (6th Cir. 1990); *Mitchell v. Stewart Oldford & Sons, Inc.*, 415 N.W.2d 224, 227 (Mich. Ct. App. 1987).

141. *See Colantuoni v. Alfred Calcagni & Sons, Inc.*, 44 F.3d 1, 3 (1st Cir. 1994).

142. *Id.* at 2.

143. *Id.*

144. *Id.* at 904.

145. *Meritor Savings Bank, FSB v. Vinson*, 477 U.S. 57, 65 (1986).

nature. Such a claim may arise, for example, when a manager forces an employee to maintain a sexual relationship to keep his or her job.

Hostile environment cases are more common. They arise when harassing conduct based upon a protected trait, such as sex or race, is severe and pervasive to the point of altering the plaintiff's workplace. Such claims frequently include accusations of sexual or racial slurs, physical misconduct, pictures or drawings, or other inappropriate workplace conduct of a sexual, racial, or other nature.

As a result of two 1998 United States Supreme Court cases, *Burlington Industries, Inc. v. Ellerth*[146] and *Faragher v. City of Boca Raton*,[147] the defenses available to employers in harassment cases are somewhat limited, particularly if the alleged harasser is the plaintiff's supervisor. These defenses require not only careful structuring of the answer but also great skill throughout the conduct of discovery.

The *Ellerth* and *Faragher* cases recognized that an employer can establish a defense by demonstrating that (1) it took reasonable steps to prevent and correct harassing conduct and (2) the plaintiff failed to take advantage of preventative or corrective opportunities by the employer.[148] These defenses have a number of serious limitations,[149] the most important of which is that they do not apply if the employee has suffered a tangible employment action, such as termination or discharge.

If no tangible employment action has been taken against an employee, an employer defendant may avoid vicarious liability for an alleged hostile environment. The defense is available to shield the employer from either liability or damages. The employer must prove that it exercised reasonable care to prevent and correct any harassing behavior and

146. 524 U.S. 742 (1998).

147. 524 U.S. 775 (1998).

148. *Burlington Indus., Inc. v. Ellerth*, 524 U.S. at 765; *Faragher v. City of Boca Raton*, 524 U.S. at 807.

149. One limitation of the *Ellerth* and *Faragher* defenses is that they may not apply to state or local law harassment claims. *See Zakrzewska v. New School*, 620 F.3d 168, 169 (2d Cir. 2010) (defenses do not apply to claims under New York City Human Rights Law).

that the employee unreasonably failed to take advantage of preventive or corrective opportunities provided by the employer.[150] In *Ellerth*, the court specifically noted that an anti-harassment policy, though not necessary as a matter of law, would be relevant to a showing that the employer exercised reasonable care to prevent and correct any harassing behavior. The court also stated that an employee's failure to use an existing complaint procedure will satisfy the defendant's burden under the defense's second element.[151]

7. Just Cause

The law is still unsettled as to whether just cause is an affirmative defense. The question of whether cause is an affirmative defense also raises the issue of which party bears the burden of proof. If cause is asserted as a defense in the answer, care should be taken to avoid denominating it as an *affirmative* defense, because doing so may be construed as a concession that the employer must establish cause.

8. Consent

In addition to defamation actions, the defense of consent is available when a plaintiff alleges assault and battery, interference with contractual relations, invasion of privacy claims, and certain statutory claims.[152] For example, the Electronic Communications Privacy Act of 1986[153] prohibits the unlawful and intentional interception of electronic communications. If an employer monitors employee e-mail, the employee may have a cause of action against the employer. If, however, the employee gives consent to the employer to intercept e-mail or access stored electronic communications, no liability will attach to

150. *Ellerth*, 524 U.S. at 765; *Faragher*, 524 U.S. at 807.

151. *Ellerth*, 524 U.S. at 765; *see also Crawford v. BNSF Ry. Co.*, 665 F.3d 978, 985 (8th Cir. 2012) (unreasonable failure to take advantage of complaint procedure when plaintiff waited eight months).

152. *See Frye v. IBP, Inc.*, 15 F. Supp. 2d 1032, 1041 (D. Kan. 1998).

153. 18 U.S.C. §§ 2510–2522 (2012).

the employer.[154] An employer may develop a monitoring policy and require employees' agreement with that policy, or may set up computer systems to secure consent before giving access to the employer's computer system.

9. *Punitive Damages Defenses*

a. Constitutionality

Constitutionality challenges to punitive damages claims, once largely unsuccessful, have recently gained a measure of acceptance, particularly as to the size of the award. In 1996, the United States Supreme Court recognized that an award could be so excessive as to be unconstitutional. In *BMW of North America, Inc. v. Gore*, the plaintiff purchased a new car without the knowledge that parts of it had been repainted after acid rain damaged the paint in transit.[155] After trial, a jury awarded him $4,000 in compensatory damages and $4 million in punitive damages.[156] The Alabama Supreme Court reduced the punitive damages award to a "constitutionally reasonable" $2 million.[157]

The United States Supreme Court determined that the $2 million was "grossly excessive" and therefore unconstitutional.[158] In declaring the $2 million award unconstitutional, the court set forth a three-part test to evaluate the constitutionality of punitive damage awards: the degree of reprehensibility of the defendant's conduct; the disparity between the harm or potential harm suffered and the punitive damage award; and the difference between the award in the instant case and the award imposed in comparable cases.[159] Taking these factors

154. *Williams v. Poulos*, 11 F.3d 271, 281–82 (1st Cir. 1993); *Payne v. Norwest Corp.*, 911 F. Supp. 1299 (D. Mont. 1995); *Shefts v. Petrakis*, 758 F. Supp. 2d 620, 631 (C.D. Ill. 2010) (president of telecommunications company consented to logging of text messages when employee manual gave company right to do so).

155. 517 U.S. 559, 563–64 (1996).

156. *Id.* at 565.

157. *Id.* at 567.

158. *Id.* at 574–75, 585–86.

159. *Id.* at 575.

into consideration on remand, the Alabama Supreme Court reduced the punitive damages to $50,000.[160] The *BMW* case was the first time the United States Supreme Court held that a punitive damages award was so large that it violated the Due Process Clause of the Fourteenth Amendment.[161]

Seven years later, in *State Farm Mutual Automobile Insurance Co. v. Campbell*, the Supreme Court again addressed the question of the size of a punitive damages award, particularly one based upon the defendant's wealth.[162] The court in that case concluded that ordinarily a punitive damages award should only be at most two or three times the size of the compensatory damages award and that in any case an award should not exceed nine times the amount of compensatory damages.[163]

b. Impact of Kolstad

In addition to constitutional challenges, there may also be a higher standard that applies to punitive damage awards under Title VII and the ADA. The United States Supreme Court held in *Kolstad v. American Dental Association* that employers who demonstrate "good faith efforts at Title VII compliance" are safeguarded from punitive damages liability, even when some of their managers may have acted in violation of Title VII.[164] Additionally, in contrast to liability for compensatory damages, liability for punitive damages cannot be based on vicarious liability.[165] To the contrary, employers who engage in "good

---

160. *BMW of North Am., Inc. v. Gore*, 701 So.2d 507, 515 (Ala. 1997).

161. *Id.* at 509.

162. 538 U.S. 408, 412 (2003).

163. *Id.* at 425. Lower courts have used the *Campbell* decision to reduce punitive damages awards, *see Mendez-Matos v. Municipality of Guaynabo*, 557 F.3d 36, 56 (1st Cir. 2009) (reducing $350,000 punitive damages award for worker's unlawful detention to $35,000), and to vacate punitive damages awards in their entirety, *see Austin v. Norfolk Southern Corp.*, 158 Fed. Appx. 374, 386 (3d Cir. 2005) (vacating punitive damages award for employee's thirty-day suspension).

164. 527 U.S. 526, 544 (1999). The Ninth Circuit allows employers to escape punitive damages if they can show that the challenged actions were taken by employees other than senior managers. *See Costa v. Desert Palace, Inc.*, 299 F.3d 838, 864 (9th Cir. 2002).

165. *Kolstad*, 527 U.S. at 545–46.

faith efforts to comply with Title VII" are safeguarded from liability for punitive damages, even if their employees or managers engage in discrimination with a malicious or reckless intent.[166]

In *Kolstad*, the Supreme Court explained that if the malice or reckless indifference of an individual were automatically imputed to the company for punitive damages purposes, it "would reduce the incentive for employers to implement antidiscrimination programs."[167] Thus, the cases in which an employer can be held liable for punitive damages in the discrimination context are limited to those cases in which an employer actually perceives that its actions are unlawful.[168] A number of circuits have determined that the *Kolstad* defense is an affirmative defense and thus does not require the employee to disprove the employer's good-faith compliance with Title VII.[169]

10. Employment at Will

The doctrine of employment at will provides that an employer may terminate an employee at any time, with or without cause.[170] This is

---

166. *Id.*; *see also Dominic v. DeVilbiss Air Power Co.*, 493 F.3d 968, 976 (8th Cir. 2007) (punitive damages inappropriate when employer had zero-tolerance anti-harassment policy and conducted thorough investigations of employee's complaints); *Harsco Corp. v. Renner*, 475 F.3d 1179, 1189–90 (10th Cir. 2007) (upholding district court's decision vacating punitive damages award when employer had comprehensive Title VII policies and training procedures with which employee's supervisors failed to comply); *but see McInnis v. Fairfield Communities, Inc.*, 458 F.3d 1129, 1138 (10th Cir. 2006) (no good-faith defense when employer had antidiscrimination policies but failed to enforce them during the course of employee's complaint).

167. 527 U.S. at 544.

168. When, for example, high-ranking personnel managers retaliate against an employee for assisting in an employment discrimination investigation, a jury may find that the employer was aware that its actions violated federal law. *McDonough v. City of Quincy*, 452 F.3d 8, 24 (1st Cir. 2006); *but see Farias v. Instructional Sys., Inc.*, 259 F.3d 91, 102 (2d Cir. 2001) (retaliatory action taken pursuant to counsel's advice that the action was consistent with federal law does not support punitive damages under *Kolstad*).

169. *See, e.g.*, *Zimmerman v. Assocs. First Capital Corp.*, 251 F.3d 376, 385 (2d Cir. 2001); *Romano v. U-Haul Int'l*, 233 F.3d 655, 670 (1st Cir. 2000); *Passantino v. Johnson & Johnson Consumer Prods., Inc.*, 212 F.3d 493, 516 (9th Cir. 2000).

170. *Mers v. Dispatch Printing Co.*, 483 N.E.2d 150, 153 (Ohio 1985).

not, strictly speaking, a defense to be raised by an employer defendant. Rather, a plaintiff must demonstrate the existence of an exception to this doctrine to recover against the employer.

11. Equal Pay Act Defenses

The Equal Pay Act (EPA) prohibits discrimination in wages on the base of sex.[171] The statute reflects, however, that it is not illegal when a pay differential exists by virtue of a seniority or merit system, a system based upon quality or quantity or work, or one based "on any other factor other than sex."[172] The employer may also be relieved of all or part of liability by demonstrating good-faith reliance upon a regulation or an administrative ruling.[173] Because these matters are affirmative defenses,[174] they should be asserted in the answer.[175]

12. FLSA Defenses

Numerous affirmative defenses exist under the Fair Labor Standards Act (FLSA).[176] These defenses range from exemptions to the act to partial and complete excuses to liability.

The law is well settled that the employer bears the burden of proving the existence of exemptions under the FLSA,[177] and that such exemptions must also be pleaded as affirmative defenses.[178] Counsel defending

---

171. 29 U.S.C. § 206(d).

172. 29 U.S.C. § 206(d)(1); *see also Corning Glass Works v. Brennan*, 417 U.S. 188, 202 (1974) (finding that bona fide job evaluation plans are not illegal, even if they result in one sex being paid less than another); *Rhoades v. Young Women's Christian Ass'n*, 423 Fed. Appx. 193, 197 (3d Cir. 2011) (pay differential justified when plaintiff merely used the computer payroll system a more highly compensated employee implemented).

173. 29 U.S.C. § 260 (Portal-to-Portal Pay).

174. *See Ryduchowski v. Port Authority of New York & New Jersey*, 203 F.3d 135, 142 (2d Cir. 2000), *cert. denied*, 530 U.S. 1276 (2000).

175. *See Kouba v. Allstate Ins. Co.*, 691 F.2d 873, 875 (6th Cir. 1982).

176. 29 U.S.C. § 201 *et seq*. This act requires, inter alia, payment of a minimum wage and overtime unless the employee is exempt.

177. 29 U.S.C. § 213; *Idaho Sheet Metal Works, Inc. v. Wirtz*, 383 U.S. 190, 209 (1966).

178. 29 U.S.C. § 213; *Diaz v. Jaguar Rest. Group, LLC*, 627 F.3d 1212, 1214 (11th

such claims should therefore carefully review not only whether the more commonly known "white collar" exemptions exist,[179] or whether other, less well-known defenses may be available as well.[180]

The FLSA also has partial or complete defenses based upon the employer's subjective capability. An employer's good faith in classifying employees may constitute a defense to liquidated (double) damages under the act.[181] If applicable, the employer should also consider asserting the common law defense of payment. Finally, if the employer has relied in good faith on a regulation or an opinion letter by the Wage and Hour Administrator, it may have a complete defense to any past liability. [182]

13. Fraud Defenses

Federal Rule of Civil Procedure 9(b) states that allegations of fraud must be stated with particularity. The requirement that plaintiff plead with particularity the circumstances of an alleged fraud serve the purpose of placing defendant on notice of the misconduct with which it is charged, and also safeguards defendants against frivolous charges of immoral or fraudulent behavior.[183] To plead fraud with particularity, some courts hold that the complaint must specify the allegedly fraudulent statements, the speaker, and where and when the statements were made, as well as provide an explanation of why the statements were

---

Cir. 2010); *Renfro v. City of Emporia*, 948 F.2d 1529, 1539 (10th Cir. 1991), *cert. dismissed*, 503 U.S. 915 (1992); *Wirtz v. C & P Shoe Corp.*, 336 F.2d 21, 26 (5th Cir. 1964).

179. *See, e.g.*, 29 U.S.C. § 213(a)(1) (exemptions for executive, administrative, and professional employees).

180. *See, e.g.*, 29 U.S.C. § 213(a)(3) (certain amusement parks); 29 U.S.C. § 213(a)(6) (certain farm labor); 29 U.S.C. § 213(a)(17) (certain computer analysts and programmers); 29 U.S.C. § 213(b) (partial exemption for numerous classes of employees, including those subject to the Motor Carriers and Railway Labor Acts).

181. 29 U.S.C. § 216(b); *Swigart v. Fifth Third Bank*, 870 F. Supp. 2d 500 (S.D. Ohio 2012). Note that even if this defense is established, the awarding of liquidated damages remains in the court's discretion.

182. 29 U.S.C. § 259(a), (b)(1). This defense must be pleaded. 29 U.S.C. § 259(a).

183. *Seville Indus. Mach. Corp. v. Southmost Mach. Corp.*, 742 F.2d 786, 791 (3d Cir. 1984).

fraudulent.[184] Other courts do not require "date, place or time" but do require precision and a measure of substantiation to any allegation of fraud.[185]

Additionally, Rule 9(b) allows "malice, intent, [and] knowledge" to be averred generally. However, plaintiffs may not use conclusory allegations or speculation to show malice.[186] Plaintiffs are still required to allege facts sufficient to give rise to a strong inference of fraudulent intent. This may be done by alleging facts showing that defendant had both motive and opportunity to commit fraud, or by alleging facts that constitute strong circumstantial behavior.[187] If the fraud allegations lack sufficient specification, the claim may be dismissed.

14. Disability Claim Defenses

a. Not Disabled / Otherwise Qualified

When alleging disability discrimination, a plaintiff must prove that he or she was, in fact, disabled. He or she may prove this in one of three ways: that he or she has a physical or mental impairment that substantially limits one or more of his or her major life activities; that he or she has a record of such impairment; or that he or she is regarded as having an impairment.[188] A major life activity can include such things as walking, seeing, hearing, and working.[189]

In the past the defendant could often argue that what the plaintiff was precluded from doing was not a major life activity.[190] With the 2008

184. *Shields v. Citytrust Bancorp., Inc.*, 25 F.3d 1124, 1127–28 (2d Cir. 1994); *Bender v. Southland Corp.*, 749 F.2d 1205, 1216 (6th Cir. 1984).

185. *Seville Indus. Mach. Corp.*, 742 F.2d at 791.

186. *Shields*, 25 F.3d at 1128.

187. *Id.*

188. 42 U.S.C. § 12102. The ADA was amended by the Americans with Disabilities Amendments Act of 2008, PL 110-325, 122 Stat. 3555. The amendment lowered the standard for showing a plaintiff has a disability.

189. 42 U.S.C. § 12102(2).

190. *See, e.g.*, *Chenowett v. Hillsborough County*, 250 F.3d 1328, 1330 (11th Cir. 2001) (occasional seizures preventing driving not a disability).

amendments to the ADA, however, which broadened the definition of a disability, these arguments are much more difficult.

Additionally, the ADA makes it unlawful to discriminate against an "otherwise qualified" individual with a disability. The plaintiff must prove that he or she was a qualified individual at the time of the discrimination. Once this is shown, the employer may argue that the plaintiff is not, in fact, qualified for the position. In one case, for instance, a shoe salesman was terminated because he had seizures in the store and stockroom.[191] The court found that because store security was an essential part of the job and the plaintiff's seizures made him unable to perform that function, he was not qualified for the job.[192] Even though he was fired because of his disability, the fact that he was not qualified to perform an essential function of his job relieved the employer of all liability.[193]

b. Direct Threat

The "direct threat" defense prevents an employer from being held liable for discriminating against an individual whose disability on the job would pose a significant risk of harm to the health or safety of the individual or others that cannot be eliminated by reasonable accommodation.[194]

The EEOC regulations setting forth the parameters of this defense raise a very high bar for the employer.[195] First, the direct threat defense must be based on medical judgment, relying on the most current medical knowledge. Second, an individualized inquiry must be made to

---

191. *Martinson v. Kinney Shoe Corp.*, 104 F.3d 683, 685 (4th Cir. 1997).

192. *Id.* at 687.

193. *Id.* at 686; *see also McFadden v. Ballard Spahr Andrews & Ingersoll, LLP*, 611 F.3d 1, 4, 5 (D.C. Cir. 2010) (affirming summary judgment for employer when legal secretary's disability prevented her from typing); *Phelps v. Optima Health, Inc.*, 251 F.3d 21, 26, 28 (1st Cir. 2001) (affirming summary judgment for employer when nurse's disability prevented her from performing the essential function of lifting).

194. 42 U.S.C. § 12113(b).

195. It is the employer's burden to show that its employee posed a direct threat to the workplace. *Branham v. Snow*, 392 F.3d 896, 906 (7th Cir. 2004).

determine the duration of the risk, the nature and severity of the potential harm, the likelihood of the potential harm, and the imminence of the harm.

Though many of the cases using this defense involve plaintiffs with communicable diseases,[196] the Supreme Court has allowed the defense when an employer refused to hire the plaintiff to work on an oil refinery after tests showed liver damage that would be aggravated by continued exposures to toxins at the refinery.[197] In this instance, the employer was concerned that performing the essential function of the job would pose a direct threat to the plaintiff's health, based on medical tests done prior to his employment. Such a concern, however, cannot be based on subjective perceptions.[198]

c. Undue Burden

In a case in which the plaintiff is seeking an accommodation from his or her employer and claims that he or she would be qualified to perform the essential functions of his or her job with such accommodation, the employer may use this defense to avoid making accommodations that would pose an undue hardship on the business of the employer.[199] The initial burden rests on the employee to propose an accommodation and to show that the proposed accommodation is objectively reasonable for that employer to make.[200] For instance, a reasonable accommodation might be to transfer a disabled employee to a vacant position, but it would pose an undue hardship to keep a disabled employee on unpaid leave until a position opens up.[201]

---

196. *See, e.g., Mauro v. Borgess Med. Ctr.*, 886 F. Supp. 1349, 1352–53 (W.D. Mich. 1995) (surgical technician terminated because he was HIV positive and posed a health risk to patients in the hospital).

197. *Chevron U.S.A. Inc. v. Echazabal*, 536 U.S. 73, 87 (2002).

198. *Hamlin v. Charter Twp. of Flint*, 165 F.3d 426, 432 (6th Cir. 1999).

199. *Hedrick v. Western Reserve Care Sys.*, 355 F.3d 444, 452 (6th Cir. 2004).

200. *Id.* at 457.

201. *Thompson v. E.I. DuPont deNemours & Co.*, 70 Fed. Appx. 332, 336–37 (6th Cir. 2003). Similarly, an employer is not required to grant disabled employees an indefinite leave of absence as a reasonable accommodation. *Peyton v. Fred's Stores of*

The determination of "undue hardship" is a fact-specific inquiry, though courts should generally weigh the risks and alternatives to determine whether an accommodation would pose an undue hardship on an employer.[202] This is not a precise mathematical calculation but a common-sense balancing of the following:

i. The nature and cost of the accommodation needed under this chapter;
ii. The overall financial resources of the facility or facilities involved in the provision of the reasonable accommodation; the number of persons employed at such facility; the effect on expenses and resources, or the impact otherwise of accommodation upon the operation of the facility;
iii. The overall financial resources of the covered entity; the overall size of the business of a covered entity with respect to the number of its employees; the number, type, and location of its facilities; and
iv. The type of operation or operations of the covered entity, including the composition, structure, and functions of the workforce of such entity; the geographic separateness and administrative or fiscal relationship of the facility or facilities in question to the covered entity.[203]

15. Preemption

Numerous federal defenses have either expressed or implied preemptive effect.[204] With respect to other statutes, preemption has been established

---

Arkansas, Inc., 561 F.3d 900, 903 (8th Cir. 2009).

202. *Nunes v. Wal-Mart Stores, Inc.*, 164 F.3d 1243, 1247 (9th Cir. 1999).

203. 42 U.S.C. § 12111(10); *see also Borkowski v. Valley Cent. Sch. Dist.*, 63 F.3d 131, 139 (2d Cir. 1995).

204. Under ERISA, the preemption is specifically provided for in the statute, 29 U.S.C. § 1144, and is extremely broad. *See, e.g.*, *Pilot Life Ins. Co. v. Dedeaux*, 481 U.S. 41, 45–46 (1987).

by courts as a means of protecting a federal statutory scheme.[205] Preemption, if is it available, should be asserted as a defense.

16. Collateral Estoppel

The doctrines of *res judicata* and collateral estoppel exist to prevent the same issue from being re-litigated between the same parties and to preclude inconsistent outcomes. Collateral estoppel, as contrasted with *res judicata*, works to preclude previously settled issues, rather than claims. In *Ryan v. New York Telephone Co.*, the plaintiff was discharged for misappropriating workplace property.[206] He applied for unemployment benefits but was denied such benefits because of the misappropriation of property.[207] The plaintiff subsequently brought an action in New York state court alleging, among other things, wrongful discharge. The court held that the second action was barred by collateral estoppel because the issue of misappropriation had already been decided.[208]

For collateral estoppel to apply, the issue must have been "material" to the first action and essential to the decision rendered, and the point "actually to be determined" in the second action.[209] The second element necessary is that the litigant be given a full and fair opportunity to litigate the issue in the first instance considering the realities of the first litigation.[210] The requirement that the issues be the same is strict; if the same factual predicate exists in two actions but the central issue to be resolved differs, then no collateral estoppel exists.[211]

---

205. *See, e.g.*, *Allis-Chalmers Corp. v. Lueck*, 471 U.S. 202, 211 (1985) (involving § 301 of the Labor Management Relations Act); *Union Pac. R.R. Co. v. Sheehan*, 439 U.S. 89, 94 (1978) (involving the Railway Labor Act).

206. 467 N.E.2d 487, 489 (N.Y. 1984).

207. *Id.* at 489.

208. *Id.* at 491.

209. *Id.* at 490.

210. *Id.* at 491.

211. *See Silberman v. Penn Gen. Agencies of New York, Inc.*, 63 A.D.2d 929, 929 (N.Y. App. Div. 1978). One state court determined that collateral estoppel barred an employee's state law public-policy claim alleging discrimination based on age and disability when a federal court had previously granted summary judgment on the employee's ADA and ADEA claims. *Youse v. Duke Energy Corp.*, 614 S.E.2d 396, 401 (N.C. Ct.

17. Judicial Estoppel

Judicial estoppel prevents an employee who assumes and successfully maintains a position in a legal proceeding from later assuming a contrary position to accommodate a changed interest.[212] Courts use three factors to determine whether the doctrine applies. First, the party's later position must be clearly inconsistent with the party's first position. Second, the party must have convinced an earlier court to accept its position, thus risking inconsistent court determinations if the second court accepts the changed position. Finally, judicial estoppel is appropriate only when accepting an inconsistent position would unfairly prejudice the opposing party.[213]

Many courts will dismiss a claim on the basis of judicial estoppel if the plaintiff fails to exercise the existence of his or her employment claims to his or her creditors in the bankruptcy proceeding.[214] Counsel should consider carefully whether to assert this claim as one specifically for "judicial estoppel" or to rely only upon the Rule 8(c) word "estoppel."

18. Resignation

The fact that the plaintiff has voluntarily resigned may prove to be a very worthwhile defense. In most such cases, an employee bringing suit will contend that he or she was the victim of "constructive discharge." For a constructive discharge, however, most courts apply an objective test and require that the employee show that a reasonable person in his or her shoes would have felt compelled to resign.[215] Though there is

---

App. 2005).

212. *New Hampshire v. Maine*, 532 U.S. 742, 749 (2001).

213. *Id.* at 750–51.

214. *Robinson v. Tyson Foods, Inc.*, 595 F.3d 1269, 1276 (11th Cir. 2010) (finding judicial estoppel as to plaintiff but not the EEOC); *EEOC v. CRST Van Expedited, Inc.*, 679 F.3d 657, 679 (8th Cir. 2012).

215. *See, e.g.*, *Meyer v. Brown & Root Constr. Co.*, 661 F.2d 369, 372 (5th Cir. 1981); *see also Torrech-Hernandez v. General Elec. Co.*, 519 F.3d 41, 52 (1st Cir. 2008) (employee's subjective belief that he would be fired if he did not voluntarily resign cannot support a claim for constructive discharge).

considerable difference among the courts as to *which* acts might constitute a constructive discharge, it is generally clear that a mere denial of a promotion or unfavorable review is not sufficient.[216]

19. After-Acquired Evidence

The after-acquired evidence defense is one that has led to a fair amount of controversy. That defense may reduce, but not necessarily eliminate, an employer's liability for a violation of the ADEA, Title VII, or Equal Pay Act, as well as for other claims. Although courts were historically divided on this topic, the parameters of the after-acquired evidence defense were set forth in *McKennon v. Nashville Banner Publishing Co.*[217] In *McKennon*, the United States Supreme Court held that employee misconduct discovered after an employee had been terminated justified limiting the type of damages an employee could recover, even when the employer had terminated the employee for an improper reason such as unlawful discrimination.[218] The Supreme Court referred to such evidence of employee misconduct as "after-acquired evidence," and its ruling that such evidence limits the damages an employee may collect is known as the after-acquired evidence doctrine.

In *McKennon*, the court indicated that the employee misconduct must be "of such severity that the employee in fact would have been terminated on those grounds alone if the employer had known of it at the time of the discharge."[219] Later decisions have applied the after-acquired evidence doctrine to résumé fraud and held that an employee's damages should be limited if the employee would not have been hired as a result of misrepresentations during the application process.[220] For

216. *See, e.g.*, *Garner v. Wal-Mart Stores, Inc.*, 807 F.2d 1536, 1539 (11th Cir. 1987); *Ross v. Michigan State Univ. Bd. of Regents*, 837 F. Supp. 2d 712, 718 (W.D. Mich. 2011) (resigning from a position because employee's appointment merely conferred a new title for the work the employee was already doing did not constitute constructive discharge).

217. 513 U.S. 352 (1995).

218. *Id.* at 360–63.

219. *Id.* at 362–63.

220. *Thurman v. Yellow Freight Sys., Inc.*, 90 F.3d 1160, 1168 (6th Cir. 1996); *Maiden*

some courts, after-acquired evidence is an affirmative defense and must be asserted in the answer.[221]

20. Mitigation of Damages

Mitigation of damages is a defense that should be used with care. More courts require not only that the employer demonstrate that the employee failed to conduct a reasonable job search, but also that comparable employment was in fact available.[222] The employer bears the burden of proof on the issue of mitigation and should consider retaining a vocational expert to demonstrate that the employee could have located acceptable employment with reasonable effort.

IV. Conclusion

Affirmative defenses are some of the most powerful weapons in an employer's arsenal in employment cases. Defense Counsel should take care to properly preserve their client's defenses and to assert them at the stage of the case that is most beneficial to the employer's interest.

---

v. APA Transp. Corp., No. C-1-00-883, 2002 U.S. Dist. LEXIS 8076, at *34–35 (S.D. Ohio May 6, 2002); *Yeary v. State of Florida, Dep't of Corrections*, No. 95-0583-CIV-J-21-C, 1997 U.S. Dist. LEXIS 8839, at *11 (M.D. Fla. 1997); *see also Kapche v. Holder*, 677 F.3d 454, 458 (D.C. Cir. 2012) (affirming denial of front pay and reinstatement due to after-acquired evidence of lack of candor during FBI investigation).

221. *Holland v. Gee*, 677 F.3d 1047, 1065 (11th Cir. 2012) (reversing district court's decision to vacate back-pay award because defendant did not assert after-acquired evidence in its answer); *but see Kapche*, 677 F.3d at 465 (declining to decide whether after-acquired evidence is an affirmative defense).

222. *Sheehan v. Donlen Corp.*, 173 F.3d 1039, 1049 (7th Cir. 1999); *Hutchison v. Amateur Elec. Supply, Inc.*, 42 F.3d 1037, 1044 (7th Cir. 1994).

CHAPTER 6
The Use and Misuse of Statistics in Employment Litigation

John Richard Carrigan Sr.

I. The Evolution of the Role of Statistics in Employment Discrimination Litigation

In 1971, Laurence Tribe, then an assistant professor at Harvard Law School, examined the use of statistical evidence in "Trial by Mathematics: Precision and Ritual in the Legal Process," concluding that the utility of mathematical methods had been greatly exaggerated.[1] Describing probability as a successor to numerology, Professor Tribe argued that the inherent conflict between mathematical techniques and

Thirty-five years ago, Frank C. Morris Jr. presciently described the developing statistical issues in his brilliant book, CURRENT TRENDS IN THE USE (AND MISUSE) OF STATISTICS IN EMPLOYMENT DISCRIMINATION LITIGATION (Equal Employment Advisory Council 1977).

1. Laurence H. Tribe, *Trial by Mathematics: Precision and Ritual in the Legal Process*, 84 HARV. L. REV. 1329 (1971).

other important values would be too great to allow general use of such techniques in criminal and civil trials.

Since that time, statistical evidence founded on mathematics has become widely accepted in employment litigation. For example, in *International Brotherhood of Teamsters v. United States*, the Supreme Court stated:

> [O]ur cases make it unmistakably clear that "(s)tatistical analyses have served and will continue to serve an important role" in cases in which the existence of discrimination is a disputed issue . . . . We have repeatedly approved the use of statistical proof, where it reached proportions comparable to those in this case, to establish a *prima facie* case of racial discrimination in jury selection cases . . . . Statistics are equally competent in proving employment discrimination.[2]

Nevertheless, Professor Tribe identifies several errors that may be made in asserting arguments based on probability, such as offering calculations based on numbers for which there is no foundation, assuming probabilities to be independent when they are not, and equating the probability a randomly chosen defendant would possess incriminating characteristics with the probability that a defendant possessing those characteristics would be innocent. His concern that "mathematical proof, far from providing any clear benefit may in fact decrease the likelihood of accurate outcomes"[3] remains pertinent in evaluating statistical argument and challenging misuse of statistics.

The term *statistical evidence* could be applied to the routine use of simple arithmetic computations such as the mean, the median, and the range. Courts have long accepted such simple statistics, and expert

---

2. 431 U.S. 324 at 339–40 (1977) (quoting *Mayor of Philadelphia v. Educational Equality League*, 415 U.S. 605, 620 (1974)).

3. Tribe, *supra* note 1, at 1358. Professor Tribe pointed out several errors encountered in misuse of mathematical techniques, as well as the danger that a false illusion of precision could be created.

testimony is unnecessary to establish them. Expert testimony often becomes necessary in employment litigation when observed results of a decision process differ from what was expected, and it is necessary to determine whether the difference may be a product of random variation. Such differences between groups may occur in average pay rates, likelihood of being hired or promoted, performance evaluations, discipline and discharge, or other employment decisions. The techniques most frequently employed are hypothesis testing and, more recently, multiple regression analysis.

What this chapter hopes to do is to describe the use and misuse of common techniques and offer some practice suggestions. Teaching statistical methods is beyond the scope of this chapter, but there are many resources to familiarize lawyers with the subject, including the *Reference Manual on Scientific Evidence, Third Edition* (The National Academies Press, Washington, D.C. 2011). Statistical evidence is well explained in the *Reference Guide on Statistics* by David H. Kaye and David A. Freedman, and multiple regression is addressed in the *Reference Guide on Multiple Regression* by Daniel L. Rubenfeld.

Statistical evidence may be important in disparate treatment claims, adverse impact claims, and "pattern and practice" claims.

II. The Use of Statistical Disparities to Prove Motivation

In claims of "disparate treatment" based on protected group membership, the employer's motive for an adverse employment action typically is the crucial issue, and employers rarely admit such motivation. Consequently, the typical disparate treatment case involves an effort to prove the employer's motivation by circumstantial evidence. An early decision under the National Labor Relations Act determining whether an employer violated Section 8(3) of the NLRA, *In re F. W. Woolworth Company*, foreshadowed the statistical evidence later to be offered in Title VII litigation, because the board discussed the unduly high proportion of union members laid off as evidence of a discriminatory motive:

> It would be expected that in a selection of employees to be laid off without regard to union affiliation the proportion of union members among those laid off would approximate the proportion in the group from which the selection was made. . . . The natural assumption would be that in any selection to which the factor of union affiliation was irrelevant, union membership would be distributed among those laid off and those retained as if by operation of chance. Of course any combination is a possible result on the basis of pure chance. Variation from the expected does not necessarily establish that the operation of chance has been frustrated by intelligent selection. *When, however, the variation is marked or is manifested consistently in repeated samplings, the hypothesis that union membership was irrelevant to the selection gives way to the inference that the selection was made on a discriminatory basis.*[4]

The underlying premise of the *F. W. Woolworth* analysis is the use of statistical techniques to test the so-called "null hypothesis," that the observed results are consistent with random variation, and that, by implication, protected group membership played no part in the challenged decisions. In analysis of disparate treatment claims under the Civil Rights Act of 1964, courts recognized that an employer's denial of an unlawful motive could be challenged by circumstantial evidence, including hypothesis testing to prove, or to rebut, accusations of improper motive.

At one end of the spectrum, evidence that women or minorities were always assigned to certain jobs, or never assigned to certain jobs, has long been accepted as strong evidence that gender or minority status affected the decisions, with or without the testimony of an expert to explain or opine. The Supreme Court in *International Brotherhood*

4. 25 N.L.R.B. 1362, 1373 (N.L.R.B. 1940) (emphasis added).

of Teamsters v. United States[5] adopted the powerful phrase "inexorable zero" from the Fifth Circuit in *U.S. v. T.I.M.E.–D.C., Inc.*, which rejected the defendants' criticism of the plaintiffs' statistical evidence and assessed the defendants' failure of proof as coming "not from a misuse of statistics but from 'the inexorable zero.'"[6] At the other end of the spectrum, courts have sometimes balked at finding discrimination based on small differences in selection rates or times to promotion, even without the benefit of "expert" opinion that such slight differences are meaningless.

Nevertheless, courts have increasingly recognized that a layperson may not be qualified to evaluate differences in average pay rates, different selection rates in relatively small samples, or single-variable comparisons where many variables are simultaneously considered in making a decision. The Fourth Circuit in *Carter v. Ball* affirmed the district court's decision to exclude evidence of the mere absence of minority employees in upper-level positions as insufficient to prove a *prima facie* case of discrimination without a comparison to the relevant labor pool.[7] The Fourth Circuit explained, "This court's broad pronouncement that statistical evidence is 'unquestionably relevant' in a Title VII case cannot be read to foreclose the exclusion of evidence with little or no probative value." The Ninth Circuit similarly rejected statistics offered by plaintiff and defendant in *Hagans v. Andrus* because the plaintiff's offer of evidence regarding the low percentage of women in high-level positions was "meaningless" without evidence of the pool of qualified women applicants, and the defendant's evidence that one of its four GS-14 positions (25 percent) was filled by a woman depended on a sample of only four, "much too small to be meaningful."[8]

A statistical analysis of the disparity and selection rates can reveal the probability that the disparity is merely a random deviation from

5. 431 U.S. 324, 342 n.23 (1977).
6. 517 F.2d 299, 315 (5th Cir. 1975).
7. 33 F.3d 450, 456 (4th Cir. 1994).
8. 651 F.2d 622, 627 (9th Cir. 1981), *cert. denied*, 454 U.S. 859 (1981).

perfectly equal selection rates. Statistics, however, cannot entirely rule out the possibility that chance caused the disparity, nor can statistics determine, if chance is an unlikely explanation, whether the more probable cause was intentional discrimination or a legitimate nondiscriminatory factor in the selection process.[9]

The elevation of statistical evidence (and statistical experts) to prominence came as a result of the Supreme Court consideration of statistical evidence in citizenship rights cases. In *Casteneda v. Partida*, the Supreme Court addressed allegations of discrimination against Mexican Americans in the selection of grand jurors in Hidalgo County, Texas.[10] The question could not be answered by reference to "the inexorable zero" because the evidence showed without dispute that 39 percent of grand jurors were Mexican Americans. However, the proportion of persons serving as grand jurors who were Mexican American (39 percent) was dramatically less than the proportion of Mexican Americans in the county (79 percent). Selection from the pool of qualified jurors should have been random. That is, each qualified juror should have had the same likelihood of being selected, where the defendant offered no evidence that Mexican Americans differed in their qualifications for jury service.[11]

The court considered a simple statistical analysis technique used commonly in social sciences to test a "null hypothesis." For purposes of random jury selection, the null hypothesis would have been that there was no difference between the likelihood of selecting a Mexican American for the grand jury or the likelihood of selecting a non–Mexican American.

---

9. *See, e.g.*, *Palmer v. Shultz*, 815 F.2d 84 (D.C. Cir. 1987) (quoting D. Baldus & J. Cole, Statistical Proof of Discrimination 290–92 (McGraw-Hill Book Co. 1980)).

10. 430 U.S. 482 (1977).

11. As discussed below, the absence of evidence that individuals differed in qualifications for jury service in *Casteneda* distinguishes *Casteneda* from most employment cases, in which differences in qualifications may be crucial.

Random selection does not produce results that are always exactly consistent with the "average" result expected. Nevertheless, as the number of selections grew, differences in the selection rate between Mexican Americans and non–Mexican Americans became more conspicuous and much less likely to be the product of random selection. Given the number of grand jurors selected, and the percentage of Mexican Americans and non–Mexican Americans selected, statistical evidence showed that the likelihood that true random selection would have produced that small a number of Mexican American selections to the grand jury was infinitesimally small. In other words, in *Casteneda*, statistical analysis showed that a process that was supposed to be random clearly was not random.[12]

Adopting the methodology used by social scientists for hypothesis testing, the Supreme Court stated that "[a]s a general rule for such large samples, if the difference between the expected value and the observed number is greater than two or three standard deviations," 420 U.S. at 497, n.15, the hypothesis that jurors were selected without regard to national origin would be "suspect."[13]

Implicit in the court's analysis was the assumption that jury selection was supposed to be random, and that the defendant had not offered evidence of differences in the proportion of persons disqualified from grand jury service. Less obvious, but embedded in the adoption of a "two or three" standard deviation test, is the court's acceptance of the certainty that genuine random selection occasionally produces results that are more than "two or three" standard deviations from the expected value.

In rough terms, something that is two standard deviations from the expected value will occur about 5 percent of the time without any discriminatory motive or impropriety in the process; a result that differs by more than three standard deviations from the expected value

12. Few employers defend their employment decisions as random.
13. 430 U.S. 496 n.17.

will occur less than 1 percent of the time, even without discrimination or any impropriety at all. The practical effect of the choice between two or three standard deviations is whether the court accepts as significant evidence of nonrandom decision processes a result that might have occurred randomly from 1 percent to 5 percent of the time. Careful analysis of the effect of the "two or three standard deviation" test was not necessary in *Casteneda*, because the observed result differed so dramatically from the expected value.

Casteneda was not an employment case, but the use of the process of hypothesis testing borrowed from social science was enthusiastically transplanted to employment discrimination cases. The most extensive use of statistical evidence has been mathematical evaluation of the possibility that the difference between observed results and expected results might be the product of random variation. If a difference could have occurred by chance, it should not be considered evidence of a discriminatory motive (for disparate treatment cases) or that a particular challenged process has "adverse impact" on a protected group.

III. Development of Adverse Impact Theories

In addition to the use of statistical disparities to prove motivation, the development of adverse impact theories as a result of *Griggs v. Duke Power Co.*[14] created liability for statistical disparity without proof of unlawful motivation. In "adverse impact" cases, where an employment practice is challenged as having a disproportionate exclusionary effect on members of a protected group, statistical evidence is essential for the plaintiff to show the exclusionary effect, and may be equally important for the defendant to show its justification for the disputed practice. Where employers have instituted employment tests and qualifications with an exclusionary effect on minority applicants, such requirements must be "shown to bear a demonstrable relationship to successful

14. 401 U.S. 424 (1971).

performance of the jobs" for which they were used.[15] Generally, as discussed below, the demonstration of such a relationship will require statistical evidence.

In *Griggs*, the Supreme Court held that employment practice that produced an "adverse impact" on members of a protected group is unlawful under Title VII unless the employer can show the practice to be justified by "business necessity." The statistical evidence upon which the Supreme Court relied in *Griggs* to reject the employer's use of a high school diploma requirement for transfer from a predominantly minority work group to a historically white work group was 1960 census data that 34 percent of white males in North Carolina had graduated from high school, but only 12 percent of African American males had graduated from high school. The court reasoned that the diploma requirement barred the advancement of a much higher proportion of African American employees than of white employees, and would therefore be unlawful under Title VII unless the employer could show business necessity for the diploma requirement.

The court has recognized that "where gross statistical disparities can be shown, they alone may in a proper case constitute *prima facie* proof of a pattern or practice of discrimination."[16] Thirty-five years later, statistics remain crucial in efforts to prove "pattern and practice of discrimination" or the existence of adverse impact.

A *prima facie* case of disparate impact discrimination has two components. First, a plaintiff must identify "the specific employment practice that is challenged."[17] Second, the plaintiff must show that the employment practice "causes a disparate impact on the basis of race, color, religion, sex, or national origin."[18] To show causation, the plaintiff

---

15. *Id.* at 431.

16. *Hazelwood Sch. Dist. v. United States*, 433 U.S. 299, 307–08 (1977) (evidence that percentage of qualified black teachers in area was at least three to four times percentage of blacks on school district's teaching staff established *prima facie* case of racial discrimination by school district).

17. *Watson v. Ft. Worth Bank & Trust*, 487 U.S. 977, 994 (1988).

18. 42 U.S.C. § 2000e-2(k)(1)(A)(i).

must present "statistical evidence of a kind and degree sufficient to show that the practice in question has caused the exclusion of applicants for jobs or promotions because of their membership in a protected group."[19]

The Court of Appeals for the District of Columbia presented a detailed analysis of the role of statistics in establishing a *prima facie* case for a class of women plaintiffs challenging discrimination in the Foreign Service of the United States State Department in *Palmer v. Shultz*.[20] The court recognized that a statistical disparity may result from causes other than unlawful discrimination:

> A disparity between the selection rates of men and women for a particular job or job benefit has one of three possible causes. . . . First, the disparity may be the product of an unlawful discriminatory animus; this is what plaintiffs are attempting to prove. Second, the disparity may have a legitimate and nondiscriminatory cause. For example, prior experience of a certain type may be an important factor in making certain employment decisions, and it may happen to be true that women on average have less of this experience than men, one would expect that women would be selected less frequently. Third, the disparity may simply be a product of chance. Even if we may properly assume that, as a general rule, women and men on average are equally qualified to be selected for a particular job or job benefit, for any particular group of men or women who happen to constitute the actual pool of eligible candidates at the time the selections are made, there may be some deviation from the general rule because the actual qualifications of men and women differ from individual to individual and any pool of eligible candidates constitutes an inherently random collection of individuals. Thus, even if selections were made entirely on the basis of qualification, without a

19. *Watson*, 487 U.S. at 994.
20. 815 F.2d 84 (D.C. Cir. 1987).

> trace of discriminatory bias, random deviations in the selection rates for men and women may result.[21]

Courts interpreting Title VII have nevertheless accepted that if the disparity between selection rates for protected and nonprotected groups is sufficiently large so that the probability that the disparity resulted from chance is sufficiently small, then courts will infer from the numbers alone that, more likely than not, the disparity was a product of unlawful discrimination. This would then require the defendant to introduce evidence of a nondiscriminatory explanation for the disparity or to rebut the inference of discrimination in some other way.[22] However useful statistical evidence may be, the U.S. Supreme Court in *International Brotherhood of Teamsters v. United States* reaffirmed the role of statistics in proving employment discrimination, with a caution:

> We caution only that statistics are not irrefutable; they come in infinite variety and, like any other kind of evidence, they may be rebutted. In short, their usefulness depends on all of the surrounding facts and circumstances.[23]

The court recognized such a rebuttal of a *prima facie* case based on statistics in *Hazelwood School District v. United States*.[24]

IV. Attacks on, and Defense of, Procedures for Hiring or Promotion Require Statistical Evidence

In the aftermath of *Griggs v. Duke Power Co.*, the Equal Employment Opportunity Commission (EEOC) and other federal agencies ultimately

21. *Id.* at 90–91.

22. *See Hazelwood School District v. United States*, 433 U.S. 299, 307–08 (1977).

23. 431 U.S. 324, 340 (1977) (citing *Hester v. Southern Ry. Co.*, 497 F.2d 1374, 1379–81 (5th Cir. 1974)).

24. 433 U.S. at 307–08 (*prima facie* statistical proof of racial discrimination in hiring by school district can be rebutted by statistics dealing with district's hiring after it became subject to Title VII in 1972).

agreed on guidelines to be used to evaluate employee-selection procedures. The Uniform Guidelines on Employee Selection Procedures were promulgated in 1976, ostensibly to address interagency conflict, particularly between the Office of Federal Contract Compliance Programs of the Department of Labor and EEOC.

Although the Uniform Guidelines might be used to evaluate a wide variety of employee selection procedures, they are most obviously applicable to test hiring and promotion procedures. If an employer uses a test to determine eligibility for employment or eligibility for promotion, the Uniform Guidelines require the employer to observe statistics from which it can be determined whether the selection procedure has adverse impact on the members of a protected group. Whether a particular selection procedure has adverse impact often cannot be determined until the selection procedure has been used extensively, which presents the employer with a dilemma. At the time a selection procedure is adopted, it may not be possible to determine whether the selection procedure has adverse impact, so the employer proceeds at its peril until adverse impact information is available. When sufficient data is available to conclude that adverse impact exists, the employer may safely continue to use the selection procedure only if the employer has evidence of the validity of the selection procedure in accordance with the Uniform Guidelines. For that reason, defense of a challenged selection procedure (such as a test used for hiring or a test used for eligibility for promotion) typically requires testimony of an expert witness concerning test validation, and the demonstration of validity typically requires statistical evidence. Criterion-related validation and construct validation require statistical evidence of the correlation between results of a selection procedure and success in the position for which the selection procedure is used.

V. Statistics May Be Used to Support Disparate Treatment Claims

Statistical evidence has a much more limited role where the issue is disparate treatment of individuals. The typical disparate treatment claim is supported by circumstantial, rather than direct, evidence. Circumstantial evidence may be of several types, most commonly a showing that the plaintiff is a member of a protected group, that the plaintiff suffered adverse employment action, and evidence of a causal connection between the protected group membership and adverse employment action. The limited application of statistical evidence in showing such a causal connection follows from mathematical and practical limitations on statistical evidence.

The treatment of a single individual, whether favorable or unfavorable, often cannot be compared with a sufficient number of similar situations to permit rejection of the "null hypothesis" under normal statistical procedures. Moreover, common sense confirms that a decision maker accused of a biased decision does not calculate or utilize statistical summaries in deciding an adverse employment action. When the crucial issue is the decision maker's motivation, information not available to the decision maker has little or no relevance to the decision maker's motivation.

VI. Limitation of Statistical Evidence

A. Sample Size May Limit the Usefulness of Statistical Analysis

The techniques of statistical inference used in social science depend upon sample sizes sufficiently large for reasonably accurate conclusions to be drawn. Whether the size of a sample is sufficiently large for useful analysis depends upon the issue presented, range of possible outcomes, and the expected frequency with which events may occur. There is no bright line to determine the minimum sample size that might be useful. However, as a general rule, the larger the sample size, the more likely that statistical analysis is to produce a useful result. In general, the courts recognize that expert opinion is necessary to establish the sample is of a sufficient size under the circumstances of a case; and if experts disagree, it is the responsibility of the fact finder to resolve that disagreement.[25]

A thoughtful discussion of the sample size issue appears in *Johnson v. Shreveport Garment Co.*:

> One major problem with the statistical showing at the two plants is the size of the statistical sample from which the Court is asked to draw its inferences. If one accepts the hypothesis that a vast disparity between the number of employed persons in a particular category of an historically underprivileged group (blacks or women) and the number of employed persons in a particular category of an historically favored group (white males) gives rise to an inference that an impermissible bias caused the disparity, as the United States Court of Appeals for the Fifth Circuit has mandated, then a *prima facie* case of unlawful discrimination consists of demonstrating the disparity statistically. However, human reason dictates that many explanations exist for a failure to place a particular person in a particular position. The probability that some other reason than race was the primary motivation in a certain group decreases as the number of persons in the population increases; it increases as the population decreases. Thus, the fewer the persons in the statistical population, the weaker is the inference to be drawn from bare statistics without accompanying testimony. For example, suppose that there are ten persons in an employer's statistical population, all of whom are white. The comparable percentage of blacks in the community population might be 20%. Therefore, the inference could be drawn that in

25. *But see Hagans v. Andrus*, 651 F.2d 622, 627 (9th Cir.), *cert. denied*, 454 U.S. 859 (1981) (rejecting defendant's evidence that one of four employees in a job classification was female because "the size of the sample (four) is much too small to be meaningful").

two employment decisions racial prejudice was the deciding factor. But considering the large number of possible factors in making the decision, the likelihood that race was determinative in two out of two or none out of two decisions is very small. The situation would give rise to a much stronger inference if there were 1,000 persons in the statistical group, 100 of which were black, with a general black population of 20%. While the percentages are greatly more disparate in the first example (0–100% as compared to 10–90%), the chance of random factors entering the decision is much less likely when 100 statistically improper decisions are made than when only two are made.[26]

B. Failure to Account for Relevant Variables May Limit the Usefulness of Statistical Evidence

There are many different measures of statistical correlation, which indicates that two or more quantities are related in some way but does not necessarily indicate that one causes the other. In *Beyond Numeracy*, John Allen Paulos illustrates the difference between correlation and causation with several apparently nonsensical examples:

> Children with bigger feet spell better.
>
> In areas of the South, those counties with higher divorce rates generally have lower death rates.
>
> Nations that add fluoride to their water have a higher cancer rate than those that don't.
>
> * * *
>
> The odd results are easily explained in this way. Children with bigger feet spell better because they are older, their greater age bringing about bigger feet, and not quite so certainly, better spelling. Age is a factor in the next example as well since those couples

26. 422 F. Supp. 526, 539–40 (W.D. La. 1976).

> who are older are less likely to have divorced and more likely to die than are those from counties with younger demographic profiles. And those nations that add fluoride to their water are generally wealthier and more health-conscious and thus, a greater percentage of their citizens live long enough to develop cancer, which is, to a large extent, a disease of old age.[27]

The point that Paulos makes is an essential one for evaluating statistical evidence in litigation. Correlation is often asserted to "prove" causation, even in cases where an unexamined factor affects both of the studied variables. Paulos's examples illustrate the possibility of a mistaken inference of causation that results from the failure to include an important variable.

College admissions, a complex decision process that takes into account high school grades, test scores, extracurricular activities, essays, letters of reference, alumni affiliation, and other factors would be subject to challenge with statistical evidence, but a comparison limited to SAT scores would be misleading and unlikely admissible. Similarly, a comparison of promotions under a labor contract that examined gender as a factor but ignored seniority might show that women are rarely promoted to senior jobs covered by the labor contract, where the basis for the difference in promotion rates is lower seniority rather than employer bias.

In employment litigation, this issue is frequently presented by multiple regression studies. A multiple regression study that omits an important variable may suggest an erroneous conclusion. However, the Supreme Court in *Bazemore v. Friday* dismissed methodological criticisms of multiple regression studies as affecting the weight, but not the admissibility, of the studies:

27. John Allen Paulos, Beyond Numeracy 56–57 (Vintage Books 1991).

> While the omission of variables from a regression analysis may render the analysis less probative than it otherwise might be, it can hardly be said, absent some other infirmity, that an analysis which accounts for the major factors "must be considered unacceptable as evidence of discrimination." . . . Normally, failure to include variables will affect the analysis' probativeness, not its admissibility. . . . [A] regression analysis that includes less than "all measurable variables" may serve to prove a plaintiff's case. . . . Whether, in fact, such a regression analysis does carry the plaintiffs' ultimate burden will depend in a given case on the factual context of each case in light of all the evidence presented by both the plaintiff and the defendant. However, as long as the court may fairly conclude, in light of all the evidence, that it is more likely than not that impermissible discrimination exists, the plaintiff is entitled to prevail.[28]

As discussed below, the acceptance in *Bazemore* of a regression analysis "less probative than it otherwise might be" places a difficult burden on the trial court in its gatekeeper function under Rule 702 of the Federal Rules of Evidence.

C. Inappropriate Aggregation or Disaggregation of Data May Limit the Usefulness of Statistical Analysis

Larger sample sizes generally make it easier to detect real differences, so plaintiffs typically prefer to examine large groups of employees, notwithstanding some dissimilarities within the groups, because the plaintiff's statistical expert is more likely to find a "statistically significant difference" in a larger data set. Conversely, it is usually to the employer's advantage to utilize small samples where, for mathematical reasons, differences are less likely to be "statistically significant." The practical forces pushing plaintiffs to large data sets and driving

28. 478 U.S. 385, 400–01 (1986).

defendants to insist on analysis of small sets or subsets (where real differences in treatment may not be detectable because of sample sizes) may obscure the importance of appropriate comparisons. Useful analysis depends upon reasonable similarities of the decisions of actions being evaluated. Comparing applicants for an entry-level data-entry or keyboarding job with each other makes sense; comparing applicants for the same data-entry job with applicants for jobs as airline pilots does not.

Typical disagreements involve geographic scope, time frame, and whether common decision makers are involved. If the hiring process is uniform in every state for a national employer, combining hiring decisions for analytical purposes may be appropriate. But if different rules are used in California than are used in Massachusetts and Florida, statistical analysis on an employer-wide basis might be inappropriate.

The chapter on statistics in the *Reference Manual on Scientific Evidence* illustrates the importance of appropriate examination of data and how statistical conclusions may result from combining data incorrectly.[29] Suppose that half of applicants to a university's engineering college (both male and female) were accepted, and one quarter of applicants to the university's business college were accepted. Each college admits applicants without regard to gender, but one college admits a higher proportion of applicants (both male and female) than the other. If the data are shown separated by the college to which the individual applied, there does not appear to be any discrimination in admissions:

Admissions by Gender and College				
Engineering			Business	
Decision	Male	Female	Male	Female
Admit	300	100	50	100
Deny	300	100	150	300

29. Reference Manual on Scientific Evidence 233–35 (3d ed., The National Academies Press 2011).

Men and women differ in this example based on the college to which they applied (more men went to engineering, more women went to business), but not in the rate at which they were accepted by the colleges of their choice. However, an illusion of gender discrimination may result if the difference in college choices and the admissions rates of the colleges are omitted, as in this table:

Total University Admissions by Gender

Decision	Male	Female	Total
Admit	350	200	550
Deny	450	400	850
Total	800	600	1400

Combined in this way, it appears that only 200/600 (33 percent) of women are selected, while 350/800 (43.75 percent) of men are selected. In the words of the *Reference Manual on Scientific Evidence*, "This example illustrates a common issue: Association can result from combining heterogeneous statistical material." In this example, the actual difference was in the college choices of the individuals, not the selection decisions of the colleges. Combining data in a way that concealed the effect of the college choice variable gave a misleading suggestion of discrimination.

An early and thoughtful discussion of the complexities of the aggregation issue by the Seventh Circuit in *Coates v. Johnson & Johnson* examined a conflict between the plaintiff's expert, who insisted that "pooling" of decisions from different years was appropriate, and the defendant's expert, who opposed pooling:

> This case illustrates the problems that can arise when experts for each side construct their own analyses using different theories and then factor various variables in or out. Statistical analysis appears to be a science and, when properly and fairly used, it can be of

> great assistance to the factfinder. On the other hand, statistics are so manipulable that some skepticism may be justified when set in the evidentiary context of the whole case. . . . In this case, for example, the two experts reached their parties' desired results, but they relied on different statistical techniques, different definitions of variables, and different statistical tests for pooling. The most apparent consistency between the two experts' testimony was their insistence that the other's study contained serious statistical flaws. Given the large number of disagreements between the experts, we can understand the district court's wariness about the weight to be assigned to these particular statistical studies.[30]

The Seventh Circuit concluded in *Coates* that resolution of the conflict between experts was left to the district court.

If the decision process under examination is changed within the time period during which decisions are examined, combining decisions under a prior process with decisions under the current process may be inappropriate. The Supreme Court considered and rejected such an approach in *Hazelwood School District v. United States*.[31] The court considered a number of statistical issues, including whether hiring decisions made before the Civil Rights Act became effective could be included for statistical analysis of hiring decisions *after* the Civil Rights Act became effective. Such aggregation was improper, because the legal issue was decisions made after the act became effective.

One of the most troublesome disagreements deals with whether analysis should be confined to a limited number of decision makers, or to cases in which a common decision maker was involved. Restricting focus too narrowly risks missing real evidence of bias because a sample size may be too small to confirm bias where it actually exists. On the other hand, different decision makers might lawfully apply

30. 756 F.2d 524, 539 (7th Cir. 1985).
31. 43 U.S. 299 (1977).

different decision-making criteria, and improper aggregation could imply discriminatory decisions where the decisions were based on non-discriminatory application of different criteria.

VII. Defeat Bad Statistics with Better Statistics, or Do Not Come Unarmed to a Gunfight

In the Academy Award-winning Western *The Unforgiven*, Sheriff Little Bill Daggett exclaims in shock to the gunman Will Munny, "You just shot an unarmed man!" The gunman replies, "Well, he should have armed himself." If statistics are an issue in an employment matter, it is dangerous to prepare a defense without appropriate statistical evidence. The plaintiff's statistical evidence may be criticized on many grounds, including errors in the source data, calculation errors, inclusion of irrelevant information, omission of relevant information, lack of practical significance, and bias of the witness. However, most judges are not statisticians,[32] so weak or even flawed statistical testimony may be admitted if there is no countervailing testimony to explain the methodological errors or to rebut inferences that might be drawn.

As the D.C. Circuit noted in *Trout v. Lehman*:

> [T]he most effective way to rebut a statistically based *prima facie* case is to present more accurate statistics. As the Supreme Court has made clear, where "the employer discerns fallacies or deficiencies in the data offered by the plaintiff, he is free to adduce countervailing evidence of his own." . . . But unquantified, speculative, and theoretical objections to the proffered statistics are properly given little weight by the trial court.[33]

32. U.S. District Judge Sam Pointer of the Northern District of Alabama was a notable exception. When Judge Pointer was not satisfied with statistical evidence offered by the parties, he performed his own statistical analyses.

33. 702 F.2d 1094, 1102 (D.C. Cir. 1983), *vacated on other grounds*, 465 U.S. 1056 (1984) (quoting *Dothard v. Rawlinson*, 433 U.S. 321, 331 (1977)). In *Trout*, on remand, the district court again rejected the defendant's statistics, 652 F. Supp. 144 (D.D.C. 1986).

The best defense against statistical evidence will be testimony by a qualified expert for the defense. Although CLE programs and the Internet are replete with experts on statistics, as on every other subject, effective experts should have the following:

- Strong academic credentials
- Prior testimonial experience in similar litigation
- No skeletons in their closets
- Strong oral presentation skills
- Sufficient understanding of the employment issue to place the statistical testimony in context and to withstand cross-examination

The sufficiency of statistical evidence to establish a *prima facie* case, or to create a genuine issue of fact, has long been discussed in appellate decisions regarding acceptance or rejection of statistical testimony in employment cases that arose from summary judgments for defendants or after bench trials before Title VII was amended to allow jury trials. Jury trials, however, present additional issues, including the possible exclusion of evidence as more prejudicial than probative, or as not meeting appropriate standards for scientific evidence.

VIII. The Role of the Trial Court as Gatekeeper, or Shootout at the Daubert Corral

Statistical evidence is properly considered scientific evidence, and Rule 702 of the Federal Rules of Evidence now formally incorporates the trial judge's gatekeeping function as articulated in *Daubert v. Merrill-Dow Pharmaceuticals Inc.*[34] Rule 702 provides the following:

> A witness who is qualified as an expert by knowledge, skill, experience, training, or education may testify in the form of an opinion or otherwise if: (a) the expert's scientific, technical, or other

34. 509 U.S. 592 (1993).

> specialized knowledge will help the trier of fact to understand the evidence or to determine a fact in issue; (b) the testimony is based on sufficient facts or data; (c) the testimony is the product of reliable principles and methods; and (d) the expert has reliably applied the principles and methods to the facts of the case.[35]

The court in *Daubert* noted:

> Faced with a proffer of expert scientific testimony, then, the trial judge must determine at the outset, pursuant to Rule 104(a), whether the expert is proposing to testify to (1) scientific knowledge that (2) will assist the trier of fact to understand or determine a fact in issue. This entails a preliminary assessment of whether the reasoning or methodology underlying the testimony is scientifically valid and of whether that reasoning or methodology properly can be applied to the facts in issue.[36]

The role of the trial court as gatekeeper defined in *Daubert* will frequently place a judge relatively unsophisticated in statistical methodology in the position of determining whether proposed expert-opinion testimony meets "scientific" standards. One tool available to assist the trial court in that function is the use of a court-appointed expert, as was employed in *Reid v. Albemarle Corp.*[37] The district court there rejected the proposed testimony of an expert whose academic credentials and publications did not show sufficient expertise in the issue before the court, and where the court's expert "cast significant doubt as to the reliability" of the conclusions of the plaintiff's expert.[38]

---

35. Fed. R. Evid. 702.
36. 509 U.S. at 592–93.
37. 207 F. Supp. 2d 499 (M.D. La. 2001)
38. *Id.* at 502.

IX. Jurors Are Not Statisticians, So Lawyers Must Make Statistics Understandable

Just as nonphysician jurors routinely consider medical testimony, non-statistician jurors must now evaluate statistical testimony. Perhaps the most vivid example may be the murder trial of O. J. Simpson, in which the prosecution presented evidence based on DNA testing, including testimony that there was a 1 in 170 million match of Simpson's DNA to DNA of a blood spot in the driveway where the crime occurred.[39] The defense relentlessly cross-examined those involved in the DNA testing process, challenging sloppy procedures, possible deliberate or inadvertent contamination, and witness credibility. The jury acquitted Simpson, despite the DNA evidence.

Although the Simpson trial was a criminal trial, and far less grueling cross-examination is likely to be allowed in a typical employment litigation matter, lessons from that case are pertinent. Witnesses may make mistakes in handling evidence, the bias of witnesses may be attacked, and the possibility of error is for the jury to decide.

Appellate decisions do not yet provide much guidance concerning jury charges regarding statistical evidence. However, in *Walther v. Lone Star Gas Company*, the Fifth Circuit considered the following disputed instruction:

> Both plaintiff and defendant have introduced statistics concerning the work force reduction of the defendant company. Statistics may be introduced for the purpose of showing motive, intent or for purpose to discriminate or to demonstrate that they did not exist.
>
> *Statistics alone may establish that the reason defendant discharged the plaintiff was because of* his age. It is for the jury to make the determination of whether they do or do not in this case.[40]

---

39. Julia Wang, *The Blood and DNA Evidence in the O. J. Simpson Trial*, FORENSIC BIOLOGY, *available at* http://www.bxscience.edu/publications/forensics/articles/dna/r-dna02.htm.

40. 952 F.2d 119, 125 (5th Cir. 1992) (emphasis in original).

The employer appellant in *Walther* challenged the specific language that "statistics alone" may establish the reason for the plaintiff's discharge. The Fifth Circuit described the statistical evidence introduced by plaintiff as "far short of the explanatory power necessary to support a finding of discrimination"[41] and acknowledged "the misleading effect of the instruction on statistics"[42] but affirmed a verdict for the plaintiff "[b]ecause the district court's instruction on statistical proof was legally correct, although not factually supported."[43] The Fifth Circuit added that the misleading effect of the instruction on statistics was mitigated by instruction to find facts "in accordance with the preponderance of all the evidence in the case, both direct and circumstantial."[44]

Jury charges for consideration of statistical evidence are not standardized, although there are examples available, including the following from *Federal Employment Jury Instructions*:

> §1:1070 Consideration of Statistics as Evidence
>
> Statistics are one form of evidence from which you may find, but are not required to find, that Plaintiff's sex was a motivating factor in Defendant's decision to [specify adverse employment action]. You should evaluate statistical evidence along with all the other evidence received in the case in deciding whether Plaintiff in this case has proven that Defendant intentionally discriminated against [him/her] because of [his/her] sex.[45]

---

41. *Id.* at 126.
42. *Id.* at 126 n.2.
43. *Id.* at 126.
44. *Id.* at 126 n.2.
45. Todd J. McNamara & J. Alfred Southerland, Federal Employment Jury Instructions (James Publishing, Inc. 2011).

CHAPTER 7
Emotional Injury and Employment Causes of Action

Kerry E. Notestine

Although plaintiffs historically have been able to recover for emotional injury in personal injury and other tort actions, these emotional injury remedies traditionally have not been available in employment actions. Remedies in employment actions were limited to back pay and reinstatement. Changes in statutory law have permitted awards of compensatory and punitive damages, which have led to an increase in the assertion of those remedies. Plaintiffs frequently also allege two types of independent emotional injury claims in employment cases: intentional infliction of emotional distress and negligent infliction of emotional distress. In addition, because emotional distress can be a significant aspect of damages, plaintiffs often pair basic employment actions with state law tort claims that permit the recovery of emotional distress damages. This chapter addresses the substantive claims

---

The author thanks Eve Mantell McFadden, Evelyn Garbett, Sharon Fast, Anissa Crumley Paddock, Ashley Smith Zimmermann, and Jillian Ballard for assistance in drafting this chapter.

that permit the recovery of emotional injury damages and the proof that plaintiffs have used to demonstrate compensable emotional injury.

I. Employment Statutes and Emotional Distress Damages

A. Statutes That Permit Awards of Emotional Distress Damages

1. The Civil Rights Acts of 1866 and 1871, 42 U.S.C. §§ 1981 and 1983

The oldest statutes prohibiting employment discrimination are the Civil Rights Acts of 1866 and 1871, which are codified at 42 U.S.C. §§ 1981 and 1983, respectively. Section 1981 prohibits discrimination based on race in the formation of contracts, including employment relationships. The decision in *Patterson v. McLean Credit Union* limited recovery to claims under these statutes to those involved in hiring and other initial formation of employment contracts.[1] Congress amended the statutes in 1991 to provide that the right to be free from racial discrimination in the making and enforcement of contracts applies to the making, performance, modification, and termination of contracts, as well as the enjoyment of all benefits, privileges, terms, and conditions of the contractual relationship.[2] Section 1983 applies only to state action (typically actions by governmental entities), and § 1981 applies to governmental and private entities; but § 1983 is broader than § 1981 because § 1983 permits recovery by litigants for any violation of the civil rights protected by the Constitution or federal statutes, whereas § 1981 is limited to race and color discrimination in the making and enforcing of contracts.[3]

In *Carey v. Piphus*, the Supreme Court considered the issue of damages available under these statutes and determined the common law

1. 491 U.S. 164, 176–78 (1989).
2. 42 U.S.C. § 1981(b).
3. 42 U.S.C. § 1983.

tort rules regarding damages to be an appropriate starting point.[4] The guiding common law principle behind awarding damages is "that a person should be compensated fairly for injuries caused by the violation of his legal rights."[5] The court explained that "the rules governing compensation for injuries caused by the deprivation of constitutional rights should be tailored to the interests protected by the particular right in question . . ."[6] The court held that mental and emotional distress damages are available under § 1983 with a showing that such injury was actually caused.[7] Thus, the Civil Rights Acts of 1866 and 1871 generally allow recovery of emotional distress damages.

Lower federal courts have applied this principle to employment disputes. For example, in *Bogle v. McClure*, Caucasian librarians brought suit against the public library system for race discrimination under § 1983.[8] The librarians' own testimony was the sole evidence of emotional distress. Generally, the plaintiffs testified that they suffered mental and emotional pain from being transferred from meaningful positions to dead-end, nonmanagerial jobs. They testified that the transfers destroyed their careers and caused some to resign or make workers' compensation claims. The librarians testified that they were depressed, humiliated, upset, embarrassed, and ashamed, and one of them testified she had become suicidal. The jury awarded each librarian $1 million in compensatory damages for emotional harm. The district court remitted the amount to $500,000 per librarian. The appellate court concluded $500,000 per librarian was not an abuse of discretion and affirmed the award.[9]

4. 435 U.S. 247, 257–58 (1978).
5. *Id.* at 257.
6. *Id.* at 259.
7. *Id.* at 264.
8. 332 F.3d 1347 (11th Cir. 2003).
9. 332 F.3d at 1358–59; *see also Kim v. Nash Finch Co.*, 123 F.3d 1046, 1065 (8th Cir. 1997) (finding sufficient evidence of emotional distress and allowing recovery of those damages under § 1981 portion of claim).

Other courts limit compensatory damages awards where the plaintiff is unable to demonstrate sufficient proof. The plaintiff in *Knussman v. Maryland* brought a sex discrimination action under § 1983, claiming the state had violated the Family and Medical Leave Act[10] and the Equal Protection Clause of the United States Constitution.[11] Knussman testified that he had sought professional help after experiencing anxiety, inability to sleep, palpitations, and chest pain. His psychologist presented corroborating medical evidence, stating that he diagnosed Knussman as suffering from both a major depressive disorder and an occupation-related adjustment disorder. Knussman noted he was "particularly disgusted" with the defendant's comments that Knussman could not qualify as a primary caregiver because he could not breastfeed and his wife would have to die or slip into a coma for him to become eligible.[12] The jury awarded Knussman $375,000 for emotional distress damages under the constitutional claim, and Maryland appealed the award as excessive. The Fourth Circuit found that Knussman was entitled to recover some damages for emotional distress; however, because a large portion of Knussman's emotional distress evidence was linked more to the litigation and the general grievance process than to the abridgement of Knussman's statutory and constitutional rights, the appellate court held that the $375,000 award was excessive, vacated it, and remanded for a new trial.[13]

Other courts have denied emotional distress damages altogether. In *Brady v. Fort Bend County*, six plaintiffs alleged they had suffered emotional distress injuries because of their employer's infringement of their First Amendment rights of free speech and association.[14] They brought an action under § 1983. The plaintiffs' own testimony was the sole source of evidence of emotional distress. The first plaintiff testified that

10. 29 U.S.C. §§ 2601–2654.
11. 272 F.3d 625 (4th Cir. 2001).
12. *Id.* at 640.
13. *Id.* at 642.
14. 145 F.3d 691 (5th Cir. 1998), *cert. denied*, 525 U.S. 1105 (1999).

the employer's refusal to hire him had resulted in marital and family problems and his not feeling like the same person. The second plaintiff testified that the employer's failure to rehire him had caused him such sleeplessness, loss of appetite, weight loss, and worry that he would not be able to find another job. The third plaintiff testified that his job loss had produced nervousness, sleeplessness, and anxiety. The fourth plaintiff testified to suffering nervousness, sleeplessness, and stress and being "highly upset" to the extent that he saw a physician. He also expressed concern that his wife would have to quit college to return to work. The fifth plaintiff experienced nervousness and sleeplessness and had to leave home to seek employment, and that was not "fun." The sixth plaintiff testified that he had gained 100 pounds, worried about job prospects at his age, and was "shocked and devastated." The lower court awarded compensatory damages for emotional distress to each plaintiff in an amount ranging from $10,000 to $25,000.[15] Fort Bend County appealed. The appellate court found it remarkable that "not one plaintiff presented medical or psychological expert testimony as to the emotional harm that was purportedly suffered," nor did any plaintiff present corroborating testimony.[16] In addition, the plaintiffs' testimony was elicited through leading questions, further weakening the testimony.[17] The *Brady* court held that this testimony was too vague and conclusory to support mental anguish damages.[18]

In *Price v. City of Charlotte*, the plaintiffs similarly brought a claim against the city under § 1983 for violating the equal protection clause.[19] The plaintiffs testified that they had been humiliated, betrayed, and deceived by the city. They had allegedly suffered ignominy as a result of the city's discriminatory promotions policy. Though the lower court sustained the jury's $3,000 award to each of the seven plaintiffs for

15. *Id.* at 697 n.1.
16. *Id.* at 719.
17. *Id.* at 720.
18. *Id.*
19. 93 F.3d 1241 (4th Cir. 1996), *cert. denied*, 520 U.S. 1116 (1997).

emotional distress damages, the Fourth Circuit Court of Appeals reversed the award, finding the plaintiffs' testimony, which was the sole evidence of emotional distress, was too vague and conclusory.[20] Thus, the federal courts have evaluated evidence of emotional distress based on the requirement in *Carey v. Piphus* that compensatory damages for emotional distress must be supported by competent evidence concerning an actual injury.[21] Plaintiffs must present evidence of particularized injury to recover emotional distress damages, and corroborating testimony from lay and expert witnesses often assists in this proof.

Similar issues of proof arise when courts evaluate emotional distress evidence presented in cases alleging violations of other statutes permitting emotional distress damages.

Next is the evaluation of statutes that permit recovery of emotional distress damages and statutes that do not permit recovery of emotional distress damages. The section concludes with a summary of the principles developed in the cases addressing recovery for emotional distress.

2. Title VII of the Civil Rights Act of 1964

Title VII of the Civil Rights Act of 1964 prohibits adverse employment actions based on race, religion, color, creed, gender, and national origin.[22] When originally enacted, Title VII permitted only equitable relief in the form of back pay and reinstatement. The statute further did not allow juries to decide the facts of the case. The Civil Rights Act of 1991[23] changed this by providing for jury trials and awards of compensatory and punitive damages for violation of Title VII as well

---

20. 93 F.3d at 1257; *see also Ernie Haire Ford, Inc. v. Atkinson*, 64 So.3d 131 (Fla. Dist. Ct. App. 2011) (finding the award of $3,579,661 for past and future pain and suffering could not stand because plaintiff failed to present any evidence that he sustained a physical injury or medical proof of his alleged emotional pain and suffering stemming from the age bias he was subjected to by the defendant).

21. 435 U.S. at 264 n.20.

22. 42 U.S.C. § 2000e *et seq.*

23. Civil Rights Act of 1991, Pub. L. No. 102-166, 105 Stat. 1071.

as the Americans with Disabilities Act[24] and the Rehabilitation Act.[25] The statute places caps on compensatory and punitive damages based on the size of the employer.[26] The cap is for both compensatory and punitive damages, so it would be possible to recover the entire amount of the cap in emotional distress damages.

To recover compensatory damages under a Title VII cause of action, the plaintiff must demonstrate intentional discrimination.[27] To prove discrimination, an individual must establish a connection between the employment condition or decision and a prohibited basis (such as race or sex). Such a connection may be established by pointing to individual instances of different or disparate treatment based on prohibited criteria. Discrimination may be proved by direct evidence (such as an acknowledgment of discriminatory intent), or indirect or circumstantial evidence.[28]

The Equal Employment Opportunity Commission (EEOC) has issued an Enforcement Guidance on compensatory and punitive damages available under the Civil Rights Act of 1991.[29] In this Enforcement Guidance, the EEOC states that emotional harm will not be presumed simply because the complaining party is a victim of discrimination.

The EEOC requires actual proof of emotional harm, manifested by such symptoms as sleeplessness, anxiety, stress, depression, marital strain, humiliation, emotional distress, loss of self-esteem, excessive fatigue, or a nervous breakdown. Although the EEOC states that emotional distress may be established solely by a claimant's own testimony,

---

24. 42 U.S.C. § 12101 *et seq.*

25. 29 U.S.C. § 701 *et seq.*

26. The caps are $50,000 for employers with 15 to 100 employees, $100,000 for employers with 101 to 200 employees, $200,000 for employers with 201 to 500 employees, and $300,000 for employers with 501 or more employees. 42 U.S.C. § 1981a(b)(3).

27. 42 U.S.C. § 1981a(a)(1).

28. *Logan v. Kautex Textron N. Am.*, 259 F.3d 635, 638–39 (7th Cir. 2001).

29. U.S. Equal Employment Opportunity Commission, Enforcement Guidance No. 915.002: Compensatory and Punitive Damages Available under § 102 of the Civil Rights Act of 1991 (1992) [hereinafter EEOC Guidance], *available at* http://www.eeoc.gov/policy/docs/damages.html.

the commission "typically require[s] medical evidence of emotional harm to seek damages for such harm."[30] Recognizing that damage "awards for emotional harm vary significantly and there are no definitive rules governing the amounts to be awarded," the EEOC's position is that damages for emotional harm should be "based on a consideration of the severity of harm and the time that the complaining party has suffered from the emotional harm."[31] The cases generally have followed this same approach in evaluating emotional distress awards based on findings of unlawful discrimination under Title VII.

Most recently, in *Lore v. City of Syracuse*, the Second Circuit upheld a $150,000 jury award for pain, suffering, and emotional distress.[32] Lore claimed employment discrimination and retaliation under Title VII against a city police officer. She also asserted intentional infliction of emotional distress and defamation. Lore claimed that she had been deprived of her police vehicle, beeper, cell phone, and opportunities for overtime and other benefits. She also alleged receiving threatening messages on her answering machine. The jury found the defendant had made negative comments about Lore to the news media, that defendant was aware at the time that she had filed an EEOC complaint, and that the comments constituted a materially adverse employment action. The court upheld jury awards against the city of $100,000 for reputational injury and $150,000 for emotional distress. Moreover, the Second Circuit found, given that the damaging publicity the defendant generated with his "retaliatory conduct," and the evidence that Lore seemed near a nervous breakdown and was being treated for depression, the district court's refusal to order remittitur was not an abuse of discretion. EEOC guidelines state that damages are available for emotional harm and other nonpecuniary losses, such as injury to professional standing and injury to character and reputation.[33] The city argued that the

30. *Id.* § II.A.2.
31. *Id.*
32. *Lore v. City of Syracuse*, 670 F.3d 127 (2d Cir. 2012).
33. *See* EEOC GUIDANCE, *supra* note 29.

appeals court should order a new trial limited to damages or a new trial unless the plaintiff agreed to accept a reduction of the emotional distress damages from $150,000 to $15,000. The court disagreed and found that the city's arguments against excess damages for emotional distress presented no basis for disturbing the judgment.

In *Thomas v. Texas Department of Criminal Justice*, the plaintiff sued her employer for alleged violations of Title VII.[34] Thomas testified to severe emotional distress, weeping while on the stand. She testified that "it hurt, it hurt" and that she was depressed, could not sleep, suffered from nausea, contemplated death, and took antidepressants. After the employer denied Thomas a promotion and retaliated against her, she felt tearful, like a failure, isolated from her coworkers, and helpless. In addition, other witnesses, including her sister, brother, a coworker, and a friend, corroborated the severity of the Thomas's distress. Regarding future emotional harm, Thomas testified that she was still angry and fearful that the lawsuit would bar her from future promotion. Thomas continued to suffer from a heart condition, fatigue, and everyday stress. Moreover, according to her sister, Thomas still had mood swings that made her melancholy and not herself. The Fifth Circuit found that Thomas presented "convincing and substantial evidence of emotional damages" and affirmed the $30,000 award for past emotional distress.[35] The *Thomas* court, however, ordered the award for $100,000 in future emotional distress to be reduced to $75,000.[36]

In one of the largest gender discrimination verdicts ever, *Velez v. Novartis Pharmaceuticals Corp.*, the jury found the company liable for sex discrimination against a nationwide class of female representatives.[37] The case was a class action lawsuit alleging gender-based discrimination against a large pharmaceutical company under Title VII.

34. 297 F.3d 361 (5th Cir. 2002).

35. *Id.* at 371.

36. *Id.* at 372.

37. *Velez v. Novartis Pharms Corp.*, No. 04 Civ. 09194, 2010 WL 4877852 (S.D.N.Y. Nov. 30, 2010).

The plaintiffs alleged that managers of the company made damaging statements, reflecting an antifemale work environment. The plaintiffs elicited testimony from current and former employees who described sexual harassment and a hostile work environment for women. Novartis tried to rebut the evidence with testimony from a number of women who had enjoyed successful careers at the company. Nonetheless, the jury imposed an exceptionally large damages award on the company, awarding $3.4 million in compensatory damages and $250 million in punitive damages. Specifically, the jury awarded twelve testifying plaintiffs $3.4 million for emotional damages. The damages paid to the testifying plaintiffs were for pain and suffering and loss of enjoyment. Subsequent settlement negotiations resulted in a claims process limiting compensatory and punitive damages under the statutory caps per person.

The plaintiff in *Salinas v. O'Neill*, in support of his Title VII claim for emotional distress, testified in detail to paranoia regarding future retaliation, multiple (over seventy) physician visits, and deteriorating relations with his wife and son.[38] Salinas offered particular manifestations of his emotional harm and health problems, and his wife corroborated with specifics. The jury awarded Salinas compensatory damages for emotional distress of $1 million. The trial court reduced the award to $300,000 and the court of appeals considered whether even the reduced award was excessive.[39] The Fifth Circuit further reduced the emotional distress award to $150,000 after a comparison with other emotional damage awards in the Fifth Circuit.[40]

Courts, however, will deny emotional distress damages if the plaintiff is unable to adduce particularized proof of emotional distress. In *Dennis v. Columbia Colleton Med. Ctr., Inc.*, the plaintiff claimed to have suffered emotional distress as a result of being denied a promotion

38. 286 F.3d 827 (5th Cir. 2002).
39. 286 F.3d at 829.
40. 286 F.3d at 833.

based on her gender.[41] The plaintiff testified at trial that she was "devastated" and "humiliated," even explaining the reasons she felt that way. As a result of purportedly having to leave the company because she had not been promoted, she allegedly had to take on multiple jobs and had less time with her children. The appellate court agreed with the trial court that the plaintiff presented no demonstrable evidence of distress, such as testimony of a physician, symptoms, or a physician's diagnosis. Because the distress seemed to relate to the plaintiff's decision to leave the company, and not the company's failure to promote, the Fourth Circuit affirmed the denial of any emotional distress damages.[42]

In addition to a plaintiff's own testimony and the testimony of family and friends who can support the claim of emotional distress, expert witnesses are often used to bolster claims for emotional distress. For example, in *Keenan v. City of Philadelphia*, the Third Circuit reviewed a jury verdict awarding $640,000 in compensatory damages for five plaintiffs.[43] The court noted, "[b]eyond the lay testimony, Dr. Robert Sadoff, an expert witness, stated that each plaintiff suffered emotional stress related to the [employment action]" and "[a]n actuary-economist, David Bunin, calculated plaintiff's economic losses which alone exceeded the jury's compensatory awards for each plaintiff."[44] Based on this testimony, the *Keenan* court affirmed, stating, "we cannot conclude that the compensatory damages were so grossly excessive as to shock our judicial conscience."[45]

3. Americans with Disabilities Act

The Americans with Disabilities Act (ADA)[46] prohibits discrimination against qualified individuals with a disability. This term is defined in

41. 290 F.3d 639 (4th Cir. 2002).
42. *Id.* at 653.
43. 983 F.2d 459, 469 (3d Cir. 1992).
44. *Id.*
45. *Id.*
46. 42 U.S.C. § 12101 *et seq.*

the act as a person with a disability who, with or without reasonable accommodation, can perform the essential functions of the job in question. The ADA goes beyond merely prohibiting discrimination based on a disability. The employer must reasonably accommodate an individual with a disability. The duty to make reasonable accommodations applies to all aspects of employment. Reasonable accommodation, according to the act, means any accommodation that the employer can adopt without undue hardship. Damages under the ADA are similar to damages under Title VII. Successful plaintiffs can recover back pay, front pay, and compensatory and punitive damages.[47] Like Title VII, an award of compensatory and punitive damages under the ADA is capped based on the size of the employer.[48]

The jury in *Giles v. Gen. Elec. Co.* awarded the plaintiff $400,000 in compensatory damages and $800,000 in punitive damages.[49] The court limited these damages to $300,000 in compliance with the statutory cap.[50] GE appealed the verdict, complaining that the evidence was insufficient to support the emotional distress award. Giles testified at trial that he had trouble sleeping, suffered headaches and marital problems, and had lost prestige and social connections as a result of losing his position at GE. His coworker testified that he appeared "despondent, depressed, down and absolutely utterly discouraged about not being able to come back to work." There were no other damages witnesses. After reviewing the evidence, the appellate court determined that a

47. One court has ruled that the Civil Rights Act of 1991 applies only to claims of unlawful discrimination and failure to reasonably accommodate brought under 42 U.S.C. § 12112 or § 12112(b)(5); emotional distress and other damages permitted by the 1991 act do not apply to retaliation claims that are covered by 42 U.S.C. § 12203. *See Kramer v. Banc of Am. Secs., LLC*, 355 F.3d 961, 964 (7th Cir. 2004); *see also Alvarado v. Cajun Operating Co.*, 588 F.3d 1261, 1269–70 (9th Cir. 2009) (ruling that based upon the plain language of the ADA, compensatory and punitive damages are not available to plaintiffs claiming retaliation under the ADA; instead, only so-called "equitable relief," such as reinstatement, back pay, or front pay, are available to persons claiming retaliation under the ADA).

48. 42 U.S.C. § 1981a(a)(2), (b)(3).

49. 245 F.3d 474 (5th Cir. 2001).

50. 42 U.S.C. § 1981a(b)(3)(D).

reasonable jury would award no more than $100,000 for emotional distress. However, to avoid substituting its judgment for the jury's, the court augmented the maximum recovery amount by 50 percent, reduced the compensatory damages award to $150,000, and gave the plaintiff the option of a new trial if he did not accept the remittance.[51]

Less specificity about the details of the emotional distress generally results in a smaller damage award. For example, in *Foster v. Time Warner Entm't Co.* the jury awarded the complainant $75,000 in emotional distress damages based on her ADA retaliation claim.[52] To prove emotional distress damages, Foster presented her husband's testimony that she had become withdrawn, could not eat, and experienced back pain, muscle stress, and stomach problems. Foster herself testified that she was devastated by being accused of collusion and terminated, that she withdrew, and that she feared she would not be able to find another job. The appellate court found this evidence sufficient to sustain the $75,000 award for emotional distress.[53]

Similarly, in *Webner v. Titan Distrib., Inc.*, the jury awarded Webner $12,500 for emotional distress damages in his ADA suit against his employer.[54] Webner's testimony was the sole basis for the award. He testified that his discriminatory job loss emotionally devastated him, made him feel "empty," like he had lost his best friend, and as if there were a "hole in his chest." He also described a fear (inability to pay his bills) and frustration based on being unable to find a job for six months. The Eighth Circuit upheld the award, finding that Webner's testimony was sufficient to support the $12,500 award.[55]

Most recently, in *Soliday v. 7-Eleven Inc.*, a federal jury awarded a deaf former manager of the 7-Eleven convenience store chain $934,000 in damages, $756,000 of which was compensatory damages for

51. 245 F.3d at 488.
52. 250 F.3d 1189 (8th Cir. 2001).
53. 250 F.3d at 1196.
54. 267 F.3d 828 (8th Cir. 2001).
55. *Id.* at 836–37.

emotional pain and mental anguish.[56] Soliday, who had worked for the company for twenty-six years, was terminated when the company would not reasonably accommodate his disability. In particular, the court noted that a new manager refused to replace the fax machine or provide a pager so Soliday could communicate with other managers. Under Florida law, the court has discretion to determine appropriate damages, thus explaining the large emotional distress award.

4. The Rehabilitation Act of 1973

Finally, the Rehabilitation Act[57] allows recovery of compensatory damages in certain cases. The Rehabilitation Act prohibits discrimination on the basis of disability in employment decisions by the federal government and federal contractors.[58] Title VII again provides the remedies for the relevant portion of the Rehabilitation Act.[59] The Civil Rights Act of 1991 also extends the availability of nonpecuniary damages under the Rehabilitation Act where unlawful, intentional discrimination is found, or where the respondent violates the regulations implemented concerning reasonable accommodations.[60] Damages awarded under this section are subject to the monetary caps in § 1981a(b)(3).

B. Federal Statutes That Do Not Provide for Emotional Distress Damage

1. The Fair Labor Standards Act and Equal Pay Act

The Fair Labor Standards Act (FLSA)[61] requires employers to provide additional compensation to "non-exempt" employees for work beyond forty hours a week and to pay at least a minimum wage.[62] The FLSA

56. *Soliday v. 7-Eleven, Inc.*, No. 2:09-CV-807-FtM-29SPC, 2010 WL 3928586 (M.D. Fla. Oct. 4, 2010).
57. 29 U.S.C. § 701 *et seq.*
58. 29 U.S.C. §§ 791, 793–794.
59. 29 U.S.C. § 794a(a)(1).
60. 42 U.S.C. § 1981a(a)(2).
61. 29 U.S.C. § 201 *et seq.*
62. 29 U.S.C. §§ 206, 207.

also prohibits retaliation for engaging in certain protected rights under the statute[63] and includes the Equal Pay Act, which prohibits pay discrepancies based on sex.[64] For violation of the minimum wage and overtime provisions of the FLSA, plaintiffs can recover unpaid wages, unpaid overtime, and an additional equal amount as liquidated damages.[65] According to the Supreme Court in *Brooklyn Savings Bank v. O'Neil*, liquidated damages are not penal in nature; rather, they are "compensation for retention of a workman's pay which might result in damages too obscure and difficult of proof for estimate other than by liquidated damages."[66] Because liquidated damages are available under the FLSA, nonpecuniary damages are not recoverable for violations of § 206 or § 207 of the FLSA.

The remedies available for retaliation are broader.[67] More specifically, they include "such legal or equitable relief as may be appropriate to effectuate the purposes of section 215(a)(3) of this title, including without limitation employment, reinstatement, promotion, and the payment of wages lost and an additional equal amount as liquidated damages."[68] Three appellate courts have addressed whether additional damages are available for violation of the FLSA's antiretaliation provisions. The Seventh Circuit held in *Travis v. Gary Community Mental Health Center, Inc.*, that "legal" relief language included compensatory and punitive damages.[69] The court noted, "[c]ompensation for emotional distress, and punitive damages, are appropriate for intentional torts such as retaliatory discharge."[70] The Ninth Circuit affirmed a compensatory damages award for retaliation in *Lambert v. Ackerley*.[71]

63. 29 U.S.C. § 215(a)(3).
64. 29 U.S.C. § 206(d).
65. 29 U.S.C. § 216(b).
66. 324 U.S. 697, 707 (1945).
67. 29 U.S.C. §§ 216(b), 215(a)(3).
68. 29 U.S.C. § 216(b).
69. 921 F.2d 108, 111–12 (7th Cir. 1990), *cert. denied*, 502 U.S. 812 (1991).
70. 921 F.2d at 111; *see also* 29 U.S.C. § 216(b).
71. 180 F.3d 997 (9th Cir. 1999), *cert. denied*, 528 U.S. 1116 (2000).

However, the court was not able to address the issue directly because the appellant failed to challenge the availability of the damages and only argued that they were excessive.[72] The Eleventh Circuit, in *Snapp v. Unlimited Concepts, Inc.*, disagreed with the *Travis* decision regarding the availability of punitive damages.[73] It did, however, permit recovery of compensatory damages for retaliation.

2. The Age Discrimination in Employment Act

The Age Discrimination in Employment Act (ADEA)[74] prohibits employment discrimination based on age.[75] The remedial provision procedures of the FLSA, with some noted exceptions,[76] apply to ADEA actions. The ADEA enforcement statute provides in pertinent part:

> Amounts owing to a person as a result of a violation of this chapter shall be deemed to be unpaid minimum wages or unpaid overtime compensation for purposes of sections 216 and 217 of this title: *Provided,* that liquidated damages shall be payable only in cases of willful violations of this chapter. In any action brought to enforce this chapter the court shall have jurisdiction to grant such legal or equitable relief as may be appropriate to effectuate the purposes of this chapter, including without limitation judgments compelling employment, reinstatement or promotion, or enforcing liability for amounts deemed to be unpaid minimum wages or unpaid overtime compensation under this section . . .[77]

---

72. It is interesting to note that the appellant did challenge the availability of punitive damages under the FLSA for retaliation. The *Lambert* court noted that only the Seventh Circuit in *Travis* had specifically addressed this issue and found punitive damages were available. The Ninth Circuit found the reasoning in *Travis* persuasive. 180 F.3d at 1011.

73. 208 F.3d 928, 934 (11th Cir. 2000), *cert. denied*, 532 U.S. 975 (2001).

74. 29 U.S.C. § 621 *et seq.*

75. 29 U.S.C. § 623.

76. 29 U.S.C. § 626(b).

77. *Id.* (emphasis in original).

Accordingly, § 626(b) authorizes damages for ADEA violations as if the employer had failed to pay overtime. It does not utilize the FLSA's antiretaliation provisions. Thus, neither punitive nor compensatory damages appear to be available.

The ADEA, however, also states that "the court shall have jurisdiction to grant such legal or equitable relief as may be appropriate to effectuate the purposes of this chapter, including without limitation judgments compelling employment, reinstatement or promotion, or enforcing liability for amounts deemed to be unpaid minimum wages or unpaid overtime compensation under this section."[78] Nevertheless, the circuit courts have unanimously held that the ADEA does not permit recovery of compensatory damages.[79] In addition, the Supreme Court acknowledged in *Commissioner of Internal Revenue v. Schleier* that despite the broad remedial mechanism in the ADEA, "the Courts of Appeals have unanimously held, and the respondent does not contest, that the ADEA does not permit a separate recovery of compensatory damages for pain and suffering or emotional distress."[80]

The Seventh Circuit held recently that a former sales manager could not recover on his age discrimination claim because his only possible remedy—front pay—was barred by his failure to link the alleged discrimination to the disability that prevented his reinstatement.[81] The appellant, who had a history of anxiety attacks, sought the award for front pay in an action for age discrimination and retaliation after the second of two psychological breakdowns he experienced while working as a sales training manager left him totally disabled. The Seventh Circuit disagreed with the district court's conclusion that front pay is

78. *Id.*

79. *Perrell v. Finance America Corp.*, 726 F.2d 654, 657 (10th Cir. 1984); *Fiedler v. Indianhead Truck Line, Inc.*, 670 F.2d 806, 809 (8th Cir. 1982); *Vazquez v. Eastern Air Lines, Inc.*, 579 F.2d 107 (1st Cir. 1978); *Naton v. Bank of California*, 649 F.2d 691, 699 (9th Cir. 1981); *Hill v. Spiegel, Inc.*, 708 F.2d 233, 235 (6th Cir. 1983); *Pfeiffer v. Essex Wire Corp.*, 682 F.2d 684, 686 (7th Cir. 1982), *cert. denied*, 459 U.S. 1039 (1982).

80. 515 U.S. 323, 326 (1995).

81. *Barton v. Zimmer Inc.*, 662 F.3d 448, 455 (7th Cir. 2011).

unavailable as a matter of law because it would amount to an award of compensatory damages for an emotional injury, which is not permitted under the ADEA. The court agreed that a front-pay award is not categorically available as a compensatory-damages remedy for an emotional injury under the ADEA's equitable remedies provision. Nonetheless, the court opined that the U.S. Supreme Court has found that front pay under Title VII is not classified as a compensatory-damages remedy under Title VII when reinstatement is impossible due to psychological injuries suffered as a result of discrimination.[82] But, even if the award were available, the plaintiff in *Barton* was unable to establish causation because his disability was caused by assignments for his new supervisor, not the previous supervisor, who had discriminated against him.

The ADEA, like the FLSA, prohibits retaliation.[83] Unlike the FLSA, the ADEA does not include a separate enforcement provision for retaliation.[84] Thus, the same types of damages are available for substantive and retaliation claims under the ADEA. Accordingly, compensatory damages are generally not recoverable under the ADEA.

3. The Family and Medical Leave Act

The Family and Medical Leave Act (FMLA)[85] prohibits employers from both interfering with an employee's right to take FMLA leave and discriminating against employees for opposing the employer's prohibited actions under the act.[86] In addition, the FMLA contains an

---

82. *Pollard v. E. I. du Pont de Nemours & Co.*, 532 U.S. 843, 846 (2001) (holding that front pay under Title VII is *not* properly classified as compensatory-damages remedy and therefore not subject to Title VII's compensatory-damages cap; front pay might be an appropriate equitable remedy where "reinstatement is not viable because of continuing hostility between the plaintiff and the employer or its workers, or because of psychological injuries suffered by the plaintiff as a result of the discrimination").

83. 29 U.S.C. § 623(d).

84. *Compare* 29 U.S.C. § 626(b), *with* 29 U.S.C. § 216(b).

85. 29 U.S.C. § 2601 *et seq.*

86. 29 U.S.C. § 2615(a).

antiretaliation provision.[87] The enforcement provision of the FMLA allows for recovery of damages of any wages, salary, employment benefits, or other compensation lost by reason of the FMLA violation.[88] Alternatively, if none of the above damages are found, any actual monetary losses sustained by the employee as a direct result of the violation up to a sum equal to twelve weeks of wages or salary may be available. Like the ADEA and the FLSA, liquidated damages are available under the FMLA for the sum equal to the amount of damages calculated.[89] Compensatory damages, accordingly, do not appear to be recoverable under the FMLA.

4. *The National Labor Relations Act*

The National Labor Relations Act (NLRA) prohibits unfair labor practices.[90] The National Labor Relations Board enforces the NLRA.[91] Where a violation is found, remedies available include reinstatement of employment and back pay.[92] Neither compensatory nor nonpecuniary damages are available under the NLRA.

C. Proof Necessary to Establish a Right to Compensatory Damages for Statutory Employment Claims

The cases cited above demonstrate that the courts have not established a structured format for the level of proof needed for compensatory damages. However, appellate courts have consistently evaluated awards for emotional distress, using some general principles derived from the Supreme Court's statement in *Carey v. Piphus* that a plaintiff must demonstrate actual injury as a result of the violation of the statute.[93] The

87. 29 U.S.C. § 2615(b).
88. 29 U.S.C. § 2617(a)(1).
89. *Id.*
90. 29 U.S.C. §§ 151–169.
91. 29 U.S.C. § 160(a).
92. 29 U.S.C. § 160(c).
93. *Carey v. Piphus*, 435 U.S. 247, 263 (1978) (addressing compensatory damages for a § 1983 claim).

Fifth Circuit, in *Brady v. Fort Bend County*, elaborated on the *Carey* holding and provided a good summary of principles related to proving/negating emotional distress injuries.[94]

To prove a claim for mental damages, there must be a "specific discernable injury to the claimant's emotional state."[95] The injury should be proven with evidence regarding the nature and extent of the harm.[96] However, "hurt feelings, anger and frustration are part of life and are not the types of harm that could support a mental anguish award."[97] Moreover, conclusory statements of emotional distress and the mere fact of a constitutional violation are insufficient to support an award of compensatory damages.[98] Furthermore, because emotional distress is fraught with vagueness and speculation, the *Brady* court noted that claims of emotional distress are easily susceptible to fictitious and trivial claims.[99]

A claimant's testimony alone, nevertheless, may at times be insufficient to show the injury.[100] Courts, accordingly, "scrupulously analyze an award of compensatory damages for a claim of emotional distress predicated exclusively on the plaintiff's testimony."[101]

Corroborating testimony or medical or psychological evidence may be necessary to prove the injury.[102] However, if the plaintiff's testimony

94. 145 F.3d 691, 718–20.

95. *Id.* at 718 (quoting *Patterson v. P.H.P Healthcare Corp.*, 90 F.3d 927, 940 (5th Cir. 1996)), *cert. denied*, 519 U.S. 1091 (1997), *abrogated on other grounds by*).

96. *Id.*

97. *Id.*

98. *Id.*

99. *Id.* at 719.

100. *Id.* at 718.

101. *Price v. City of Charlotte, N.C.*, 93 F.3d 1241, 1251 (4th Cir. 1996), *cert. denied*, 520 U.S. 1116 (1997); *see also Sloane v. Equifax Information Services, Inc.*, 510 F.3d 495, 503 (4th Cir. 2007) (stating a plaintiff is required to reasonably and sufficiently explain the circumstances of the injury and not resort to mere conclusory statements; the court will distinguish between plaintiff testimony that amounts only to conclusory statements and plaintiff testimony that sufficiently articulates true demonstrable emotional distress).

102. *Brady*, 145 F.3d at 718.

is "particularized and extensive, such that it speaks to the nature, extent, and duration of the claimed emotional harm in a manner that portrays a specific and discernable injury, then that testimony alone may be sufficient."[103] Moreover, a court may require less evidence of damages when the deprivation of a substantial right is evident.[104] The cases cited above provide some examples of the evidence that the courts have considered sufficient and insufficient to support claims of emotional distress under federal employment statutes.

The scope of this chapter does not allow an analysis of state statutes prohibiting discrimination in employment, but many states have such statutes that permit the recovery of emotional distress damages. In general, those statutes follow the principles used with the federal statutes, although practitioners must be mindful of differences between state statutes and similar federal laws. We now turn to another issue of state law: the recovery of emotional distress damages under nonstatutory claims.

II. Emotional Injury in the Context of State Law and Employment-Related Claims

There has been a steady increase in new tort claims and causes of actions in connection with wrongful discharge over the last several years. The claims that an employer can expect to face when a former employee complains of a discharge include wrongful discharge, tortious interference with a contract, defamation, and intentional and negligent infliction of emotional distress. It is important to understand the type of conduct that underlies such claims and recognize the liabilities that can result from them.

---

103. *Id.* at 720.

104. *Foster v. MCI Telecommunications Corp.*, 773 F.2d 1116, 1120–21 (10th Cir. 1985), *abrogated on other grounds by Branson v. Price River Coal Co.*, 853 F.2d 768, 771 n.6 (10th Cir. 1998).

A. Independent Claims for Emotional Distress: Intentional and Negligent Infliction of Emotional Distress

To avoid the statutory caps placed on compensatory and punitive damages in cases involving federal employment statutes, many plaintiffs assert claims for intentional and negligent infliction of emotional distress. The elements for the tort of intentional infliction of emotional distress vary from state to state, but most follow the general provisions detailed in the Restatement (Second) of Torts, which provides:

> One who by extreme and outrageous conduct intentionally or recklessly causes severe emotional distress to another is subject to liability for such emotional distress, and if bodily harm to the other results from it, for such bodily harm.[105]

The elements of proof generally are: (1) the defendant intended to inflict emotional distress or recklessly disregarded whether its acts would result in the infliction of emotional distress; (2) the acts caused severe emotional distress; and (3) the acts constituted outrageous and extreme conduct.[106]

The intent element refers to the defendant's intent to cause severe emotional distress rather than intentionally acting in a way that causes severe emotional distress.[107] Thus, intent to terminate typically would not be sufficient for this claim. Probably the most addressed element of this claim is the requirement of "outrageous" conduct.[108] Courts also reference the Restatement standard for outrageous conduct:[109]

---

105. Restatement (Second) of Torts § 46(1).

106. *McGanty v. Staudenraus*, 901 P.2d 841, 849 (Or. 1995); *ComSouth Teleservices, Inc. v. Liggett*, 531 S.E.2d 190, 191 (Ga. Ct. App. 2000); *Benitez v. KFC Nat'l Mgmt. Co.*, 714 N.E.2d 1002, 1006 (Ill. App. Ct. 1999).

107. *McGanty v. Staudenraus*, 901 P.2d 841, 849 (Or. 1995).

108. *See, e.g.*, *Petyan v. Ellis*, 200 Conn. 243, 254 n.5 (1986)

109. *Wilson v. Monarch Paper Co.*, 939 F.2d 1138, 1143 (5th Cir. 1991) (citing *Dean v. Ford Motor Credit Co.*, 885 F.2d 300, 306 (5th Cir. 1989)).

> Liability has been found only where the conduct has been so outrageous in character, and so extreme in degree, as to go beyond all possible bounds of decency, and to be regarded as atrocious, and utterly intolerable in a civilized community. Generally, the case is one in which the recitation of the facts to an average member of the community would arouse his resentment against the actor, and lead him to exclaim, "Outrageous!" . . . The liability clearly does not extend to mere insults, indignities, threats, annoyances, petty oppression, or other trivialities.[110]

The elements of outrageous conduct and severe emotional distress are mirror images of each other. One would not expect severe emotional distress without outrageous conduct. Thus, some states have defined conduct as extreme and outrageous when it results naturally in intense humiliation, embarrassment, or fright.[111] Outrageous conduct is that which is beyond the bounds of socially tolerable conduct: "[T]he tort does not provide recovery for the kind of temporary annoyance or injured feelings that can result from friction and rudeness among people in day-to-day life . . . [s]imilarly, insults, harsh or intimidating words, or rude behavior ordinarily do not result in liability."[112]

The employer-employee relationship is a relevant factor in determining whether conduct is outrageous. Often, employers have a higher duty than strangers to avoid inflicting emotional distress.[113] But criticism of an employee's job performance, abrasive interrogations, unjustified reprimands, opposition to unemployment benefits, excess supervision, or negative evaluations alone do not constitute conduct beyond the bounds of socially acceptable behavior.[114] Similarly, the emotional distress that

---

110. Restatement (Second) of Torts § 46 cmt. d.

111. *Moses v. Prudential Ins. Co.*, 369 S.E. 2d 541, 543 (Ga. 1988).

112. *Hall v. May Dep't Stores Co.*, 637 P.2d 126, 129 (Or. 1981), *abrogated on other grounds by McGanty v. Staudenraus*, 901 P.2d 841 (Or. 1995).

113. *Id.* at 130.

114. *See, e.g.*, *Ali v. Douglas Cable Commc'ns*, 929 F. Supp. 1362 (D. Kan. 1996) (monitoring employees' calls at work and terminating employees in retaliation for their

usually results from a termination of employment is not sufficient to support a claim of intentional infliction of emotional distress.[115]

Because this tort requires a showing of severe emotional distress based on outrageous conduct, emotional distress awards can be significant. For example, in *Wilson v. Monarch Paper Co.*, the plaintiff prevailed in his claims of age discrimination and intentional infliction of emotional distress.[116] The Fifth Circuit affirmed the trial court's judgment for the plaintiff, citing, among other facts, that the employer had stripped the plaintiff of his job duties and demoted him from an executive position to a warehouse supervisor. This job required him to sweep floors in the warehouse and clean up after employees in the cafeteria. The court indicated that the "degrading and humiliating" way the employer treated him in an apparent effort to get him to quit justified the damage award, which included approximately $622,000 in past emotional distress, $225,000 in future emotional distress, and $2.25 million in punitive damages. The court determined that the defendant's actions were beyond the realm of an ordinary dispute and were outrageous conduct. The plaintiff presented evidence that the employer's treatment had caused him to be involuntarily hospitalized with a psychotic manic episode, and that he suffered a severe and long-lasting emotional illness.[117] The court found that the plaintiff's evidence

complaints is not actionable); *Barber v. Whirlpool Corp.*, 34 F.3d 1268 (4th Cir. 1994) (human resource manager's verbal abuse of an employee regarding the employee's alleged theft did not rise to the level of being atrocious); *Spence v. Maryland Casualty Co.*, 995 F.2d 1147 (2d Cir. 1993) (employer's continual criticisms of plaintiff and continual threats to discharge plaintiff were not actionable); *Brown v. Freedman Baking Co.*, 810 F.2d 6 (1st Cir. 1987) (president's report to Division of Employment Security that employee was fired for willful misconduct, which delayed but did not deny award of unemployment benefits, was not outrageous where state statutes require such reporting).

115. *Muniz v. Kravis*, 757 A.2d 1207 (Conn. App. Ct. 2000); *see also Worster v. Carlson Wagonlit Travel, Inc.*, No. 3:02 CV 167 EBB, 2005 WL 1595596, at *3 (D. Conn. 2005) (noting intentional infliction of emotional distress arises only where it is based upon the defendant's unreasonable conduct in the termination process).

116. 939 F.2d 1138 (5th Cir. 1991).

117. *Id.* at 1141.

was sufficient to support the emotional distress award. The court also affirmed the damage awards under the ADEA, including back pay.[118]

Several states also recognize the tort of negligent infliction of emotional distress. The elements of this claim are generally the same as intentional infliction of emotional distress, except for the fact that intent is not required.[119] Only several states recognize this tort, because the workers' compensation laws of most states preempt negligence claims, including claims of negligent infliction of emotional distress.[120]

Some states recognize negligent infliction of emotional distress claims when the state workers' compensation statute does not cover the alleged emotional distress suffered by the employee. For example, in *Chea v. Men's Wearhouse*, the plaintiff alleged racial harassment and discrimination, plus negligent infliction of emotional distress, based on an event in which a supervisor grabbed him by his coat lapels and shouted obscenities at him.[121] The supervisor, however, had made no racial remarks during this incident. The plaintiff filed a workers' compensation claim, but the workers' compensation commission denied the claim, finding no specific compensable injury. He then filed a lawsuit and recovered $45,000 for racial harassment, $27,000 for negligent infliction of emotional distress, and $22,500 in punitive damages for racial harassment. The court of appeals affirmed the emotional distress award, finding that the claim was separate from the harassment claims because it was based on acts separate from the racial harassment evidence, which permitted an independent recovery for negligent infliction of emotional distress.[122]

Similarly, the Montana Supreme Court in *Onstad v. Payless Shoesource* held that a plaintiff could recover for negligent infliction of emotional distress because the state workers' compensation statute

118. *Id.* at 1148.
119. *Muniz v. Kravis*, 757 A.2d at 1211–12.
120. *See, e.g., Prescott v. CSPH, Inc.*, 878 S.W.2d 692, 694 (Tex. Ct. App. 1994).
121. 932 P.2d 1261 (Wash. Ct. App. 1997).
122. *Id.* at 1262.

specifically excluded recovery for emotional or mental stress and, therefore, could not preempt the negligent infliction of emotional distress claim.[123] Moreover, based on the testimony from the plaintiff, her mother, a counselor, and a psychologist, the court affirmed the $500,000 award for emotional distress to the plaintiff, who had been sexually assaulted by a customer while working alone at a company store.[124]

Other courts have considered this tort and required more than mere employment decisions to sustain the claim. For example, in *Snyder v. Medical Service Corp. of Eastern Washington*, the plaintiff pursued a variety of claims based on an alleged hostile environment involving a supervisor intimating the plaintiff, embarrassing her in front of her peers, poking her in the chest, and accusing her of insubordination.[125] The Washington Supreme Court affirmed the dismissal of the negligent infliction verdict claim, stating that employers are not obligated to provide a "stress free" workplace.[126] The courts also have denied negligent infliction claims where the duty allegedly breached was too attenuated to justify relief.[127]

---

123. 9 P.3d 38 (Mont. 2000), *overruled on other grounds by Johnson v. Costco Wholesale*, 152 P.3d 727 (2007).

124. *Id.* at 43.

125. 145 Wn2d 233, 35 P.3d 1158 (Wash. 2001).

126. 35 P.3d at 1164.

127. *See Ky. Fried Chicken of Cal., Inc. v. Super. Ct.*, 927 P.2d 1260 (Cal. 1997) (because an employee has no duty to comply with a robber's unlawful demands in order to avoid unreasonably increasing the risk of harm to a customer, the customer who suffered emotional distress as a result of being held hostage in a holdup could not state a claim for negligent infliction of emotional distress); *Robblee v. Budd Serv.*, 525 S.E.2d 847 (N.C. 2000) (emotional distress suffered by employee as a result of shootings by former co-employee was not a reasonably foreseeable consequence of any negligent conduct on the part of employer's security company and, therefore, employee did not establish claim for negligent infliction of emotional distress); *Govito v. W. Jersey Health Sys., Inc.* 753 A.2d 716 (N.J. Super. Ct. App. Div. 2000) (negligent infliction of emotional distress could not be used to circumvent restrictions imposed on what essentially was a defamation claim).

B. Wrongful Discharge and Emotional Injury

Every state has legislative and judicially defined exceptions to the general rule that employment can be terminated at the will of the employer. The exceptions generally fall into one or more of the following categories: (1) an express or implied contract to discharge only for cause; (2) a judicially recognized public policy prohibiting discharge in particular circumstances; (3) an implied covenant of good faith and fair dealing. The states vary considerably in the extent to which they recognize these exceptions. In addition, plaintiffs frequently "tag on" to and/or sometimes substitute for wrongful discharge claims with intentional or negligent infliction of emotional distress claims.

As a general matter, emotional distress damages are not available for contract-based claims such as express or implied contracts to discharge only for cause and implied covenants of good faith and fair dealing. Courts typically will not permit plaintiffs to circumvent the prohibition against emotional distress damages in contract-based actions by pairing these claims with intentional or negligent infliction of emotional distress claims based on the same underlying facts. For average employment disputes, termination alone typically does not support a plaintiff's emotional injury claim.[128] A few courts, however, will allow emotional distress damages for willful and wanton breach of contract.[129]

This is not necessarily the case for claims of wrongful termination based on a violation of public policy. Courts generally characterize this claim as an intentional tort and allow emotional distress damages, which generally are available for intentional tort claims.[130] For example, the West Virginia Supreme Court of Appeals affirmed an award of $50,000 in emotional distress to the plaintiff, who had been terminated

128. *Larson v. Koch Ref. Co.*, 920 F. Supp. 1000, 1003–04 (D. Minn. 1996).

129. *See, e.g.*, *Allabashi v. Lincoln Nat'l Sales Corp.*, 824 P.2d 1 (Colo. App. 1991) (affirming emotional distress award of $250,000 based on breach of employment contract).

130. *Chavez v. Manville Prods Corp.*, 777 P.2d 371 (N.M. 1989); *Cagle v. Burns & Roe, Inc.*, 726 P.2d 434 (Wash. 1986).

from his position in retaliation for asserting rights under the Veterans' Reemployment Rights Act, including a claim for back pay. The court found that there was sufficient indicia of intent to violate public policy, which justified the award of emotional distress as part of compensatory damages.[131] Similarly, the Washington Supreme Court in *Cagle v. Burns & Roe, Inc.*, has held that an award of $87,896 in emotional distress damages was appropriate based on a wrongful termination in violation of public policy.[132] There, the employer terminated the plaintiff in violation of public policy by terminating her after she told a supervisor that she would complain to the Nuclear Regulatory Commission if the supervisors continued to direct her to violate procedures applicable to construction of the nuclear power plant.

C. Tortious Interference with a Contract

Tortious interference in the employment context generally arises when an employer does something to hinder the plaintiff's employment with another employer. Tortious interference may occur when an employer attempts to enforce an overbroad noncompetition agreement with a former employee that prevents him or her from working for a competitor, or when an employer attempts to interfere with an employee's prospective employment by providing a poor employment reference. It may also occur when an employer seeks to bar another company's employee from doing business on the employer's premises, such as when the employer does not wish to deal with a particular salesperson. A plaintiff generally may plead two separate causes of action for tortious interference: one for interference with an existing contract and one for interference with a prospective business relationship.[133]

---

131. *Mace v. Charleston Area Med. Ctr. Found.*, 422 S.E.2d 624, 630–31 (W. Va. 1992).

132. *Cagle*, 726 P.2d at 438.

133. *Juliette Fowler Homes, Inc. v. Welch Assocs. Inc.*, 793 S.W.2d 660, 664 (Tex. 1990).

To establish a claim of tortious interference with an existing contract, the plaintiff must show (1) the existence of a contract subject to interference, (2) an act of interference that was willful and intentional, (3) an intentional act that was the proximate cause of plaintiff's damage, and (4) actual damage or loss.[134] The elements generally are the same for a claim of tortious interference with prospective business relations or contracts, except when the interference relates to an opportunity to contract. In some states, a plaintiff may pursue a tortious interference claim even if the employment relationship is terminable at will.[135] In addition, the interference must be by a third party. The employer that terminates the contract and the employees acting in the course and scope of employment generally are not third parties that can interfere with the employment relationship.[136]

Emotional distress damages typically are available for tortious interference with contract claims. A Florida appellate court, in *Albritton v. Gandy*, addressed a case involving actions by a county commissioner who had induced the plaintiff's termination as an ombudsman at a county hospital and forced a county administrator to remove the plaintiff from eligibility to be called to work as a relief emergency medical technician (EMT).[137] The court affirmed (1) a $35,000 award for past and future loss of wages and earnings; (2) $300,000 for injury to reputation and mental and emotional distress based on the interference in the EMT position; and (3) $1 million in punitive damages based on a finding of tortious interference with contract. The court determined that the $300,000 award for nonpecuniary relief was not "clearly arbitrary

---

134. *Appleton v. Board of Educ.*, 757 A.2d 1059, 1063 (Conn. 2000); *Powell Indus., Inc. v. Allen*, 985 S.W.2d 455, 456 (Tex. 1998).

135. *Michaelson v. Minnesota Mining & Mfg. Co.*, 474 N.W.2d 174, 181 (Minn. Ct. App. 1991), *aff'd*, 479 N.W.2d 58 (Minn. 1992); *Riley v. Dow Corning Corp.*, 767 F. Supp. 735, 738 (M.D. N.C. 1991); *Beyda v. USAir, Inc.*, 697 F. Supp. 1394, 1398 (W.D. Pa. 1988).

136. *Lichtie v. U.S. Home Corp.*, 655 F. Supp. 1026, 1027–28 (D. Utah 1987); *Creel v. Davis*, 544 So.2d 145, 146 (Ala. 1989).

137. 531 So.2d 381 (Fla. Dist. Ct. App. 1988).

or so great as to be shocking," even though the plaintiff made only $104.75 to $346.70 per week in her job as a part-time EMT.[138] The court, however, reversed the trial court's directed verdict on the interference related to the ombudsman position and remanded the case to the trial court to make a determination of whether the jury's award of $145,000 for past and future loss of wages and $700,000 for injury to reputation and mental and emotional distress was appropriate or excessive.[139]

D. Defamation

The release of inaccurate, misleading, or occasionally even truthful information about an employee or former employee may lead to an employer being sued for defamation. Defamation encompasses any false and unprivileged communication, either oral (slander) or written (libel), that has a tendency to injure a person in his or her occupation or reputation.[140] Generally, to maintain a cause of action for defamation, a plaintiff must prove: (1) false and defamatory statement of fact, (2) statement regards the plaintiff, (3) statement was published to a third party by the defendant, and (4) statement resulted in injury to the plaintiff.[141] A plaintiff need not prove the final element, damages, if the alleged defamatory statements concern one of the following: (1) the commission of a criminal offense; (2) infection with a loathsome, communicable disease; (3) an inability to perform or want of integrity in the discharge of the duties of office or employment; or (4) lack of ability in one's trade, profession, or business. In such cases, the statements are "defamatory *per se*" and a jury may presume damages have

138. 531 So.2d at 388.

139. *Id.* at 389–90.

140. *Snyder v. AG Trucking, Inc.*, 57 F.3d 484, 489 (6th Cir. 1995); *Jensen v. Hewlett-Packard Co.*, 18 Cal. Rptr. 2d 83 (Cal. Ct. App. 1993); *Schneider v. Pay'N Save Corp.*, 723 P.2d 619, 623 (Alaska 1986).

141. *Smith v. Maldonado*, 72 Cal. App. 4th 637 (1999); *Northern Ind. Pub. Serv. Co. v. Dabagia*, 721 N.E.2d 294 (Ind. Ct. App. 1999).

been suffered.[142] Because statements that tend to disparage or injure a plaintiff in his or her trade or profession are slanderous or libelous per se, the employment context is especially susceptible to per se defamation allegations.[143]

Defamation can support a finding of compensatory damages. For example, the Supreme Court of Alaska upheld compensatory and punitive damages in a defamation case, citing the company's bad behavior, in which it defamed an employee after that employee attempted to uncover her supervisor's misappropriation of funds.[144] When the supervisor discovered the employee's probe, he accused the employee of "(1) breaking into Association offices; (2) illegally accessing the Association's computers; (3) stalking [the supervisor]; (4) making death threats; and (5) retaliating against the Association by accusing [the supervisor] of wrongdoing after she was suspended."[145] The Alaskan court upheld the jury's award of $15,000 in emotional distress and $20,000 in reputational harm, stating that "[g]iven the Association's and the [supervisor's] conduct and motives in this case, we find that [the compensatory and punitive damages awards] are not excessive."[146]

E. Invasion of Privacy

Most states recognize four types of invasion of privacy claims. The tort of "public disclosure of private facts," under which an employee can sue an employer who discloses true but embarrassing private facts about the employee, is perhaps the most commonly asserted one.[147] A plaintiff alleging "public disclosure of private facts" must prove that

---

142. *See, e.g., Celle v. Filipino Reporter Enters.*, 209 F.3d 163, 179 (2d Cir. 2000).

143. *Hayes v. Sweeney*, 961 F. Supp. 467, 479 (W.D.N.Y. 1997); *Matta v. May*, 118 F.3d 410 (5th Cir. 1997), *cert. denied*, 523 U.S. 1136 (1998).

144. *Central Bering Sea Fishermen's Ass'n. v. Anderson*, 54 P.3d 271 (Alaska 2002).

145. *Id.* at 276.

146. *Id.* at 285. *But see Northern Ind. Pub. Serv. Co. v. Dabagia*, 721 N.E.2d 294 (Ind. Ct. App. 1999) (racial slurs are not defamatory per se and reversing $500,000 award for defamation based on this claim).

147. *Washington State Human Rights Comm'n v. Seattle*, 607 P.2d 332 (Wash. Ct. App. 1980).

the challenged disclosure would be highly offensive to a reasonable person, not to him or her subjectively.[148]

A second type of invasion of privacy claim arises from investigations or surveillance the employee feels was overly invasive.[149] In order for a plaintiff to establish a cause of action for this type of invasion of privacy, he or she must first have a reasonable expectation of privacy as to the subject matter of the intrusion.[150] It is more difficult for an employee to establish an invasion of privacy claim where the employer's actions are taken in good faith as part of an investigation.[151]

The remaining types of privacy claims are intrusion upon seclusion and false-light invasion of privacy. Intrusion upon seclusion requires that a plaintiff show that the defendant invaded a sphere of seclusion where the plaintiff had a reasonable expectation of privacy.[152] A false-light invasion of privacy claim can be brought where publication of information places the plaintiff in a false light. False light exists when one attributes to the plaintiff views he or she does not hold or actions he or she did not take. The false light must be something objectionable to a reasonable person under the circumstances.[153]

The personal nature of the invasion of privacy tort lends itself to a finding of emotional distress in many instances. In general, a court

---

148. *Armstrong v. Freedom of Info. Comm'n*, 1997 Conn. Sup. LEXIS 1991, at *4 (Conn. Sup. Ct. July 23, 1997).

149. *Melton v. United States Steel Corp.*, 8 IER Cas. (BNA) 687, 1993 U.S. Dist. LEXIS 17233 (N.D. Ind. 1993).

150. *Doe v. Kohn Nast & Graf, P.C.*, 866 F. Supp. 190 (E.D. Pa. 1994).

151. *Shattuck-Owen v. Snowbird Corp.*, 16 P.3d 555 (Utah 2000).

152. *See, e.g., Stengart v. Loving Care Agency, Inc.*, 990 A.2d 650, 665 (N.J. 2010) (health care service executive who used a company laptop to exchange messages with her attorney on a personal password-protected e-mail account had an expectation of privacy that was violated when the employer retrieved and read the e-mail messages from the computer hard drive); *see also Benitiez v. KFC Nat'l Mgmt. Co.*, 714 N.E.2d 1002, 1006 (Ill. App. Ct. 1999) (allegations by former female employees of fast-food restaurant that coworkers and supervisor poked holes in ceiling of women's bathroom and viewed the female employees disrobing and using restroom facilities supported a claim for unreasonable intrusion upon seclusion).

153. *See, e.g., Dominguez v. Davidson*, 974 P.2d 112, 121 (Kan. 1999).

will examine whether the emotional or mental distress alleged "is of a kind that normally results from such an invasion."[154] For example, the court in *Levias v. United Airlines* upheld a jury's finding of emotional distress and an award of $14,000 after the plaintiff, whose medical history had been disclosed unnecessarily to her supervisor, testified that she experienced substantial emotional distress from these disclosures.[155] This distress included "embarrassment, anxiety, headaches, and an adverse effect on her marital relations."[156] Furthermore, the plaintiff claimed that "her emotional reaction temporarily elevated her blood pressure, causing her to take medication for that condition."[157] Though the court determined that this evidence was enough to support a verdict for compensatory damages, it distinguished compensatory damages from a claim of intentional infliction of emotional distress.[158] "Unlike an action for intentional or negligent infliction of emotional distress, the plaintiff need not prove a debilitating injury to recover for an invasion of privacy."[159]

In *Kjerstad v. Ravellette Publ'ns, Inc.*, the South Dakota Supreme Court reversed and remanded a directed verdict in the defendant's favor after reviewing the plaintiffs' testimony.[160] The plaintiffs in *Kjerstad* testified that upon the discovery that the owner of the publishing company was spying on them in the ladies room through a hole in the wall, they suffered severe emotional distress. The court reviewed the evidence supporting the emotional distress, including the plaintiffs' visits to a doctor and their counseling sessions.[161] One plaintiff also testified that "she vomited when she saw the [Peeping Tom] observe [another plaintiff]. She later developed diarrhea, headaches and stomach sickness.

154. *Rohrbaugh v. Wal-Mart Stores, Inc.*, 572 S.E.2d 881, 888 (W. Va. 2002).
155. 500 N.E.2d 370, 374 (Ohio 1985).
156. *Id.*
157. *Id.*
158. *Id.*
159. *Id.*
160. 517 N.W.2d 419, 428–29 (S.D. 1994).
161. *Id.* at 429.

[Another plaintiff] testified that she had nightmares as a result of the incident."[162] Based on this evidence, the court determined that there was "sufficient evidence to create a jury question as to whether or not [the defendant's] conduct intentionally or recklessly caused the plaintiffs an extreme disabling emotional response."[163] Accordingly, the court reversed the directed verdict and remanded the case.[164]

F. Assault and Battery

Assault and battery are separate torts that are sometimes alleged in cases of sexual harassment or where there has been some other alleged physical contact between the employee and the employer (or a co-employee). Battery is defined as intentional contact by one person with the person of another that is either harmful or offensive. The intent required refers only to the intent to make physical contact; the defendant need not intend that his or her contact be offensive or harmful.[165] To successfully prove the tort of assault, a plaintiff must at least demonstrate: (1) intent to cause a harmful or offensive contact with the other person by the defendant and (2) apprehension of such injury by the plaintiff.[166] The fact that the tortfeasor may not have had the present ability to inflict injury is irrelevant as long as the plaintiff had a reasonable apprehension of injury.[167]

An employer generally is not liable for assault and battery committed by an employee, because most assaults or batteries are not committed within the scope of employment.[168] Conduct may be within the scope of

162. *Id.*
163. *Id.*
164. *Id.* at 430.
165. Restatement (Second) of Torts § 16(1).
166. Restatement (Second) of Torts § 21(1).
167. Restatement (Second) of Torts § 33; *Lowry v. Standard Oil Co.*, 146 P.2d 57 (Cal. Ct. App. 1944) (defendant committed assault when he pointed an unloaded gun at plaintiff and cocked the gun).
168. *Vinsonhaler v. Quantum Residential Corp.*, 73 P.3d 930 (Or. Ct. App. 2003); *Dia CC v. Ithica City Sch. Dist.*, 758 N.Y.S.2d 197 (N.Y. App. Div. 2003); *Partridge v. Harvey*, 805 So.2d 668 (Miss. Ct. App. 2002).

employment for purposes of determining whether an employer is liable for such intentional torts committed by its employee, if the employer authorized or ratified the conduct or the employee acted under the authority of the employer.[169] In contrast, a court may find no employer liability in a situation in which the employee has a desire to serve his or her own interests, and the assault is adverse to the employer's interests.[170]

When a plaintiff alleges assault or battery in the employment context, courts appear to be willing to affirm awards of emotional distress damages to employees found to be victims of assault, particularly when the assault is in conjunction with a sexual harassment claim. Plaintiffs who prove sexual assault may recover mental anguish damages without a showing of physical injury.[171] In *Valdez v. Church's Fried Chicken, Inc.*, the court awarded the plaintiff $10,000 for mental anguish related to plaintiff's sexual assault claim, though plaintiff suffered no physical manifestation of emotional distress.[172] The *Valdez* court reasoned: "sexual assault, by its nature, assures that plaintiff will suffer some mental injury."[173] However, some states hold that their workers' compensation statutes bar emotional distress damages arising from assault and battery tort claims.[174]

---

169. *Partridge v. Harvey*, 805 So.2d at 672.

170. *Hubbard v. Lakeland Nursing Home*, 734 So.2d 1280, 1282 (La. Ct. App. 1999).

171. *See Priest v. Rotary*, 634 F. Supp. 571, 584 (N.D. Cal. 1986) (holding that under California law, plaintiff who alleged a number of state law torts against employer, including assault and battery stemming from sexual harassment by employer, may recover for mental suffering whether or not "it is occasioned by physical pain").

172. 683 F. Supp. 596, 613 (W.D. Tex. 1988); *see also Gilardi v. Schroeder*, 672 F. Supp. 1043, 1047 (N.D. Ill. 1986) (upholding award to plaintiff for $100,000 on her assault and battery and intentional infliction of emotional distress claims and noting that trier of fact may specifically take into account injury to plaintiff's psyche with regard to assault and battery claims).

173. 683 F. Supp. at 613.

174. *See, e.g., Newman v. Hansen & Hempel Co.*, 19 IER Cas. (BNA) 781, 2002 WL 31455990 (N.D. Ill. Oct. 30, 2002).

III. Defenses and Strategy

A. Failure to Meet Burden of Proof: Summary Judgment Challenges

Defendants frequently obtain summary judgment dismissing intentional and/or negligent infliction of emotional distress claims. Employers have been able to obtain summary judgment where, for example, the plaintiff fails to plead sufficiently "severe" emotional distress, that is, distress so severe that a normal person could not be expected to endure it. Normally, physical injury must be alleged.[175]

As demonstrated above, courts must determine whether the plaintiff has met the requirements of the claim that permit recovery of emotional distress damages. In certain instances, the nature of the employment law action, such as tortious interference with a contract, can influence the perception of an emotional injury claim.[176]

Although a jury must determine whether the alleged conduct is outrageous enough to generate severe emotional distress for purposes of intentional infliction of emotional distress, a court must first decide whether reasonable persons could disagree on whether the conduct was outrageous and the resulting distress was severe.[177] Accordingly, once the employer has completed enough discovery to uncover the evidence supporting the plaintiff's allegations, the defendant may be able to demonstrate to the court that reasonable minds could not disagree over whether its conduct was atrocious and utterly intolerable in a civilized community or would cause an average member to exclaim, "outrageous!" thus giving rise to *severe* emotional distress.[178] Given the

---

175. *Hanson v. Hancock Cnty. Mem'l Hosp.*, 938 F. Supp. 1419, 1442–43 (N.D. Iowa 1996) (extended periods of crying were not sufficiently severe to state a claim for emotional distress).

176. *See supra*, Section II.C.

177. *Bell v. Board of Educ.*, 739 A.2d 321, 327 (Conn. App. Ct. 1999); *see also Walker v. Boeing Corp.*, 218 F. Supp. 2d 1177, 1184 (C.D. Cal. 2002) (finding defamatory accusation that plaintiff had engaged in sexual harassment was insufficient to give rise to an action for intentional infliction of emotional distress).

178. Restatement (Second) of Torts § 46 cmt. d.

extreme difficulty in proving that employment actions rise to this level, many claims can be dismissed through a summary judgment motion.

B. Failure to Demonstrate Causation: Expert Challenges

As discussed above, plaintiffs can use expert witnesses to support claims for emotional injury.[179] At times, a plaintiff does not even need an expert witness to establish emotional injury damages.[180] When a plaintiff uses an expert witness, however, an employer can challenge that expert witness to undermine the support for an emotional injury claim.

Before a court can admit expert testimony, it must first investigate whether the expert's testimony is relevant and reliable.[181] In this hearing, the court should consider whether the theory or medicine that forms the expert's testimony (1) can be and has been tested; (2) has been subjected to peer review and publication; (3) has a high known or potential rate of error and standards controlling its operation; and (4) is generally accepted within the relevant scientific or technical community.[182] "[W]hether *Daubert's* specific factors are, or are not, reasonable measures of reliability in a particular case is a matter that the law grants the trial judge broad latitude to determine."[183] Courts conduct this inquiry "to make certain that an expert, whether basing testimony upon professional studies or personal experience, employs in the courtroom the same level of intellectual rigor that characterizes the practice of an expert in the relevant field."[184]

Based on the standards set forth by the U.S. Supreme Court in *Daubert*, a plaintiff may have difficulty supporting an emotional injury

179. *See Keenan v. City of Phila.*, 983 F.2d 459, 469 (3d Cir. 1992).

180. *Bolden v. SEPTA*, 21 F.3d 29, 34–35 (3d Cir. 1994).

181. Fed. R. Evid. 702; *Kumho Tire Co. v. Carmichael*, 526 U.S. 137, 147–49 (1999); *Pipitone v. Biomatrix, Inc.*, 288 F.3d 239, 244 (5th Cir. 2002). Under the seminal case, *Daubert v. Merrell Dow Pharms.*, 509 U.S. 579 (1993), a party may request a hearing to determine whether an expert is reliable.

182. *Daubert*, 509 U.S. at 593–94.

183. *Kumho*, 526 U.S. at 153.

184. *Id.* at 152.

claim because these claims involve evaluations of subjective symptoms.[185] Furthermore, an employer can challenge a plaintiff's emotional injury experts if the witness bases his or her opinion on theories that are not generally accepted within the medical community (as frequently happens in actions with emotional injury claims). Also, employers can challenge whether the employment action caused the plaintiff's distress by probing into the basis of the expert's opinion and reasons for associating distress with an employment event.

Moreover, the employer may gain additional support for its causation challenge by requesting an independent mental and/or physical examination under Rule 35 of the Federal Rules of Civil Procedure. To request such an examination, the employer must file a motion showing good cause for the examination and that the mental or physical condition of the plaintiff is in controversy.[186] The plaintiff's mental and/or physical condition is in controversy if the plaintiff has pleaded mental or physical injury to support his or her position.[187] Though general allegations of mental and/or physical injury will not place the plaintiff's condition in controversy, a separate tort claim for emotional distress will.[188] An employer may only request an independent examination for the parties involved in the lawsuit; a court may not order an independent examination for nonparties.[189]

C. Settlement and Taxation of Emotional Injury Claims

Taxation of emotional injury damages is an important consideration for damage awards, and in strategic settlement planning and negotiation

185. *E.E.O.C. v. Fox News Network*, 806 F. Supp. 2d 128, 137 (D.D.C. 2011) (finding "purely subjective" emotional distress injuries are legally insufficient to constitute materially adverse employment actions).

186. Fed. R. Civ. P. 35(a); *Schlagenhauf v. Holder*, 379 U.S. 104, 118 (1964).

187. *Schlagenhauf*, 378 U.S. at 119.

188. *Gattegno v. Price WaterhouseCoopers, LLP*, 204 F.R.D. 228, 231–32 (D. Conn. 2001); *Turner v. Imperial Stores*, 161 F.R.D. 89, 97–98 (S.D. Cal. 1995).

189. *Scharf v. U.S. Attorney Gen.*, 597 F.2d 1240, 1243 (9th Cir. 1979); *Caban ex rel. Crespo v. 600 E. 21st Street Co.*, 200 F.R.D. 176, 181 (E.D.N.Y. 2001) (court does not have "inherent authority" to order a nonparty to submit to an independent examination).

(discussed more fully in chapter 10), briefly, a jury's award typically can be allocated between economic loss and compensatory damages by the verdict form used. In settlement negotiations, the parties may (should) agree to allocate settlement proceeds along the same lines. Regardless, the parties must determine whether amounts a plaintiff receives are taxable under the Internal Revenue Code (IRC) and, if so, to what extent.

Prior to 1996, plaintiffs and defendants relied upon IRC § 104(a)(2) to shield payments for emotional distress damages from taxation. The pre-1996 version of Section 104(a)(2) excluded from income any damages received because of a "personal injury or sickness." The U.S. Supreme Court construed this section to apply to both physical and nonphysical injuries.[190] In determining whether damages were excludable under the pre-1996 version of Section 104(a)(2), courts looked at (a) whether the damages arose from a personal injury and (b) whether the damages stemmed from a "tort-like" claim.[191] Pre-1996, employees and employers alike considered an emotional distress claim as qualifying as a "personal injury or sickness" under Section 104(a)(2), making it nontaxable.

In 1996, Congress amended Section 104(a)(2) to exclude payments made on account of "personal *physical* injuries or *physical* sickness."[192] Congress also added language to Section 104(a), stating: "For the purposes of [Section 104(a)(2)], emotional distress shall not be treated as a physical injury or physical sickness."[193] This amendment effectively eliminated any exclusion from income for emotional distress damages in employment law cases. Emotional distress damages arising out of an employment law claim are now taxable to the plaintiff under Amended Section 104(a)(2) as ordinary income. Accordingly, the vast majority of payments made to plaintiffs for emotional distress damages in

190. *U.S. v. Burke*, 504 U.S. 229 (1992); *C.I.R. v. Schleier*, 515 U.S. 323 (1995).

191. *Burke*, 504 U.S. at 236; *Schleier*, 515 U.S. at 333–34; *Dotson v. U.S.*, 87 F.3d 682, 685 (5th Cir. 1996).

192. 26 U.S.C. § 104(a)(2) (emphasis added).

193. *Id.* § 104(a)(5) (emphasis added).

employment lawsuits will be taxable based on the 1996 amendments to Section 104(a)(2). A possible exception to this amendment may exist where the emotional distress claim arises out of an underlying personal physical injury, such as a sexual assault, that causes the plaintiff emotional distress. There is also an exception in Section 104(a) for any damages "paid for medical care attributable to emotional distress."[194]

Payments for emotional distress claims that are not excluded from income under Section 104(a)(2) are part of an employee's gross income. Accordingly, claims for emotional distress damages are not wages but are ordinary income. If such damages were wages, then they would be subject to withholding requirements under the Federal Insurance Contributions Act (FICA) or the Federal Unemployment Tax Act (FUTA). Instead, the employer should designate the emotional distress damages part of the settlement or judgment and complete the requisite Internal Revenue Service (IRS) 1099 Form to account for this part of the settlement or judgment. The employer should be realistic in this designation, because the IRS will not allow a disproportionate designation of such damages.[195]

IV. Conclusion

Plaintiffs are finding more ways to add emotional injury claims to their employment actions, either under statutory provisions or under state common law. Proof for these claims remains difficult under both statutory and common law. For independent claims of emotional injury, the

194. *Id.* "Medical care" is described in I.R.C. § 213(d)(1) (defining "medical care" as amounts paid (A) for the diagnosis, cure, mitigation, treatment, or prevention of disease, or for the purpose of affecting any structure or function of the body; (B) for transportation primarily for and essential to medical care; (C) for qualified long-term care services; or (D) for insurance covering medical care referred to in subparagraphs (A) or (B) or for any qualified long-term care insurance contract).

195. In order for the allocation in a settlement agreement to be respected, it must be entered into (1) in an adversarial relationship, (2) at arm's length, and (3) in good faith. It is not enough for the parties to reach a settlement figure in an adversarial relationship; rather, the allocation must also be based on adversarial positions. *See Robinson v. C.I.R.*, 102 T.C. 116, 126–27 (1994).

elements of outrageous and extreme conduct and severe emotional distress have proved difficult to satisfy. Although legitimate, supportable emotional injury claims exist in the area of labor and employment law, these claims will most likely be subjected to scrutiny and challenges.

CHAPTER 8
Back Pay, Front Pay, Compensatory and Punitive Damages Standards, and Defense of Claims Seeking Same

Roxella T. Cavazos

Back pay is the basic measure of "damages" for persons who claim unlawful employment discrimination or wrongful termination of employment. Few plaintiffs who litigate employment claims, however, are content to settle for or satisfied with an award consisting solely of back pay, reinstatement, and other injunctive relief. Instead, plaintiffs routinely seek damages beyond back pay. Legal and equitable relief routinely has been available under the Civil Rights Act of 1876, codified at 42 U.S.C. § 1981.[1] The passage of the Civil Rights Act of 1991 (CRA)[2] made compensatory and punitive damages generally available

1. *Johnson v. Railway Express Agency, Inc.*, 421 U.S. 454 (1975); 42 U.S.C. § 1981 (allows all persons to make and enforce contracts enjoyed by white citizens; interpreted to prohibit race and national origin discrimination in employment).
2. 42 U.S.C. § 1981a.

in employment discrimination claims brought under Title VII of the Civil Rights Act of 1964 (Title VII),[3] the Americans With Disabilities Act of 1990 (ADA),[4] and the Rehabilitation Act of 1973.[5] Defense lawyers today must focus on determining and limiting damages from the inception of a claim. This chapter is a summary of the basics of equitable and legal relief under federal antidiscrimination laws.[6]

I. Back Pay

A. Entitlement to Back Pay

Federal antidiscrimination laws are designed "to make persons whole for injuries suffered on account of unlawful employment."[7] In a Title VII context, the U.S. Supreme Court noted over thirty years ago that back pay is awarded in furtherance of the objectives of Congress in enacting Title VII to create employer incentives to ensure equality of employment opportunities.[8] Title VII provides for back pay as follows:

> If the court finds that the respondent has intentionally engaged in or is intentionally engaging in an unlawful employment practice charged in the complaint, the court may enjoin the respondent from engaging in such unlawful employment practice, and order such affirmative action as may be appropriate, which may include, but is not limited to, reinstatement or hiring of employees, with

---

3. 42 U.S.C. § 2000e *et seq.*
4. 42 U.S.C. §§ 12101–12117.
5. 29 U.S.C. §§ 791–794a.
6. In most instances, only cases decided after 1995 are cited.
7. *Albemarle Paper Co. v. Moody*, 422 U.S. 405, 421–22 (1975) (a Title VII case); *Nassar v. Tex. S.W. Med. Ctr.*, 674 F.3d 448, 455 (5th Cir. 2012) (back-pay award and all damages under Title VII should make whole the injured party by placing that individual in the position he or she would have been in but for the discrimination); *EEOC v. Massey Yardley Chrysler Plymouth, Inc.*, 117 F.3d 1244, 1251 (11th Cir. 1997) (an age discrimination case).
8. *Albemarle Paper Co.*, 422 U.S. at 418–19.

> or without back pay, or any other equitable relief as the court deems appropriate.[9]

If a plaintiff unreasonably refuses an offer of reinstatement from his or her employer, there should be no award of back pay or it should be reduced.[10]

The ADA and Rehabilitation Act expressly adopt the remedies provided by Title VII.[11] Many state antidiscrimination statutes expressly state that they are patterned after Title VII and therefore adopt the same remedies contained in Title VII.[12]

The Age Discrimination in Employment Act (ADEA) is enforced under the provisions of the Fair Labor Standards Act (FLSA).[13] The ADEA literally states that amounts owed to a person as a result of a violation of the statute shall be deemed to be unpaid minimum wages or unpaid overtime compensation.[14] In practice, monetary relief under the ADEA is not so limited, and the courts consider back pay a mandatory element of damages.[15]

---

9. 42 U.S.C. § 2000e-5(g)(1).

10. *Ford Motor Co. v. EEOC*, 458 U.S. 219, 231 (1982).

11. 42 U.S.C. § 12117(a).

12. *See, e.g.*, Texas Commission on Human Rights Act, TEX. LAB. CODE § 21.001 (adopting the remedies of Title VII and ADA); *Quantum Chem. Corp. v. Toennies*, 47 S.W.3d 473 (Tex. 2001). *But see* LA. R.S. 1006 and 51:2264 (remedies identical to Title VII in general but unlimited compensatory damages and no punitive damages).

13. 29 U.S.C. § 626(b) (ADEA); 29 U.S.C. §§ 216, 217 (FLSA).

14. 29 U.S.C. § 626(b).

15. *Franzoni v. Hartmarx Corp.*, 300 F.3d 767, 773 (7th Cir. 2002) (under the ADEA, a plaintiff may recover monetary damages in the form of back pay); *Tyler v. Union Oil of California*, 304 F.3d 379, 401 (5th Cir. 2002) (the purpose of ADEA back-pay compensation is to restore the plaintiff to the position he or she would have been in absent the discrimination); *Garcia v. S.U.N.Y. Health Sciences Center of Brooklyn*, 280 F.3d 98, 111 (2d Cir. 2001) (where a plaintiff proved that he was discharged because of his age in violation of the ADEA, he is entitled to recover, at a minimum, any back pay lost as a result of the violation); *EEOC v. Massey Yardley Chrysler Plymouth, Inc.*, 117 F.3d at 1251 (the ADEA is designed solely to ensure proper compensation for individuals whose rights are violated).

B. Determination of Back Pay

Back pay is determined by the court because it is an equitable remedy.[16] But under Rule 39(c) of the Federal Rules of Civil Procedure, the court upon motion or *sua sponte* may try the issue of back pay with an advisory jury.[17] It is wholly within the discretion of the trial court whether to accept or reject in whole or in part the verdict of an advisory jury.[18]

C. Components of Back Pay

Back pay includes lost wages and lost benefits, including health insurance, accidental death or dismemberment insurance, matching 401(k) contributions, vacation, and holidays.[19]

D. Calculation of Back Pay

Once liability is established, a plaintiff is presumptively entitled to back pay from the date of discharge to the date of judgment, unless the plaintiff obtains or could have obtained substantially equivalent work before that time.[20] If the employer blocked a plaintiff from obtaining a higher-paying position, the salary of that position may be used to compute back pay.[21] Back pay should be denied only for reasons that, if

---

16. *Robinson v. Metro-North Commuter R.R. Co.*, 267 F.3d 147, 160 (2d Cir. 2001); *Hine v. Mineta*, 238 F. Supp. 2d 497, 498 (E.D.N.Y. 2003).

17. Fed. R. Civ. P. 39(c); *Black v. Pan American Labs., LLC*, 646 F.3d 254, 263 (5th Cir. 2011) (a district court need not empanel an advisory jury but can decide the back-pay issue itself absent the parties' agreement to the correct amount) (citing *West v. Nabors Drilling USA Inc.*, 330 F.3d 379, 394–95 (5th Cir. 2003)); *Hine*, 238 F. Supp. 2d at 498.

18. *Hine*, 238 F. Supp. 2d at 499.

19. *Webber v. Int'l Paper Co.*, 239 F. Supp. 2d 88, 97 (D. Me. 2003) (accidental death or dismemberment insurance and matching 401(k) contributions are elements of back pay); *Horn v. Specialized Servs., Inc.*, 241 F. Supp. 2d 994, 1014 (S.D. Iowa 2003) (vacation and holidays are elements of back pay); *Patterson v. P.H.P. Healthcare Corp.*, 90 F.3d 927, 937 (5th Cir. 1996) (back pay refers to wages and other benefits the employee would have earned if the unlawful event that affected the employee's job-related compensation had not occurred).

20. *Albemarle Paper Co. v. Moody*, 422 U.S. 405, 421–422 (1975); *U.S. EEOC v. Massey Yardley Chrysler Plymouth, Inc.*, 117 F.3d 1244, 1251 (11th Cir. 1997).

21. *Nassar v. Univ. of Texas Southwestern Med. Ctr.*, 674 F.3d 448, 455 (5th Cir.

applied generally, would not frustrate the central statutory purposes of eradicating discrimination throughout the economy and making persons whole for injuries suffered through past discrimination.[22] Back pay is not denied in constructive discharge cases, unless there is no showing of a constructive discharge.[23]

Back pay in a discharge case is computed from the day of the adverse employment decision to the day of final judgment.[24] Back pay in a failure-to-promote case where the plaintiff is still employed may be calculated in a manner dependent on whether the plaintiff was promoted to the position sought. For example, in one case in which the plaintiff was denied a promotion and eventually transferred to another department, back pay was calculated from the date of the denial of the promotion to the date she transferred to another department at the rate paid to the employee who received the promotion.[25] Back-pay liability does not accrue from a date more than two years prior to the filing of a charge of discrimination with the EEOC.[26]

Absent special circumstances, ongoing accrual of back-pay liability is tolled when a claimant rejects the job he or she originally sought.[27] The same is true if a claimant quit subsequent employment or failed to

---

2012).

22. *Bergerson v. New York State Office of Mental Health*, 652 F.3d 277, 287 (2d Cir. 2011) (denial of back pay because the court believed the award of compensatory damages was sufficient was error; an award of back pay is the rule, not the exception, where liability if found); *Dennis v. Columbia Colleton Med. Ctr., Inc.*, 290 F.3d 639, 651 (4th Cir. 2002).

23. *Dennis*, 290 F.3d at 651; *Nassar*, 674 F.3d at 455; *Mallinson-Montague v. Pocrnick*, 224 F.3d 1224, 1236 (10th Cir. 2000) (no back-pay award because plaintiffs resigned and jury rejected constructive discharge claims).

24. *Dennis*, 290 F.3d at 651 (back pay was calculated from the date of the denial of the promotion, which is the date of the constructive discharge to the date of final judgment); *Patterson*, 90 F.3d at 651 (back pay was calculated from the date of the constructive discharge to the date the plaintiff rejected the employer's first unconditional offer of reinstatement, where employee sought other employment with little success).

25. *David v. Caterpillar, Inc.*, 324 F.3d 851 (7th Cir. 2003).

26. 42 U.S.C. § 2000e-5(g).

27. *Ford Motor Co. v. EEOC*, 458 U.S. 219, 238 (1982).

seek employment.[28] The reopening of a position that was the subject of a discrimination case does not toll a back-pay period.[29] An employer who offers reinstatement is released from the back-pay obligation from the date the offer was rejected.[30]

II. Front Pay

A. Entitlement to Front Pay

Front pay is an exceptional award; reinstatement should be the norm.[31] A front-pay award that is not supported by a finding that reinstatement was impractical or impossible will be vacated.[32] Stated differently, when reinstatement is impractical or impossible, front pay may be appropriate.[33]

According to the Supreme Court, front pay is simply money awarded for lost compensation during the period between judgment and reinstatement or in lieu of reinstatement.[34] When an appropriate position for the plaintiff is not immediately available without displacing an incumbent employee, courts have ordered reinstatement upon the opening of such a position and have ordered front pay to be paid until reinstatement occurs.[35]

Front pay in lieu of or as a substitute for reinstatement is appropriate when reinstatement is not a viable option because of continuing

---

28. *Warnke v. CVS Corp.*, 265 F.R.D. 64, 69 (E.D.N.Y. 2010) (citing *Hawkins v. 1115 Legal Serv. Care*, 163 F.3d 684, 695 (2d Cir. 1998)).

29. *Dennis*, 290 F.3d at 652.

30. *EEOC v. Massey Yardley Chrysler Plymouth, Inc.*, 117 F.3d 1244, 1252 (11th Cir. 1997); *Alexander v. Local 496, Laborers Int'l Union of North America*, 177 F.3d 394, 411 (6th Cir. 1999); *NLRB v. Huntington Hospital, Inc.*, 550 F.2d 921, 924 (4th Cir. 1977); *Webber v. International Paper Co.*, 239 F. Supp. 2d 88, 97 (D. Me. 2003).

31. *Kucia v. Southeast Arkansas Cmty. Action Corp.*, 284 F.3d 944, 948 (8th Cir. 2002).

32. *Id.* at 949.

33. *Bergerson v. New York State Office of Mental Health*, 652 F.3d 277, 287 (2d Cir. 2011).

34. *Pollard v. E. I. du Pont de Nemours & Co.*, 532 U.S. 843, 846 (2001).

35. *Id.* (citing *Waldorf v. Board of Comm'rs*, 857 F.2d 1047, 1053–1054 (5th Cir. 1988)); *King v. Staley*, 849 F.2d 1143, 1145 (5th Cir. 1988).

hostility between plaintiff and employer or because of psychological injuries suffered by plaintiff as a result of discrimination.[36] The converse is true. Front pay may be denied when there is no finding that the animosity is so extreme that it makes an amicable and productive work relationship impossible.[37]

Front pay is a supplement to back pay, not a substitute for it.[38] Front pay is granted to compensate "victims of discrimination for the continuing future effects of discrimination until the victim can be made whole."[39]

Front pay serves to make a plaintiff whole when the plaintiff mitigated his or her damages but has no prospect of finding comparable or suitable employment, immediate promotion cannot occur because there are no positions available, or reinstatement is not available and the plaintiff is making less money at the current job.[40] Front pay is excluded in mixed-motive cases.[41] If the after-acquired evidence doctrine applies, front pay is not an appropriate remedy.[42] A plaintiff who cannot be reinstated because of a psychological disability is not entitled to front pay unless there is a causal connection between the adverse action and the psychological disability.[43]

---

36. *Pollard*, 532 U.S. at 846; *Schick v. Illinois Dep't of Human Servs.*, 307 F.3d 605, 614 (7th Cir. 2002) (a Title VII case); *Van Horn v. Specialized Support Servs., Inc.*, 241 F. Supp. 2d 994, 1014 (S.D. Iowa 2003) (a Title VII case); *Abuan v. Level 3 Commc'ns, Inc.*, 353 F.3d 1158, 1176 (10th Cir. 2003) (an ADEA case).

37. *Tadlock v. Powell*, 291 F.3d 541, 548 (8th Cir. 2002) (reinstatement and denial of front pay is affirmed because employer's actions evidenced poor judgment more than hostility or animus toward the plaintiff).

38. *Pitre v. Western Elec. Co.*, 843 F.2d 1262, 1279 (10th Cir. 1988).

39. *Id.* at 1278.

40. *Padilla v. Metro-North Commuter R.R.*, 92 F.3d 117, 126 (2d Cir. 1996); *Carter v. Sedgwick County*, 929 F.2d 1501, 1505 (10th Cir. 1991).

41. 42 U.S.C. § 2000e-5(g)(2)(B).

42. *Sellers v. Mineta*, 358 F.3d 1058, 1064 (8th Cir. 2004) (after-acquired evidence precludes award of front pay).

43. *Barton v. Zimmer, Inc.*, 662 F.3d 448, 455 (7th Cir. 2011) (plaintiff was not entitled to front pay because his psychological disability was caused by an unrelated job assignment from his new supervisor).

B. Calculation of Front Pay

Front pay is not an element of compensatory damages for purposes of the Civil Rights Act of 1991 and, thus, is not subject to the CRA's statutory caps discussed below.[44] Like back pay, front pay is an equitable remedy and is awarded only at the sound discretion of the court.[45] Front-pay awards are targeted at compensating the plaintiff for the reasonable time from the conclusion of trial that it would take to obtain comparable employment.[46] The court, however, is not supposed to catapult the plaintiff into a better position that he or she would have enjoyed in the absence of discrimination.[47] Front pay, thus, is an alternative for finite, not indefinite, periods during which reinstatement is unavailable.[48] Some courts take the position that front pay is only designed to compensate a plaintiff for the lost earnings from his or her old job for as long as he or she may have been expected to hold it.[49] Intent to remain in the defendant's employ until retirement does not entitle a plaintiff to front pay for the remainder of his or her work life.[50] Periods during which a plaintiff is not available for work, such as a period of imprisonment, justify the reduction of a front-pay award.[51] The greater the period of time upon which a front-pay award is calculated in a case involving an at-will employee, the less likely it is that the loss of future earnings can be demonstrated with any degree

---

44. *Pollard v. E. I. du Pont de Nemours & Co.*, 532 U.S. 843, 846–47 (2001); 42 U.S.C. § 1981a(b)(3).

45. *EEOC v. W & O, Inc.*, 213 F.3d 600, 618–619 (11th Cir. 2000); *McCue v. Kansas*, 165 F.3d 784, 791 (10th Cir. 1999); *Reed v. A. W. Lawrence & Co.*, 95 F.3d 1170, 1182 (2d Cir. 1996).

46. *Schick v. Illinois Dep't of Human Servs.*, 307 F.3d 605, 614 (7th Cir. 2002); *Williams v. Pharmacia*, 137 F.3d 944, 953–54 (7th Cir. 1998); *Selgas v. American Airlines, Inc.*, 104 F.3d 912 (1st. Cir. 1997); *Horney v. Westfield Gage Co.*, 211 F. Supp. 2d 291, 322 (D. Mass. 2002).

47. *Ford Motor Co. v. EEOC*, 458 U.S. 219, 234 (1982).

48. *Selgas v. American Airlines, Inc.*, 104 F.3d 9, 13–14 (1st. Cir. 1997) (eighteen-month back-pay award was found reasonable).

49. *Schick*, 307 F.3d at 614; *Williams*, 137 F.3d at 953–54.

50. *Peyton v. DiMario*, 287 F.3d 1121, 1129 (D.C. Cir. 2002).

51. *Schick*, 307 F.3d at 614 (time spent in prison is deducted from front pay).

of certainty or can reasonably be attributed to the illegal conduct of the employer.[52]

Because future damages, such as front pay, are inherently speculative, courts keep a close eye on the circumstances of the particular case.[53] Although front pay is not subject to a federal statutory damage cap, some circuits have overturned speculative and excessively lengthy front-pay awards under federal law.[54] Trial courts, moreover, may condition the denial of a motion for a new trial on the filing by the plaintiff of a remittitur in a stated amount that would be the maximum that would be upheld by the trial court as not excessive. This is called the least intrusive method.[55]

Front pay should be denied when the plaintiff has not sought other suitable employment or alternative employment.[56] Front pay should be denied when the plaintiffs resign and the jury rejects constructive discharge claims.[57] If the employer shows that the plaintiff failed to make a reasonable effort to seek comparable employment, the employer

---

52. *Donlin v. Phillips Lighting North America Corp.*, 581 F.3d 73, 88 (3d Cir. 2009) (court's reduction of advisory jury's front-pay award for twenty-five years to ten years to a temporary employee who was not hired was not an abuse of discretion and was affirmed); *Cummings v. Standard Register Co.*, 265 F.3d 56, 66 (1st Cir. 2001) (upholding a $665,000 award that constituted fourteen years of front pay based on an open-ended state law); *see Peyton v. DiMario*, 287 F.3d 1121, 1128–1129 (D.C. 2002) (vacating award of front pay for twenty-six years and stating that the longer the front-pay period, the more speculative the damages become).

53. *Arban v. West Publishing Corp.*, 345 F.3d 390 (6th Cir. 2003) (an FMLA case); *Tyler v. Union Oil Co. of California*, 304 F.3d 379 (5th Cir. 2002) (an ADEA case; front pay was denied because such an award would have required the court to speculate on whether the employees would have been hired by the new entity); *Torres v. White*, 45 Fed. Appx. 738 (6th Cir. 2002) (Title VII case; court will not disturb jury's failure to award front pay because the jury is the trier of fact on damages).

54. *Peyton*, 287 F.3d at 1128-29 (vacating award of front pay for 26 years); *Horney v. Westfield Gage Co.*, 211 F. Supp. 2d 291, 322 (D. Mass. 2002) (vacating award of front pay for 28 years to healthy young worker).

55. *Conjugal Partnership Re Jones & Jones v. Conjugal Partnership Re Pineda & Pineda*, 22 F.3d 391, 397 (1st Cir. 1994); *Earl v. Bouchard Transp. Co.*, 917 F.2d 1320, 1328–30 (2d Cir. 1990).

56. *Hine v. Mineta*, 238 F. Supp. 2d 497, 501 (E.D.N.Y. 2003).

57. *Mallinson-Montague v. Pocrnick*, 224 F.3d 1224, 1236 (10th Cir. 2000).

is relieved of the burden to prove that suitable work existed.[58] Front pay should not be awarded when the calculation method is unduly speculative.[59] A plaintiff need not accept employment that is an unreasonable distance from his or her residence. What is reasonable is a question of fact.[60]

III. Compensatory Damages

A. Entitlement to Compensatory Damages

The CRA makes compensatory and punitive damages available under Title VII for unlawful intentional discrimination in individual disparate-treatment cases, provided that the complaining party cannot recover under 42 U.S.C. § 1981. Such damages are available in addition to any other relief authorized by Title VII. Compensatory damages under the CRA may be sought in a lawsuit brought by the Equal Employment Opportunity Commission (EEOC) or the Attorney General of the United States.[61]

The CRA excludes the availability of compensatory and punitive damages from claims involving an employment practice that is unlawful because of its disparate impact.[62] Except for the § 1981 condition, which does not apply to the ADA or the Rehabilitation Act, the CRA also makes compensatory and punitive damages available under the ADA and Rehabilitation Act under the same conditions as in Title VII.[63]

---

58. *Shannon v. Fireman's Fund Ins. Co.*, 136 F. Supp. 2d 225, 228 (S.D.N.Y. 2001).

59. *Sagendorf-Teal v. County of Rensselaer*, 100 F.3d 270, 277 (2d Cir. 1996); *Brenlia v. La Sorsa Buick Pontiac Chevrolet, Inc.*, No. 00-5207, 2002 WL 1059117 (S.D.N.Y. May 28, 2002).

60. *Puchalski v. Sch. Dist. of Springfield*, 161 F. Supp. 2d 395, 412 (E.D. Pa. 2001) (whether failure to accept one of twenty-two coaching positions available in three years, which involved at least a 45-mile commute when plaintiff/coach was discharged from position that was five minutes away from home, was a question of fact regarding mitigation).

61. 42 U.S.C. § 1981a(d).

62. 42 U.S.C. § 1981a(a)(1) and (b)(4).

63. 42 U.S.C. § 1981a(a)(2).

Compensatory damages for emotional distress, mental pain, mental anguish, and the like are not available under the ADEA.[64]

B. Components of Compensatory Damages

General tort principles apply to Title VII cases so that a plaintiff may only recover damages proximately caused by the defendant's conduct.[65] Compensatory damages under the CRA include future pecuniary losses, emotional pain, suffering, inconvenience, mental anguish, loss of enjoyment of life, and other nonpecuniary losses.[66] Compensatory damages under the CRA shall not include back pay, interest on back pay, or any other relief authorized by § 2000e-5(g).[67]

The most-sought item of compensatory damages is emotional distress. A plaintiff's own testimony is sufficient to establish humiliation or emotional distress, especially when there is evidence of indifference on the part of the employer.[68]

A pre-existing condition, such as being raped or subjected to sexual abuse prior to employment, may not relieve an employer of liability for emotional distress.[69] Some courts take the position that a defendant

---

64. *Comm'r of Internal Revenue v. Schleier*, 515 U.S. 323, 326 (1995); *Barton v. Zimmer, Inc.*, 662 F.3d 448, 454 (7th Cir. 2011); *Villescas v. Abraham*, 211 F.3d 1253, 1259 (10th Cir. 2002); *Smith v. Berry Co.*, 165 F.3d 390, 396 (5th Cir. 1999).

65. *Schick v. Illinois Dep't of Human Servs.*, 307 F.3d 605, 615 (7th Cir. 2002) (plaintiff cannot recover for damages resulting from his conviction and incarceration for robbing a convenience store).

66. 42 U.S.C. § 1981a(b)(3); *Horn v. Specialized Support Servs., Inc.*, 241 F. Supp. 2d 994, 1014 (S.D. Iowa 2003).

67. 42 U.S.C. § 1981a(b)(2).

68. *Horn*, 241 F. Supp. 2d at 1015 (plaintiff's testimony on the sexual harassment and assault by the employer's client, the indifference of the employer after concerns were expressed, and the continued aggressive conduct of the client were sufficient to establish emotional distress); *Kucia v. Southeast Arkansas Cmty. Action Corp.*, 284 F.3d 944, 947–48 (8th Cir. 2002) (an award of compensatory damages based on plaintiff's testimony and remitted within the applicable statutory cap was not so excessive as to shock the conscience because the court knew the community standards); *but see Forshee v. Waterloo Indus., Inc.*, 178 F.3d 527, 531 (8th Cir. 1999) (verdict for $9,631 for emotional distress was reversed for insufficiency of evidence).

69. *Shea v. Icelander*, 925 F. Supp. 1014, 1025 (S.D.N.Y. 1996) (it is well settled that aggravation of a preexisting condition gives rise to liability); *McClelland v. Montgomery*

takes the plaintiff as it finds him or her.[70] This would include a plaintiff with a history of a troubled childhood, including sexual molestation, abandonment, and foster homes.[71] Other courts have limited damages for aggravation of a pre-existing condition to those above and beyond the pre-existing condition.[72] In determining the remittitur of a compensatory damages award, courts review awards in other cases.[73] Because of the statutory language, the specific items of compensatory damages are sometimes not identifiable, and an award in an amount deemed reasonable for the discrimination alleged is upheld.[74] Courts have awarded compensatory damages for mileage representing a longer commute than when the plaintiff was employed by the defendant

---

Ward & Co., No. 95-C-23, 1995 WL 571324 (N.D. Ill. Sept. 25, 1995) (evidence of preadolescent or adolescent parental sexual, physical, or emotional abuse and the psychological or mental conditions resulting from such abuse are admissible to determine compensatory damages for emotional distress and suffering caused by the defendant's conduct).

70. *Lockard v. Pizza Hut, Inc.*, 162 F.3d 1062, 1076 (10th Cir. 1998) (plaintiff's sexual abuse as a teenager was a pre-existing condition that was aggravated by the sexual harassment); *Horn*, 241 F. Supp. 2d at 1015 (plaintiff's rape as a child was a pre-existing condition that aggravated the sexual harassment).

71. *See Hurley v. Atlantic City Police Dep't*, 933 F. Supp. 396 (D.N.J. 1996).

72. *Hurley*, 933 F. Supp. at 424–25 (compensatory damages award was reduced from $575,000 to $175,000 because plaintiff's difficulties were rooted in a troubled childhood, physical abuse by two husbands, and personal problems, all unrelated to the work environment); *Kennedy v. City of St. Paul*, No. CX-99-259, 2000 WL 290425 (Minn. Ct. App. Mar. 21, 2000) (many of plaintiffs' symptoms or injuries from past abuse pre-dated the sexual harassment, and therefore, plaintiffs failed to mitigate their damages by not obtaining psychological treatment earlier).

73. *Meacham v. Knolls Atomic Power Lab.*, 185 F. Supp. 2d 193, 220 (N.D.N.Y. 2003) (in determining whether a jury's award of compensatory damages was excessive, the court reviewed awards in cases in which a plaintiff's emotional distress consisted of shock, sleepless nights, nightmares, and the like, but the plaintiff did not require treatment); *Hurley*, 933 F. Supp. at 423–24 (court reviewed cases in which awards for emotional distress were remitted or vacated).

74. *Connor v. Schroder-Bridgeport Int'l, Inc.*, 227 F.3d 179, 202 (4th Cir. 2000) (compensatory damages award of $20,000 for sexually hostile work environment experienced was reasonable); *Kimzey v. Wal-Mart Stores, Inc.*, 107 F.3d 568, 570 (8th Cir. 1997) (compensatory damages award of $35,000 for sexual harassment was reasonable).

and compensation at the hourly rate of pay for the time spent in a longer commute.[75]

IV. Punitive Damages

A. Entitlement to Punitive Damages

There is no vested right to punitive damages in Title VII or ADA cases, no matter how egregious the defendant's conduct.[76] Under the CRA, however, a complaining party may recover punitive damages against a respondent (other than a government, government agency, or political subdivision) if the complaining party demonstrates that the respondent is intentionally engaged in one or more discriminatory practices with malice or with reckless indifference to the federally protected rights of an aggrieved individual.[77] Punitive damages may be sought in a lawsuit brought by the EEOC or the Attorney General of the United States.[78] Some circuits hold that punitive damages are available in the total absence of compensatory damages because nothing in the plain language of the CRA conditions an award of punitive damages on an underlying award of compensatory damages.[79]

If the ADEA is violated, an employer is liable for the back pay plus an equal amount of liquidated damage in cases of willful violations.[80]

---

75. *Horn v. Specialized Support Servs., Inc.*, 241 F. Supp. 2d 994, 1014 (S.D. Iowa 2003).

76. *McKinnon v. Kwong Wah Restaurant*, 83 F.3d 498, 508 (1st Cir. 1996).

77. 42 U.S.C. § 1981a(b)(1); *Kolstad v. American Dental Ass'n*, 527 U.S. 526, 535 (1999) (punitive damages are limited to cases in which the employer has engaged in intentional discrimination and has done so with malice or with reckless indifference to the federally protected rights of an aggrieved individual).

78. 42 U.S.C. § 1981a(d).

79. *Corti v. Storage Tech. Corp.*, 304 F.3d 336, 341 (4th Cir. 2002) (punitive damages award in the absence of an award of compensatory damages was upheld because back pay was awarded); *EEOC v. W & O, Inc.*, 213 F.3d 600, 615 (11th Cir. 2000); *Provencher v. CVS Pharmacy*, 145 F.3d 5, 11 (1st Cir. 1998); *Timm v. Progressive Steel Treating, Inc.*, 137 F.3d 1008, 1010 (7th Cir. 1998).

80. 29 U.S.C. § 216; 29 U.S.C. § 626(b).

Liquidated damages under the ADEA and FLSA, which enforces the ADEA, are considered punitive in nature.[81]

B. Standard for Punitive Damages

Malice and *reckless indifference* refer not to the egregiousness of the employer's conduct or its awareness that it is engaging in discrimination, but rather to the employer's knowledge that it may be acting in violation of federal law.[82] A failure to take complaints seriously or to take prompt remedial action, as well as discharging the employee in retaliation, satisfies the standard for awarding punitive damages.[83] A failure to establish a sexual harassment policy is evidence of reckless indifference.[84] A cover-up of the true reason for a discriminatory discharge, when the cover-up was planned prior to the discharge, is evidence of a recognized risk of violating the law and is sufficient to support the award of punitive damages.[85] Malice and reckless indifference may be inferred when a manager responsible for setting or enforcing policy in the area of discrimination does not respond to complaints, despite knowledge of serious harassment.[86] Good deeds taken by the employer

---

81. *Trans World Airlines, Inc. v. Thurston*, 469 U.S. 111, 125 (1985); *EEOC v. Massey Yardley Chrysler Plymouth, Inc.*, 117 F.3d 1244, 1250 (11th Cir. 1997) (liquidated damages are designed to punish employers whose conduct constituted a willful violation).

82. *Kolstad*, 527 U.S. at 535; *David v. Caterpillar, Inc.*, 324 F.3d 851 (7th Cir. 2003) (court was required to reduce punitive damages award of $750,000 to no more than $250,000 because the compensatory award was $50,000 and the applicable statutory cap was $300,000); *Deters v. Equifax Credit Info. Servs.*, 202 F.3d 1262, 1269 (10th Cir. 2000).

83. *Horn v. Specialized Support Servs., Inc.*, 241 F. Supp. 2d 994, 1015 (S.D. Iowa 2003).

84. *Harris v. L & L Wings, Inc.*, 132 F.3d 978, 983 (4th Cir. 1997).

85. *Juarez v. ACS Government Solutions Group, Inc.*, 314 F.3d 1243, 1247 (10th Cir. 2003).

86. *Deters v. Equifax Credit Information Services, Inc.*, 202 F.3d at 1269 (punitive damages award affirmed because management not only did not respond to plaintiff's complaints but also minimized and disregarded them so as to protect the "revenue producers"); *Baty v. Williamette Industries, Inc.*, 172 F.3d 1232, 1244–45 (10th Cir. 1999).

after it has made an unlawful employment decision do not insulate the employer from an award of punitive damages.[87]

According to the doctrine of *respondeat superior*, employer malice or reckless indifference in failing to remedy or prevent a hostile or offensive work environment of which management-level employees knew or should have known is premised on direct liability, not derivative liability.[88] Because the CRA provides for the recovery of punitive damages against a respondent, it requires a determination of who qualifies as the employer for purposes of determining direct punitive liability.[89] It does not matter whether the allegedly wayward employee is a sufficiently highly ranked manager or policy maker such that her or his knowledge would be imputed as a matter of law to the employer. It is sufficient that the employer has specifically designated the allegedly wayward employee as a final representative of the company to implement the harassment policy and process complaints of harassment.[90]

V. Defenses to Back Pay and Front Pay

A. Failure to Mitigate

A victim of discrimination has a duty to mitigate damages, including back pay, by using "reasonable diligence in finding other suitable employment."[91] Title VII is interpreted to require mitigation of damages because it provides for the reduction of damages as follows:

---

87. *David*, 324 F.3d 851 (7th Cir. 2003) (punitive damages award was appropriate even if employer treated plaintiff well after discriminatory action and ultimately promoted plaintiff).

88. *Deters*, 202 F.3d at 1270 (citing *Adler v. Wal-Mart Stores*, 144 F.3d 664, 673 (10th Cir. 1998) (discussing direct liability in the context of compensatory damages)).

89. *Id.*; 42 U.S.C. § 1981a(b)(1).

90. *Deters*, 202 F.3d at 1270 (punitive damages could be awarded because the sexual harassment policy designated any human resources officer as a final representative, the employee who received the complaints was an HR officer, and information provided to such officer is knowledge to the company).

91. *Ford Motor Co. v. EEOC*, 458 U.S. 219, 231 (1982); *Miller v. AT&T Corp.*, 250 F.3d 820, 838 (4th Cir. 2001); *Hine v. Mineta*, 238 F. Supp. 2d 497, 498 (E.D.N.Y. 2003).

> Interim earnings or amounts earnable with reasonable diligence by the person or persons discriminated against shall operate to reduce the back pay otherwise allowable.[92]

The same is true of the ADA because it expressly adopts the powers, remedies, and procedures of Title VII.[93] By case law, the ADEA requires the mitigation of damages.[94]

The failure diligently to seek new employment precludes an award of back pay completely or for the period during which employment was not sought.[95] An inability to work, including an inability to be available for work because of the receipt of workers' compensation benefits, precludes an award of back pay.[96] The duty to mitigate is not without limits. For example, a plaintiff need not go into another line of work, accept a demotion, or take a demeaning position.[97]

The employer bears the burden of demonstrating that the plaintiff has failed to fulfill the duty to mitigate damages.[98] But once the employer proves that an employee has not made reasonable efforts to obtain work, the employer also does not have to establish the availability of substantially equivalent employment.[99] The jury may reduce damages, provided that the defendant-employer makes certain show-

---

92. 42 U.S.C. § 2000e-5(g)(1); *Hawkins v. 115 Legal Serv. Care*, 163 F.3d 684, 695 (2d Cir. 1998); *Hine*, 238 F. Supp. 2d at 500.

93. 42 U.S.C. § 12117(a).

94. *West v. Nabors Drilling USA, Inc.*, 230 F.3d 379, 393 (5th Cir. 2003); *Yancy v. Weyerhaeuser Co.*, 277 F.3d 1021, 1025 (8th Cir. 2002); *Gotthardt v. National R.R. Passenger Corp.*, 191 F.3d 1148, 1157 (9th Cir. 2000).

95. *Miller*, 250 F.3d at 838; *Hine*, 238 F. Supp. 2d at 500 (plaintiff who was a traffic-controller trainee was denied back pay because she did not search for employment for more than seven years, other than a three-month clerical job).

96. *Hine*, 238 F. Supp. 2d at 501 (plaintiff was denied back pay because she failed to search for a job for seven years and received workers' compensation benefits during that time in the amount of $310,000).

97. *Ford Motor Co.*, 458 U.S. at 231.

98. *Duty v. Norton-Alcoa Proppants*, 293 F.3d 481, 496 (8th Cir. 2002); *Peyton v. DeMario*, 287 F.3d 1121, 1128 (D.C. Cir. 2002); *Miller*, 250 F.3d at 838; *EEOC v. Yardley Chrysler Plymouth, Inc.*, 117 F.3d 1244, 1251 (11th Cir. 1997).

99. *West*, 230 F.3d at 393 (an ADEA case).

ings. To meet its burden that damages should be reduced, an employer must demonstrate that (1) substantially equivalent work was available, and (2) the employee did not exercise reasonable diligence in obtaining employment.[100] For example, a showing that other employees who were laid off obtained comparable jobs at a university, that the employee declined the university's offer of job-search help, and that the employee, despite attending a job fair, produced only two job rejection letters covering a fifteen-month period satisfied the burden to reduce an employee's claim for back pay.[101]

With respect to a plaintiff who has decided to forgo a search for employment and become a full-time student, the court will consider whether an individual's furtherance of his or her education is consistent with the responsibility to use reasonable diligence in finding other suitable employment.[102] If a plaintiff opts to attend school to obtain greater future benefits, such as leaving nursing to attend law school, the plaintiff has failed to mitigate damages, and a back-pay award may be reduced or denied.[103] Back-pay awards ordinarily will not be denied if the plaintiff enrolled in school only after a diligent but fruitless search for employment, and if the plaintiff did not voluntarily absent him- or herself from the active job market because he or she believed his or her ultimate earning potential would be enhanced with the benefit of further education.[104]

---

100. *Le v. Univ. of Pennsylvania*, 321 F.3d 403, 407 (3d Cir. 2003); *Conetta v. Nat'l Hair Care Ctrs., Inc.*, 236 F.3d 67, 77 (1st Cir. 2001).

101. *Le*, 321 F.3d 407.

102. *Miller*, 250 F.3d at 838; *Dailey v. Society Generale*, 108 F.3d 451, 456–57 (4th Cir. 1997).

103. *Floca v. Homecare Health Servs., Inc.*, 845 F.2d 108, 112–13 (5th Cir. 1988) (front pay denied to plaintiff who left nursing to attend law school); *Miller v. Marsh*, 766 F.2d 490, 492–93 (11th Cir. 1985) (back pay denied to plaintiff who abandoned temporary stenographer job in order to enroll in law school); *Taylor v. Safeway Stores, Inc.*, 524 F.2d 263, 267–68 (10th Cir. 1975) (back-pay award reduced to plaintiff who enrolled in school full time).

104. *Miller*, 250 F.3d at 839 (plaintiff did not fail to mitigate damages by going to school where the position for which the plaintiff trained while in school was not a "step up" to the prior position and the plaintiff earned less in the new position than at the

Moreover, reducing the back-pay award because the plaintiff moved to another state after she or he could not find work in the home state is improper where the plaintiff continued to look for a job in the new state. In such a situation, the court has the discretion to increase the amount of the jury's award to cover the period from the date of the constructive discharge to the date the plaintiff rejected the defendant's unconditional offer of reinstatement.[105] This is because the courts are not deemed to have violated the rule of *Dimick v. Schwedt* [106] when the jury has found the underlying liability and there is no genuine issue as to the correct amount of damages.[107]

As in back-pay situations, a plaintiff seeking front pay has the duty to exercise reasonable diligence in mitigating damages by seeking other suitable or alternative employment.[108] A plaintiff fails to mitigate when there is substantially equivalent work available and he or she has not exercised reasonable diligence in finding new work.[109] On the other hand, a plaintiff who claims that he or she looked for employment but did not apply for any jobs because he or she could not find substantially

---

prior position) (citing *Dailey v. Society Generale*, 108 F.3d 451, 456–57 (4th Cir. 1997) (plaintiff who enrolled in school after six-month job search was unsuccessful did not fail to mitigate damages); *Smith v. Am. Serv. Co. of Atlanta, Inc.*, 796 F.2d 1430, 1432 (11th Cir. 1986) (plaintiff who enrolled in school after unsuccessfully seeking employment for seven months and who worked part time while in school did not fail to mitigate damages); *Hanna v. Am. Motors Corp.*, 724 F.2d 1300, 1308–09 (7th Cir. 1984) (plaintiff who enrolled in school but who applied for and was willing to accept full-time employment did not fail to mitigate damages).

105. *EEOC v. Massey Yardley Chrysler Plymouth, Inc.*, 117 F.3d at 1252.

106. *Dimick v. Schwedt*, 293 U.S. 474, 486–87 (1935) (this case holds that the Seventh Amendment to the U.S. Constitution prevents a court from increasing a jury's award or conditioning the denial of a new trial on the defendant's acquiescence to an additur).

107. *EEOC v. Massey Yardley Chrysler Plymouth, Inc.*, 117 F.3d at 1252.

108. *Hine v. Mineta*, 238 F. Supp. 2d at 501; *Reed v. A. W. Lawrence & Co.*, 95 F.3d 1170, 1182 (2d Cir. 1996).

109. *Booker v. Taylor Milk Co.*, 64 F.3d 860, 864 (3d Cir. 1995) (a Title VII case); *Puchalski v. Sch. Dist. of Springfield*, 161 F. Supp. 2d 395, 411 (E.D. Pa. 2001) (an ADEA case).

comparable job openings may be found to have mitigated his or her damages.[110]

B. Offset for Unemployment Benefits

In *NLRB v. Gullet Gin Co.*,[111] the Supreme Court affirmed an NLRB decision not to deduct unemployment benefits from a back-pay award obtained from an employer found to have discriminated on the basis of union membership. The court, in so doing, noted that unemployment benefits are a collateral source and do not have to be deducted from back pay, even when the employer paid for some part of the unemployment benefits through its contributions.

District courts have the same discretion as the NLRB to determine whether to deduct unemployment benefits from back-pay awards.[112] If the defendant provides a benefit to the plaintiff specifically to compensate him or her for an injury, the benefit does not constitute a collateral source, and the payments may be offset against a back-pay award. By contrast, a payment is from a collateral source and should not be offset if the defendant does not provide the benefit to the plaintiff as compensation for his or her injury.[113] In practice, the majority of courts has held that unemployment benefits are a collateral source of compensation and should not be deducted from or offset against

110. *Ellerbrook v. City of Lubbock*, 465 Fed. Appx. 324 (5th Cir. 2012) (*per curiam*) (jury's award of three years of back pay plus benefits, which was the total amount requested by plaintiff, was an implied finding that plaintiff did not fail to mitigate her damages).

111. 340 U.S. 361 (1951).

112. *Toro v. Sanchez*, 141 F. Supp. 2d 195, 199 (D.P.R. 2002); *Daily v. Society Generale*, 108 F.3d 451, 460 (2d Cir. 1997); *Hunter v. Allison-Chambers Corp. Engine Div.*, 797 F.2d 1417, 1428 (7th Cir. 1986); *Hill v. Airborne Freight Corp.*, 2003 WL 366641 (S.D.N.Y. Feb. 20, 2003); *Leidel v. Ameripride Servs., Inc.*, 276 F. Supp. 2d 1138, 1144 (D. Kan. 2003); *Hilton v. Entemann's Sales Co., Inc.*, 2002 WL 1821666 (N.D. Ill. Aug. 8, 2002); *Doherty v. Crow*, 2001 WL 722090 (S.D. Ind. Apr. 20, 2001).

113. *Sloas v. CSX Transp., Inc.*, 616 F.3d 380, 389–90 (4th Cir. 2010) (disability benefits were collateral and could not be offset).

a back-pay award.[114] Yet some courts have allowed the deduction.[115] State law should be consulted if the case is being tried under the state antidiscrimination statute.[116]

---

114. *See Daily v. Society Generale*, 108 F.3d 451, 460–61 (2d Cir. 1997) (under the circumstances, unemployment benefits were not to be deducted from the back-pay award); *Leidel v. Ameripride Servs., Inc.*, 276 F. Supp. 2d at 1144 (citing *EEOC v. Sandia Corp.*, 639 F.2d 600, 624–26 (10th Cir. 1990)); *Hill v. Airborne Freight Corp.*, 2003 WL 366641 (S.D.N.Y. Feb. 20, 2003) (noting that sister circuits have expressed the view that a district court has compelling reasons not to offset unemployment compensation); *Doherty v. Crow*, 2001 WL 722090 (S.D. Ind. Apr. 20, 2001) (citing cases where the district courts in the Seventh Circuit have declined to deduct unemployment benefits from a back-pay award); *Rivera v. Hollow Corp.*, 1999 WL 219910 (S.D.N.Y. Apr. 15, 1999) (the prevailing practice among the courts in this district is to follow the collateral source doctrine and not give defendants the benefit of plaintiff's compensation from a third party); *see also McLean v. Runyon*, 222 F.3d 1150, 1155–56 (9th Cir. 2000) (the collateral source rule does not apply to workers' compensation benefits); *Hamlin v. Charter Twp. of Flint*, 165 F.3d 426, 433–34 (6th Cir. 1999) (ADA case in which pension benefits were deemed to be a nondeductible collateral source).

115. *Naton v. Bank of California*, 649 F.2d 691, 700 (9th Cir. 1981) (district court did not abuse its discretion in deducting unemployment benefits from back-pay award; application of the collateral source rule is not necessary to ensure a full recovery to an injured party); *Miles-Hackman v. David Powers Homes, Inc.*, 613 F. Supp. 872, 890 (S.D. Tex. 2009) (unemployment benefits were considered interim earnings that were subject to offset); *Palma v. Pharmedia Commc'ns, Inc.*, 2003 WL 22750547 (D. Conn. Sept. 30, 2003) (plaintiff's consulting actuary testified that he reduced plaintiff's lost future income by the value of plaintiff's part-time jobs and unemployment benefits received, and therefore, the jury's verdict deducting unemployment benefits was not erroneous); *Pennsylvania Nurses Ass'n, Local 729, OPEIU AFL/CIO v. John F. Kennedy Med. Ctr.*, 247 F. Supp. 2d 265, 676 (E.D. Pa. 2003) (it maybe proper for an arbitrator to offset unemployment benefits, but there is no authority for an arbitrator to penalize an employee financially for failing to mitigate); *Grave v. Georgia Gulf Corp.*, 2002 WL 31455701 (M.D. La. Sept. 30, 2002) (FMLA case in which court found that had plaintiff proven that she was entitled to damages, the award would have been offset by any sums the plaintiff received from other sources, such as unemployment benefits); *EEOC v. Yellow Freight Sys., Inc.*, 2002 WL 31011859 (S.D.N.Y. Sept. 9, 2002) (court approved deduction of unemployment benefits because plaintiff included the deduction in his damages computation); *Higdon v. Entemann's Sales Co., Inc.*, 2002 WL 1821666 (N.D. Ill. Aug. 8, 2002) (plaintiff complained that the jury improperly deducted unemployment compensation from his back-pay award; court denied plaintiff's motion to alter or amend judgment because plaintiff failed to show he had not been made whole by the jury); *Sherman v. AI/FOCS, Inc.*, 113 F. Supp. 2d 65, 76 (D. Mass. 2000) (FMLA case).

116. For example, section 21.258(c) of the Texas Labor Code provides that "Interim earnings, worker's compensation benefits, and unemployment compensation benefits received operate to reduce the back pay otherwise allowable."

C. The After-Acquired Evidence Doctrine

Evidence of employee wrongdoing acquired after wrongful termination may limit an award of back pay and disentitle an employee to front pay and reinstatement when the employer establishes that the employee in fact would have been terminated on those grounds alone if the employer had known of it at the time of the discharge.[117] The after-acquired evidence doctrine balances the need to enforce national employment policy by deterring and punishing employer misconduct, while taking "due account of the lawful prerogatives of the employer in the usual course of its business and the corresponding equities that it has arising from the employee's wrongdoing."[118]

The employer must show that (1) it did not know of the employee's misconduct prior to the allegedly actionable employment decision, (2) the misconduct was severe, and (3) it would have made the same adverse employment decision based on the severe misconduct alone.[119] The after-acquired evidence doctrine limits back pay from the date of the discovery of the wrongdoing or misconduct. The doctrine does not bar liability.[120]

---

117. *McKennon v. Nashville Banner Publishing Co.*, 513 U.S. 352, 361–63 (1995); *Sellers v. Mineta*, 358 F.3d 1058, 1065 (8th Cir. 2004) (after-acquired evidence precludes award of front pay); *Miller v. AT&T Corp.*, 250 F.3d 820, 838 (4th Cir. 2001) (after-acquired doctrine applies to chronically absent employee's claim, but back pay cannot be reduced because employer did not show that plaintiff was not entitled to FMLA leave for the absences and employer in fact would have terminated plaintiff based on the absences); *but see Jones v. Nissan North America, Inc.*, 438 Fed. Appx. 388 (6th Cir. 2011) (*McKennon v. Nashville Banner* rule did not apply to plaintiff's search for a new job because were it not for Nissan's wrongful imposition of medical restrictions rendering plaintiff unfit for any position at Nissan, plaintiff would not have been in the position of seeking new employment without Nissan's permission).

118. *McKennon*, 513 U.S. at 361.

119. *Id.* at 362–63.

120. *Id.* at 361; *see Chang v. Cargill, Inc.*, 168 F. Supp. 2d 1003 (D. Minn. 2001) (plaintiff falsified his employment application by lying about his college major, cumulative grade point average, and college grades in math and computer programming classes).

The after-acquired evidence defense may be asserted in federal and state law claims, including the FMLA, as well as state common law wrongful discharge claims.[121]

D. The Statute of Limitations and Continuing Violations

Plaintiffs generally have 300 days, or in nondeferral jurisdictions 180 days, within which to file a Charge of Discrimination.[122] The continuing violation doctrine is an equitable exception that allows employees to seek damages for otherwise time-barred allegations if they were deemed part of an ongoing series of discriminatory acts.[123]

The Supreme Court in *National Railroad Passenger Corp. v. Morgan*[124] distinguished discrete discriminatory acts from a hostile work environment and explained why the two claims should have different limitation periods. "A discrete retaliatory or discriminatory act occurs on the day that it happened. A party, therefore, must file a charge within either 180 or 300 days of the date of the act or lose the ability to recover for it."[125]

Stated another way, a discrete discriminatory act happens only at the time it takes place, even if it was related to acts that were filed in a timely manner, and each discrete discriminatory act starts a new clock for filing charges alleging that act.[126] The Supreme Court in *Morgan* held that "discrete acts, such as termination, failure to promote, denial

121. *McKennon*, 513 U.S. 352 (ADEA case); *O'Neal v. City of New Albany*, 293 F.2d 998 (7th Cir. 2002) (Title VII and ADA case); *Woods v. Champion Chevrolet*, 35 Fed. Appx. 453 (9th Cir. 2002) (Title VII case); *Miller v. AT&T Corp.*, 250 F.3d 820, 838 (4th Cir. 2001) (FMLA case); *Wal-Mart Stores, Inc. v. Amos*, 79 S.W.3d 178 (Tex. Ct. App. 2002).

122. *See* 42 U.S.C. § 2000e-5(1) (a charge must be filed with the EEOC within 180 days, or 300 days in a deferral state, after the alleged unlawful employment practice occurred).

123. *Riviera v. Puerto Rico Aqueduct & Sewers Authority*, 331 F.3d 183, 188 (1st Cir. 2003); *O'Rourke v. City of Providence*, 235 F.3d 713, 730 (1st Cir. 2001).

124. 536 U.S. 101, 110 (2001).

125. *Id.* at 110.

126. *Nat'l R.R. Passenger Corp. v. Morgan*, 536 U.S. 101, 112 (2002); *Riviera*, 331 F.3d at 188.

of transfer, or refusal to hire, constitute separate actionable unlawful employment practices." Thus, if the discrete acts are not the subject of a charge filed in a timely manner with the EEOC or the deferral agency, they are time barred.[127]

A claim for hostile work environment is different from a discrete discriminatory act because by its very nature it involves repeated conduct, and recovery may be had for the whole period as long as the charge has been filed within 180 or 300 days of any act that was part of the hostile work environment.[128] Since *Morgan*, the courts have held that the incidents that make up a hostile work environment constitute a single unlawful employment practice, and the employer may be liable for all acts that are part of this single claim. In order for the hostile work environment charge to be timely, however, the employee must file a charge within 180 or 300 days of any act that is part of the hostile work environment.[129]

The requirement of filing a charge of discrimination within 180 or 300 days of the alleged unlawful employment practice is subject to equitable doctrines, such as tolling, estoppel, or waiver. Courts may evaluate whether it would be proper to apply such doctrines, although they are to be applied sparingly.[130]

---

127. *Morgan*, 536 U.S. at 114 (plaintiff's discrete discriminatory acts were not filed in a timely manner and were not actionable); *Riviera*, 331 F.3d at 188–89 (plaintiff's transfers more than 300 days before she filed her charge were discrete acts and time barred, and plaintiff could not show pretext for the reason for the transfers); *Cherosky v. Henderson*, 330 F.3d 1243, 1248 (9th Cir. 2003) (employer's rejection of a proposed accommodation was a discrete act for which no charge was filed; a policy that remained in effect during the limitations period was insufficient to establish a continuing violation).

128. *Morgan*, 536 U.S. at 120–21; *see also Madison v. IBP, Inc.*, 330 F.3d 1051, 1060–61 (8th Cir. 2003) (hostile work environment claims were not time barred).

129. *Boyler v. Cordant Techs., Inc.*, 316 F.3d 1137, 1140 (10th Cir. 2003) (overruling Tenth Circuit cases holding that recovery in a Title VII hostile work environment case is not available for acts taken outside the statutory time period, where the plaintiff knew or should have known the conduct was discriminatory when the acts occurred; plaintiff's hostile work environment claims filed outside the 300-day time period could proceed under continuing violation theory).

130. *Morgan*, 536 U.S. at 113 (*citing Zipes v. Trans-World Airlines, Inc.*, 455 U.S. 385, 393 (1982) and *Baldwin Cty. Welcome Ctr. v. Brown*, 466 U.S. 147, 152 (1984)

E. Failure to Exhaust Administrative Remedies

As set forth above, under Title VII, the ADA, and the ADEA, a charge must be filed with the EEOC within 180 days, or within 300 days in a deferral state, after the alleged unlawful employment practice occurred.[131] If a charge is not filed, the court lacks subject matter jurisdiction and should dismiss the claims that would have been the subject of the charge.[132]

F. Prompt Remedial Action and Other Defenses to Harassment Claims

In two sexual harassment cases decided in 1998, the Supreme Court held that an employer is subject to vicarious liability to a victimized employee for an actionable hostile environment created by a supervisor with immediate (or successively higher) authority over the employee.[133] When no tangible employment action is taken by a supervisor, a defending employer may raise an affirmative defense to liability or damages that (1) it exercised reasonable care to prevent and promptly correct any sexually harassing behavior, and (2) the plaintiff unreasonably failed to take advantage of any preventive or corrective opportunities provided by the employer or to avoid harm otherwise.[134]

(*per curiam*)); *see also Manning v. Chevron Chemical Co.*, 332 F.3d 874 (5th Cir. 2003) (discussing justifications for equitable tolling). The Fifth Circuit has repeatedly rejected equitable tolling arguments where plaintiffs had knowledge of the facts or where the employer did not conceal or misrepresent facts so as to deter plaintiffs from exercising their rights. *See Ramirez v. City of San Antonio*, 312 F.3d 178 (5th Cir. 2002); *McGregor v. Louisiana State Univ. Bd. of Supervisors*, 3 F.3d 850 (5th Cir. 1993); *Conaway v. Control Data*, 955 F.2d 358 (5th Cir. 1992); *Blumberg v. HCA Mgmt. Co.*, 848 F.2d 642 (5th Cir. 1988); *Pruet Prod. Co. v. Ayles*, 784 F.2d 1275 (5th Cir. 1986).

131. 42 U.S.C. § 2000e-5(1).

132. *Robinson v. Front-Line Security, Inc.*, No. 02-7859, 2003 WL 21510424 (2d Cir. July 1, 2003); *Howard v. Seaway Food Town, Inc.*, 63 Fed. Appx. 837 (6th Cir. 2003); *Cochren v. Barnes*, 55 Fed. Appx. 505 (10th Cir. 2003).

133. *Faragher v. City of Boca Raton*, 524 U.S. 775, 778 (1998); *Burlington Indus. v. Ellerth*, 524 U.S. 742 (1998).

134. *Faragher*, 524 U.S. at 807; *Ellerth*, 524 U.S. at 745.

Although proof that an employer had promulgated an anti-harassment policy with complaint procedure is not necessary in every instance as a matter of law, the need for a stated policy suitable to the employment circumstances may appropriately be addressed in any case when litigating the first element of the defense.[135] Proof that an employee failed to fulfill the corresponding obligation of reasonable care to avoid harm is not limited to showing an unreasonable failure to use any complaint procedure provided by the employer. But a demonstration of such failure will normally suffice to satisfy the employer's burden under the second element of the defense.[136]

No affirmative defense is available when the supervisor's harassment culminates in a tangible employment action, such as discharge, demotion, failure to promote, reassignment with significantly different responsibilities, or a decision causing a significant change in benefits.[137]

In a sexual or other harassment case in which the harassment was perpetrated by a non-supervisory coworker, the employer is liable only if the plaintiff can demonstrate that the employer (1) knew or should have known of the harassing conduct and (2) failed to implement prompt and appropriate action.[138] Consequently, a defense that the employer did not know or could have known of the harassing conduct, or that prompt remedial action was taken, may be raised by the employer in a coworker harassment case. Actual notice is established by proof that management knew of the harassment, whereas constructive notice will be found when the harassment was so severe and pervasive that management should have known of it.[139] The factors to be considered in

---

135. *Faragher*, 524 U.S. at 807; *Ellerth*, 524 U.S. at 745; *see also Reed v. MBNA Marketing Systems, Inc.*, 333 F.3d 27, 32 (1st Cir. 2003).

136. *Faragher*, 524 U.S. at 807–08; *Ellerth*, 524 U.S. at 745; *see also Reed*, 333 F.3d at 32.

137. *Faragher*, 524 U.S. at 808; *Ellerth*, 524 U.S. at 745.

138. *Crowley v. L.L. Bean, Inc.*, 303 F.3d 387, 401 (1st. Cir. 2002) (a sexual harassment case where prompt remedial action was not established); *Miller v. Kenworth of Dothan, Inc.*, 277 F.3d 1269, 1278 (11th Cir. 2002) (race discrimination case where affirmative defense was not established).

139. *Miller*, 277 F.3d at 1278.

determining constructive notice of the harassment are (1) the remoteness of the location of the harassment as compared to the location of management, (2) whether the harassment occurred intermittently over a long period of time, (3) whether the victims were employed on a part-time or full-time basis, and (4) whether the instances of harassment were few and discrete.[140] Prompt remedial action shields an employer from liability when the harassing conduct is committed by a coworker rather than a supervisor.[141]

For purposes of supervisor and nonsupervisor harassment cases, prompt remedial action obligates an employer to take the action reasonably calculated to end the harassment and not necessarily to terminate the employment of an employee who engages in sexual harassment.[142] Prompt remedial action that eliminates the allegedly intolerable working conditions operates as a complete defense to a claim of constructive discharge.[143] Prompt remedial action is not established if there is a failure to investigate the complaint.[144] Prompt remedial action may not

---

140. *Miller*, 277 F.3d at 1278–79.

141. *Meriwether v. Caraustar Packaging Co.*, 326 F.3d 990, 993 (8th Cir. 2003) (summary judgment to employer affirmed where employer's initial suspension of harasser for two days and then five days after the investigation was completed, requiring the harasser to undergo training, and warning the harasser about termination of employment if another incident occurred, was prompt and effective remedial action).

142. *Woodford v. Federal Express Corp.*, 2004 WL 234396 (D. Minn. Jan. 21, 2004) (prompt remedial action defense established where the employer's investigation was prompt; the perpetrator was suspended without pay pending the investigation, reprimanded in writing, ordered to avoid contact with the complainant, and required to attend diversity training; and complainant was given an office job where she had little contact with the drivers); *Scarberry v. ExxonMobil Oil Corp.*, 328 F.3d 1255 (10th Cir. 2003) (summary judgment to employer affirmed where employer promptly investigated incidents of sexual harassment and took progressively more serious remedial action that not only ended harassment by specific employees but also was reasonably calculated to demonstrate to all employees that its policy against sexual harassment would be enforced); *see also EEOC Guidance on Vicarious Liability for Unlawful Harassment by Supervisors*, Fair Employment Practices Manual 405:7651 (BNA).

143. *Lee-Crespo v. Schering-Plough Del Caribe Inc.*, 354 F.3d 34, 45 (1st Cir. 2003).

144. *Homesley v. Freightliner Corp.*, 61 Fed. Appx. 105, 2003 WL 1908744 (4th Cir. 2003) (failure to investigate suggested that the employer was not interested in preventing, let alone correcting, sexual harassment in the workplace).

be established if the remedy is inadequate under the circumstances, such as when the offensive conduct has occurred on a long-term basis, or the employer failed to comply with its policies designed to correct sexually harassing behavior.[145]

The practitioner should request jury instructions if the affirmative defenses to harassment are pled or tried by consent.[146]

G. ADEA Defenses

An employer may assert the good-faith defense in an ADEA case to avoid liability for liquidated damages that are automatically imposed in cases of willful violations.[147] A violation is willful if the employer knew or showed reckless disregard for whether its conduct was prohibited by the ADEA.[148]

An employer who knowingly relies on age in reaching an employment decision does not invariably commit a knowing and reckless ADEA violation.[149] If an employer incorrectly but in good faith and nonrecklessly believes that the ADEA permits particular age-based decisions, then liquidated damages should not be imposed.[150]

---

145. *Homesley v. Freightliner Corp.*, 61 Fed. Appx. 105 (4th Cir. 2003) (moving the sexual harasser 100 feet away from the complainant was considered inadequate to stop the harasser's stalking and glaring; first element of affirmative defense is not established); *Jackson v. Quanex Corp.*, 191 F.3d 647, 664 (6th Cir. 1999) (a racial harassment case; reprimand of the supervisor was inadequate where the supervisor engaged in racial slurs for years and finally was told that the conduct was not acceptable anymore).

146. *See Homesley*, 61 Fed. Appx. 105 (lengthy discussion of the jury instructions that the appellate court held correctly stated the law).

147. 29 U.S.C. § 626(b).

148. *West v. Nabors Drilling USA, Inc.*, 230 F.3d 381, 391 (1st Cir. 2000); *Smith v. Berry Co.*, 165 F.3d 390, 395 (5th Cir. 1999) (citing *Trans World Airlines, Inc. v. Thurston*, 469 U.S. 111, 128 (1985)).

149. *Tyler v. Union Oil Co. of California*, 304 F.3d 379, 398 (5th Cir. 2002).

150. *West*, 230 F.3d at 391 (employer's testimony that plaintiff was discharged because of his age was contrary to a good-faith belief, and jury's finding of willfullness was upheld); *Tyler*, 304 F.3d at 398 (quoting *Hazen Paper Co. v. Biggins*, 507 U.S. 604, 616 (1993)); *Minshall v. McGraw Hill Broadcasting Co.*, 323 F.3d 1273, 1283 (10th Cir. 2003) (employer's testimony that no one under the age of forty be hired to replace plaintiff meant that the employer was aware of the ADEA, and the award of liquidated damages was affirmed); *but see Carberry v. Monarch Marking Sys., Inc.*, 30 Fed.

In an ADEA action, the employer should determine whether one of the enumerated defenses applies. For example, the ADEA states that it shall not be unlawful to take any action otherwise prohibited by the statute where age is a bona fide occupational qualification reasonably necessary to the normal operation of the particular business, where the differentiation is based on reasonable factors other than age, or where such practices involve an employee in a workplace in a foreign country and compliance with the ADEA would cause such employer or a corporation controlled by such employer to violate the laws of the country in which such workplace is located.[151]

Another defense provides that it shall not be unlawful to take any action otherwise prohibited under the ADEA to observe the terms of a bona fide seniority system that is not intended to evade the ADEA, except that no such seniority system shall require or permit involuntary retirement of any individual specified by § 631(a) because of the age of such individual.[152]

A third defense enumerated under the ADEA provides that it shall not be unlawful to take any action otherwise prohibited under the ADEA to observe the terms of a bona fide employee benefit plan: (1) where for each benefit or benefit package, the actual amount of payment made or cost incurred on behalf of the older worker is no less than that made or incurred on behalf of a younger worker as permitted under 29 C.F.R. § 1625.10; or (2) that is a voluntary early retirement incentive plan consistent with the relevant purpose of the ADEA.[153]

Finally, the ADEA also provides other defenses pertaining to firefighters, law-enforcement officers, and employee pension benefit plans.[154]

Appx. 386 (6th Cir. 2002) (*per curiam*) (no evidence was presented that the employer's supervisors believed that their decision, based upon a somewhat visceral sense of which candidate was the "right fit" for the position advertised, violated the ADEA; award of liquidated damages was reversed).

151. 29 U.S.C. § 623(f)(1).
152. 29 U.S.C. § 623(f)(2)(A).
153. 29 U.S.C. § 623(f)(2)(B).
154. 29 U.S.C. § 623(j) and (1).

VI. Defenses to Compensatory and Punitive Damages

A. Statutory Caps Under Title VII, ADA, and the Rehabilitation Act

The CRA provides limitations (caps) on the amounts of compensatory and punitive damages awarded in a Title VII or ADA case. Under the CRA, the sum of the amount of compensatory damages awarded for future pecuniary losses, emotional pain, suffering, inconvenience, mental anguish, loss of enjoyment of life, and other nonpecuniary losses, and the amount of punitive damages awarded shall not exceed the following amounts for each complaining party:

A. In the case of a respondent who has more than 14 and fewer than 101 employees in each of 20 or more calendar weeks in the current or preceding calendar year, $50,000;
B. In the case of a respondent who has more than 100 and fewer than 201 employees in each of 20 or more calendar weeks in the current or preceding calendar year, $100,000;
C. In the case of a respondent who has more than 200 and fewer than 501 employees in each of 20 or more calendar weeks in the current or preceding calendar year, $200,000; and
D. In the case of a respondent who has more than 500 employees in each of 20 or more calendar weeks in the current or preceding calendar year, $300,000.[155]

The purpose of statutory caps is to deter frivolous lawsuits and protect employers from financial ruin as a result of unusually large awards.[156] The statutory caps apply per plaintiff (that is, per party, per litigant) and not per claim.[157] Punitive damages are unlimited under 42 U.S.C.

155. 42 U.S.C. § 1981a(b)(3).
156. *Luciano v. Olsten Corp.*, 110 F.3d 210, 221 (2d Cir. 1997).
157. *Black v. Pan American Labs., LLC*, 646 F.3d 254, 264 (5th Cir. 2011) (following sister circuits); *Hudson v. Reno*, 130 F.3d 1193, 1200 (6th Cir. 1997); *Fogg v.*

§ 1981.[158] In determining punitive damages, the jury is to be guided by the traditional principles of whether an amount is necessary to punish the defendant for its conduct and to deter the defendant and other employers from engaging in such activity in the future.[159]

If the complaining party seeks compensatory or punitive damages under the CRA, any party may demand a jury trial, and the court shall not inform the jury of the limitations (caps) on damages described in § 1981a(b)(3).[160]

If a plaintiff is awarded compensatory damages alone or in combination with punitive damages in excess of the applicable statutory caps, the defendant should immediately move for a remittitur, in addition to requesting other relief it deems appropriate, such as judgment notwithstanding the verdict or motion for a new trial. If the sum of the compensatory and punitive damages awarded by the jury exceeds the relevant cap, the district court is required to reduce the award to ensure that it conforms to the applicable statutory cap.[161]

Appellate review of an award of compensatory damages involves three inquiries:

(1) Whether the award is monstrously excessive;
(2) Whether there is no rational connection between the award and the evidence;
(3) Whether the award is roughly comparable to awards made in similar cases.[162] An employer should request a jury instruction

---

Ashcroft, 254 F.3d 103, 106–08 (D.C. Cir. 2001).

158. *Claiborne v. Illinois Central R.R. Co.*, 583 F.2d 143, 153–54 (5th Cir. 1978), *reh'g denied*, 588 F.2d 828 (5th Cir. 1978), *cert. denied*, 442 U.S. 934 (1978); *Skinner v. Total Petroleum, Inc.*, 859 F.2d 1439, 1443 (10th Cir. 1988).

159. *Luciano v. Olsten Corp.*, 110 F.3d 210, 221 (2d Cir. 1997).

160. 42 U.S.C. § 1981a(c).

161. *Luciano*, 110 F.3d at 221 (award of $5 million in punitive damages was reduced to $300,000).

162. *David v. Caterpillar, Inc.*, 324 F.3d 851 (7th Cir. 2003) (remittitur of compensatory damages award from $100,000 to $50,000 was upheld based on district court's review of awards in comparable as well as more egregious cases); *E.E.O.C. v. AIC Sec.*

that compensatory damages do not include back pay, lost wages, or lost benefits.[163]

B. Compliance with Title VII

In the context of punitive damages, an employer may not be vicariously liable for the discriminatory employment decisions of managerial agents when those decisions are contrary to the employer's good-faith efforts to comply with Title VII.[164] This principle advances the purposes of Title VII by encouraging the remediation and prevention that lie at the heart of the statute's goals. Those purposes would be defeated if an employer were held strictly liable for the acts of rogue managers when it has made every effort to comply with the Title VII requirements.[165] Widespread good-faith antidiscrimination efforts, including the implementation of an organization-wide antidiscrimination policy, grievance policy, and diversity training program, may relieve an employer of liability for punitive damages.[166] An employer's prompt investigation of a complaint and prompt remedial action constitutes good-faith efforts to comply with Title VII and should be pled as an affirmative good-faith defense. The good-faith defense does not apply to cases premised on direct liability; it is negated by a showing of direct malice or reckless indifference to federally protected rights.[167]

Investigations, Ltd., 55 F.3d 1276, 1285 (7th Cir. 1995).

163. *Corti v. Storage Technology Corp.*, 304 F.3d 336, 341 (4th Cir. 2002).

164. *Kolstad v. American Dental Ass'n*, 527 U.S. 526, 545 (1999) (establishing a three-part inquiry governing the recovery of punitive damages and providing for a good-faith defense of compliance with Title VII).

165. *Id.*

166. *Bryant v. Aiken Regional Med. Ctrs., Inc.*, 333 F.3d 536 (5th Cir. 2003) (hospital was not vicariously liable for its managerial employee's discriminatory decisions, which were contrary to the hospital's good-faith efforts, and no punitive damages could be awarded under Title VII or § 1981); *but see Fischer v. UPS, Inc.*, 390 Fed. Appx. 465 (6th Cir. 2010) (the *Kolstad* good-faith defense was denied because UPS presented no evidence from which a reasonable juror could conclude that UPS effectively advanced its policies).

167. *Deters v. Equifax Credit Info. Servs., Inc.*, 202 F.3d 1262, 1269 (10th Cir. 2000) (punitive damages award affirmed because management not only did not respond to

A punitive damages award alone or in combination with compensatory damages in excess of the applicable statutory caps is subject to remittitur.[168]

An employer should argue the remittitur of a punitive damages award because it is excessive.[169] In considering whether a punitive damages award is constitutionally excessive, a court will review the reprehensibility of the defendant's conduct, the ratio of the punitive damages to the actual harm inflicted on the plaintiff, a comparison of the punitive damages award with the civil or criminal penalties that could be imposed for comparable misconduct, and the goal of deterrence.[170] The Supreme Court has reiterated that courts must ensure that the measure of punishment is both reasonable and proportionate to the amount of harm to the plaintiff and the general damages recovered.[171] When the ratio of punitive damages to compensatory damages exceeds single digits, the damages award may not satisfy due process

---

plaintiff's complaints but also minimized and disregarded them to protect the "revenue producers").

168. *David v. Caterpillar, Inc.*, 324 F.3d 851 (7th Cir. 2003) (punitive damages award of $750,000 was appropriately reduced to $150,000 to maintain a reasonable relationship between the award and the particular harm that resulted from the employer's conduct); *Connor v. Schroder-Bridgeport Int'l, Inc.*, 227 F.3d 179, 202 (4th Cir. 2000) (amount of punitive damages was excessive by law and was remanded for factual development); *Deters*, 202 F.3d at 1269 (punitive damages award of $1,000,000 was reduced to $295,000, which was the remainder of the statutory cap because the plaintiff was awarded $5,000 in compensatory damages).

169. *EEOC v. Service Temps, Inc.*, 679 F.3d 323, 337–38 (5th Cir. 2012) (jury award of $150,000 in punitive damages was remitted to $68,800, which was one half of the back-pay and compensatory award); *Kim v. Nash Finch Co.*, 123 F.3d 1046, 1067 (8th Cir. 1997) (an award of $7 million for punitive damages is excessive, but an award of $300,000 is not, based on the applicable statutory cap and the size and assets for the employer).

170. *Deters*, 202 F.3d at 1269 (under the circumstances, a punitive damages award of $295,000, which was $5,000 below the statutory cap, was not disproportionate and did not shock the conscience) (citing *BMW of North America v. Gore*, 517 U.S. 559 (1996)).

171. *State Farm Mut. Auto Ins. Co. v. Campbell*, 538 U.S. 408, 424 (2003) (reversing punitive damages award with a ratio of 145 to 1 as excessive and not comporting with due process).

considerations.[172] Ratios greater than those that the Supreme Court has upheld may comport with due process when a particularly egregious act has resulted in only a small amount of economic damages.[173] A ratio of 4:1 of punitive damages to compensatory damages is considered "close to the line."[174]

C. Good-Faith Reasonable Accommodation

If the ADA or Rehabilitation Act claim involves the provision of a reasonable accommodation under § 12112(b)(5) of the ADA or the regulations of the Rehabilitation Act, compensatory and punitive damages under the CRA may not be awarded under certain circumstances. More specifically, no award is appropriate if the employer demonstrates good-faith efforts, in consultation with the person with the disability who has informed the covered entity that accommodation is needed, to identify and make a reasonable accommodation that would provide such individual with an equally effective opportunity and would not impose an undue hardship on the operation of the business.[175]

VII. Special Issues Regarding Back Pay and Damages

A. Damages in Class Actions

Class actions are categorized according to the nature or effect of the relief sought. Rule 23(b)(2) of the Federal Rules of Civil Procedure governs cases in which broad, class-wide injunctive or declaratory relief is necessary. Rule 23(b)(3) disposes of all other cases in which a class action would be convenient and desirable, including those involving larger-scale, complex litigation for money damages.[176] Compensa-

172. *Id.* at 425.

173. *Id.*

174. *BMW of North America v. Gore*, 517 U.S. 559 (1996); *Pacific Mut. Life Ins. Co. v. Haslip*, 499 U.S. 1 (1991).

175. 42 U.S.C. § 1981a(a)(3).

176. *Smith v. Texaco, Inc.*, 263 F.3d 394, 405 (5th Cir. 2001).

tory and punitive damages are available only in individual disparate treatment cases involving intentional discrimination; they are not available in disparate treatment cases.[177] But individual class members may seek damages.

To contain the relief sought, defense counsel should challenge class certification and ascertain the relief sought. The main inquiry is whether common issues predominate over individual issues, as required by Rule 23(b) of the Federal Rules of Civil Procedure.[178] If the common issues do not predominate over the individual issues, then the class action degenerates in practice into multiple lawsuits separately tried.[179] Class actions in which the employer has engaged in a pattern or practice of intentional discrimination ordinarily are handled in bifurcated proceedings imposing different burdens of proof in the respective phases.[180]

During the first or "liability" stage, plaintiffs seek to prove a pattern or practice of invidious class-based determination.[181] When successful individual class members benefit from a presumption of back pay, the back pay is determined during the second or "remedial" stage.[182] To obtain back pay, class members need only prove that they were denied employment opportunities and the extent of their loss. The burden then shifts to the employer to demonstrate that the denial was for legitimate reasons.

This process involves individual hearings and may be streamlined by employing special masters.[183]

Recovery of punitive damages in a class action is restricted to class members who allege that they were harmed by the employer's proven pattern or practice of discrimination.[184] A consent decree that preserves

177. 42 U.S.C. § 1981a (a)(1) and (2).
178. *Smith*, 263 F.3d at 409.
179. *Id.* at 410.
180. *Id.* at 404; *Shipes v. Trinity Indus.*, 987 F.2d 311, 318 (5th Cir. 1992).
181. *Smith*, 263 F.3d at 404.
182. *Id.* at 405.
183. *Id.*
184. *Beck v. Boeing Co.*, 60 Fed. Appx. 38 (9th Cir. 2003).

the right of class members to bring claims for actual damages may not be modified unilaterally by the district court in its order approving the consent decree.[185]

B. Offer of Judgment

The Federal Rules of Civil Procedure provide for an offer of judgment, which in the proper case may limit damages and the costs and fees associated with litigation.[186] Rule 68 of the Federal Rules of Civil Procedure provides generally that if at any time more than ten days before trial begins, a party defending against a claim may serve upon the adverse party an offer to allow a judgment to be taken against the defending party for the money specified in the offer. If the offer is accepted and the judgment finally obtained by the offer is not more favorable than the offer, the offeree must pay the costs incurred after the offer is made. An offer of judgment under Title VII includes lawyers' fees in the definition of costs.[187] As long as the offer does not implicitly or explicitly provide that the judgment does not include costs, an offer is valid, and it is presumed the defendant will pay costs.[188]

C. Arbitration Agreements[189]

The amounts of back pay, front pay, and compensatory damages cannot be limited under an arbitration agreement. Such limitation-of-remedies provisions are considered unenforceable because they undermine the

185. *Molski v. Gleich*, 318 F.3d 937, 946 (9th Cir. 2003) (the consent decree memorialized an enforceable settlement and was also the final judgment of the district court).

186. Fed. R. Civ. P. 68.

187. 42 U.S.C. § 2000e-5(k) (in any action under Title VII, the court, in its discreation, may allow the prevailing party, other than the commission or the United States, a reasonable lawyer's fee (including expert fees) as part of the costs).

188. *Marek v. Chesny*, 473 U.S. 1, 9 (1985) (lawyer fees sought under 42 U.S.C. § 1988 are a part of costs); *Le v. Univ. of Pennsylvania*, 321 F.3d 403, 409 (3d Cir. 2003) (offer of $50,000 plus costs and citation to *Marek* decision to state that such costs, including lawyers' fees, are sufficient to make offer of judgment valid).

189. For a lengthy discussion, see Ellis B. Murov & Beverly Aloisio, *Arbitration of Employment Disputes Before and After* Circuit City, 17 Lab. Law., no. 2 (2001).

remedial and deterrent principles of federal employment discrimination laws.[190] It is well established that a party does not forgo the substantive rights afforded by a statute when she or he agrees to arbitrate a statutory claim but only submits to its resolution in an arbitral, rather than a judicial, forum.[191]

VIII. Conclusion

The issue of damages should be considered from the inception of the litigation even if it appears that there is no or limited liability. The pattern jury instructions for the applicable circuit also should be consulted from the inception of the case. The applicable defenses should be asserted in the affirmative or permissive form. Discovery should be conducted on all aspects of economic and noneconomic damages. To avoid being blindsided close to trial, a letter should be sent to opposing counsel to request supplementation by a certain date. Trial preparation should include drafting witness examination on the defenses to damages, drafting jury instructions that follow the law, and computing the damages in a manner that can be understood by the jury. Research on issues as they are discovered or become relevant should be conducted. At trial, the testimony must be followed closely to prevent instructions and questions on damages where no evidence was presented, especially on the factors related to punitive damages, and to include instructions and questions on the defenses.

---

190. *Morrison v. Circuit City Stores, Inc.*, 317 F.3d 646, 670 (6th Cir. 2003); *Perez v. Global Airport Sec. Servs. Inc.*, 253 F.3d 1280, 1286 (11th Cir. 2001).

191. *Gilmer v. Interstate/Johnson Lane Corp.*, 500 U.S. 20, 26 (1991); *Morrison v. Circuit City Stores, Inc.*, 317 F.3d 646, 670 (6th Cir. 2003).

CHAPTER 9
Litigation of EPLI Claims

Margaret J. Grover

Once litigation begins, the employer-employee dispute can have one of three possible outcomes: the employer or the employee prevails through summary judgment; the case is resolved amicably, through settlement discussions, mediation, or another form of alternative dispute resolution; or the case is resolved through an adversarial proceeding, such as trial or arbitration. Because any of these methods of dispute resolution is possible, defense counsel must keep all three in mind when crafting the litigation strategy.

I. Evidence Preservation

As soon as a lawyer is aware of litigation or threatened litigation, steps should be taken to preserve all relevant evidence, including electronic evidence. "[W]hen a company or organization has a document retention or destruction policy, it 'is obligated to suspend' that policy and 'implement a 'litigation hold' to ensure the preservation of relevant documents' once the preservation duty has been triggered."[1] "The obligation to

1. *Victor Stanley, Inc. v. Creative Pipe, Inc.*, 269 F.R.D. 497, 524 (D. Md. 2010) (quoting references omitted).

preserve evidence arises when the party has notice that the evidence is relevant to litigation or when a party should have known that the evidence may be relevant to future litigation. Identifying the boundaries of the duty to preserve involves two related inquiries: *when* does the duty to preserve attach, and *what* evidence must be preserved?"[2]

The scope of a party's preservation obligation can be described as follows: once a party reasonably anticipates litigation, it must suspend its routine document retention/destruction policy and put in place a "litigation hold" to ensure the preservation of relevant documents. As a general rule, that litigation hold does not apply to inaccessible backup tapes (for example, those typically maintained solely for the purpose of disaster recovery), which may continue to be recycled on the schedule set forth in the company's policy. On the other hand, if backup tapes are accessible (that is, actively used for information retrieval), then such tapes *would* likely be subject to the litigation hold.

However, it does make sense to create one exception to this general rule. If a company can identify where particular employee documents are stored on backup tapes, then the tapes storing the documents of "key players"[3] to the existing or threatened litigation should be preserved if the information contained on those tapes is not otherwise available. This exception applies to *all* backup tapes.[4]

At least one court has held that "the failure to issue a written litigation hold in a timely manner amounts to gross negligence."[5]

Failure to produce evidence when initially requested, failure to preserve evidence, or destruction of evidence may result in serious penalties, including sanctions payable to the court or opposing party, shifting of

2. *Zubulake v. UBS Warburg*, 220 F.R.D. 212, 216 (S.D.N.Y. 2003) (emphasis in original).

3. *Id.* at 218.

4. *Id.*

5. *Pension Comm. of the Univ. of Montreal Pension Plan v. Banc of Am. Sec., LLC*, 685 F. Supp. 2d 456, 488 (S.D.N.Y. 2010), *abrogated by Chin v. Port Auth. of N.Y. & N.J.*, 685 F.3d 135 (2d Cir. 2012) (finding that failure to institute litigation hold did not constitute gross negligence per se).

costs of retrieving and producing evidence, the party failing to produce the evidence bearing costs of additional depositions, evidence preclusion, an adverse inference instruction, contempt, or even dismissal of the party's claims or defenses.[6]

As soon as counsel is aware of litigation or a threatened claim, she or he should take reasonable steps to advise the client of the duty to preserve all relevant evidence. If the client has implemented a litigation hold before retaining counsel, counsel may wish to confirm that the hold is sufficiently broad in scope to preserve all relevant evidence. An effective litigation hold typically requires the following steps:

- Understand the client's document and data retention practices;
- Identify one or more persons within the organization who will be responsible for assuring that litigation-hold procedure is followed;
- Explain the client's duty to preserve information, including the obligation to refrain from automatic or routine destruction of files and information, including paper files, digital files, backup files, and other electronic storage media;
- Identify the likely topics and scope of discovery in the action;
- Prepare a list of documents and data that client must preserve;
- Consult with client's information technology department or other information technology consultant to assure that electronically stored information is being preserved; and
- Make reasonable efforts to recover recently deleted information.

II. Discovery[7]

Discovery provides defense counsel with the opportunity to discern the scope of the plaintiff's claims and shape the employer's defenses to meet those claims. As courts restrict the amount and scope of discovery, establishing a discovery plan becomes increasingly critical. Discovery

6. *Victor Stanley, Inc.*, 269 F.R.D. at 533–41; *Zubulake*, 220 F.R.D. at 219–22.
7. Pleading strategies are addressed in chapter 5.

must be focused, and all available forms of discovery should be evaluated to determine which tools will be most useful in obtaining relevant information.

Defense counsel will want to begin discovery as early as possible so that there will be sufficient time to bring a motion for summary judgment, conduct follow-up discovery, or resolve the case through settlement or alternative dispute resolution. When the trial date is several months, or even a year, in the future, counsel may be tempted to delay discovery. However, discerning the strengths and weaknesses of your case early in the litigation process will allow the greatest opportunity to reach a favorable resolution.

A. Initial Disclosures

In federal court, the parties are generally not permitted to conduct discovery until after the initial disclosures have been made under Rule 26 of the Federal Rules of Civil Procedure. Federal Rule 26(a)(1)(A) requires the parties to provide the following discovery without awaiting a discovery request:

> (i) The name and, if known, the address and telephone number of each individual likely to have discoverable information—along with the subjects of that information—that the disclosing party may use to support its claims or defenses, unless the use would be solely for impeachment;
>
> (ii) A copy—or a description by category and location—of all documents, electronically stored information, and tangible things that the disclosing party has in its possession, custody, or control and may use to support its claims or defenses, unless the use would be solely for impeachment;
>
> (iii) A computation of each category of damages claimed by the disclosing party, which must also make available for inspection and copying as under Rule 34 the documents or other evidentiary material, unless privileged or protected from disclosure, on

which each computation is based, including materials bearing on the nature and extent of injuries suffered; and

(iv) For inspection and copying as under Rule 34, any insurance agreement under which an insurance business may be liable to satisfy all or part of a possible judgment in the action or to indemnify or reimburse for payments made to satisfy the judgment.

Rule 26(a)(1)(C) also provides that "[a] party must make the initial disclosures at or within 14 days after the parties' Rule 26(f) conference unless a different time is set by stipulation or court order, or unless a party objects during the conference that initial disclosures are not appropriate in this action and states the objection in the proposed discovery plan."

Rule 26(f) obligates the parties to confer about several items, including making or arranging for the Rule 26 disclosures and developing a proposed discovery plan. Rule 26(f)(2) specifies that, during the conference, "the parties must consider the nature and basis of their claims and defenses and the possibilities for promptly settling or resolving the case; make or arrange for the disclosures required by Rule 26(a)(1); discuss any issues about preserving discoverable information; and develop a proposed discovery plan. The attorneys of record and all unrepresented parties that have appeared in the case are jointly responsible for arranging the conference, for attempting in good faith to agree on the proposed discovery plan, and for submitting to the court within 14 days after the conference a written report outlining the plan." Rule 26(f)(3) specifies that the discovery plan must include the parties' views and proposals on:

(A) What changes should be made in the timing, form, or requirement for disclosures under Rule 26(a), including a statement of when initial disclosures were made or will be made;

(B) The subjects on which discovery may be needed, when discovery should be completed, and whether discovery should be conducted in phases or be limited to or focused on particular issues;

(C) Any issues about disclosure or discovery of electronically stored information, including the form or forms in which it should be produced;

(D) Any issues about claims of privilege or of protection as trial-preparation materials, including—if the parties agree on a procedure to assert these claims after production—whether to ask the court to include their agreement in an order;

(E) What changes should be made in the limitations on discovery imposed under these rules or by local rule, and what other limitations should be imposed; and

(F) Any other orders that the court should issue under Rule 26(c) [protective orders] or under Rule 16(b) and (c) [scheduling and pretrial conferences].

The standing orders in many district courts modify the schedule and procedures for initial disclosures. Counsel should carefully review any standing order or initial case management orders to confirm the dates by which the Rule 26(f) conference must be held and initial disclosures are to be completed.

B. Plaintiff's Deposition

The plaintiff's deposition is typically the key element of the employer's discovery plan. In preparation for the plaintiff's deposition, defense counsel will want to gather all available evidence regarding the claims and defenses. Typically, documentary evidence will include the plaintiff's personnel file and any separate files maintained on the plaintiff, such as medical records, workers' compensation claims files, attendance records, requests for accommodation and medical leave of absence, the supervisor's working file, the company's employee handbook, any company policies or procedures, and records of any investigation in which the plaintiff was involved. The plaintiff's electronic mail (e-mail) messages may provide important evidence regarding the plaintiff's job performance. E-mail may also reveal that the plaintiff engaged in non-work activities on the job or violated company policies. Counsel should verify that the company has provided the handbook, policies, and procedures that were in effect during the time of the alleged events.

Company representatives should also be interviewed regarding the plaintiff's job performance, attendance, and reasons for the adverse action. Defense counsel will probably want to interview the plaintiff's immediate supervisor, the plaintiff's coworkers, the company human resources representative, and all persons involved in the decision-making process.

A company representative and any individual defendant should attend the deposition. If the plaintiff testifies regarding an incident about which counsel has only limited knowledge, the presence of a company representative to fill in the details from the company's perspective can be invaluable. In addition, many lawyers believe that the plaintiff will have a more difficult time lying or exaggerating if he or she is looking across the table at someone else who is also familiar with the events.

Areas of questioning for the plaintiff typically include:

- Documents reviewed by plaintiff and individuals with whom he or she spoke about the deposition;
- Educational background;
- Employment history;
- Reasons for leaving prior jobs;
- Involvement in other litigation and prior testimony at depositions or trial;
- Plaintiff's application process with employer;
- Plaintiff's employment application, including any at-will language;
- Company employee handbook, including at-will language and antidiscrimination/anti-harassment policies;
- Plaintiff's assessment of her or his performance;
- Plaintiff's performance evaluations;

- Plaintiff's promotions, demotions, or other changes of position while plaintiff worked for the employer;
- Plaintiff's contentions regarding discriminatory, harassing, retaliatory, or otherwise wrongful conduct. This area is perhaps the most critical portion of the deposition. Counsel should be careful to exhaust plaintiff's recollection of the events, including exploring whether there are documents that will refresh plaintiff's recollection;
- Actions that the plaintiff claims were inappropriate or wrongful;
- Statements that the plaintiff heard or knew of that he or she contends indicate a discriminatory or retaliatory motive;
- Witnesses to each act plaintiff contends was discriminatory, harassing, or otherwise wrongful;
- Documents recording any act plaintiff contends was discriminatory, harassing, or otherwise wrongful;
- Termination of plaintiff's employment, including witnesses and documents;
- Plaintiff's efforts to locate other work after termination;
- Plaintiff's employment, earnings, and benefits after termination;
- Plaintiff's physical and emotional condition, including any history of medical or psychiatric treatment for conditions similar to those plaintiff claims;
- Changes in plaintiff's medical and mental condition during and after working with employer; and
- Any other damages plaintiff is claiming.

In the most effective depositions, the areas of inquiry are carefully tailored to the particular case. In a case where the plaintiff is claiming harassment, counsel should explore not only inappropriate actions directed at the plaintiff but also inappropriate actions directed to others that the plaintiff observed or with which he or she was familiar. If the plaintiff is claiming retaliation, questions should be directed to the timing and nature of the plaintiff's complaint or other protected activity.

In a case alleging disability discrimination, or failure to accommodate, questions should be designed to determine the plaintiff's medical condition, what information was provided to the employer regarding the plaintiff's medical condition, what accommodations were discussed with the employer, the employer's response, and whether any accommodations were provided.

C. Defending Depositions of Company Representatives

Good preparation is essential for the company representatives to make their best possible appearance at deposition. Many company representatives will never have been exposed to the trial or deposition process. A thorough explanation of the deposition process will help the company representative to be at ease and focused during the deposition process. At a minimum, in preparing the company representative for deposition, defense counsel should:

- Describe the deposition process, including the formal nature of the deposition, the question and answer format, and the need to listen carefully and respond directly to any questions;
- Explain objections, what they mean, and how to respond; and
- Review anticipated areas of questioning.

It will be very helpful if defense counsel has taken the plaintiff's deposition before company representatives are deposed. Defense counsel can then review with the company representative the key areas of the plaintiff's testimony in support of his or her claims. Defense counsel can explore the similarities and differences between the company's position and the plaintiff's description of events. In addition, if the plaintiff's testimony contained inconsistencies or the plaintiff did not recall certain areas, those areas should be explored in preparation for the defendant's deposition to determine if the company representatives have a better recollection or can provide a clear explanation.

Before showing specific documents to the company representatives during deposition preparation, counsel should understand how the jurisdiction handles documents that are reviewed. Some federal courts have held that the selection of documents for review constitutes work product, and the witness will not need to identify those documents,[8] especially if those documents have not been disclosed or are privileged. In other jurisdictions, any document that the witness uses to refresh her or his recollection in preparation for deposition becomes discoverable.[9]

The better practice is for defense counsel to review the documents him- or herself and summarize the key provisions for the witness.

Any company representative who will be deposed should be prepared to respond to questions in the following areas:

- Plaintiff's job performance, reviews or annual evaluations, and other documents in plaintiff's personnel files;
- Comparison of the plaintiff's performance with other employees in the same work group, people who reported to the same supervisor;
- Reasons for termination of plaintiff's employment, including disciplinary history, oral and documented warnings, opportunities for improvement, and the plaintiff's response to warnings;
- Company policy, including policies to prevent discrimination or harassment and any policy explaining the "at-will" nature of the employment relationship;
- Whether the plaintiff made any complaints of discrimination, harassment, or retaliation while employed and, if so, how the company responded;

---

8. *See Sporck v. Peil*, 759 F.2d 312, 317–18 (3d Cir. 1985); *Nutramax Labs., Inc. v. Twin Labs., Inc.*, 183 F.R.D. 458, 469–70 (D. Md. 1998).

9. *See, e.g.*, CAL. EVID. CODE § 771(a) ("if a witness, either while testifying or prior thereto, uses a writing to refresh his memory with respect to any matter about which he testifies, such writing must be produced at the hearing at the request of an adverse party and, unless the writing is so produced, the testimony of the witness concerning such matter shall be stricken").

- Any internal investigation of the plaintiff's allegations. Note that if the internal investigation was conducted entirely in anticipation of litigation, and the employer does not intend to assert a good-faith investigation as an element of its defense, investigations conducted by or at the direction of counsel may be protected by the attorney-client privilege. However, when the employer places its investigation at issue, even investigations conducted by or at the direction of counsel may be discoverable.[10] Moreover, factual information gathered during an investigation, such as identities of persons who had information or had made statements relating to claims or defenses in the case, substance of information they possessed, and statements they had made, may not be protected from disclosure under lawyer work-product doctrine.[11]
- Any similar complaints of discrimination, harassment, or retaliation and the company's response to those complaints; and
- Composition of the workforce in terms of race, gender, age, religion, national origin, or any other issue raised by the litigation.

If the plaintiff's lawyer deposes multiple corporate representatives, each representative should be aware of the company's position. In preparing corporate representatives, counsel may wish to disclose key points of the testimony offered by other representatives. If the corporate representatives provide conflicting or inconsistent testimony, defense counsel will need to determine whether there are plausible explanations for these differences.

---

10. *See Johnson v. Rauland-Borg Corp.*, 961 F. Supp. 208, 211 (N.D. Ill. 1997); *Harding v. Dana Transp., Inc.*, 914 F. Supp. 1084, 1094 (D.N.J. 1996); *Peterson v. Wallace Computer Servs., Inc.*, 984 F. Supp. 821, 825 (D. Vt. 1997).

11. *Equal Employment Opportunity Comm'n v. Jewel Food Stores, Inc.*, 23 F.R.D. 343, 346–47 (N.D. Ill. 2005).

D. Interrogatories

Defense counsel can use interrogatories to flesh out the plaintiff's allegations. Contention interrogatories, which ask the plaintiff to identify all facts supporting a particular allegation, can require the plaintiff to detail the facts supporting his or her claims and identify the witnesses and documents relevant to each claim.

Interrogatories can also be useful in determining whether the plaintiff had a history of mental or physical ailments similar to those that he or she attributes to the adverse employment action. The plaintiff's treating physicians and mental-health care providers can be identified through interrogatories.

Finally, some defense counsel use interrogatories to obtain information that the plaintiff could not recall at the time of his or her deposition or to ask questions following up those asked during deposition.

E. Requests for Production of Documents

Document requests to the plaintiff should be drafted broadly to obtain all documents relevant to the plaintiff's claims. Employees may prepare detailed notes of perceived wrongs or save electronic mail communications, interoffice memoranda, and other informal documents that the employer has not retained. These documents can prove invaluable in cross-examination, particularly when the plaintiff exaggerates his or her claims or makes statements that are inconsistent with prior writings.

The employer's document request should include documents that could reveal malfeasance by the plaintiff, such as use of the employer's trade secrets, removal of the employer's documents, or the plaintiff's providing information or services to a competitor while still working for the defendant. Document requests may also provide after-acquired evidence that could limit the plaintiff's ability to recover damages, such as documents showing that the plaintiff misrepresented his or her education, prior employment, or other qualifications during the application process.[12]

Defense counsel may wish to include the following categories in any document request directed to the plaintiff:

- Plaintiff's application for employment;
- Any written employment agreement between plaintiff and the employer;
- Documents relating to the terms of any agreement between the plaintiff and the employer;
- Documents relating to the terms and conditions of plaintiff's employment;
- Plaintiff's job description or other documents relating to plaintiff's duties and responsibilities;
- Plaintiff's performance reviews or other documents relating to plaintiff's job performance;
- Documents relating to each specific allegation of wrongdoing identified in plaintiff's complaint;
- Any complaint made by the plaintiff during the course of his or her employment;
- Documents relating to the employer's knowledge or ratification of the alleged wrongdoing;
- Plaintiff's administrative charge and all documents plaintiff submitted to the administrative agency;
- Documents relating to plaintiff's search for alternative employment;
- Documents relating to plaintiff's income from the date of termination until the date of the deposition;
- Plaintiff's calendars, date books, appointment books, log books, diaries, or other similar documents in which plaintiff recorded notes or appointments; and

12. *See, e.g., McKennon v. Nashville Banner Publ'g Co.*, 513 U.S. 352, 362 (1995).

- Plaintiff's medical records, including work releases, medical statements regarding limitations on work or other activities, referrals, prescriptions, and billings.

F. Requests for Admissions

Defense counsel may use requests for admissions to narrow the areas of dispute. Admissions can also be particularly helpful in motions for summary judgment.

Plaintiffs may acknowledge the truth of documents, including their own job applications, job description, employee handbooks, disciplinary memoranda, and wage and hour records. Facts that may be admitted will vary from case to case but may include matters of little dispute, such as the plaintiff's dates of employment, job title, job duties, and compensation.

Admissions are difficult to obtain because the employee's counsel will be looking for any reason to deny the request. Defense counsel should draft requests for admission carefully. Each request should ask the plaintiff to admit a single fact so that he or she cannot deny the entire request because a portion of it is incorrect.

G. Psychological Examination of the Plaintiff

Most plaintiffs claim that the alleged discrimination, harassment, or other wrongful act caused them to suffer emotional distress. Plaintiffs will often introduce expert testimony from a health care provider, including psychiatrists, psychologists, and mental health counselors. Rule 35 of the Federal Rules of Civil Procedure controls the defendant's right to obtain an independent medical or psychiatric evaluation of the plaintiff. Rule 35 provides, in part, that:

> The court where the action is pending may order a party whose mental or physical condition—including blood group—is in

> controversy to submit to a physical or mental examination by a suitably licensed or certified examiner.[13]

To obtain a mental examination of the plaintiff under Rule 35, the defendant must demonstrate both that the plaintiff's mental state is in controversy and that there is good cause for the examination. The motion seeking a mental examination must demonstrate the good cause and "specify the time, place, manner, conditions, and scope of the examination, as well as the person or persons who will perform it."[14]

Courts then engage in a case-by-case analysis to determine whether good cause exists:

> [T]he "in controversy" and "good cause" requirements of Rule 35 . . . are not met by mere conclusory allegations of the pleadings—nor by mere relevance to the case—but require an affirmative showing by the movant that each condition as to which the examination is sought is really and genuinely in controversy and that good cause exists for ordering each particular examination. Obviously, what may be good cause for one type of examination may not be so for another. The ability of the movant to obtain the desired information by other means is also relevant.[15]

Courts will not necessarily compel a mental examination of a former employee who seeks to recover damages for the stress normally associated with the wrongful termination or other alleged wrong.[16] In evaluating motions to compel a mental examination, courts have looked at a variety of factors, including whether the plaintiff has alleged an independent cause of action for intentional infliction of emotional

---

13. FED. R. CIV. P. 35(a)(1).
14. FED. R. CIV. P. 35(a)(2).
15. *Schlagenhauf v. Holder*, 379 U.S. 104, 118 (1964).
16. *See, e.g.*, *Bowen v. Parking Auth. of City of Camden*, 214 F.R.D. 188, 194–95 (D.N.J. 2003).

distress, whether the plaintiff claims ongoing mental injury, and whether the plaintiff will support his or her claims with psychiatric testimony.[17]

If the plaintiff requests a copy of the psychiatric report, the defendant must deliver "a copy of the examiner's report, together with like reports of all earlier examinations of the same condition."[18] For a discussion of expert disclosure requirements and discovery procedures, see section V. below.

H. Third-Party Depositions and Document Requests

The importance of third-party depositions, including custodian of records depositions, will vary from case to case. In some instances, records obtained from the educational institutions attended by the plaintiff or his or her prior employers may disclose that plaintiff made false statements on his or her job application. The employer can use such after-acquired evidence to eliminate or reduce the plaintiff's damages claims. If discovery reveals evidence that the employee had engaged in wrongdoing that would have led to termination of employment in any event, this may provide a partial or complete defense to the plaintiff's claims.[19] To take advantage of the after-acquired evidence, the employer must prove that it would, in fact, have fired the plaintiff for the newly discovered misconduct.[20]

The plaintiff's medical and mental-health care providers can help evaluate the plaintiff's claims of emotional distress and consequential physical harm. If the plaintiff's former coworkers are no longer employed by the company, their testimony may be very persuasive to the jury. To prepare the case, defense counsel will need to determine how these former coworkers will testify. If the former employee left

17. *Nuskey v. Lambright*, 251 F.R.D. 3, 6–7 (D.D.C. 2008); *Gattegno v. Pricewaterhouse Coopers, LLP*, 204 F.R.D. 228, 230 (D. Conn. 2008); *Lahr v.Fulbright & Jaworski L.L.P.*, 164 F.R.D. 196, 199–201 (N.D. Tex. 1995), *aff'd*, 164 F.R.D. 204.

18. Fed. R. Civ. Proc. 35(b)(1).

19. *See McKennon v. Nashville Banner Publ'g Co.*, 513 U.S. 352, 362 (1995).

20. *O'Day v. McDonnell Douglas Helicopter Co.*, 79 F.3d 756, 759 (9th Cir. 1996).

on amicable terms, counsel may be able to obtain statements through informal interviews. However, if a former employee was terminated or is a personal friend of the plaintiff's, defense counsel will have to conduct depositions to ensure that the former employee provides an accurate statement.

III. Alternative Dispute Resolution

Court congestion, rising jury verdicts, and the costs of extended litigation have caused many employers to turn to alternative dispute resolution to resolve employer-employee disputes. Most courts urge, or mandate, that the parties engage in at least one form of alternative dispute resolution.

Typically, use of alternative dispute resolution is a consensual process and the means of resolution can be structured in whatever manner the parties agree upon. Although there are certain typical procedures in any form of alternative dispute resolution, any of them can be modified or abandoned when doing so would fit the parties' needs. Preliminary matters such as timing, location, cost sharing, and number of neutrals can be selected by agreement.

Counsel should carefully evaluate which form of alternative dispute resolution is most likely to lead to success in the particular case. Alternative dispute resolution is most likely to succeed when all parties are committed to resolving the dispute. The procedures within the dispute-resolution process should also be selected carefully. The procedures can even be modified during the resolution process at the suggestion of the neutral or any party, as long as all parties agree to the changes.

The potential benefits and disadvantages of mediation, as well as mediation strategies and tactics, are discussed more fully in chapter 11. Only binding arbitration, nonbinding arbitration, neutral evaluations, and mini-trials are discussed in this chapter.

A. Binding Arbitration

Arbitration may be required by an agreement entered between the employee and employer at the outset of the employment relationship. If the employee has signed an arbitration agreement, the employer should immediately move to enforce that agreement. Failure to do so may result in waiver.[21]

Even when the employee has not accepted arbitration as a condition of employment, the parties may agree to binding arbitration when the claim arises because it provides parties with an adjudication that is easier, faster, less formal, and less expensive than trial. Many employees' lawyers are reluctant to submit to binding arbitration voluntarily because they believe that an employee will receive more favorable treatment from a jury. However, the speed and finality of the arbitration decision enable the employee who has been wronged to obtain relief more quickly, without having to pay for expensive pretrial proceedings or waiting years for an appellate issue to be resolved.

Arbitration may be used to resolve the entire claim or to resolve only limited issues, depending upon the parties' agreement. The parties typically agree to present their claims before a single arbitrator. However, when the parties are not able to reach agreement, or the matters are complex, a panel composed of three arbitrators may serve. Retired judges and lawyers often serve as arbitrators. However, individuals with relevant business or industry backgrounds may also be selected to fill the neutral role.

Discovery before the arbitration is usually more limited than pretrial discovery. The parties may exchange documents voluntarily or limit

---

21. *Compare Snelling & Snelling, Inc. v. Reynolds*, 140 F. Supp. 2d 1314, 1321–23 (M.D. Fla. 2001) (finding waiver when Reynolds litigated for fourteen months and did not seek to arbitrate until after the close of discovery), *with Siam Feather & Forest Prods., Inc. v. Midwest Feather Co.*, 503 F. Supp. 239 (S.D. Ohio 1980), *aff'd*, 663 F.2d 1073 (6th Cir. 1981) (filing answer and asserting counterclaim not enough to waive arbitration). Thus, the more discovery the parties conduct, the more likely it is that one of them can void an agreement to arbitrate based on waiver.

the number of written discovery requests. In addition, there may be an agreed-upon limit to the number, length, or scope of depositions.

The arbitrator presides at a private evidentiary hearing, which may take one or several days. The rules of evidence provide a foundation for admitting testimony, but they are not generally followed rigorously. The arbitrator can issue subpoenas to compel the attendance of witnesses or presentation of documents. Evidence is presented through direct examination and cross-examination of witnesses. A good arbitrator maintains control of the hearing in a balanced, impartial manner.

At the conclusion of evidence, the parties may present their summaries orally, through a closing argument, or in written submissions. The arbitrator will issue a written decision on the merits. Most arbitrators will provide a legal analysis and explain how the facts of the case support the conclusions. Arbitration awards are final, legally binding, and enforceable in most jurisdictions. The Federal Arbitration Act (FAA) provides for enforcement of arbitration agreements and awards in interstate commerce and international contracts.[22]

Arbitration awards may be challenged only on very limited grounds. The FAA enumerates the following grounds for vacating the decision:

> 1. Where the award was procured by corruption, fraud, or undue means;
>
> 2. Where there was evident partiality or corruption in the arbitrators, or either of them;
>
> 3. Where the arbitrators were guilty of misconduct in refusing to postpone the hearing, upon sufficient cause shown, or in refusing to hear evidence pertinent and material to the controversy; or of any other misbehavior by which the rights of any party have been prejudiced; or

22. 9 U.S.C. § 9.

4. Where the arbitrators exceeded their powers, or so imperfectly executed them that a mutual, final, and definite award upon the subject matter submitted was not made.[23]

The grounds for vacating arbitration awards are interpreted narrowly to promote the concept of finality in the arbitration process.

B. Nonbinding Arbitration

The parties may agree to participate in nonbinding arbitration, and many state and federal courts provide nonbinding arbitration programs. The procedures for nonbinding arbitration are similar to those used in binding arbitration.

As with binding arbitration, when the parties agree to nonbinding arbitration, they have the opportunity to establish procedures appropriate to the case. Because the parties have the right to reject the decision, they may agree to limit rigorously the scope and amount of discovery conducted before the hearing. This can expedite the arbitration process. If the parties accept the arbitrator's decision, the discovery limits may significantly reduce the amount of lawyer's fees expended by the parties.

At the hearing, the arbitrator will hear evidence and render a decision. To streamline the process, evidentiary standards may be relaxed. For example, the parties may agree to permit declarations in lieu of testimony, to allow hearsay evidence, or to consider documents without laying a foundation. Indeed, the parties may agree to waive a hearing and provide the arbitrator only with written documents, declarations, and written briefs.

Following the hearing, the arbitrator will render an award, which typically includes deciding the issues of liability, damages, and lawyer's fees. The agreement or court procedures under which the nonbinding arbitration is being conducted will generally provide a time frame and procedure for acceptance or rejection of the arbitrator's award.

23. 9 U.S.C. § 10.

If all parties accept the arbitrator's award, it will become a judgment. If either party rejects the arbitrator's award, the claims then proceed through the judicial process as though the arbitration had not occurred. The award then typically becomes the starting point for settlement discussions. The arbitrator's award, even if rejected, gives the parties insight into the relative strengths and weaknesses of their cases, which enables them to make a more informed decision about the settlement value of the action.

C. Early Neutral Evaluation

Early neutral evaluation is not designed to resolve the entire case. Instead, it is a process designed to assist the parties in evaluating their case. The evaluator may also assist the parties in reaching areas of agreement with respect to either the litigation procedure or the substantive claims.

In advance of early neutral evaluation, both parties typically present letter briefs or other informal position papers. The evaluator meets with all parties and counsel in an informal session, during which both evidence and argument may be presented. The evaluator writes a private evaluation of the lawsuit, which usually includes an assessment of the relative strengths and weaknesses of the parties' cases. The evaluation also includes an estimate of the likelihood of liability and provides an estimate of the range of damages.

After writing the evaluation, and before sharing it with the parties, the evaluator will offer to conduct settlement discussions. If settlement discussions do not resolve the action, the evaluator may suggest limitations on discovery or stipulations the parties could enter to narrow the dispute and reduce the cost of litigation. At the close of the early neutral evaluation, the evaluator will disclose his or her private evaluation. Often the evaluation will spur further settlement discussions between the parties, with or without the assistance of the evaluator.

Many courts offer a panel of attorneys who will provide early neutral evaluation of the claims and defenses asserted in a lawsuit. The evaluator should have expertise in employment matters.

D. Mini-Trial

Mini-trials provide a procedure designed to lead to consensual resolution of a claim. They are more akin to mediation, with the opportunity to present evidence to a neutral. In a mini-trial, the parties select a neutral. Ideally, the neutral should have experience as both a mediator and an arbitrator, as well as familiarity with litigation of employment practices claims.

The neutral presides over a summary presentation of evidence and will hear legal argument. However, in a mini-trial, the neutral is not authorized to make a binding decision. After hearing the evidence, the neutral may either render an advisory opinion or provide the parties with an analysis of the strengths and weaknesses of their respective positions. The neutral will then step into a mediator-like role and attempt to help the parties reach a negotiated, consensual resolution of the dispute.

IV. Summary Judgment

Summary judgment is often the most potent weapon in the defense counsel's arsenal. Even if the entire case cannot be resolved through summary judgment, partial summary judgment may eliminate causes of action or elements of damage that will enable counsel to reach a reasonable settlement for the remaining claims.

A. Standard for Summary Judgment

Summary judgment is appropriate when there is no genuine issue regarding any material fact and the moving party is entitled to judgment as a matter of law. Under Rule 56(a) of the Federal Rules of Civil Procedure:

> A party may move for summary judgment, identifying each claim or defense—or the part of each claim or defense—on which summary judgment is sought. The court shall grant summary judgment if the movant shows that there is no genuine dispute as to any material fact and the movant is entitled to judgment as a matter of law.[24]

"Unless a different time is set by local rule or the court orders otherwise, a party may file a motion for summary judgment at any time until 30 days after the close of all discovery."[25]

A party seeking summary judgment always bears the initial burden of establishing the absence of a genuine issue of material fact.[26] The moving party can satisfy this burden in two ways: (1) by presenting evidence that negates an essential element of the nonmoving party's case or (2) by demonstrating that the nonmoving party failed to make a showing sufficient to establish an element essential to that party's case, on which that party will bear the burden of proof at trial.[27]

However, once the employer meets this initial burden, the employee cannot defeat summary judgment by merely demonstrating "that there is some metaphysical doubt as to the material facts."[28] Rather, the employee must "go beyond the pleadings and by her own affidavits, or by 'the depositions, answers to interrogatories, and admissions on file,' designate 'specific facts showing that there is a genuine issue for trial.'"[29] In order to defeat a summary judgment motion, the employee

---

24. FED. R. CIV. P. 56(a).
25. FED. R. CIV. P. 56(b).
26. *See Celotex Corp. v. Catrett*, 477 U.S. 317, 323 (1986).
27. *Id.* at 322–23.
28. *Matsushita Elec. Indus. Co., Ltd. v. Zenith Radio Corp.*, 475 U.S. 574, 586 (1986); *see also Triton Energy Corp. v. Square D Co.*, 68 F.3d 1216, 1221 (9th Cir. 1995) ("The mere existence of a scintilla of evidence in support of the non-moving party's position is not sufficient.") (citing *Anderson v. Liberty Lobby, Inc.*, 477 U.S. 242, 252 (1986)).
29. *Celotex Corp.*, 477 U.S. 324 (quoting FED. R. CIV. P. 56(e)).

must present some evidence on every material issue for which he or she will bear the burden of proof at trial.[30]

B. Attacking the *Prima Facie* Case

In Title VII and retaliation cases, attacking the *prima facie* case is the simplest approach to summary judgment. When the plaintiff does not have sufficient facts to make a *prima facie* case, courts are more likely to grant an employer's motion for summary judgment than in other circumstances.

To establish a *prima facie* case of discrimination in the terms and conditions of employment, "the plaintiff must provide evidence that (1) she was a member of a protected class; (2) she was qualified for the position she sought or was performing competently in the position she held; (3) she suffered an adverse employment action, such as termination, demotion, or denial of an available job; and (4) some other circumstance suggests discriminatory motive."[31]

The *prima facie* case may be stated differently, depending upon the nature of the allegedly wrongful act. In a case of discriminatory termination, "a plaintiff must show: (1) she is a member of a protected minority; (2) she was performing her job in a satisfactory manner; (3) she suffered an adverse employment action; and (4) she was replaced by an individual outside the protected class with equal or inferior qualifications, that similarly situated employees outside the protected class were treated more favorably or at least that her termination occurred under circumstances giving rise to an inference of race discrimination."[32]

"In order to establish *a prima facie* case of discriminatory refusal to hire, a plaintiff must prove: (1) that he belongs to a protected minority group; (2) that he applied for and was qualified for a job for which the employer was seeking applicants; (3) that despite his

30. *Id.*
31. *See McDonnell Douglas Corp. v. Green*, 411 U.S. 792, 802–04 (1973).
32. *Crawford v. MCI Worldcom Commc'ns*, 167 F. Supp. 2d 1128, 1132 (S.D. Cal. 2001).

qualifications he was rejected; and (4) the position remained open and the employer continued to seek applicants from persons with the plaintiff's qualifications."[33]

The employer may obtain summary judgment by attacking any element of the *prima facie* case. For example, the employer may rely on the first prong to defeat claims of so-called "reverse age discrimination" if the plaintiff is under forty years old.

The second prong is commonly the focus of a motion for summary judgment in failure to hire cases. The employer is in the best position to demonstrate that the employee was not qualified when it had objective, written criteria for applicants; the criteria were reasonably designed to predict success on the job; the criteria were applied to all applicants and did not disproportionately eliminate members of the protected category; and the applicant did not meet the criteria.

In cases where the employee is still at work, or resigned, the employer's counsel may prevail by demonstrating that the complained-of action was not an adverse employment action:

> "[A]n action is cognizable as an adverse employment action if it is reasonably likely to deter employees from engaging in protected activity." In context, this is, at least in part, a subjective standard because the EEOC manual speaks of "any adverse treatment that is based on a retaliatory motive and is reasonably likely to deter *the charging party* or others from engaging in protected activity."[34]

The Seventh Circuit recognized that neither unfavorable performance evaluations nor oral or written reprimands implicated sufficiently "tangible job consequences" to constitute an independent basis of liability

---

33. *McDonnell Douglas Corp.*, 411 U.S. 8024; *Sandoval v. Saticoy Lemon Ass'n*, 747 F. Supp. 1373, 1390 (C.D. Cal. 1990).

34. *Vasquez v. County of Los Angeles*, 349 F.3d 634, 646 (9th Cir. 2003) (emphasis in original) (quoting references omitted).

under Title VII.[35] Similarly, no adverse employment action existed when the employee was denied training, was not invited to staff meetings, was required to work outside his or her area of expertise, was denied compensatory time off, and was not provided performance feedback.[36]

In *Patterson v. Avery Dennison Corp.*[37] summary judgment was granted because the employee had failed to fulfill the fourth prong of the *prima facie* case. The Seventh Circuit explained that, to establish the fourth prong of the *prima facie* case, a plaintiff must show that similarly situated persons outside the protected class were treated more favorably. In *Patterson*, the employee failed to make this showing because the male employees that she compared herself to were not directly comparable in all material respects. The court rejected Patterson's assertion that she could satisfy the fourth prong by demonstrating that male employees took over her job responsibilities after her termination because the plaintiff's job functions were not absorbed; these functions had ceased to exist.

C. Burden Shifting

If the employee can demonstrate a *prima facie* case of discrimination or retaliation, the analysis moves to the burden-shifting approach of *McDonnell Douglas Corp. v. Green.*[38] This burden shifting is described as follows:

1. The plaintiff must establish a *prima facie* case of retaliation,
2. The defendant can then articulate a legitimate nonretaliatory explanation for its acts, and

35. *Oest v. Illinois Dep't of Corrs.*, 240 F.3d 605, 613 (7th Cir. 2001).

36. *Johnson-Carter v. B.D.O. Seidman, LLP*, 169 F. Supp. 2d 924, 938 (N.D. Ill. 2001).

37. 281 F.3d 676 (7th Cir. 2002).

38. 411 U.S. 792 (1973).

3. To prevail, the plaintiff must prove that the defendant's proffered explanation is merely a pretext for the illegal action.[39]

Once the plaintiff has established a *prima facie* case, "the burden of *production* only shifts briefly to the employer to explain why it took the challenged action, if not based on the protected characteristic. In practice, employers quickly rebut the presumption, and it 'drops from the case.' . . . The burden of production then shifts back to the plaintiff to introduce evidence from which the factfinder could conclude that the employer's proffered reason was pretextual. The burden of *persuasion* always remains with the employee to prove the ultimate Title VII violation—unlawful discrimination."[40]

The plaintiff—once the employer produces sufficient evidence to support a nondiscriminatory explanation for its decision—must be afforded the opportunity to prove by a preponderance of the evidence that the legitimate reasons offered by the defendant were not its true reasons but were a pretext for discrimination.[41] "To avoid summary judgment, [plaintiffs] 'must do more than establish a prima facie case and deny the credibility of the defendant's witnesses.'"[42] Three types of evidence can be used to show pretext: (1) direct evidence of discrimination or retaliation, such as statements or admissions, (2) comparative evidence, and (3) statistics.[43]

Plaintiffs often rely upon one or two comments in the workplace to show pretext. If the comments were not related to the decision at issue, were remote in time, or were not uttered by the decision maker,

39. *Id.* at 802–04; *see also Texas Dep't of Cmty. Affairs v. Burdine*, 450 U.S. 248, 252–53 (1981).

40. *Costa v. Desert Palace, Inc.*, 299 F.3d 838, 855 (9th Cir. 2002), *aff'd*, 539 U.S. 90 (2003) (emphasis in original); *see also McDonnell Douglas Corp.*, 411 U.S. 792; *Texas Dep't of Cmty. Affairs*, 450 U.S. 248.

41. *Reeves v. Sanderson Plumbing Prods., Inc.*, 530 U.S. 133, 143 (2000).

42. *Bradley v. Harcourt, Brace & Co.*, 104 F.3d 267, 270 (9th Cir. 1996) (quoting *Wallis v. J. R. Simplot Co.*, 26 F.3d 885, 890 (9th Cir. 1994)).

43. *Penk v. Oregon State Bd. of Higher Educ.*, 816 F.2d 458, 462 (9th Cir. 1987).

defense counsel should ask the court to disregard the comments as stray remarks. In *Nesbit v. Pepsico, Inc.*,[44] the Ninth Circuit concluded that the employer was entitled to summary judgment in an age-discrimination claim, although the plaintiff had produced evidence that one supervisor had told the plaintiff, "We don't necessarily like grey hair," and the senior vice president of personnel had stated, "We don't want unpromotable fifty-year-olds around." The comments were not tied directly to the plaintiff's termination and fell short of creating an inference of age discrimination.[45]

D. Affirmative Defenses

Defense counsel may also assert various affirmative defenses to obtain summary judgment or partial summary judgment. The affirmative defenses more commonly raised on a motion for summary judgment include:

- Failure to exhaust administrative remedies;
- Claim was not filed in a timely manner;[46]
- Defendant was not plaintiff's employee;[47]
- In harassment cases, the three-pronged approach that (1) plaintiff suffered no tangible employment action, (2) the employer had exercised reasonable care to prevent and correct promptly any harassing behavior, and (3) the plaintiff employee unreasonably failed to take

44. 994 F.2d 703 (9th Cir. 1993).

45. *Id.* at 705; *see also Price Waterhouse v. Hopkins*, 490 U.S. 228, 251 (1989) (O'Connor, J., concurring); *Krystek v. Univ. of Southern Mississippi*, 164 F.3d 251 (5th Cir. 1999); *Bahl v. Royal Indem. Co.*, 115 F.3d 1283 (7th Cir. 1997).

46. "A discrete retaliatory or discriminatory act 'occurred' on the day that it 'happened.' A party, therefore, must file the charge within either 180 or 300 days of the date of the act or lose the ability to recover for it." *Nat'l R.R. Passenger Corp. v. Morgan*, 536 U.S. 101, 108 (2002).

47. This defense typically applies when plaintiff sues multiple entities, claiming they are joint employers or an integrated enterprise. For cases rejecting these theories, see *Sizova v. Nat'l Institute of Standards & Technology*, 282 F.3d 1320 (10th Cir. 2002); *Hukill v. Auto Care, Inc.*, 192 F.3d 437 (4th Cir. 1999); *Swallows v. Barnes & Noble Book Stores, Inc.*, 128 F.3d 990 (6th Cir. 1997).

advantage of any preventive or corrective opportunities provided by the employer or to avoid harm otherwise;[48]

- Failure to mitigate damages, useful to minimize the recovery when the plaintiff has not searched for replacement employment; and
- Punitive damages are not appropriate.

These and other affirmative defenses are discussed more fully in chapter 5.

V. Selection and Use of Experts

Both sides in an employment dispute will typically engage the services of experts. Depending upon the nature of the case, expert testimony could encompass a wide variety of issues. Employer's counsel may wish to use one or more of the following types of experts:

- Psychiatrist or psychologist: to testify about the plaintiff's emotional condition and possible alternative causes of any emotional distress;
- Physician: to testify about the plaintiff's physical condition. This may be relevant in cases under the Americans with Disabilities Act or when the plaintiff's physical ailments contribute to or are caused by his or her medical condition;
- Economist or accountant: to minimize the plaintiff's claim for future lost wages and benefits;
- Vocational rehabilitation counselor: to testify about the plaintiff's job options, the job market, and when the plaintiff should reasonably secure comparable alternative employment;
- Ergonomics consultant: to testify about whether the workplace contained adequate accommodations or whether further accommodation was reasonable;

---

48. *Burlington Indus., Inc. v. Ellerth*, 524 U.S. 742 (1998); *Faragher v. City of Boca Raton*, 524 U.S. 775 (1998).

- Management-practices consultant: to testify to the adequacy of the employer's policies and practices, adequacy of the investigation of any complaints made by the plaintiff, or other management practices or human resources matters. Some judges will allow management-practices consultants to testify about ultimate issues, such as whether the alleged behavior constitutes discrimination or harassment; and
- Statistician: to explain statistical evidence, such as whether the workforce composition is within the statistically expected range given the ethnic distribution in the surrounding community or the applicant pool.

Expert selection should include evaluation of a number of factors. First, is the expert qualified in the field? Second, has the expert testified so frequently or primarily for one side that he or she will appear to be a hired gun, rather than an impartial explainer? Third, has the expert offered opinions inconsistent with those he or she will be offering at trial? Fourth, are the expert's opinions consistent with and supportive of the employer's position and theme of the case? Finally, is the expert a good "explainer"? That is, can she or he educate the jury in a clear, persuasive manner, without relying on technical jargon or terms that will be boring or that the jurors will have difficulty understanding?

In federal courts, admissibility of expert testimony is governed by Rule 702 of the Federal Rules of Evidence, which states:

> A witness who is qualified as an expert by knowledge, skill, experience, training, or education may testify in the form of an opinion or otherwise if:
>
> (a) the expert's scientific, technical, or other specialized knowledge will help the trier of fact to understand the evidence or to determine a fact in issue;

(b) the testimony is based on sufficient facts or data;

(c) the testimony is the product of reliable principles and methods; and

(d) the expert has reliably applied the principles and methods to the facts of the case.

If scientific, technical, or other specialized knowledge will assist the trier of fact (that is, the judge or jury) to understand the evidence or to determine a fact in issue, a witness qualified as an expert by knowledge, skill, experience, training, or education may testify thereto in the form of an opinion or otherwise.

Under Rule 702, expert witness testimony is admissible only when:

- The expert has knowledge, skill, experience, training, or education necessary to form the proffered opinions;
- The expert opinion concerns scientific, technical, or other specialized knowledge;
- The opinion is relevant to the case;
- The opinion will assist the trier of fact to understand the evidence or determine a fact issue; and
- The opinion is based on reliable methodology or analysis and not subjective belief or unsupported speculation.[49]

In determining whether to admit proffered expert testimony, federal courts evaluate a number of factors, including whether it (1) can be tested; (2) has been subjected to peer review; (3) has a high known or potential rate of error; and (4) has attained general acceptance within the scientific community.[50]

49. *See Daubert v. Merrell Dow Pharm.*, 509 U.S. 579, 590–95 (1993); *Kumho Tire Co., Ltd. v. Carmichael*, 526 U.S. 137, 149 (1999).

50. *Kumho Tire Co., Ltd.*, 526 U.S. at 149–50.

Many state courts follow what is known as the *Frye*[51] standard in ruling on admissibility of expert testimony. Under *Frye*, the court evaluates whether the evidence is "generally accepted" in the relevant scientific community. The party offering scientific evidence must show general acceptance by offering scientific publications, judicial decisions, evidence of practical use, or testimony by scientists on their peers' position regarding the evidence in question.

Courts have the power to set a date for expert disclosure. If no specific disclosure date is established, all parties must disclose their experts ninety days before the trial date. Counsel should retain the expert well in advance of the disclosure date. Expert disclosure includes both the identity of the expert witnesses who will be testifying and a written report prepared and signed by the witness. The report shall contain a complete statement of all opinions to be expressed and the basis and reasons therefor; the data or other information considered by the witness in forming the opinions; any exhibits to be used as a summary of or support for the opinions; the qualifications of the witness, including a list of all publications authored by the witness within the preceding ten years; the compensation to be paid for the study and testimony; and a listing of any other cases in which the witness has testified as an expert at trial or by deposition within the preceding four years.[52]

Failure to provide the report, or an incomplete report, can limit or significantly eliminate the expert's ability to testify at trial.

Effective expert witness testimony is the result of detailed preparation of the expert. The expert should be familiar with defense counsel's theory or theme of the case so that the expert opinions are consistent with the employer's approach. Because communications between defense counsel and the expert are discoverable, counsel must take care to avoid any statements that could be construed as instructing the expert to form a particular opinion. In general, counsel should ask the

51. *Frye v. United States*, 293 F. 1013 (D.C. Cir. 1923).
52. Fed. R. Civ. P. 26(a)(2)(B).

expert to form opinions on particular areas. For example, a psychiatric expert might be asked to evaluate the nature, extent, causation, and expected duration of any emotional distress the plaintiff is claiming. Defense counsel will generally also want the retained experts to comment upon the reports and conclusions of plaintiff's experts.

All relevant documents should be provided to the expert. If the expert reviews the complete deposition transcript, rather than a summary or excerpts, he or she can determine what information is relevant. Ask the expert what additional documents might be helpful. If the expert is engaged early in the process, counsel can propound additional discovery requests or subpoena additional documents that the expert would like to evaluate in forming his or her opinion. If the expert admits that there were additional documents or information that he or she would have liked to review in forming an opinion, it will undermine the expert's credibility with the jury.

VI. Pretrial Submissions

In federal court, judges typically require the parties to exchange and file trial pleadings in advance of the trial. Rule 16 of the Federal Rules of Civil Procedure authorizes courts to set dates for the identification of witnesses and documents, to schedule filing and exchanging of pretrial briefs, to establish reasonable limits on the time for presenting evidence, and to take other measures that facilitate the just, speedy, and inexpensive disposition of the action, including a pretrial conference:

> The court may hold a final pretrial conference to formulate a trial plan, including a plan to facilitate the admission of evidence. The conference must be held as close to the start of trial as is reasonable, and must be attended by at least one attorney who will conduct the trial for each party and by any unrepresented party.

> The court may modify the order issued after a final pretrial conference only to prevent manifest injustice.[53]

A. *Voir Dire* Questions

Many courts ask the parties to submit questions for the jurors in advance of trial. Some judges will even ask the parties to agree on the basic questions that will be asked of each juror. When the case is one involving sensitive matters, or which may engender passion, the parties may often agree to use a juror questionnaire as the basis for a preliminary screening. The questionnaire can elicit a substantial amount of information about each juror's beliefs and experiences without having the jurors discuss private matters in the presence of all prospective jurors. In addition, questionnaires can be a time-saving device, because the jurors can complete and turn in the questionnaires and be released until the next court day. Some lawyers do not use questionnaires because they believe the written responses may mask the jurors' reaction to sensitive subjects involved in the case, or because they want to use the *voir dire* process to create a bond with the prospective panel members.

When the court will be conducting preliminary *voir dire*, the following questions provide basic information about the prospective juror's experience and background:

(1) Do you know any of the parties or lawyers: [state names of parties and lawyers]?
(2) Do you know any of the following potential witnesses: [state names of anticipated witnesses]?
(3) What was your age on your last birthday?

53. Fed. R. Civ. P. 16(e).

(4) Do you currently own a home, rent, live with relatives, live with friends, or live with someone else? (If other, please have potential juror explain.)

(5) Does anyone live with you? [If so]: What is your relationship to each person with whom you live?

(6) Do you have children? [If so]:

a. How many children do you have?

b. Please state the age, gender, and occupation (if applicable) of each of your children.

c. Do any of these children live with you? If so, indicate which ones.

(7) About how long have you lived at your current address?

(8) What is your current marital status? [If potential juror has never married, please skip to question 9.] How many times have you been married?

(9) What is your educational background?

(10) What is the highest level of school from which you graduated?

(11) Did you attend school beyond the level identified in question 10 but not graduate? (If so, please have potential juror explain.)

(12) Have you received any technical/vocational certifications? (If so, please specify in which field.)

(13) Do you have any specialized knowledge, training, or experience in any of the following fields: Education? Business management? Nonprofit organizations? Financial planning? Accounting? Human resources? Law enforcement? Law?

a. Please describe the source or background of your knowledge, training, or experience in any of these areas.

b. Does anyone close to you have specialized knowledge, training, or experience in any of those fields?

(14) Are you employed, a homemaker, retired, a student, or not currently working?

a. If employed, what is your primary occupation? If not, are you away from work because you are retired, a student, on strike, laid off, on leave, or on disability? (If necessary, please have potential juror explain.)

b. Are you currently working full time or part time?

c. Are you self-employed?

d. Are you currently collecting any welfare benefits?

(15) For your current or most recent job, who is/was your employer, and what is/was your position? [If potential juror has never been employed full time, please skip to question 16.]

a. What are or were your job responsibilities?

b. How long have you had / did you have this job?

c. Does this job reflect your overall work experience? [If not]: What type of job does your work experience best qualify you to do?

d. Does this job have any supervisory or managerial responsibilities? (If so, please have potential juror explain.)

(16) Do you now or have you ever worked for local, state, or federal government? (If yes, please have potential juror explain.) [Please ask question 17 only if potential juror is currently married or living with someone.]

(17) What is your spouse's or partner's current employment status?

a. For your spouse's or partner's current or most recent job, who is/was the employer, and what is/was the position?

b. How long did your spouse or partner have this job?

(18) Have you or your spouse been terminated from a job or laid off in the last five years? (If yes, please have potential juror explain.)

(19) Have you ever been a party to a lawsuit, either as a plaintiff, defendant, or a witness? [Please skip to question 20 if potential juror has never been involved in a lawsuit.]

For each lawsuit:

a. Who was suing (who was the plaintiff)? Who was being sued (who was the defendant)?

b. Please describe your role in the case, and how it came into being.

c. What was the outcome of the case? Were you satisfied with it?

(20) Has any member of your immediate family ever been involved in a lawsuit, either as a party or as a witness? If so, who were the parties and what were the circumstances?

(21) Have you ever served as a juror? [Please skip to question 22 if potential juror has never served as a juror.]

a. What was the year of your *most recent* service?

b. Was the trial in civil court or criminal court?

c. Was the trial in the United States District Court, a California State Court, or some other court? (If other, please explain.)

d. What was the case about?

e. Was a verdict reached? If so, was it "guilty or liable," or "not guilty or not liable"?

f. If a verdict was reached, were you satisfied with it? (Repeat for other cases.)

g. Have you ever served as a foreperson on a jury?

(22) Have you ever been a member of a labor or trade union? (If yes, please explain.)

(23) Have you ever (on your own, or through your union) filed any type of formal complaint or grievance at work? (If yes, please explain.)

(24) Have you personally or has anyone close to you ever been subjected to discrimination in the workplace? (If yes, please explain.) Did you any or anyone close to you sue the employer for this alleged conduct?

(25) Have you personally or has anyone close to you ever been subjected to harassment in the workplace? (If yes, please explain.) Did you or anyone close to you sue the employer for this alleged conduct?

(26) Have you personally or has anyone close to you ever been subjected to retaliation in the workplace? (If yes, please explain.) Did you or anyone close to you sue the employer for this alleged conduct?

(27) Have you, your spouse, a family member, or a close friend ever been a victim of what you consider to be unethical or immoral conduct by an employer? (If yes, please explain for each occurrence.) Did you or any of those listed above sue the employer for this alleged conduct?

(28) Have you personally or has anyone close to you ever received treatment for a mental disability? (If yes, please explain.)

(29) Have you personally or has anyone close to you ever relocated residences for an employment opportunity? (If yes, please explain.)

(30) Do you agree that employers have a right to set and enforce performance goals for their employees and to terminate employees who fail to meet these goals?

(31) Do you agree that employers have a right to set and enforce personnel policies for their employees and to terminate employees who violate these policies?

(32) Do you believe that no employee should be terminated without a formal warning from an employer and an opportunity to improve his or her performance?

(33) Do you believe that large companies tend to take advantage of employees?

(34) Do you believe that taxes for corporations should be increased?

(35) Do you believe that large companies tend to discriminate against people based upon the employee's race?

(36) Do you believe that large companies would be more likely than other companies to discriminate against employees based upon their race?

(37) Have you ever had a serious dispute with an [insert employer's line of business, for example, bank, retail establishment, manufacturing plant]? (If yes, please explain.)

(38) Have you ever had any problem with any [insert employer's line of business, for example, bank, retail establishment, manufacturing plant]?

(39) Has anyone in your immediate family or any close friend ever worked for any [insert employer's line of business, for example, bank, retail establishment, manufacturing plant]? (If so, please have potential juror explain, including the reason, if applicable, why this family member or friend no longer works for the [insert employer's line of business, for example, bank, retail establishment, manufacturing plant].)

(40) This case involves allegations against the [insert name(s) of defendant(s)]. Do you have any negative feelings or experiences related to the [insert name(s) of defendant(s)], or [insert line of business of defendant(s)] in general, that could prevent you from giving this case a fair and unbiased hearing? (If yes, please explain.)

(41) Have you ever had any contacts with the [insert name(s) of defendant(s)], either as a customer, applicant, or an employee? (If so, please have potential juror explain.)

(42) Are there any situations in your life that are currently affecting you emotionally in such a way that it would make it difficult for you to concentrate on the evidence in this case?

(43) Do you believe that you should be excused from serving on a jury, or that serving on a jury would cause you unusual hardship? Why?

(44) Do you believe that when a lawsuit is filed, there is usually a good reason for it?

(45) Do you believe that an individual who does something dishonest in one matter in his or her life is more likely to be dishonest or untrustworthy in other matters than someone who has not been shown to be dishonest?

(46) What are your major outside interests or hobbies—things that you spend a great deal of time on outside of work (for example, clubs, groups, watching TV, and so on)?

B. Trial Brief

Trial briefs should provide the judge with the necessary framework to evaluate the legal arguments and evidence that will be presented at trial. The trial brief need not be lengthy or extremely detailed. It may contain a two- to four-page statement of the facts of the case, organized in a logical and persuasive manner. The trial brief should also explain the causes of action being asserted, the affirmative defenses being raised, and the essential elements of each.

If the parties have entered any stipulations during the course of the litigation, these can be pointed out in the trial brief. In addition, the controlling authorities, including both statutes and decisions, for each claim and affirmative defense should be discussed briefly. It is useful to attach any stipulations and the applicable statutes and key cases, so the court and parties have the relevant authority easily at hand.

Employer's counsel have differing opinions as to whether the trial brief should discuss the plaintiff's alleged damages. Some lawyers are concerned that a discussion of damages will be viewed as an admission that the plaintiff has some right to recover damages. Other defense counsel believe it is important to provide a persuasive statement explaining why, if the employee proves liability, the recoverable damages are minimal.

Separate mini-briefs on key legal issues, to be presented as the factual or legal issues arise during the course of trial, can be beneficial. Addressing critical issues in separate briefs allows the judge to focus on the single issue presented. Having the detailed discussions of these issues in another pleading also allows counsel to have a more concise trial brief. Finally, when the critical issues arise, the trial judge will already have heard arguments and evidence and will, therefore, have a greater understanding of the framework of the dispute.

C. *In Limine* Motions

Motions *in limine* are pretrial motions seeking evidentiary rulings. Parties will ask the court to exclude evidence in advance of the trial to avoid having the jury hear damaging testimony that is not admissible. In some jurisdictions, the courts also permit motions *in limine* asking the court to determine, before the trial, that certain evidence can be admitted.

In limine motions should identify the precise testimony or evidence counsel is seeking to exclude. The motion should be supported by a short brief containing citations to rules of evidence and decisions supporting the exclusion. Some motions will also need to be supported by evidence, such as deposition testimony, explaining why the evidence should be excluded. For example, counsel may attach an expert's curriculum vitae and deposition testimony in support of a motion seeking to keep the expert from testifying because he or she lacks the qualifications or has opinions that are not well founded. The plaintiff's testimony about his or her failure to conduct a reasonable job search may be attached in seeking to exclude lost wages and benefits.

The primary grounds for motions *in limine* are as follows:

- Relevance: The anticipated evidence has no "tendency to make a fact more or less probable than it would be without the evidence" and the evidence has no "consequence in determining the action."[54]
- Unfair prejudice: "The court may exclude relevant evidence if its probative value is substantially outweighed by a danger of one or more of the following: unfair prejudice, . . ."[55]
- Confusing the issues.[56]
- Misleading the jury.[57]
- Undue delay or wasting time.[58]
- Needless presentation of cumulative evidence.[59]

54. Fed. R. Evid. 401.
55. Fed. R. Evid. 403.
56. *Id.*
57. *Id.*
58. *Id.*
59. *Id.*

At the pretrial conference, the court may rule on the motions or take them under submission. "Once the court rules definitively on the record—either before or at trial—a party need not renew an objection or offer of proof to preserve a claim of error for appeal."[60] Note that in some states, the party must renew the objection when the evidence is offered during the trial to preserve the question for appeal.

If the judge does not rule on a motion *in limine*, counsel should ask the court to instruct the parties to refrain from mentioning the objectionable evidence during opening statements, or until after the motion is decided. During trial, counsel seeking to admit the evidence should lay the necessary foundation, then ask for a ruling on admissibility. Whenever evidence is excluded, counsel seeking to have the evidence admitted should make an offer of proof, explaining what the evidence would be, to preserve the record for appeal.

Counsel should advise each witness about the *in limine* rulings, instructing the witness to refrain from blurting out information that has been excluded. In addition, if the court has granted a motion *in limine* to exclude damaging evidence, the party who filed the motion must avoid offering evidence that would "open the door" to that evidence by creating a basis for admitting the evidence, such as attacking the credibility of a witness or providing an explanation contrary to the reasons put forth by the employer.

D. Jury Instructions

The parties are entitled to have jury instructions given regarding each cause of action and affirmative defense raised by the evidence. Counsel has the obligation to request particular jury instructions. In federal court, failure to give a jury instruction that is not requested cannot be grounds for appeals.[61]

60. FED. R. EVID. 103(b).
61. FED. R. CIV. P. 51.

Jury instructions should be written in lay language and organized logically. One common method of organization is as follows:

- Preliminary instructions, such as those on duty of jurors, relevance, direct and circumstantial evidence, and burden of proof;
- Introduction of a cause of action, followed by instructions setting forth the elements of that cause of action;
- Elements of each affirmative defense;
- Damages, including instructions on when damages are appropriate, how to calculate damages, and avoiding multiple recovery;
- Instructions on punitive damages, which should include a separate burden of proof instruction; and
- Concluding instructions, such as the jurors' duty to deliberate.

Many jurisdictions have model jury instructions, which should be used when appropriate.[62] When no model instruction is available, jury instructions can be crafted based upon language in controlling authority, such as statutes and cases. Some judges are more likely to read a jury instruction that contains an exact quotation of the relevant authority. Other judges prefer to have the language modified so that it is more understandable to the average juror, as long as the meaning is not affected.

Each jury instruction should contain only a single concept. If the court decides that a portion of an instruction containing multiple ideas is not supported by the cumulative evidence, not supported by the law, or otherwise improper, the decision not to give the instruction may also eliminate other important aspects of the instruction.

---

62. *See, e.g.*, Ninth Circuit Manual Of Model Civil Jury Instructions, *available at* http://www3.ce9.uscourts.gov/web/sdocuments.nsf/civ.

E. Special Verdicts

Many courts require special verdict forms to be submitted before the final pretrial conference. Special verdicts can help the jury focus on the proper issues. From the employer's perspective, use of special verdicts can reduce the risk that a verdict will be entered because the jurors feel sorry for the plaintiff. Special verdicts are governed by Rule 49 of the Federal Rules of Civil Procedure, which provides, in part, the following:

> The court may require a jury to return only a special verdict in the form of a special written finding on each issue of fact. The court may do so by:
>
> A. submitting written questions susceptible of a categorical or other brief answer;
> B. submitting written forms of the special findings that might properly be made under the pleadings and evidence; or
> C. using any other method that the court considers appropriate.[63]

> The court may submit to the jury forms for a general verdict, together with written questions on one or more issues of fact that the jury must decide. The court must give the instructions and explanations necessary to enable the jury to render a general verdict and answer the questions in writing, and must direct the jury to do both.[64]

A good special verdict form will require the jurors to decide whether the plaintiff has established elements of his or her claim before they

63. Fed. R. Civ. P. 49(a)(1).
64. Fed. R. Civ. P. 49(b)(1).

reach a decision on liability. A properly drafted special verdict form can help avoid errors in damage calculations, such as those caused by awarding cumulative damages for each cause of action. When punitive damages are requested, courts will often allow the employer to incorporate the higher burden of proof required for awarding punitive damages within the special verdict.

VII. Trial

The "theme of the case" should be incorporated into all aspects of the employer's presentation. Seasoned trial lawyers start thinking about possible themes early in discovery so that evidence supporting the theme can be gathered or developed. Themes, however, may develop during trial as evidence is admitted. Johnnie Cochran provided an outstanding example of responding to evidence by adopting the theme, "If it doesn't fit, you must acquit," in his closing argument for the criminal trial of O. J. Simpson. The opportunity for this theme arose during trial, when the prosecutor asked Mr. Simpson to try on a glove left at the crime scene.

A theme should be a simple, persuasive explanation of the employer's position. It should be stated in a single sentence and provide a plausible explanation for the events. The theme can be incorporated into both the opening statement and closing argument. In determining what evidence to present, the trial lawyer should select facts, documents, and witnesses that support or enhance the theme. In some instances, expert opinions can be crafted to incorporate or repeat the theme of the case.

The employer's witnesses, such as the immediate supervisor, human resources representative, or individual who made the termination decision, may be helpful in deciding the theme of the case. A theme that is not supported by the employer's witnesses will not be persuasive.

Employer's themes may often be based on one of the following concepts, common to many defenses:

- The employee was not doing his or her job;
- Others in the protected class did not have any problems;

- The employee did not want to be treated like everyone else; he or she wanted special benefits;
- Tough economic times require difficult choices;
- The employee's job was no longer needed;
- The employee's absences, attitude, or nonperformance was making everyone else work harder;
- The employer provides a good place to work;
- The employee never complained while she or he was working, even though the company had policies and procedures to prevent just the type of conduct the employee is now complaining about;
- The employee is greedy and is trying to take advantage of the judicial system.

A. Selecting Jurors

Experienced employer's counsel have two goals in conducting *voir dire.* One purpose is to learn about the past experiences, prejudices, and biases of potential jurors. This information can be used to evaluate which jurors will be predisposed to the employer's position. The second and, some would say, equally important purpose is to educate the jurors about the case by communicating the employer's position. This approach educates and persuades the jurors, even before the panel is selected.

Well-crafted jury questions can accomplish both information gathering and persuasion. Questions can incorporate the expected evidence in the case, asking the juror about past experiences in similar situations. The open-ended questions should be designed to evaluate whether the prospective juror has biases about the issues that will arise in the case, including overarching attitudes about employers and supervisors; beliefs regarding the frequency of discrimination or harassment; acceptance of the employer's ability to terminate employment at will; beliefs that progressive discipline is warranted in all circumstances; and what actions the panel member expects from a good and fair employer. In addition to the work-related questions, counsel can ask questions that commit the juror to evaluate the evidence fairly, such as: "You will be hearing from the employee first, and the employer will not be able to respond to the employee's allegations until after the employee has finished presenting her entire case. Can you wait until all of the evidence is in, and the employer's witnesses have testified, before you make any decision on this matter?" and "If you decided that the employer had not violated any laws, could you set aside any feelings of sympathy you may have for the employee and enter a verdict in the employer's favor?"

Counsel's effort to educate the jury should not, however, go so far as to precondition the jury to render a particular verdict. It is clear that "it is not proper to propound hypothetical questions purporting to embody testimony that is intended to be submitted, covering all or any aspects of the case, for the purpose of ascertaining from the juror how he will vote on such a state of the testimony. Such questions are improper, regardless of whether or not they correctly epitomize the testimony intended to be introduced."[65]

In questioning the jury, lawyers should be professional but warm. Use each juror's name in the course of questioning. Preparing a chart that depicts each seat in the jury box and filling in the names as panel members are seated will enable the lawyer to recall each name. The employer should be humanized when possible. Be sure to use the employer's name and the names of the key witnesses so the jurors begin to think about the individuals involved in the decision-making process, rather than a faceless corporate employer. Listen carefully to the responses. Incorporating a portion of the response into a follow-up question will tell the panel member that his or her answers are important. At the same time, it will allow the lawyer to verify that his or her understanding of the answer is correct.

In federal court, jury selection is governed by Rule 47 of the Federal Rules of Civil Procedure, which allows the court to conduct the examination of prospective jurors itself or permit lawyers to conduct

65. *Dicks v. State*, 93 So. 137 (Fla. 1922).

the examination. "If the court examines the jurors, it must permit the parties or their attorneys to make any further inquiry it considers proper, or must itself ask any of their additional questions it considers proper."[66]

The parties may challenge jurors either for cause or through peremptory challenges. Jurors are dismissed for cause only under the narrow statutory grounds of actual, implied, or inferable bias concerning a party or issue in the case.[67] Counsel need not have a reason for exercising a peremptory challenge. However, peremptory challenges cannot be used to exclude potential jurors because of their membership in a protected class.[68] In civil cases, each party is entitled to three peremptory challenges.[69] Several defendants or several plaintiffs may be considered as a single party for the purposes of making challenges, or the court may allow additional peremptory challenges and permit them to be exercised separately or jointly.

The panel is bound to include more subordinates than supervisors. The employee will certainly excuse most individuals likely to have viewpoints favorable to an employer, such as small-business owners, managers, or human resource professionals. The employer will not be able to eliminate every panel member who expresses employee-favorable sentiment. In deciding which jurors to retain, employer's counsel should evaluate both the strength of the prospective juror's beliefs and the likelihood that he or she will be a leader. A juror who is vocal or demonstrates strong leadership characteristics, and who holds beliefs inconsistent with the employer's position, should be excused from the panel if the employer has any peremptory challenges remaining.

---

66. FED. R. CIV. P. 47(a).

67. *See United States v. Torres*, 128 F.3d 38, 43 (1997).

68. *J. E. B. v. Alabama ex rel. T.B.*, 511 U.S. 127, 129 (1994) (gender); *Batson v. Kentucky*, 476 U.S. 79, 89 (1986) (race). However, in a sexual harassment case, the employer was permitted to use peremptory strikes to eliminate all three women from the jury panel when the employer was able to provide plausible explanations, unrelated to gender, for its decisions. *Alverio v. Sam's Warehouse Club, Inc.*, 253 F.3d 933, 942 (7th Cir. 2001).

69. 28 U.S.C. § 1870.

B. Opening Statement

Opening statement is defense counsel's first opportunity to explain the employer's position to the jury. Jurors form first impressions of the case during the opening statement. Once a juror reaches an opinion, he or she perceives the evidence in the light most supportive to that opinion. Because the jurors' first impressions can be difficult to change during the course of the trial, counsel must carefully prepare the opening statement.

Many jurisdictions permit the defendant to defer the opening statement until after the close of the plaintiff's case. Most defense counsel, however, want to explain the defense at the earliest possible moment. This keeps the jurors from dwelling exclusively on the plaintiff's theme during the duration of the plaintiff's case. In addition, providing the jurors with a defense-oriented framework early in the case allows them to understand how or why certain evidence is important. Testimony and evidence key to the employer's case are often introduced during the plaintiff's case. However, they may be underplayed or introduced in a disjointed fashion. The jurors are more likely to understand the importance of particular documents or facts, and thus to recall them, if they are anticipating the evidence.

In planning the opening statement, defense counsel must keep in mind that this is the jury's introduction to the case and the parties. The jurors will need enough information about the employer, the plaintiff, and the breakdown in the employment relationship to understand the evidence as it comes in. Too often, counsel who are intimately familiar with the facts and witnesses will omit the basic facts necessary to provide a clear picture for the jurors. Another common fault is at the other end of the spectrum, when counsel provide too much minutiae and the jurors' eyes glaze over.

The opening statement must be well organized. A very common organizational tool is to present a chronology. Another method of organization is to introduce the witnesses and explain each person's anticipated testimony. This technique works best when there will be one or two key witnesses who will present the employer's story.

Employer's counsel wants to humanize the employer during the opening statement. This can be accomplished by giving a brief background of the key employer witnesses, such as the plaintiff's immediate supervisor or the human resources representative who was involved in the discipline and termination decisions. In discrimination or harassment cases, it is generally important to establish that the company is a good employer and that people like working there. This evidence can be highlighted during the opening statement.

Counsel may not argue during the opening statement. The facts should be presented in a persuasive manner, using positive language to describe the employer's actions. The structure and facts selected should support the employer's theme of the case, without overstatement. If the employer's counsel is not able to prove what is promised in the opening statement, the employee's counsel will almost certainly point out the failure during closing argument—even if the unproven fact has no bearing on the outcome of the case.

C. Cross-Examining the Plaintiff

Cross-examining the former employee can be one of the highlights of the employer's case. If it goes badly, however, the cross-examination can sound the death knell for the defense.

Preparation is critical to conducting a good cross-examination. If the trial lawyer did not take the plaintiff's deposition, he or she must gain a thorough understanding of both the testimony and the former employee's demeanor. The trial lawyer should carefully review the transcripts or, better yet, videotapes of the deposition. In the review process, the trial lawyer should identify those areas of deposition testimony supporting the employer's theory of the case, inconsistencies in the employee's story, inconsistencies between documents prepared or adopted by the employee and the employee's testimony, and inconsistencies between the employee's testimony and statements the employee made to third parties, such as an investigator, medical care provider, or psychotherapist. These critical areas should be identified and indexed so that the trial lawyer can refer to them easily during the cross-examination.

Employer's counsel should construct the entire cross-examination before asking any questions. First, elicit any testimony that will assist the employer or further its theory of the case. The witness will be more open to questions right after he or she has finished direct examination and before his or her credibility is attacked. In addition, a successful attack on the witness's credibility will undermine the testimony that follows. Pick the two or three points that are most helpful to the employer and have the witness adopt them.

Avoid asking the former employee any questions to which you do not know the answer. Cross-examination should be conducted with leading questions that direct and control the witness. The best questions are short and suggest the answer. Open-ended questions that provide the witness with an opportunity to explain can easily leave the witness, rather than the lawyer, in control.

Defense counsel should determine in advance whether to attack the employee's credibility. If the witness has not contradicted him- or herself and has been sympathetic during direct testimony, an attack may only increase the jury's sympathy. This is particularly true when the case is based upon discrimination, harassment, or some other fact pattern likely to cause emotional trauma. The jury may well perceive any attack upon the witness's credibility as just another step in the employer's plan to harm the witness. In these cases, the focus of cross-examination should be limited to bringing forth helpful testimony. The weakness in the plaintiff's case will have to be left to other witnesses.

In some circumstances, however, challenging the former employee's testimony is necessary and helpful. For example, if the employee is bringing a claim for racial harassment and failed to complain until after he or she was terminated, and changed key details in his or her description of events, the lack of action and inconsistencies will need to be brought out on cross-examination.

Often the employee's testimony can be undermined by an indirect approach. Good cross-examination can be used to set up a closing argument attacking the employee's motives in bringing the lawsuit. For example, having the employee admit that he or she was disciplined can raise the possibility that the employee was angry at his or her superior, and having the employee acknowledge that he or she did not receive a raise or promotion can raise the possibility that the employee was angry at the company. Also, having the employee admit that he or she failed to use internal dispute-resolution mechanisms can be used to argue that the employee did not want to resolve the issue but just wanted to have the employer pay him or her for not working. Each case will differ, but the key to good cross-examination in every case is thorough preparation.

D. Presenting Company Witnesses

Good direct examination is often the most difficult part of the trial. Company witnesses must be prepared before trial so that they are comfortable testifying and know what questions to expect. Any witness who has been deposed should carefully review his or her deposition transcript as part of preparing to testify. Counsel should then review the expected questions and exhibits, conducting mock direct and cross-examinations of the witness. Videotape can provide effective feedback, allowing the witness to understand how his or her style and demeanor will be perceived, and to correct problem areas in the presentation.

Direct examination should be conversational, relying upon open-ended questions that allow the witness to tell his or her story. Although counsel is anticipating the information to be presented by each witness, listening to the responses is critical. If an answer is not what counsel expected, follow-up questions or directing the witness to a particular document may help keep the examination on track.

The opening and closing series of questions for each witness should be carefully identified. When a new witness takes the stand, jurors are ready to hear what the witness has to say. These valuable initial questions should be used to convey critical information, rather than to provide witness background or other testimony that is merely helpful. A powerful series of concluding questions is more likely to help the jury recall the witness.

E. Expert-Witness Examinations

Direct and cross-examination of expert witnesses typically follow much the same procedure as that used for fact witnesses. Counsel must be familiar with the expert's report and the area in which the expert is testifying.

When cross-examining the employee's expert, defense counsel should structure the examination to make positive points before attacking the witness. Having the employee's expert agree with points that the employer's expert will make can emphasize those points and give the employer's expert more credibility when he or she testifies. The employee's expert should not be given the opportunity on cross-examination to explain responses or repeat favorable testimony. Defense counsel must remain in control of the examination by using short, directed questions that suggest the answer. Giving the experienced expert the opportunity to explain by asking an open-ended question or, worse yet, a question to which the examiner does not know the answer, will give the expert the opportunity to take over the examination and reinforce opinions already offered.

On direct examination, the employer's expert witnesses should be asked open-ended questions that permit him or her to explain fully the conclusions and reasons for the conclusions. The expert's qualifications should be presented in an interesting manner. Rather than providing a laundry list of degrees, jobs, articles, and speaking engagements, ask the expert what factors in his or her professional background make him or her uniquely qualified to testify in the case. Many lawyers like to have the court confirm that the individual is qualified as an expert. Certainly, if the employee's experts have been certified, the defense experts should likewise be.

Though you may need to provide the expert's qualifications first, the expert's key conclusions should be brought out as soon as possible. In preparing your expert to testify, make sure that he or she understands the theory of the case and will answer questions consistently with that theory. Work with your expert so that his or her testimony is given in easily understandable lay terms, without talking down to the jury. If prompted, many experts can provide real-world examples, which can be particularly helpful in explaining differences between the expert's approaches and conclusions.

F. Closing Argument

The closing argument is the employer's final opportunity to persuade the jurors. The closing argument should be planned well before the trial begins, as part of the overall trial strategy. The theme of the case should be emphasized during the closing argument. In addition, having the closing prepared before the evidence is admitted will help counsel to develop the examinations of witnesses and introduction of evidence that support the planned closing argument.

Effective closing arguments are short and focused. Many courts will impose time limitations on the arguments. Even if the court does not restrict the time for argument, a short argument is preferable. Jurors have a limited attention span and, by the close of the trial, are ready to complete their service. Many trial judges report that the jurors' most common criticism of trials is that the lawyers are repetitive, which the jurors may view as an insult to their intelligence.

Counsel should build the closing argument around the theme of the case. The closing should have a logical structure, with a powerful introduction and conclusion. Both the legal theories and the key facts should be incorporated into a persuasive presentation. Exhibits important to the employer should be highlighted. Use of exhibits, or audiovisual materials specially prepared for the closing, will help hold the jury's attention. The employer's counsel should not be afraid to provide the ultimate conclusion being sought—a defense verdict or, when liability is admitted, a modest damage award.

Arguments phrased in affirmative language are more persuasive than negative phrasing. Many defense counsel tend to argue that the plaintiff failed to meet his or her burden of proof. Certainly, the employer's counsel should acknowledge the weaknesses and explain why they are not important. More importantly, however, the argument should focus on the strengths of the employer's case, providing a positive, compelling explanation for the employer's actions.

Though each lawyer will need to develop his or her style of argument, compelling arguments should be made with a minimum of notes, while maintaining eye contact with the jurors. Variations in speed, volume, and tone of voice will keep the jurors interested.

A number of techniques may be incorporated in a closing. In deciding whether to use any particular construct, counsel should evaluate whether it will enhance the likelihood that the jurors will remain engaged with the closing argument and retain the information provided. Some of the more common techniques are as follows:

- *Quote Jury Instructions.* Reading the jury instructions can give counsel credibility. In addition, explaining how the facts apply to particular instructions helps the jury analyze.
- *Storytelling.* Use of a memorable analogy or story can emphasize key points or enhance the logic of your conclusions.
- *Rhetorical Questions.* Questions can allow the jurors to reach their own conclusions, which they are likely to retain much longer than they would if counsel thrust the reasoning upon them. Defense counsel should, however, carefully test any rhetorical questions to ensure that they cannot be answered in a way favorable to the employee.
- *Understating Case.* Some lawyers can effectively underplay key conclusions, arguing the facts and law to a point just short of the

conclusion. Before attempting this approach, counsel must examine the logic to ensure that no alternative conclusions can be reached.

Employer's counsel should anticipate and respond to the employee's rebuttal argument. Counsel should refrain from overstating what the evidence showed or providing other opportunities for the employee's lawyer to attack the credibility of the employer's position.

G. Trial and Post-Trial Motions

During trial, the employer's counsel may wish to move for entry of judgment as a matter of law under Rule 50(a) of the Federal Rules of Civil Procedure. A motion for judgment challenges the legal sufficiency of the evidence supporting the opposing party's claims.[70] The employer may make such a motion after opening statements, at the conclusion of the plaintiff's case, or after both sides have rested.

The most common post-trial motions are a renewed motion for judgment as a matter of law, under Rule 50, and a motion for a new trial, under Rule 59. Rule 50 requires a court to render judgment as a matter of law when a party has been fully heard on an issue, and there is no legally sufficient evidentiary basis for a reasonable jury to find for that party on that issue.[71] In ruling on motion, the court must draw all reasonable inferences in favor of the nonmoving party and may not make credibility determinations or weigh the evidence.[72]

A party may not bring a post-trial motion for judgment as a matter of law unless it first made the motion before the case was submitted

70. Rule 50(a)(1) of the Federal Rules of Civil Procedure provides: "If a party has been fully heard on an issue during a jury trial and the court finds that a reasonable jury would not have a legally sufficient evidentiary basis to find for the party on that issue, the court may: (A) resolve the issue against the party; and (B) grant a motion for judgment as a matter of law against the party on a claim or defense that, under the controlling law, can be maintained or defeated only with a favorable finding on that issue."

71. *Reeves v. Sanderson Plumbing Prods., Inc.*, 530 U.S. 133, 149 (2000).

72. *Id.* at 149.

to the jury.[73] The post-trial motion must be made within twenty-eight days following entry of judgment.[74]

A new trial motion, made under Rule 59, is often filed together with the post-trial motion for judgment as a matter of law. Rule 59 authorizes courts to grant a new trial "(A) after a jury trial, for any reason for which a new trial has heretofore been granted in an action at law in federal court; or (B) after a nonjury trial, for any reason for which a rehearing has heretofore been granted in a suit in equity in federal court."[75] "Generally courts have interpreted this language to mean that a new trial is warranted when a jury has reached a 'seriously erroneous result' as evidenced by: (1) the verdict being against the weight of the evidence; (2) the damages being excessive; or (3) the trial being unfair to the moving party in some fashion, i.e., the proceedings being influenced by prejudice or bias."[76] In ruling on a motion for a new trial, the court may reweigh the evidence and grant the motion if the verdict is against the great weight of the evidence or it is quite clear that the jury has reached a seriously erroneous result."[77]

---

73. *See* FED. R. CIV. P. 50(b).
74. *Id.*
75. FED. R. CIV. P. 59(a)(1).
76. *Holmes v. Massillon*, 78 F.3d 1041, 1045–46 (6th Cir. 1996).
77. *Johnson v. Paradise Valley Unified Sch. Dist.*, 251 F.3d 1222, 1228–29 (9th Cir. 2001).

CHAPTER 10
Settlement Issues and Strategies for EPL Claims

Michael Corey

Although settlement of employment-related claims can be complicated by a number of substantive and political issues, the settlement of EPL-covered claims presents additional challenges as well. This chapter highlights several of the settlement issues routinely encountered in defending and settling EPL-covered claims, and provides some insight into other common settlement issues that often arise in resolving employment discrimination claims.

I. Policy Provisions Regarding Settlement

A. The Different Interests of Insurers and Insureds

Whether the insured or the insurer controls the settlement discussions is, perhaps, the first and most critical settlement issue encountered in EPL claims. For example, the tension between the insurer's desire to

---

The editor and author would like to thank Thomas E. Deer of Ogletree, Deakins, Nash, Smoak & Stewart, P.C. for his significant contributions to chapter 10 in the second edition of this book.

settle quickly and cost effectively may conflict with the insured's desire to fight the claim in employment-related cases, which are often emotional and viewed as precedent setting by the insured. Conversely, in certain cases, insureds want to settle early and for their own reasons and the carrier resists. As different types of EPL policies may have substantially different control provisions, the language of the policy is, of course, paramount. In these circumstances, defense counsel should ensure from the outset of the engagement that everyone understands who will control settlement discussions.

B. Who Has Settlement Authority?

Most EPL policies will make clear, by their terms, who has control over settlement. Over time, since the introduction of EPL policies, insureds have gained more settlement control. In fact, many insureds negotiate settlement-control provisions when purchasing their EPL policies because insureds have a particularly strong interest in controlling settlement discussions, particularly where the retainage or deductible is substantial.[1] In other situations, such as when injunctive relief is sought, a number of EPL policies provide "defense expenses only" coverage, thereby in effect increasing the insured's settlement control for such claims.

C. Consent Provisions and Hammer Clauses

Certain EPL policies provide that the insurer, in its sole and exclusive discretion, has the right to settle claims, without the consent of the insured. Because these provisions, though often cost effective for the insurer, can lead to substantial conflict with the insured, they have lost favor over time.[2] "Consent" provisions, which allow the insurer

---

1. In situations where a conflict has arisen between the insured and insurer, or in a situation where the insured is defending under a reservation of rights, separate counsel may be required or appropriate for the insured. In such cases, the insurer may lose whatever control it might have had over settlement of the case.

2. The right to control settlement should not be confused with the duty to defend

to settle claims up to policy limits with the consent of the insured, are more common now.

Policies containing such provisions also generally provide that the insured's consent may not be "unreasonably" withheld.[3]

As a way to subtly (or perhaps not so subtly) encourage insureds to agree to a settlement endorsed by the insurer, many EPL policies contain "hammer" clauses. These clauses transfer the risk of not settling the claim back to the insured. A typical hammer clause caps the liability of the insurer at the limit for which the case could have been settled and may also provide that defense costs beyond that point are the responsibility of the insured as well. As defense costs are often as much, if not more, than the judgment value in employment-related claims, hammer clauses are a powerful inducement to settlement.[4]

D. Cooperation Clauses and Protesting a Proposed Settlement

Insureds can incur some risk of losing their coverage altogether if they reject a proposed settlement offered by the insurer. In such cases, the insurer may claim that the rejection constitutes a violation of the "cooperation" clause, which is a staple of almost every insurance policy.[5]

---

or indemnify. Although certainly not common, some EPL policies do not contain a duty to defend at all. Because of the high cost of defending employment-related suits, such policies are fairly uncommon. Most policies contain a clear statement regarding the duty to defend, and, because an insurer will generally defend all counts of a complaint if even one count falls within coverage, such policies are highly desirable for the insureds.

On the flip side, some policies cover only the costs of defense, but not any payout, judgment, or other liability. Even under these policies, however, an insurer may be willing to contribute to a settlement brokered by the insured, on the theory that the settlement contribution will be much cheaper than the expected costs of defense going forward.

3. For a discussion of certain sample EPL provisions covering settlement, *see* The EPL Book 205–14 (Gary W. Griffin ed., 2001).

4. Certain insurers include less draconian hammer clauses that require the insured to pay a percentage of the defense costs or indemnity beyond the rejected settlement amount.

5. A typical duty of cooperation clause reads in essence as follows:

(1) In the event of a Claim, or after giving the Underwriter notice of a Potential Claim, the Insureds must provide the Underwriter with all information, assistance and

Insureds, therefore, should not categorically object to settlement. Rather, they should consider each proposal on a case-by-case or offer-by-offer basis.

As a practical matter, often the best course of action for an insured who objects to the insured's settlement proposal is to wait for the plaintiff's response. If the insured remains silent, and the plaintiff rejects the settlement overture from the insurer, the insured has not placed its coverage at risk. Such an approach also limits the danger of the insurer offering a minimal offer it knows is objectionable to the insured for the purpose of putting the coverage obligations in play.[6]

II. Crafting Settlements

A. Allocation of Proceeds Between Covered vs. Uncovered Claims

Counsel must clearly understand claims that are covered and those that are not covered when allocating settlement proceeds,[7] because the allocation may determine which proceeds are paid by the insurer and which are borne by the insured. Allocation decisions may even affect the propriety of coverage itself, and thereafter the taxability of the settlement proceeds.

In the context of coverage, perhaps the most vivid reminder of the importance of this issue comes from *Glen Lincoln, Inc. v. Zurich Insurance Co.*[8] In *Glen Lincoln*, after the insured settled the underlying

---

cooperation as the Underwriter may reasonably request.

(2) The Insureds may do nothing to prejudice the Underwriter's position or the Underwriter's potential or actual rights of recovery in the event of a Claim.

6. *See also* Lisa E. Chang, *Litigating with Employment Practices Liability Insurance*, PRAC. LITIGATOR (A.L.I-A.B.A.), November 1999.

7. Of course, at the outset of the litigation, defense counsel should explore all possible sources of insurance coverage, whether under a CGL policy, a D&O policy, a workers' compensation policy, or even homeowner's insurance. If an argument for possible coverage can be made under one or more of these policies as well as the EPL policy, such issues should be explored as early as possible in the litigation. *See generally* Joan Dolinsky & Barbara O'Donnell, *Employment Practices Liability Coverage*, THE BRIEF (A.B.A.), Fall 2001.

8. 945 F. Supp. 844 (E.D. Pa. 1996), *aff'd in part, rev'd in part*, 142 F.3d 428 (3d

discrimination claim, the insured sought indemnification from Zurich under its comprehensive general liability policy, which covered "discrimination, which is not deemed unlawful under state or federal law."

Zurich assessed that the settlement of the case by the employer/insured constituted an admission that the actions of the employer were unlawful and, therefore, outside the scope of coverage. Though the appellate court rejected Zurich's contention that the settlement constituted an admission because the language was ambiguous, on remand, and after hearing extrinsic evidence, the district court found Zurich had a duty to defend, but not indemnify.

Areas of particular concern where a settlement may go beyond the policy terms include whether the EPL policy in question covers equitable claims, emotional distress claims, physical injuries, punitive damages, back pay, or the corporation itself (as opposed to just the employees of the corporation). In these situations, the lawyers crafting the settlement must pay particular attention to the claims asserted, the coverage afforded with respect to those specific claims, and the consequences of the proposed settlement language on the coverage question.[9]

B. Taxability of Settlements

1. Introduction

Depending on which party to an employment dispute you are representing, the tax consequences of a settlement payment are quite different. Therefore, a well-prepared lawyer will be familiar with not only the tax consequences of a settlement payment to his or her client, but also the tax consequences of the same settlement payment to the opposing party. Importantly, understanding the taxation of settlement payments

---

Cir. 1998), *remanded to* No. 95-5621, 1999 WL 58587 (E.D. Pa. Jan. 13, 1999).

9. In these cases, D&O insurance coverage cases are instructive. Courts have generally used (1) the relative liability exposure approach or (2) the larger settlement test. In the former approach, payments are allocated based on the relative exposure of the covered and noncovered claims; in the latter approach, payments are allocated based on the extent to which the noncovered claims increased the loss.

allows a lawyer representing the plaintiff to know in advance the "net" settlement payment that his or her client will receive and allows a lawyer representing the defendant to be cognizant of any taxes that the defendant will have to pay in addition to the negotiated settlement payment.[10] Moreover, by understanding both sides of the equation, a lawyer not only protects his or her client's own best interests and bottom line, but may also be able to find creative solutions or acceptable compromises to tax-related stalemates. Rest assured, one need not be a seasoned tax lawyer to understand the basic concepts related to the taxation of settlement payments.

As a premise, every settlement agreement should include an express allocation of the settlement payments to be received by the plaintiff, as well as a discussion of the expected tax treatment of such payments by the defendant, including the appropriate federal and state income tax and employment tax withholdings that the parties intend and agree upon when structuring the agreement. This is of particular importance because the Internal Revenue Service (IRS) and state tax authorities will generally respect an express allocation contained in a settlement agreement if the agreement was negotiated at arm's-length and in good faith by adversarial parties.[11] Thus, explicitly addressing and providing for an allocation of settlement payments and the related tax consequences helps not only to avoid future disputes and inconsistencies between the parties about the characterization of the settlement payments, but also helps protect against future scrutiny by the IRS and state taxing authorities. Settlement payments without express allocation provisions are often treated as entirely taxable (often as wages) by the IRS and state taxing authorities.

---

10. For purposes of this discussion, it is assumed that the employee or former employee is the plaintiff and the employer or former employer is the defendant. In certain cases, it is possible that the insured may make payments directly to the plaintiff, rather than the defendant.

11. *See, e.g.*, *Robinson v. Comm'r*, 102 T.C. 116 (1994), *aff'd on this issue*, 70 F.3d 34 (5th Cir. 1995); *Gross v. Comm'r*, 80 T.C.M. (CCH) 648 (2000); *Burditt v. Comm'r*, 77 T.C.M. (CCH) 1767 (1999).

The following discussion is intended to provide lawyers settling employment litigation disputes with a general understanding of the federal and state income tax and employment tax consequences of most payments made pursuant to settlement agreements. Issues to be covered herein include the following:

- Distinguishing between taxable and nontaxable income, including the proper tax treatment of damages for "emotional distress" (section 2);
- Whether all or a portion of a settlement payment should be characterized as "wages," including the proper characterization of back pay and front pay (section 3);
- Determining the proper treatment of lawyers' fees (section 4); and
- Model language to be considered when drafting settlement agreements (section 5).[12]

2. *Taxable vs. Nontaxable Settlement Payments*

In determining the proper federal and state income tax and employment tax treatment of amounts paid pursuant to a settlement agreement, the threshold inquiry should be whether such payments constitute taxable or nontaxable income to the plaintiff.

Taxable income is just that—income that is subject to federal and state income tax in the hands of the plaintiff. Taxable income generally must be reported by the defendant to the IRS and to the plaintiff. Nontaxable income is not taxable to the plaintiff and is not reported by the defendant to the IRS or to the plaintiff. This commonly results in friction.

---

12. Though this discussion provides a good starting point (especially for nontax lawyers) with respect to the federal and state income tax and employment tax consequences of entering into a settlement agreement, it does not purport to address every issue or contention that may arise. Therefore, one should consult with a tax lawyer prior to finalizing any settlement agreement. Nonetheless, the basic concepts presented herein should prove most useful in negotiating, drafting, and understanding the tax consequences of settlement payments.

Logic dictates that the plaintiff wants the entire settlement agreement to be nontaxable; however, portions or all of the vast majority of EPL settlements are taxable, and consequently, the employer is exposed to potential tax liability (including penalties and interest) for failing to withhold on and report to the IRS and to the plaintiff, the amount of taxable payments made to the plaintiff. Thus, counsel must understand what is and is not taxable income to the plaintiff.

Code Section 104(a)(2)[13] provides that the amount of any damages (other than punitive damages) received, whether by suit or agreement, and whether as lump sums or as periodic payments, on account of (i) personal physical injuries or (ii) physical sickness, are excluded from gross income (that is, nontaxable).[14] "[E]motional distress" is *not* considered a physical injury or physical sickness.[15] For this purpose, "emotional distress" includes physical symptoms (for example, insomnia, headaches, stomach disorders) that may result from emotional distress.[16] Accordingly, most damages received for emotional distress (including the physical symptoms of emotional distress) are taxable, except to the extent amounts paid for medical care attributable to such emotional distress that were not otherwise deducted by the plaintiff on his or her current or previous income tax returns.[17]

However, "[i]f an action has its origin in a physical injury or physical sickness, then all damages (other than punitive damages) that flow therefrom are treated as payments received on account of physical injury

---

13. All "Code Section" references are to the Internal Revenue Code of 1986, as amended, or to the Treasury Regulations ("Treas. Reg. §") promulgated thereunder.

14. Code Section 104(a)(2) generally applies to amounts received after August 20, 1996, unless amounts are received after August 20, 1996, pursuant to a written binding agreement, court decree, or mediation award in effect on (or issued on or before) September 13, 1995. Pub. L. No. 104-188, I.R.C. § 104.

15. I.R.C. § 104(a) (flush language).

16. Staff of Joint Comm. on Taxation, 104th Cong., 2d Sess., General Explanation of Tax Legislation Enacted in the 104th Congress 222–24 (1996) [hereinafter Bluebook].

17. I.R.C. § 104(a) (flush language); Bluebook at 222–23.

or physical sickness, and, therefore, are not taxable."[18] Thus, damages received for emotional distress and other nonphysical injuries or sickness are nontaxable only to the extent that they are directly attributable to a personal physical injury or a physical sickness.

Thus, for example, emotional distress damages arising out of a claim of employment discrimination or injury to reputation are taxable. However, the exclusion from gross income under Code Section 104(a)(2) would apply to the amount of damages received based on a claim of emotional distress attributable to physical sickness or personal physical injury.[19]

The IRS has privately ruled that payments for damages properly attributable to direct unwanted or uninvited physical contact are treated as personal physical injuries under Code Section 104(a)(2) only if the contact results in observable bodily harm, such as bruises, cuts, swelling, or bleeding.[20] Conversely, taxable payments (that is, those not attributable to personal physical injuries or physical sickness excludable under Code Section 104(a)(2)) generally include wage payments, liquidated damages, punitive damages (whether or not attributable to personal physical injuries or physical sickness), and interest.

In order to characterize settlement payments as taxable or nontaxable income, lawyers settling employment-related cases should look to (i) the claims made by the plaintiff in any pleadings; (ii) the causes of action raised by the plaintiff; (iii) the types of relief available to the plaintiff under the statute; (iv) the types of relief available to the plaintiff under common law; and (v) any other documents or evidence supporting those (or other) claims, including correspondence between the parties and contract formulas for allocating damages.[21]

---

18. BLUEBOOK at 223.

19. *Id.* at 223–24.

20. I.R.S. P.L.R. 200041022 (Oct. 13, 2000).

21. *See, e.g.*, *Robinson v. Comm'r*, 102 T.C. 116 (1994), *aff'd on this issue*, 70 F.3d 34 (5th Cir. 1995); *Miller v. Comm'r*, 65 T.C.M. (CCH) 1884 (1993), *aff'd*, 76 A.F.T.R. 2d 95-5718 (4th Cir. 1995) (unpublished).

In most employment discrimination cases, however, the key issue is not whether the settlements are taxable to the plaintiffs (which they usually are), but rather the extent to which such payments constitute "wages," from which the defendant must withhold for federal and state income taxes and employment taxes. Thus, the pertinent inquiry in most employment-related cases is whether the settlement payments represent "wage" or "nonwage" payments, both of which are subject to federal and state income taxes in the hands of the plaintiff, but only "wage" payments are subject to upfront income and employment tax withholdings by the defendant.

3. Wage vs. Nonwage Payments

On the portion of any settlement payment treated as wages, the defendant must withhold applicable federal and state income and employment taxes. For this purpose, wages are generally defined as all remuneration for services performed by an employee for his or her employer.[22]

Treasury Regulation § 31.3121(a)-1(i) further provides that remuneration for employment is considered wages "even though at the time paid the relationship of employer and employee no longer exists between the person in whose employ the services were performed and the individual who performed them." Employees include former employees receiving settlement payments in connection with their current or previous employment, but it is unclear whether wages may be paid to a person with whom an employment relationship was never established (for example, a person who was not hired).[23]

22. *See* I.R.C. §§ 3121(a), 3401(a).

23. *See, e.g., Newhouse v. McCormick & Co., Inc.*, 157 F.3d 582 (8th Cir. 1998), *aff'd in part, rev'd in part*, 910 F. Supp. 1451 (D. Neb. 1996) (back pay and front pay awarded under an ADEA claim were not "wages" for income tax and employment tax purposes where the plaintiff was not hired for the position sought); *but see* Rev. Rul. 78-176, 1978-1 C.B. 303 (payments received in settlement of a suit brought under Title VII by job applicants who allegedly were wrongfully refused employment were "wages" for purposes of FICA, FUTA, and income tax withholding, although no actual or previous employment relationship existed).

Furthermore, back pay and front pay constitute taxable wage payments.[24] On the other hand, "taxable non-wage payments" generally consist of all payments paid to a plaintiff that do not constitute (i) payment on account of personal physical injuries or physical sickness under Code Section 104(a)(2) or (ii) "wages."

a. Tax Treatment of Wage Payments

Once a settlement payment is characterized as wages, the defendant may withhold federal income tax at a flat 27 percent rate on such wage payments, or if the settlement amount is very large, the defendant may consider allowing the plaintiff to reduce the amount of federal income tax withholding by filing a new Form W-4 claiming additional exemptions and determining the income tax withholding based on tables published by the IRS.[25] If the latter alternative is chosen, careful scrutiny under treasury regulations must be given to Form W-4s claiming more than ten exemptions.[26] Wages payments are also subject to state (and local where applicable) income tax withholding.

In addition to federal and state income tax withholdings, employers must withhold from any wage payments the employee's share of FICA taxes and then match the amount to cover the employer's share

---

24. *See, e.g.*, Rev. Rul. 96-65, 1996-2 C.B. 6 (which indicates in holding number 3 that back pay in an employment discrimination case under Title VII constitutes "wages" for federal income tax and FICA purposes); *Johnson v. United States*, 85 A.F.T.R. 2d 2000-1563 (April 11, 2000) (back pay and front pay received under an ADA claim are "wages" subject to income tax and employment tax withholding); *Associated Electric Coop. Inc. v. United States*, 42 Fed. Cl. 867 (1999) (certain termination payments paid pursuant to a voluntary separation program were "wages" subject to employment tax withholding); *Gerbec v. United States*, 164 F.3d 1015 (6th Cir. 1999) (portion of award for back pay and front pay constituted "wages" subject to employment taxes); *Abrahamsen v. United States*, 44 Fed. Cl. 260 (1999) (downsizing payments received by former employees were "wages" subject to income tax and employment tax with-holding). *But see United States v. Quality Stores, Inc.*, 693 F.3d 605 (6th Cir. 2012) (SUB payments are not wages for purposes of FICA taxation).

25. *See* Treas. Reg. § 31.3402(g)-l.

26. *See* Treas. Reg. § 31.3402(f)(2)-1(g).

of FICA taxes. For this purpose, wage payments are treated as being paid in the year received by the plaintiff, notwithstanding that they may represent back pay, front pay, or otherwise relate to a year other than that in which they are being paid.[27]

Wage payments are subject to current-year tax rates and FICA caps.[28] For wage payments made in 2003, a defendant must withhold 7.65 percent from the first $87,000 of wage payments paid to a defendant and 1.45 percent from wages in excess of $87,000, and must also pay a matching amount from its own funds.[29] The employer must also pay (but not withhold) the employer's portion of federal unemployment taxes (FUTA) and any state unemployment taxes. The defendant reports wage payments to the IRS and to the plaintiff on a Form W-2 in the year in which such wages are paid to the plaintiff.[30]

Importantly, the appropriate federal and state income tax and FICA withholdings on the portion of the settlement amount constituting taxable wages will be deducted from the settlement payment. Accordingly, the amount of any settlement constituting wages that will be received by the plaintiff should be "net" of taxes, which means that the plaintiff will generally receive only about 65 percent of the amount of wages agreed upon pursuant to the settlement agreement.[31] Additionally, the defendant will be required to pay an additional 6.2 percent of the amount of wages paid to the plaintiff up to $87,000 and an extra 1.45 percent of all wages paid above that amount.

---

27. *United States v. Cleveland Indians Baseball Co.*, 523 U.S. 200 (2001).

28. *See* Treas. Reg. §§ 31.3101-2(c), -3; 31.3111-2(c), -3.

29. FICA taxes are divided between Social Security and Medicare taxes. The Social Security tax rate is 6.2 percent each for both an employer and an employee for a total rate of 12.4 percent on the first $87,000 of wages paid in 2003 (this amount is indexed annually for inflation). The Medicare tax is 1.45 percent each for both an employer and an employee for a total rate of 2.9 percent of all wages paid in 2003.

30. *See generally* I.R.C. § 6051.

31. Depending on the plaintiff's tax situation, the plaintiff may recoup some of these taxes in connection with the filing of his or her federal and state income tax returns for the year of payment. Plaintiff's counsel may wish to consult a tax lawyer or accountant to better understand a plaintiff's tax situation prior to finalizing the settlement agreement containing a wage component.

Thus, counsel should first factor in these costs when structuring a settlement agreement that contains a wage component and then ensure that the release adequately defines/describes the payments.

b. Tax Treatment of Taxable Nonwage Payments

Other taxable settlement payments (that is, "taxable non-wage payments") will be received by the plaintiff in their full amounts with no income or employment taxes being withheld by the defendant (unless income tax withholding is requested by the plaintiff and agreed upon by the defendant), although such amounts will generally be subject to federal and state income taxation and need to be reported on the plaintiff's federal and state income tax returns. For this purpose, taxable nonwage payments generally consist of all payments paid to a plaintiff that do not constitute (i) payment on account of personal physical injuries or physical sickness excludable under Code Section 104(a)(2) or (ii) wages. These payments include, among other items, punitive damages, liquidated damages, lawyers' fees, and interest. Taxable nonwage payments will be reported by the defendant to the plaintiff and the IRS on a Form 1099.

4. Lawyer Fees

There was a split of authority over whether contingency fees paid directly to lawyers are included in a client's gross income, because such fees are in essence income to the lawyer and not to the client. The Fifth, Sixth, and Eleventh circuits excluded contingency fees from a client's gross income,[32] whereas the Third, Fourth, Seventh, Ninth, Tenth, and Federal circuits included contingency fees in a client's gross income.[33]

---

32. *Davis v. Comm'r*, 210 F.3d 1346, 1347 (11th Cir. 2000) (*per curiam*); *Estate of Clarks v. United States*, 202 F.3d 854, 858 (6th Cir. 2000); *Cotnam v. Comm'r*, 263 F.2d 119, 126 (5th Cir. 1959).

33. *See Hukkanen-Campbell v. Comm'r*, 274 F.3d 1312, 1314 (10th Cir. 2001), *cert. denied*, 553 U.S. 1056 (2002); *Kenseth v. Comm'r*, 259 F.3d 881, 885 (7th Cir. 2001); *Young v. Comm'r*, 240 F.3d 369, 379 (4th Cir. 2001); *Coady v. Comm'r*, 213 F.3d 1187, 1191 (9th Cir. 2000), *cert. denied*, 532 U.S. 972 (2001); *Baylin v. United States*,

In 2005, the Supreme Court resolved the circuit split by holding that "when a litigant's recovery constitutes income, the litigant's income includes the portion of the recovery paid to the attorney as a contingent fee."[34]

The tax consequences of including lawyer fees warrants a brief explanation. Specifically, counsel representing a plaintiff should keep in mind that if lawyer fees are included in a plaintiff's gross income, the plaintiff will generally have to pay income tax on some portion of such fees, notwithstanding that they may never in fact receive any of the proceeds under the fee agreement with the lawyer. This is the case because the lawyer fees, which are an itemized deduction for federal income tax purposes, are deductible by a plaintiff only to the extent that they exceed 2 percent of the plaintiff's adjusted gross income for the taxable year,[35] and are not deductible at all in determining alternative minimum tax (if applicable to the plaintiff).[36] If the lawyer fees are included in a plaintiff's gross income, the defendant will generally report such fees to both the plaintiff and plaintiff's counsel on a Form 1099.

Regardless of whether the lawyer fees are includable in, or excludable from, a plaintiff's gross income, such fees should be expressly identified in the settlement agreement to avoid the risk that some portion of the lawyer fees will be improperly characterized by the parties. Thus, although plaintiff's counsel does not always want to disclose its fees to the opposing party, such disclosure is generally necessary to both properly exclude the lawyer fees from a plaintiff's gross income in circuits where such treatment is appropriate and, in circuits where the lawyer fees are included in a plaintiff's gross income, to properly allocate the settlement payments between the various payment components,

---

43 F.3d 1451, 1454 (Fed. Cir. 1995); *O'Brien v. Comm'r*, 319 F.2d 532 (3d Cir. 1963) (*per curiam*).

34. *Comm'r v. Banks*, 543 U.S. 426, 430 (2005).

35. *See* I.R.C. § 67 (relating to the 2 percent floor on miscellaneous itemized deductions).

36. *See* I.R.C. § 56 (relating to adjustments in computing alternative minimum tax).

including lawyer fees (this is especially true when there is a wage component in the settlement). In this respect, plaintiff's counsel may have to "fall on their sword" to protect their client's best interest.

5. Model Language for Settlement Agreement

As discussed above, every settlement agreement should include an express allocation of the payments to be received by the plaintiff, as well as a discussion of the expected tax treatment of the settlement payments. Below is some simple yet very decisive and powerful language that counsel should consider including when drafting settlement agreements:

- Allocation of Settlement Payments:
  "$_ shall be allocated and paid as nontaxable income under Code Section 104(a)(2)." [Very unusual in employment disputes]

  "$_ shall be allocated and paid as back and/or front pay."

  "$_ shall be allocated and paid as liquidated damages."

  "$_ shall be allocated and paid as [insert other damages—for example, emotional distress]."

  "$_ shall be allocated and paid as interest."

  "$_ shall be allocated and paid as lawyers' fees payable to____."

- Federal, State, and Local Income and Employment Tax Reporting and Withholding:
  "The [defendant] will report as wages on Form W-2 and will withhold applicable federal, state, and local income taxes and the plaintiff's share of FICA taxes (based on rates as currently in effect)

with regard to the payment of wages, including the payment of back pay and/or front pay."

"The [defendant] will report on Form 1099 the balance of the settlement payment, including any lawyers' fees, as nontaxable wages, with the exception of any amounts designated as nontaxable income under Code Section 104(a)(2)."

"[The defendant] will provide the [plaintiff] and [plaintiff's counsel] with the appropriate federal and state tax forms reporting the settlement payments and any taxes withheld as required by law."

"The [plaintiff] acknowledges and represents that neither the [defendant], nor [counsel for the defendant], has made any representations regarding the income tax treatment of these settlement payments and that, except for withholding, reporting, and payment of FICA taxes and federal, state, and local income tax withholdings, the [plaintiff] is responsible for reporting and paying any taxes associated with these payments under relevant law."

- Additional Language to Consider:
  "The [plaintiff] and/or [plaintiff's counsel] agrees to indemnify and hold the [defendant] harmless for any taxes, penalties, interest, and legal fees incurred by the [defendant] as a result of not withholding federal, state, and local income taxes and/or FICA taxes on the settlement payment." [Pro-defendant]

  "No payment provided for and paid pursuant to this settlement agreement shall be treated as wages for purposes of any employee benefit plan of the [defendant]." [This provision may be dependent on the terms of the defendant's employee benefit plan or collective bargaining agreement.]

III. Offers of Judgment

A. Introduction

Rule 68, or the offer of judgment rule, is a double-edged sword that provides an effective tool for encouraging the settlement of all claims, including those claims that are employment related.[37] The rights and liabilities of both plaintiff and defendant occupy opposite edges of the sword where misapplication of the rule, or ignoring the rule entirely, can convert a winning judgment into a financial loser for the prevailing plaintiff. This section provides a summary of the rule and addresses how it operates so that a litigant does not become the Pyrrhic victor at the end of the day.

B. The Rule

Rule 68 permits a defendant in litigation to make an offer of judgment to the plaintiff, and if the offer is not accepted, and the plaintiff's award is not more favorable than the defendant's offer, the defendant will not be liable for any costs that accrue after the date of the offer, even though the defendant remains liable for the judgment. The rule, in pertinent part, is as follows:

> At any time more than 10 days before the trial begins [or at the end of trial and 10 days prior to the commencement of hearings to determine liability], a party defending against a claim may serve upon the adverse party an offer to allow judgment to be taken against the defending party for the money or property or to the effect specified in the offer, with costs then accrued. . . . An offer not accepted shall be deemed withdrawn . . . [but i]f the judgment finally obtained by the offeree is not more favorable than the offer, the *offeree must pay the costs incurred after the making of the offer.*[38]

37. Fed. R. Civ. P. 68.
38. Fed. R. Civ. P. 68 (emphasis added).

The right to offer judgment under Rule 68 applies only to offers by the defending party to a claim. "The Rule has no application to offers made by the plaintiff," except that a plaintiff defending a counterclaim or other claim may invoke the rule in that defendant capacity.[39]

The fundamental purpose of Rule 68 is to encourage the settlement of litigation.[40] Because both parties face adverse consequences if they lose the litigation, there is an incentive for them to settle, even under ordinary circumstances. This incentive is powerfully increased under the operations of Rule 68, such that each party stands to gain or suffer significant benefits or detriments.[41]

For the defendant's part, by making an offer of judgment, he or she acknowledges wrongdoing and accepts an adverse judgment. However, the defendant also "benefits" by mitigating the overall potential judgment realized from a verdict after full trial. Furthermore, the defendant can avoid court costs if the plaintiff rejects the offer and the judgment at trial is not more favorable than the offer itself. For the plaintiff's part, a rejection of the defendant's offer can mean loss of many of the benefits of the victory if the recovery is less than the offer. Finally, the benefits of Rule 68 also inure to the courts by eliminating the burden of litigation on the system.

C. The Primary Cases

Two Supreme Court cases provide significant guidance on the scope and applicability of Rule 68: *Delta Air Lines, Inc., v. August*[42] and *Marek v. Chesney.*[43] The first Supreme Court case to articulate Rule 68 was

---

39. *Delta Air Lines, Inc. v. August*, 450 U.S. 346–50 (U.S. 1981); *Simon v. Intercontinental Transp. (ICT) B.V.*, 882 F.2d 1435–40 (9th Cir. 1989) (applying Rule 68 in counterclaim against plaintiff); *Garnes v. Bed Bath & Beyond, Inc.*, 2010 U.S. Dist. LEXIS 101639 (E.D. Mich. 2010).

40. *Delta Air Lines*, 450 U.S. at 350.

41. *Id.* at 352.

42. *See id.* at 346.

43. 473 U.S. 1 (1985).

Delta Air Lines, in which the court decided that Rule 68 does not apply when the defendant prevails in a cause of action.[44]

Delta Air Lines involved a wrongful discharge claim under Title VII. Approximately four months after the complaint was filed, the defendant made an offer of judgment for $450, including costs and lawyers' fees "then accrued." The plaintiff declined the offer and lost the case. The defendant filed a motion to recover costs under Rule 68. Both the district court and Seventh Circuit Court of Appeals declined to apply Rule 68, holding that an offer of less than $500 before trial is not of such significance in the context of this case as to justify serious consideration by the plaintiff.[45] The Supreme Court articulated the plain meaning of Rule 68, noting that it only applies in circumstances where the plaintiff prevails.[46] Otherwise, the court held, any defendant could make a meaningless offer and avoid imposition of costs under Rule 54(d).[47]

In *Marek v. Chesny*, the court held that all costs, including lawyers' fees, are includable as costs under the rule *if such costs are provided for in the underlying fee statute*, thus depriving a winning plaintiff recovery of all post-offer rejection fees.[48]

D. Lawyer Fees

At first impression, the inducement to settle from the plaintiff's point of view does not seem that strong; that is, until the plaintiff realizes that "costs" *could* also include lawyers' fees. The potential of losing lawyers' fees is the ultimate "Hobson's choice" for the plaintiff. The plaintiff's acceptance of the defendant's offer of judgment can translate into a lower post-verdict recovery, but rejecting the offer and proceeding to trial risks the potential of losing costs in terms of lawyers' fees that

44. 450 U.S. at 352.

45. *August v. Delta Air Lines, Inc.*, 600 F.2d 699–700 n.3 (7th Cir. 1979).

46. *Delta Air Lines*, 450 U.S. at 353.

47. *Id.* at 353–54; *see* Fed. R. Civ. P. 54(d) (granting a judge equitable discretion in awarding fees).

48. *Marek*, 473 U.S. at 9.

are amassed during protracted trial proceedings. These costs could far exceed the amount of recovery under the judgment itself.

A caveat to the recovery of lawyers' fees is that such fees can only be cut off with certitude through Rule 68 if fees are defined as "costs" through an underlying statute or contract in the cause of action.[49]

Federal courts applying state law will also look to that state's applicable statutes to determine if lawyers' fees are textually included as costs.[50] Otherwise, the cutoff, if any, will be measured at the discretion of the judge under Federal Rule 54(d).[51]

E. Operation of Rule 68

The *Marek* and *Delta* decisions outline the protocol a defendant needs to follow in making an offer of judgment and what a plaintiff must do to accept or reject that offer.

---

49. *Id.* at 44–48; *see also Util. Automation 2000, Inc. v. Choctazuhatchee Electric Coop., Inc.*, 298 F.3d 1238–45 (11th Cir. 2002) (noting that *Marek*'s reference to "other authority" also includes contracts); *accord Kessler v. Superior Care, Inc.*, 127 F.R.D. 513, 518 (N.D. Ill. 1989); *But see Cedars-Sinai Med. Ctr. v. United Healthcare Ins.*, 2010 U.S. Dist. LEXIS 125125 (C.D. Cal. 2010) (holding that a mere allegation of a violation will not suffice in establishing a Rule 68 violation); *see, e.g., Webb v. James*, 147 F.3d 617, 622–23 (7th Cir. 1998) (holding that because the ADA does not define costs to include fees, Rule 68's cost-shifting device does not apply to lawyers' fees under the ADA); *accord Wyatt v. Ralphs Grocery Co.*, Nos. 02-55571, 02-55750, 2003 WL 1193809 at *2 (9th Cir. March 14, 2003); *see, e.g., Le v. Univ. of Pa.*, 321 F.3d 403, 406–07 (3d Cir. 2003) (holding that Title VII only includes lawyers' fees as costs where the plaintiff's claim was frivolous, and thus Rule 68 does not generally operate as a bar to recovery of lawyers' fees); *accord Crossman v. Marcoccio*, 806 F.2d 329, 334 (1st Cir. 1986); *O'Brien v. City of Greers Ferry*, 873 F.2d 1115, 1120 (8th Cir. 1989); *EEOC v. Bailey Ford, Inc.*, 26 F.3d 570, 571 (5th Cir. 1994); *see, e.g., Dalal v. Alliant Techsystems, Inc.*, No. 94-1483, 1995 WL 747442 at *5 (10th Cir. Dec. 18, 1995) (holding that costs do not include lawyers' fees in ADEA claims); *accord, remanded to, Dalal v. Alliant Techsystems, Inc.*, 927 F. Supp. 1374, 1378 (D. Colo. 1996).

50. *MRO Commc'ns v. AT&T*, 197 F.3d 1276 (9th Cir. 1999) (holding that the Nevada statute including lawyers' fees as costs applied even though the offer of judgment did not specify the rule in the statute applied). However, where the statue defines costs and lawyers' fees separately, the cutoff may not apply. *See Haworth v. State of Nev.*, 56 F.3d 1048 (9th Cir. 1996), *cert. denied*, 519 U.S. 993 (offer does not cut off plaintiff's entitlement to lawyers' fees because FLSA defines lawyers' fees separately from costs).

51. *Delta Air Lines*, 450 U.S. at 343.

The most important component of any offer of judgment is that it permits judgment to be entered against the defendant for damages and costs accrued.[52] Thus, the defendant's offer to settle by itself without also allowing judgment would not constitute an offer under Rule 68.[53] The offer of judgment must be made after the litigation has commenced.[54] Offers of judgment made prior to the filing of pleadings will be disregarded as mere settlement overtures.[55]

Furthermore, federal courts have held that offers of judgment, along with "costs then accrued," must be unconditional, in writing, and served on the plaintiff or adverse party.[56] Moreover, the writing of the offer must contain a definite sum or other equitable relief for which judgment is being entered. However, the offer does not have to separately state the costs being assessed. "As long as the offer does not implicitly or explicitly provide that the judgment not include costs, a timely offer will be valid."[57]

The *Delta Airlines* decision never addressed the logic of the lower courts' decisions that an offer of judgment must be reasonable (both courts held that such offers must be reasonable). Thus, whether an offer of judgment carries a "good faith" component is unknown.

---

52. *Marek v. Chesny*, 473 U.S. 1 (1985).

53. *Clark v. Sims*, 28 F.3d 420, 424 (4th Cir. 1994); *Grosvenor v. Brienen*, 801 F.2d 944, 948 (7th Cir. 1986) (holding that oral offer of settlement does not satisfy an offer of judgment under Rule 68).

54. *Clark* at 424.

55. *Id.*

56. *Cole v. Wodziak*, 169 F.3d 486 (7th Cir. 1999) (denying oral offer of judgment as inconsistent with Rule 68); *Clark*, 28 F.3d at 424 (holding that "Rule 68 offer of judgment must be in writing"); *Grosvenor*, 801 F.2d at 948 (holding that "although Rule 68 does not specify that an offer of judgment be in writing, the requirement that the offer be served upon the plaintiff makes no sense unless it means that the offer must be written"); *Knoeffler v. Town of Mamakating*, 126 F. Supp. 2d 305–15 (S.D.N.Y. 2000) (oral offer to settle does not rise to offer of judgment pursuant to Rule 68).

57. *Marek*, 473 U.S. at 6–7; *see also Pelkowski v. Highland Managed Care Group, Inc.*, No. 01-2335, 2002 WL 1836509 (7th Cir. Aug. 9, 2002) (granting lawyers' fees as costs under 42 U.S.C. § 2000e(k) was appropriate, even though lawyers' fees were not specifically mentioned in the offer) (unpublished decision).

An offer of judgment may also include equitable relief. In *Marek*, the court held that Rule 68 applies to all claims of relief, including non-monetary, injunctive-type relief under the language of the rule allowing judgment "for money or property or to the *effect specified.*"[58]

Finally, offers of judgment are generally irrevocable unless the plaintiff fails to respond within ten days of receiving service of the written offer or at the discretion of the court to avoid mistake.[59]

Rule 68 provides that a plaintiff or adverse party may accept an offer of judgment by serving written notice of acceptance on the defendant within the prescribed ten-day period. The acceptance of the offer must be unconditional.[60] Moreover, noting an absence of extension language in the rule, courts have refused to extend the Rule 68 time period beyond the ten days.[61]

As already noted, the rejection of an offer of judgment has no adverse consequences for the defendant but can be very damaging to the plaintiff or adverse party. The plaintiff or adverse party stands to lose, even if he or she wins, by rejecting an offer of judgment that is more favorable than the ultimate judgment rendered at trial. Courts are in agreement that the consequences of rejecting an offer of judgment are immutable, and courts do not have the discretion to mitigate the potential impact.[62]

---

58. FED. R. CIV. P. 68 (emphasis added); *see also Chathas v. Local 134 IBEW*, 233 F.3d 508–11 (7th Cir. 2000) (affirming applicability of offer of judgment to cases in equity).

59. *See Webb v. James*, 147 F.3d 617, 622 (7th Cir. 1998) (defendant's omission was not due to mistake).

60. *Grosvenor*, 801 F.2d at 949.

61. *See Martino v. Massachusetts Bay Transp. Auth.*, 230 F. Supp. 2d 195, 203 (D. Mass. 2002) (refusing extension of offer of judgment in whistleblower claim); *Grosvenor*, 801 F.2d at 948–49; *Staffend v. Lake Cent. Airlines, Inc.*, 47 F.R.D. 218–20 (N.D. Ohio 1969) (holding that "[n]o sensible defendant would make an offer of judgment if he knew the offer might be kept open for an indefinite period of time, even though the value of the litigation might change.").

62. *See U.S. v. Trident Seafoods Corp.*, 92 F.3d 855, 859 (9th Cir. 1996), *cert. denied*, 519 U.S. 1109 (1997) ("Rule 68 leaves no room for the court's discretion"); *Simon v. Intercontinental Transp. (ICT) B.V.*, 882 F.2d 1435, 1439 (9th Cir. 1989) ("the mandatory cast of the rule 'leaves no room for district court discretion'") (*citing Liberty Mut. Ins. Co. v. EEOC*, 691 F.2d 438, 442 (9th Cir. 1982)).

Thus, upon receiving an offer of judgment, a plaintiff should run the necessary financial evaluations to determine the approximate cost-risk ratio of going to trial and winning, but receiving a judgment that is equal to or less than what the plaintiff would have received in the offer.

In conclusion, in settling EPL claims, either party—plaintiff or defendant—must be mindful of Rule 68 and its potential to cut both ways if a party is not knowledgeable about the scope of the rule. After two consistent Supreme Court pronouncements, it appears that it is here to stay, and courts will apply the rule according to its plain meaning.

CHAPTER 11
MEDIATION AND RELEASES

Sandra R. McCandless

Both plaintiff and employer representatives often approach the settlement of employment cases from a highly emotional point of view, even in cases of lesser value, when emotionalism may not seem warranted to the neutral outside observer. The presence in a lawsuit of individually named defendants, a common occurrence in certain types of employment cases, also plays an important role and is a complicating factor in any settlement process. Though employment practices liability (EPL) insurance provides a monetary benefit to the employer-defendant and a potential source of money for the plaintiff from a party with a more dispassionate view of the case than the defendant, the overlay of EPL insurance to an already volatile and complicated mix requires that counsel understand and take the interests of all parties into account in moving toward a desirable settlement.

As the percentage of employment cases covered by EPL insurance increased in recent years, the use of mediation in such cases also spread across the United States. Although reaching settlement without the facilitation of a neutral mediator may take weeks or even months of back-and-forth discussion, the most effective mediators are often able to settle employment cases, even in vitriolic situations, in one long day.

When counsel on both sides of a case are experienced and reasonable and there are no serious client control issues, it may be possible to value a case and attain a timely and cost-effective settlement without the use of a mediator. But such cases are the exception rather than the rule. So the attainment of a settlement sufficiently palatable to all of the necessary decision makers requires that counsel select a knowledgeable and effective mediator and know and utilize the most effective mediation techniques.

The preparation for and appearance at mediation of a lawyer on behalf of a plaintiff or defendant requires many of the usual litigation skills: attention to detail, organization and mastery of the facts and related law, sufficient rapport with and understanding of those who will appear with the lawyer at the mediation to enable their adequate preparation, eloquence in presentation of the client's position on the facts and the law, and persuasiveness with the mediator. The successful advocate in the mediation process must also have an additional skill; he or she must have the ability to temper the forceful presentation of the client's legal position to further the mutual interest shared with the opposing party of working together toward the common goal of settlement. When a good mediator has been selected, but mediation nevertheless breaks down, it is often the lack of realism and/or practicality in one of the opposing lawyers that has caused the failure of the process. The advocate in mediation must couple vigorous representation of the client with the facilitation of a constructive dialogue to enable the parties to compromise their interests.

Many advocates make the mistake of approaching the mediation process unprepared, as if it were an easy and informal one. This is a serious mistake. The mediation process can sometimes be more difficult than actual litigation because of the need to further the competing interests of persuasive advocacy and the attainment of compromise. The unprepared mediation advocate may fail to persuade the mediator and/or damage the client's case by presenting the evidence in a deficient or inappropriate manner. The unprepared mediation advocate may fail to reach a desired resolution because of lack of preparation alone.

Before any actual mediation appearance, lawyers should engage in sufficient work to be well prepared on the facts and the applicable law; educate their clients about the mediation process and the characteristics of the mediator, opposing counsel, and the opposing representatives and witnesses; discuss with their clients the role each representative will play in the process; amass and analyze potential documentary evidence; and consider the negotiating tactics to be used in the particular matter at hand. In employment cases, the advocate must additionally take into account the emotional attributes of the clients as they affect the relationships between the parties and the role those attributes will play in the mediator's assessment of the case and the negotiating process.

The role the EPL carrier for an insured defendant will play in this process is a subject for serious discussion between the lawyer for the insured and the carrier representative. If the existence of EPL coverage was previously unknown to plaintiff's counsel, bringing such coverage to the attention of the plaintiff and plaintiff's counsel may drive up the monetary demand, particularly if the employer is a small entity that appears to have limited financial resources. On the other hand, a solo plaintiff's counsel may in some circumstances be even more eager to attain settlement when a large company defendant has EPL coverage from an equally large insurer.

Though court-supervised settlement processes often require the carrier representative to be present in person at a settlement conference, mediation allows more flexibility. If the plaintiff is unaware of the existence and role of EPL insurance in the particular matter, the lawyer and the EPL insurer may decide that it is better not to have the insurer representative involved in a visible way at the mediation. The lawyer for the insured will need in such a case to time the premediation and mediation events in a way that allows for insurer approval and involvement without having the insurer representative present either in person or by telephone. If more than one insurer is involved in the case, the lawyer will need to discuss who will play what role in the mediation proceedings, not only with the EPL carrier representative but with the representative of any other involved insurer.

The following outline is intended to assist the advocate in an employment case in determining when and before whom to mediate, to outline some of the preparatory work to be done in advance of the mediation, to make suggestions for participation in the actual mediation process, and to provide some hints about how to reach successful closure.

I. When to Mediate?

A. Potential Benefits of Alternative Dispute Resolution

Privacy is a key benefit for all parties resolving an employment dispute through alternative dispute resolution. From the employer's perspective, the privacy inherent in alternative dispute resolution can eliminate the risk of negative publicity. An employer can prevent damage to its public image as a progressive or equal opportunity employer. Privacy may be particularly important if the alleged wrongdoer is in a high-profile or sensitive position.[1]

For the employee, a private forum may also be a substantial benefit. The victim of unlawful harassment or discrimination will often experience serious emotional trauma. Replaying the events before a judge and a jury, in open court, can renew or intensify the stress.

Resolving a claim through alternative dispute resolution can also create substantial savings of time and costs for the employer. Alternative dispute resolution is often conducted with limited discovery and before the other expenses typical of protracted litigation are incurred. Legal fees are also typically reduced by a substantial amount when a

---

1. The retirement, resignation, or termination of certain principal executive, financial, or operating officers of a public company are reportable events that must be filed on a Form 8-K with the U.S. Securities and Exchange Commission within four business days of the event. This requirement must be taken into account when an anticipated dispute with a high-ranking executive of a public company first arises. The privacy of mediation may be very attractive to both employer and employee in such a situation.

claim is resolved through alternative dispute resolution. The dispute can usually be resolved at a relatively early stage, with the neutral's fees well below the lawyer's fees that would be expended in protracted litigation.

The benefit of more rapid resolution of the dispute may create a significant benefit for the employer by avoiding business disruption, workforce "downtime," and negative employee relations. Many employment claims, such as claims of discrimination or harassment, cause divisiveness in the work unit, with employees siding with either the complaining party or the alleged wrongdoer. Prompt and amicable resolution of a dispute can minimize damage to workforce relationships and the time spent in discussions or gossip about the claims. It also benefits the employee plaintiff who wishes to avoid being the subject of discussion and speculation for an extended period of time after the dispute arose.

The experienced neutral provides the parties and their lawyers with an early evaluation of the relative merits of their claims and defenses. Thus, even if a full resolution does not occur, the issues may be significantly narrowed, minimizing the expense of further litigation.

B. Potential Drawbacks of Alternative Dispute Resolution

If neither party is committed to resolving the process through alternative dispute resolution, or if the resolution process fails, there may be drawbacks to having participated in it. In alternative dispute resolution, the parties often expose both the weaknesses and the strengths of their claims. Opposing counsel may use the resolution session as an inexpensive means of conducting discovery. The risks of improper use of information gained through alternative dispute resolution efforts can be minimized by signing an appropriate and strongly worded confidentiality agreement prior to participation.[2] However, once the information is disclosed, obtaining the same information through narrowly drafted formal discovery is a relatively easy matter.

2. *See* a sample form of Mediation Confidentiality Agreement at Appendix 1.

Before beginning an alternative dispute resolution process, the client should be advised in a case where the mediation outcome seems uncertain that, if unsuccessful, the parties' prior participation in mediation may add complexity and difficulty to later or continuing litigation. However, the skillful advocate will work toward a mediation strategy that avoids such an outcome.

The financial cost of preparing for and participating in mediation and paying the mediator should normally not be a disincentive to mediation, because the cost is small as compared to the cost of full-blown litigation. Given the benefits of an early, amicable resolution, the additional expense of mediation should not be a significant deterrent.

The parties to a dispute often divide the fees of the alternative dispute resolution provider. In employment cases, however, the economic disparity between the parties may dictate that the employer agrees to pay a larger portion of fees. Yet, even recognizing that the employee or former employee may have a limited income, the process works best if all parties contribute to the costs and feel that they have "invested" in the alternative dispute resolution process. Nonetheless, plaintiff's employment counsel often ask that the employer-defendant pay the entire cost of mediation, and the employer sometimes agrees. When this does not happen, the request that the employer pay the mediator's fee in full is typically renewed and often accepted in the course of successful settlement negotiations.

C. Settlement Discussions

Discussing settlement one on one with opposing counsel is often an effective means of resolving claims, particularly if settlement discussions proceed before the parties engage in hard-fought litigation. If the lawyers are experienced and have a reasonably good relationship, they can discuss the strengths and weaknesses of their respective cases and evaluate the merits and damages without the need to educate a neutral third party. In recent years, however, parties have come to rely routinely on the services of a neutral in helping them evaluate and settle their cases.

In employment cases in particular, there may be many valid reasons to turn to a third party who can assist the parties in feeling "heard" and thereby facilitate resolution. Typically, a plaintiff will make an initial settlement demand at least double and often many times higher than the amount his or her counsel expects to receive in settlement. The parties then engage in a number of rounds of offers and counteroffers. As the gap narrows, the plaintiff's demand may drop significantly between one demand and the next. This drop often signals the plaintiff's desire to resolve the case and will generally be near the amount the plaintiff expects to receive in settlement. However, a hardening of the plaintiff's position also usually follows the drop. If the defense does not make an offer that is in the range of the plaintiff's anticipated settlement, settlement discussions may then come close to failure. It is at that time that the presence of an experienced and persuasive neutral will be most needed and most helpful in reaching resolution.

D. Mediation

The informal and resolution-oriented atmosphere of mediation often enhances the chances of settling an employment-practices claim and providing a resolution satisfactory to all parties. However, achieving a satisfactory mediation result takes careful planning.

The mediation process is the most flexible form of dispute resolution, offering options for timing, format, scope, and available results. Counsel should take advantage of this flexibility when establishing the mediation procedures to enhance the settlement potential.

Mediation can be conducted at any stage of a proceeding, even before a lawsuit is filed. A neutral investigation can be conducted prior to the mediation to provide the parties and mediator with impartial information regarding the claims being asserted. The mediation is typically held in neutral territory, such as a conference room in the mediator's offices.

Careful selection of the mediator increases the likelihood of settlement. The mediator's ability to appear fair and impartial and to establish rapport with and be highly persuasive to both sides is critical.

The parties to employment cases sometimes desire to select mediators for reasons that are less critical than the mediator's basic skills in bringing the parties to resolution. For example, in sexual harassment cases, parties are sometimes of the simplistic view that a mediator of the same sex as the plaintiff will have greater credibility with the plaintiff than an opposite-sex mediator. However, if counsel provides the client with sufficient information on the various reasons to choose a particular mediator, the party may be convinced to be more open minded in choosing the mediator.

Client participation is greater in mediation than in any other form of dispute resolution. The structure of the mediation should also be designed to facilitate agreement. Often, the mediation begins with a meeting of all parties and the mediator, where each party explains his or her position. This allows the client to hear the opposition's story directly. The parties may also be asked to exchange position papers and key documents before the start of the mediation.

However, this pattern may not be best for discrimination or harassment claims, which typically involve highly charged emotions. If animosity exists between the parties, a mediation structured to avoid having the parties face off at the outset and instead meet for extended periods alone with the mediator for informal discussions, seeing each other only after very significant progress has been made, is the better approach. When the parties meet individually with the mediator, the opportunity to speak to a neutral outsider can provide a much-needed outlet for pent-up emotions. The ability to vent complaints at the outset may be key to moving negotiations forward.

In addition, because of their direct participation in the process, the parties can better understand how achieving dispute resolution will benefit them. The parties can then articulate their goals and fashion a resolution tailored to fit their ongoing needs. It is commonly accepted that solutions reached through mediation are more likely to endure, perhaps because the solution is based upon and addresses the parties' concerns, rather than being externally imposed. A mediated resolution typically leads to full closure because the parties' participation in the process causes them to feel committed to it and obliged to fulfill the resulting agreement.

Confidentiality is also an essential element of making mediation work. For the parties to engage in frank discussions of the weaknesses of their positions, they must understand that anything they disclose will not be used against them should mediation fail. Entering the required written confidentiality agreement before mediation helps to ensure that disclosures made during the proceedings are neither used improperly by the parties nor disseminated to third parties.

Traditional litigation tends to focus on how much a claim is worth, whereas a mediator can look for a creative solution that may include discipline of an offender, an agreement by the complaining party and the accused harasser not to disparage each other, training, an updated complaint process, or definition of terms of the future relationship between the parties (such as what the employer will say in the event of a request for an employment reference and who the employer spokesperson will be). The mediator can explore the core issues, determine the parties' goals, and suggest alternative courses of action that satisfy those goals.

Mediation is often the best method of resolving a complaint when the employee/employer relationship is expected to continue. Litigation and other forms of dispute resolution designed to determine rights and obligations, or rights and wrongs, may destroy a relationship. Mediation offers the parties an opportunity to control their destiny and craft a sensible solution that allows both sides to process the need for and acceptance of change, while still working together in the context of a continuing relationship. And parties having a continuing relationship with each other are more likely to adhere to agreement reached through their direct participation.

The lawyer anticipating a mediation should know the case facts and applicable law so well *before* the mediation that there are few surprises, if any, in the process. Unless precluded by cost constraints or a desire to avoid discovery that will substantially weaken the parties' cases, mediation should be preceded by sufficient witness interviews, document review, and, as appropriate, discovery to allow a persuasive presentation to the mediator to be made. Plaintiff's counsel should anticipate facts and arguments the defendant is likely to present and be prepared to counter them. A defendant-employer is potentially in a better position in most cases than the plaintiff to learn all of the relevant background facts to a case, but is not aided by that position if it does not learn and make use of those facts prior to the mediation. A defendant that has not only learned those background facts but also taken the plaintiff's deposition and obtained admissions countering the plaintiff's version of events stated in the complaint is much more likely to obtain a favorable result than the defendant that has done neither. In mediation, as in other aspects of the legal process, there is no substitute for "doing one's homework."

Sometimes a lawyer is forced—because of cost constraints or because discovery will likely bring damaging facts, information, or documents to the attention of the other party—to mediate without much, if any, discovery. In such a case the early portion of the mediation process can be used as a discovery tool to obtain information not yet known but helpful both on the merits and in the negotiation and settlement process. Conversely, counsel should work toward forestalling the adversary from using the mediation as its own discovery tool.

The dynamics of the mediation process are such that, once the parties engage in an unsuccessful mediation, it may become more difficult later to settle the case at an acceptable price. Although a mediation that ends in a stalemate, with the mediator declaring that no settlement can be achieved, may sometimes have served to advance a party's discovery objectives, it also is often harmful to the objective of a later reasonable settlement. Thus, for the party with the objective of achieving a mediated resolution, mediation should occur only at the point that opposing counsel and his or her client appear to be willing to move toward a realistic and reasonable position and no sooner.

II. Selection of the Mediator

Selection of the mediator may well be the most important step in the entire process of mediation. Selection of a mediator who will not be effective at persuading the parties to temper their positions or prepared to expend the extra effort it will take to achieve closure will doom the process and may even hurt the parties' ability later to achieve an early settlement by other means. Some of the considerations in the selection of a mediator for a particular case include the following:

- What is the mediator's background?
- Is the mediator experienced in the particular areas of the law in the case?
- Has the mediator been successful in achieving settlement in prior mediations?
- What is the mediator's attitude toward "going the distance," that is, continuing to work with the parties to achieve resolution as long as necessary, whether by working until midnight on the day of the mediation or in the days following the scheduled mediation until the case is settled?

Some lawyers prefer using retired judges as mediators, on the assumption that a retired judge will seem a more credible mediator to one or more of the party representatives than a mediator who has never been on the bench. Mediation requires subtle negotiating skills and great persistence in a forum where there is no decision-making authority. Some former judges have those skills, and some do not. The lawyer selecting a mediator should consider the attributes of various mediators and select one with good negotiating and "closing" skills who will have rapport with plaintiff and defense counsel and their clients and who will also deal creatively with the issues that arise.[3]

3. Though the mediation of employment class actions is beyond the scope of this chapter, it bears noting that the selection of a mediator or mediators to assist in the

III. Preparation for Mediation

The mediator will spend minimal time in mediation preparation, and opening statements are typically brief. Therefore, providing the mediator with a well-written, easy-to-read mediation brief containing a persuasive, nonargumentative statement of the facts in support of the client's position and of the law applicable to those facts is very helpful to the advocate in the process of helping the mediator to see the client's view of the case. Although the preparation of such a brief can be expensive, and there are many cases in which either case strategy or cost factors dictate a different approach, a persuasive and thorough mediation brief is an effective means of convincing the mediator of the strength of the client's position early in the mediation. The brief will also be helpful to client representatives in understanding the strong points of the client's case and in demonstrating how the client representatives should focus any factual presentation they may be required to make in response to mediator questioning during the course of the mediation. Supporting documentation (to the extent that such documentation is favorable to the party presenting it) should be attached as exhibits to the mediation brief. The provision to the mediator of an excellent brief will enable the advocate to be somewhat more conciliatory if there is a joint session and opening statement phase of the mediation than would be the case in the absence of a compelling written presentation.

An employment mediation brief that is intended to facilitate and result in settlement should typically include a detailed chronology of the facts presented from that party's point of view, with specific citations to attached documents or deposition testimony. Presentation of the facts in such an organized fashion greatly facilitates the mediator's

---

complexities of class action resolution requires even more consideration than does the selection of a mediator in a one-plaintiff or even multi-plaintiff case. Though the mediator of an individual employment case may be able to rely on his or her "people" and practical skills, leaving any argument over the applicable substantive law to the parties' counsel, a class action mediator must be experienced in the applicable procedural and substantive law to provide meaningful assistance to the parties in settling their class action dispute.

understanding of the case and expedites the mediation process. If the opposing party then fails to provide a persuasive brief, the opposing party is in a disadvantageous position with the mediator. Often, the parties exchange mediation briefs; in some cases, the briefs are submitted confidentially to the mediator and not provided to the other party. In most cases the former is the better practice in that, if the brief is persuasive, counsel obtains the benefit of having opposing counsel see the strengths of his or her client's case by having opposing counsel read the brief. If the case seems unlikely to settle in any event, however, counsel may understandably be unwilling to allow opposing counsel to see counsel's factual presentation and legal theories in the format of a brief to the mediator. Before drafting any mediation brief, the advocate should decide whether mediation briefs will be exchanged and build that determination into the drafting process.

Counsel should work with the insured and the carrier to decide which representative(s) will attend the mediation and the role each will play in the process. Critical to this decision are the abilities of potential representatives and witnesses to be articulate, unemotional (or emotional) when necessary, and credible, and the anticipation of how a given representative or witness will "play" in the process. Attendees at the mediation should be selected to play up the strengths of the case and to downplay its weaknesses. If the presence of an individually named defendant at the mediation will make the company's case look weaker and/or make it more difficult to settle, a decision may be made to conduct the mediation with that person absent. Those who will attend will need to be counseled on proper mediation conduct, such as the avoidance of statements or body language that will unnecessarily alienate the opposing party. If a decision is made not to have the ultimate settlement decision maker present in person, either for strategy reasons or because of unavailability, the lawyer should have access to the necessary representative(s) by telephone throughout the mediation.

Part of counsel's work in preparing for mediation is to educate the client about the mediation process. Many clients approach mediation without understanding the mechanics of the process. After engaging in the necessary discussion to provide a framework for the client about the process in general, counsel should explain his or her style and strategy; advise the client about the role the client will be expected to play; describe what may be anticipated from the mediator and the opposition; and convey the danger in talking too much or too informally in what appears on its face to be an informal process. Then, any client representative who will be asked to speak at the mediation, particularly in any joint session, should be prepared to present a persuasive rendition of the facts and to anticipate questions that may be asked by the mediator.

Effective mediation preparation includes preparation for both the expected monetary give and take and for the nonmonetary proposals that may arise. Preparation on the monetary front will require an opening negotiating number and a strategy for monetary movement toward a desired result. The tax implications of a settlement should be addressed with the client, the carrier, and opposing counsel early in the process, because the ultimate amounts to be paid by the defense and recovered by the plaintiff will be tied to after-tax amounts by the plaintiff and plaintiff's counsel. Nonmonetary terms, which are often discussed only as the parties get close to resolution, may include a neutral reference (or even a reference letter), a nondisparagement provision, an offer of outplacement, or an agreement to replace a termination with a designation of the termination as a resignation or layoff. Counsel for each party will have to decide before and during the course of the mediation when and whether to make the demand for the desired nonmonetary items to the other party.

IV. Participation in the Mediation Process

In contrast to court proceedings or arbitration, it is not improper to speak with the mediator before the mediation. If counsel has not previously worked with a particular mediator, it is critical to ask the mediator how he or she intends to conduct the overall process and to confirm that the mediator will remain with the process as long as the parties desire the mediator's participation. A specific question to ask before any mediation with an unfamiliar mediator is exactly how the mediator intends to begin the mediation session, because mediator methodologies vary. If the mediator intends to have counsel deliver opening statements, counsel will need to prepare such a statement ahead of time. If no such statements will be delivered, counsel should avoid the expense of preparing an opening statement. A flexible mediator will ask counsel's view of what approaches will be desirable in a particular case, and having a premediation discussion with the mediator will make it possible for dialogue on this subject to occur.

The mediator will have counsel and the parties sign a confidentiality agreement at the beginning of the mediation.[4] This agreement prevents the parties from using information disclosed at the mediation in another forum. Often, however, counsel shares with the mediator certain information that is not to be disclosed to the other party or its counsel. Before disclosing to the mediator information that counsel does not wish to be disclosed to the opposing party, the lawyer should obtain assurance from the mediator that he or she will, indeed, maintain such confidentiality.

If there is an initial joint session before the parties are separated and negotiations begin, the effective mediation advocate will make a brief presentation demonstrating the strength of the client's legal position without unnecessarily alienating the opposing party. Mediation counsel sometimes present their opening statements as if they were at trial before a jury or in court making an appellate argument. Counsel should, instead, present the client's position with attention to the type of proceeding at hand and to its ultimate objective. A good opening case presentation need not be a strident case presentation.

The mediation advocate should engage in active listening to and watching of the opposing lawyer, his or her client, and the interaction

4. *See* Appendix 1 for a sample Mediation Confidentiality Agreement.

between the two. Mediation presents an ideal opportunity to size up the opponent. If weaknesses are discerned, these can be pointed out to the mediator in the process of advocating for one's position later in the mediation.

Most of the mediation will be conducted in separate caucuses, with the mediator moving back and forth between parties. Once separated from the opposing party, counsel should be prepared to begin to provide the information needed by the mediator to understand the client's position and counsel's view of the motivation and position of the opposing party. On the assumption that the lawyer has selected a mediator in whom he or she feels trust and confidence, negotiating constraints and alternative possibilities for settlement movement can be discussed openly with the mediator.

Some mediators shut counsel, the carrier representative, and/or the client out of the process. Examples of such techniques are the mediator who has the client sit in an outside room throughout a large part of the mediation or the mediator who takes the carrier representative or the representative of the defendant aside and tries to run the negotiations on that basis. This might be warranted on an occasion in which a lawyer is impeding the process when everyone else present is moving in good faith toward a settlement, but it is seldom an effective technique. Effective mediation counsel should not be faced with this technique, but, if it occurs, the lawyer should politely and privately make his or her objection to that tactic known to the mediator.

As the mediation process unfolds, counsel should work with the mediator to strategize about how to communicate the client's position and settlement offers, how much to raise or lower a monetary position at a given time, and how to reach ultimate agreement. The skillful lawyer will be able to use the mediator's authority to move the client or the carrier away from an unrealistic or overly emotional position or to learn the true "bottom line" of the opposing party. In that process the lawyer should ensure that the client's important interests are not compromised.

Mediation is a successful process because it enables the parties to feel that they have been "heard" by a neutral. When conducted well, the rancor present at the opening of the mediation often disappears. At some point in time, a joint session or sessions may become helpful and may even help to expedite the process. Because each and every mediation is different, counsel should throughout mediation approach the process creatively and flexibly, anticipate surprises, and "roll with the punches."

V. Reaching Closure

Cases frequently settle in mediation when the prospects for settlement initially seemed bleak. A positive and patient approach is often successful in the end. It is the job of the advocate, whose client is motivated to settle in the typical case in which the parties' monetary evaluations are widely divergent, to attempt to understand the opposing party's assumptions, interests, and motivations and to consider creative solutions. A second mediation session or follow-up telephone calls with the mediator are usually an option. In multiparty cases counsel will need to work in tandem with the more constructive of the other counsel and/or parties to reach overall resolution.

Before making a closing proposal, the lawyer should seek reasonable assurance from the mediator that the proposal will settle the matter. The mediator can provide assistance not only in reaching monetary agreement but in reducing crucial terms to writing and moving the process forward after the mediation if and when the agreement-drafting process breaks down or other issues arise. Though it is desirable to reach a written agreement on critical terms before the conclusion of the mediation, and signature by all necessary parties to the release agreement is sometimes possible at the mediation, counsel should be careful to ensure that the final settlement agreement is not drafted under such time pressure that omissions of necessary language occur or drafting mistakes are made.

In contrast to many settlements negotiated without mediation, the overall mediation process involves and requires the active participation of the parties, and in an EPL case, of any carrier representative who is present at the mediation in person or by telephone.[5] The plaintiff or the company representative may be queried directly by the mediator on an informal basis about case facts, sometimes in the presence of the opposing party. The informal and participatory nature of mediation means that the lawyer who mediates on behalf of a client must be prepared, flexible, and persuasive, while determining ongoing strategy on a continuous basis with the client and its carrier as the audience. The mediation lawyer must in a very brief period of time initiate, conduct, and close a strategy that brings the opposing party much closer to the client's position, while demonstrating to the client and carrier representative the effectiveness of his or her advocacy. The flexibility and creativity required in the mediation process has added one more skill set to those required of a successful litigator.

VI. Documenting the Settlement

Unless a case ends with a voluntary dismissal, summary judgment, or trial verdict, an employment case will conclude, whether after mediation or otherwise, with the drafting and signing of a settlement and release agreement. Like mediation, this is a process that too many counsel take as a simple one requiring neither much thought nor much skill. The document that finalizes the matter for all involved parties is as critical as anything else in the case and, indeed, is the most critical aspect

---

5. The sophistication and experience of carrier representatives in EPL cases varies widely from carrier to carrier. Some claims representatives are lawyers; others are not. Some are willing to provide early settlement authority when requested; others may be reluctant even when the case facts point toward the need for early settlement. In each case, counsel must establish rapport with the claims representative as well as the employer representatives early in the proceedings and be prepared to inform (and, as appropriate, educate) the claims representative about the settlement value of the case and the reasons for that settlement value in preparation for and during the mediation.

of the case at its final stage. Every section of a settlement and release agreement requires careful thought and skillful drafting.[6]

A. The Parties

A settlement and release agreement generally begins by listing the parties to the agreement. Who should be the actual parties to the release agreement, given the nature of the particular dispute and the identity and involvement of any third parties?

A release agreement in an employment case is obviously made between the employer and the former or current employee. Many releases, however, contain much broader language. For example, plaintiff's counsel may request an extremely broad statement of the parties to the settlement agreement, to the effect that it is entered by the employee with the employing entity, each and every affiliated entity, and the officers and employees of all of those entities. Though the employer may understandably require a broad release of all these parties, employer counsel should take care not to bind more entities and individuals as actual defense parties to a release agreement than is absolutely necessary. Thus, for example, employer counsel should not agree to a release agreement that purports to be entered between the plaintiff or claimant and all affiliated companies and/or employees of the employer. When individual defendants have been sued and have appeared in the case, however, plaintiff's counsel may rightfully request that such individuals be parties to a settlement and release agreement. The identity of the parties to a release agreement will therefore vary from case to case.

B. The Financial Terms

Counsel sometimes believe at the conclusion of a mediation that they have reached agreement on all essential points, only to realize in the

6. Appendix 2 contains a simple form of release agreement for an employee over age forty. Although every release agreement is different, the attached form and the commentary in this chapter are intended to provide a roadmap of some of the issues to consider in drafting the release agreement in a particular case.

course of documenting the settlement that there are further terms to be discussed. The following roadmap for drafting the financial terms of employment releases is also a useful tool for the nuances of the financial terms to be addressed in the course of a mediation:

- Will there be one check paid to the plaintiff or claimant, or more? Will there be one payment, payment made over time, or a lump sum plus additional payment over time? Will the entire payment be made in the current tax year?
- How will lawyers' fees be paid? And will any check from the employer to the lawyer be written to the lawyer or to the plaintiff or claimant?
- What are the tax implications of the settlement and its component parts? Will there be a Form 1099 issued to the plaintiff in addition to a Form W-2, and, if so, for how much of the settlement payment?[7]
- What are the conditions precedent to payment of the plaintiff and his or her lawyers (for example, prior or simultaneous dismissal of the lawsuit)?

Some of these factors will be affected by the level of trust among the various parties to the settlement. Defense counsel may accept a dismissal following the payment of the settlement proceeds if he or she has a high degree of trust in plaintiff's counsel, while insisting upon prior dismissal in another case. Plaintiff's counsel who has become distrustful of the client and concerned about actually receiving agreed-upon

7. For an informed understanding of the tax implications of employment settlements, *see* IRS Instructions for 1099-MISC, *available at* http://www.irs.gov/pub/irs-pdf/i1099msc.pdf; IRS Lawsuits, Awards, and Settlements Audit Techniques Guide (Rev. May 2011), *available at* http://www.irs.gov/Businesses/Small-Businesses-&-Self-Employed/Lawsuits,-Awards,-and-Settlements-Audit-Techniques-Guide; and Robert W. Wood, *Termination Pay Withholding Issues*, 134 Tax Notes, No. 7 (Feb. 13, 2012), 869–872, *available at* http:// www.woodllp.com/Publications and numerous authorities cited therein.

lawyers' fees may ask for a sum subject to a Form 1099 to be deposited first into counsel's trust account for the benefit of the client rather than allowing an entire settlement check to be written directly to the plaintiff.

Consideration for a release is that which is not otherwise due to the employee or former employee. Inexperienced counsel sometimes draft releases that "muddy" the difference between the financial consideration for the release and money otherwise due to the employee or former employee, such as vacation pay. The distinction between what is consideration for a release of claims and what is not should be clear in the release.

The financial terms of a release often include some provision related to continued employee benefits. Counsel should take great pains to ensure that, in the drafting of any such provision, the terms of the release are in compliance and not inconsistent with the provisions of any applicable employee benefit plan. For example, though an employer may agree to pay a former employee's COBRA premium for some period of time after separation, it would be incompatible with the terms of the employer's medical plan to treat the former employee as if he or she were still employed. Plaintiff's counsel sometimes asks for benefits entitlements not allowed by the relevant plans as part of a settlement. It is the job of defense counsel to resist such requests but to find creative ways of achieving the sought-after objectives without violating the terms of the applicable plans.

C. Operative Release Language

Counsel for the employer should carefully tailor the release language to have the release of claims cover all related business entities of the employer and the individuals affiliated with the employer and those entities. A typical release in favor of the employer might cover the employer "and each and every past and present parent, subsidiary, associated, affiliated, predecessor, and successor company, and the officers, directors, owners, employees, insurance carriers, contractors, attorneys, and agents of each, and each of them."

The prudent plaintiff's lawyer will request a mutual release to which the employer-defendant may, if it wishes to settle the matter, have to agree. Often, however, plaintiff's counsel overreaches, asking for a release of the plaintiff by all of the parties whom the plaintiff is releasing. In other words, if the plaintiff is releasing all former coworkers in return for the settlement payment, plaintiff's counsel may ask defense counsel to agree that all such former coworkers release the plaintiff from any claims as part of the release agreement. Defense counsel must beware of entering into overly broad releases of the plaintiff on behalf of unrepresented parties. When asked to pare down the release of the plaintiff to those parties for whom it makes legal and practical sense, the employee's counsel will generally agree to do so.

Although various typical provisions of employment releases are "boilerplate," each and every well-drafted release is different. Defense counsel typically insert references not only to the release of statutory and common law claims specifically made in a particular suit but also to those claims that could have been made by the particular plaintiff. Although a release for a plaintiff who had been out on disability leave should reference the release of Americans with Disabilities Act and Family and Medical Leave Act claims, there may be no need to complicate a release with reference to those particular statutes for a former employee whose employment history at no point in time ever even potentially implicated those statutes in any way. Similarly, any exceptions to the broad release of claims should be tailored to the particular situation. Possible exclusions include a pending workers' compensation claim, a future unemployment claim, or a right to a vested employee benefit. To avoid later disputes about what is or is not legally covered by a release, it is desirable for both claimant and employer counsel to work out in the release-drafting process the exact exclusions from the release language in the particular case.[8]

---

8. Employment counsel should be thoroughly familiar with current Equal Employment Opportunity Commission policy documents stating the EEOC's position on the

D. Releases for Workers over Age Forty

An understanding of the requirements of the Older Workers' Benefit Protection Act (OWBPA) is critical to the final negotiating phase of an employment settlement involving a worker over age forty. The OWBPA,[9] adopted in 1990, created a need for employers to have two vastly different types of settlement agreements, one type for workers under forty and a second for over-forty workers whose employers wish to have age-discrimination claims released along with all other claims.

OWBPA requires, among other things, that a release of age-discrimination claims by an employee over age forty must be written in understandable language; advise the employee in writing to consult a lawyer before executing the release; specifically refer to rights arising from the Age Discrimination in Employment Act; and provide that (1) the employee will be given at least twenty-one days to consider the agreement and (2) the agreement will not be enforceable until the expiration of at least seven days after execution, during which period the

---

enforceability of release agreements. *See* UNDERSTANDING WAIVERS OF DISCRIMINATION CLAIMS IN EMPLOYEE SEVERANCE AGREEMENTS, (July 2009, Appendix B revised April 2010) and EEOC ENFORCEMENT GUIDANCE ON NON-WAIVABLE EMPLOYEE RIGHTS UNDER EEOC ENFORCED STATUTES (April 1997), both *available at* http://www.eeoc.gov/policy/docs. As articulated by the EEOC to employees in the later of the two policy statements:

> Although your severance agreement may use broad language to describe the claims that you are releasing . . . , you can still file a charge with the EEOC if you believe you were discriminated against during employment or wrongfully terminated. In addition, no agreement between you and your employer can limit your right to testify, assist or participate in an investigation, hearing, or proceeding conducted by the EEOC under the ADEA, Title VII, the ADA, or the EPA. Any provision in a waiver that attempts to waive these rights is invalid and unenforceable. (Section III, *Validity of Waivers—In General*, answer to question 3)

The EEOC policy statement continues at footnote 13, however, to state, "Although your right to file a charge with the EEOC is protected, you can waive the right to recover from your employer either in your own lawsuit, or in any suit brought on your behalf by the Commission." As a sample of the type of release agreement language that takes into account both the nonwaivable nature of certain employment rights and the employer's ability to require the waiver of right to recovery, see the last sentence of paragraph 2 of Appendix 2.

9. 29 U.S.C. § 626(f).

employee may revoke the agreement. There are more stringent requirements under OWBPA for employees asked to sign releases as part of a program offered to a group or class of employees.[10]

Technically, the OWBPA requirement for provision of a twenty-one-day consideration period and seven-day revocation period does not apply when a lawsuit has actually been filed (as opposed to a situation in which a settlement occurs prior to suit), as long as the individual has been given a "reasonable period of time within which to consider the settlement agreement."[11] However, in any dispute over whether the provisions of OWBPA have been met, the party asserting the validity of a release has the burden of proving that a waiver was knowing and voluntary.[12] Therefore, to avoid any later dispute, it is the better practice to write the twenty-one-day consideration and seven-day revocation period into all release agreements for individuals over forty, whether or not suit has been filed. This is particularly true in the case of a mediation, where the release may be executed as early as the end of the day or days of mediation. Although OWBPA allows an individual over forty to sign a release "on the spot" if he or she so desires, and as long as the twenty-one-day consideration period is written into the release, the seven-day revocation period is not waivable. Cautious defense counsel will provide for payment to an individual over forty no earlier than the eighth day after the individual's execution of the release agreement, even when suit has been filed.

E. Miscellaneous Release Provisions

1. Nonadmission of Liability

Defense counsel will almost always want a clause in which the defendant states that its payment of consideration to the plaintiff or claimant pursuant to the release does not constitute an admission or concession

10. 29 U.S.C. § 626(f)(1)(F)(ii), 626(f)(1)(H).
11. 4.29 U.S.C. § 626(2)(B). 5.29 U.S.C.
12. § 626(3).

of liability and that it expressly denies such liability. Seldom is there any reason for plaintiff's counsel to object to this standard language.

2. *Nondisclosure of Settlement*

Another common settlement term is one in which the plaintiff or claimant agrees not to disclose the contents of the settlement to any third party, with the exception of his or her personal financial and legal advisors. Once a case settles, plaintiffs, almost without exception, do tend to abide by such a provision, although employers tend to be skeptical that such will be the case.

The plaintiff may also request a mutual nondisclosure provision. As is the case with the identity of the defense parties to a release and of the employer-related parties who are releasing the plaintiff, employer counsel should take care not to make nondisclosure commitments on behalf of individuals over which it has no control, such as rank-and-file employees of the defendant. To the extent it references individuals affiliated with the employer, the employer's nondisclosure commitment should be limited to those with actual knowledge of the matter, such as the company's officers and/or members of its human resources department. Thus, any mutual nondisclosure of terms of settlement provisions should be carefully drafted by defense counsel.

3. *Nondisparagement of One Party by the Other*

Another provision that raises similar issues about who employer counsel should agree will be bound is a nondisparagement provision. Often, employer representatives may not care what the employee has to say about them at the conclusion of a settlement. On other occasions, particularly when the plaintiff has been in a high-ranking position and is able to do damage to the employer by making adverse statements to third parties about it, employer representatives may care a great deal what the employee has to say about them or the employer in the future. In the latter case, the employer may wish to have the former employee sign a nondisparagement provision. Such provisions are inherently vague and potentially raise problems of enforceability, but, as is the case with a confidentiality provision, most people who agree to and sign them do abide by the agreement.

However, the employer who asks for a nondisparagement provision is then more often than not asked for a mutual provision by which employer representatives agree not to disparage the former employee. Often, the process of negotiating a mutual nondisparagement provision begins with a plaintiff's request that no one in any way affiliated with the employer will disparage the plaintiff and requires a process of whittling the mutual nondisparagement provision, to which the employer will commit, down to a manageable promise (for example, the officers of X company agree not to disparage the plaintiff). The employer should be aware that any request for a nondisparagement provision will be met with a similar request from the plaintiff and should decide whether its request is of sufficient importance to engage in the ensuing give and take on that point.

4. Tax Indemnity

If a portion of the payment is being made pursuant to an IRS Form 1099, the employer should include a tax indemnity provision in the release agreement. Such a provision might read as follows:

> Employee understands and confirms that the payment to be made to him pursuant to this release shall be reported on an IRS Form 1099. Employee agrees that any tax payable on said payment shall be his responsibility, and he agrees to indemnify, defend, and hold Company harmless from and against any liability or claim for any tax or other governmental contribution or any penalty or interest thereon that may be incurred or demanded as a result of receipt of the consideration provided by this release.

Though many plaintiffs have insufficient resources to provide indemnity to the employer in the event of a later dispute over the nonpayment of taxes on a settlement, such an indemnity provision serves to advise the plaintiff of the need to pay the required taxes and provides strong encouragement to do so.

5. Confidentiality of Employer Information

Defense counsel should discuss with counsel's client whether to include a provision confirming the employee's obligation to maintain the confidentiality of information the employee learned by virtue of his or her employment. Such a provision is advisable if the plaintiff was a high-ranking employee and may be totally unnecessary if the employee was not. The release agreement may list the types of information the employer wishes to protect from disclosure by the former employee, such as financial information, sales and customer lists, technical information, and confidential personnel information. If a decision is made to list specific types of employer information to be protected from future disclosure, counsel should discuss with the employer what types of information it is concerned about in the particular case and make mention of those types of information in the release agreement. The release agreement may also reference and reconfirm the validity of any agreement regarding the employer's confidential information previously signed.

6. Future Employment-Related Matters

Employment releases often address employment-related matters that might be expected to arise between the parties in the future. The employer may wish to confirm that the former employee has no expectation of future employment with the employer and any related or affiliated companies, and that the employee will not aid, abet, assist, or encourage any other person to file suit or to make a claim against the employer, except as required by subpoena or other legal process. The employee, on the other hand, may wish to specify what the employer representative will say in the event the employer is contacted as a reference for the employee by a prospective employer. A common term of an employment release agreement is one providing that, if asked for an employment reference by a prospective employer, the former employer will state that its policy is to provide only dates of employment and position held.

7. Provisions Common to All Releases

A well-drafted employment release will, of course, include provisions common to other types of releases, such as (1) a clause providing that none of the released claims have been transferred or assigned by the signatory to the release, (2) an integration clause providing that the release contains all of the understandings between the parties and supersedes any prior oral or written agreement, (3) a provision allowing enforceability of the remaining provisions of the release if one provision is later deemed unenforceable, and (4) a provision stating which jurisdiction's law is applicable to the release. Such provisions would also include any uniquely required by a particular state jurisdiction. In particular, for example, California law requires that the provisions of California Civil Code Section 1542 be specifically referenced and waived for a release executed under its law to be binding and enforceable. Thus, all releases for California employees should include language along the following lines:

> Employee acknowledges that he is familiar with the provisions of California Civil Code Section 1542, which provides as follows:
>
> A GENERAL RELEASE DOES NOT EXTEND TO CLAIMS WHICH THE CREDITOR DOES NOT KNOW OR SUSPECT TO EXIST IN HIS OR HER FAVOR AT THE TIME OF EXECUTING THE RELEASE, WHICH IF KNOWN BY HIM OR HER MUST HAVE MATERIALLY AFFECTED HIS OR HER SETTLEMENT WITH THE DEBTOR.
>
> EMPLOYEE, BEING AWARE OF SAID CODE SECTION, HEREBY EXPRESSLY WAIVES ANY RIGHTS HE OR SHE MAY HAVE THEREUNDER.

Whereas a successful mediation ends a particular dispute, a release agreement is intended to end disputes between the particular parties for all time. The test of a good release agreement is that it leaves no outstanding matters to be decided but, instead, states in clear and understandable language who the parties are, what is being paid and how, who is being released, and what other obligations exist between the parties to the release at the time of its signing and in the future. If counsel for the parties carefully draft an easily understandable release agreement as the final act of representation in a particular employment dispute, there should be no later dispute between the parties over postrelease matters.[13]

13. The author acknowledges the contribution of lawyer Margaret J. Grover to this chapter.

CHAPTER 11: APPENDIX A
Mediation Confidentiality Agreement

[Case Name]
[Court] Case No. [______]

Consistent with [insert applicable federal or state rule], all parties to this mediation agree as follows:

I. Mediation is intended to assist the parties in reaching a mutually acceptable agreement. The mediator is a neutral person who facilitates communication between the parties to assist in reaching a mutually acceptable agreement. The mediator does not act as an advocate for any party.

II. All communications, negotiations, or settlement discussions by and between participants in the course of a mediation or a mediation consultation shall remain confidential.

III. No evidence of anything said or any admission made for the purpose of, in the course of, or pursuant to a mediation or a mediation consultation is admissible in evidence or subject to discovery, and disclosure of the evidence shall not be compelled. The mediator shall not be compelled to disclose or to testify in any proceeding as to documents received, information disclosed, or representations made in the course of the mediation.

IV. Unless otherwise provided by law, no writing that is prepared for the purpose of, in the course of, or pursuant to, a mediation or a mediation consultation is admissible in evidence or subject to discovery, and disclosure of the writing shall not be compelled in any arbitration, administrative proceeding, or civil action.

V. Because the parties are disclosing sensitive information in reliance upon this agreement of confidentiality, any breach of this agreement would cause irreparable injury for which monetary damages would be inadequate. Consequently, any party to this agreement may obtain an injunction to prevent disclosure of any such confidential information in violation of this agreement.

VI. Any party breaching this agreement shall be liable for and shall indemnify the nonbreaching parties and the mediator for all costs, expenses, liabilities, and fees, including lawyers' fees, which may be incurred as a result of such breach.

VII. The parties agree that the mediator has no liability for any act or omission in connection with the mediation.

Dated: ___________, 20__, and signed before commencement of the mediation by each of the persons whose signatures appear below.

Mediator

____

____

____

____

____

____

____

____

CHAPTER 11: APPENDIX B
General Release and Separation Agreement

This General Release and Separation Agreement ("General Release") is made by and between John Smith, an individual, and his heirs, executors, administrators, and assigns (collectively "Smith"), on the one part; and Jones Company, a [insert state of incorporation] corporation ("Jones"), on the other part.

WHEREAS, Smith has been employed by Jones;

WHEREAS, Smith was separated from employment with Jones on __________, 20__;

WHEREAS, Jones has agreed at Smith's request that his separation from employment be characterized as a [layoff] [resignation] [retirement] from Jones;

WHEREAS, Smith wishes to receive consideration from Jones as provided in this General Release; and

WHEREAS, Smith and Jones mutually desire that any and all outstanding matters between Smith and Jones shall be fully and finally resolved on an amicable basis;

NOW, THEREFORE, Smith and Jones agree as follows:

(1) On the next regularly scheduled payroll date following the effective date of this General Release as referenced in paragraph 7 below, Jones shall pay to Smith the total amount of $__, the equivalent of __ months of Smith's base salary at the time of his separation from employment, in a lump sum less applicable withholding deductions. Jones shall also pay the COBRA premiums for medical and dental coverage (assuming continued COBRA eligibility) for the __ months commencing ________ 20__ and ending ________ 20__ or until Smith becomes eligible for other medical/dental coverage, whichever comes first, directly to [medical carrier] and [dental carrier] on behalf of Smith. **[Carefully consider and draft payment terms to former employee and his or her counsel and tax implications of same. If 1099 payment is allowable, require tax indemnity provision running from former employee to employer.]**

(2) In exchange for the consideration provided by Jones in paragraph 1 above, the adequacy of which is hereby acknowledged, Smith, on behalf of himself and his heirs, executors, administrators, and assigns, hereby releases and forever discharges Jones, and each and every past and present subsidiary, associated, affiliated, predecessor, and successor company, and the employees, officers, directors, lawyers, contractors, agents, insurance companies, administrators, assigns, and owners of each, and each of them, from any and all claims for damages, demands, causes of action, obligations, lawyers' fees, costs, damages, and liabilities of whatever kind or nature, in law or in equity, known or unknown, suspected or unsuspected (all hereinafter referred to as "claims"), which he ever had, now has, or may hereafter claim to have had, arising on or before the date of Smith's signature to this General Release, including, but not limited to, claims arising out of or in any way related to Smith's employment with Jones or his separation from that employment. Released claims include, but are not limited to, claims under Title VII of the Civil Rights Act of

1964, as amended, the Age Discrimination in Employment Act of 1967, as amended, the Older Workers' Benefit Protection Act, the Americans with Disabilities Act, the [state of residence of employee] Human Rights Act, the [city of residence of employee if there is applicable city ordinance], [state of employer's principal place of business, if different from employee's residence], or any other federal, state, or local laws; common law claims arising under contract or tort theories; or claims for payments under Jones's policies, practices, and/or promises and/or under Smith's [employment agreement] [offer letter], which he signed on ________, 20__. In signing this General Release, Smith represents and warrants that he has no outstanding court, agency, or administrative claims for damages against any person or entity released herein and that no such claims will be filed. Except as otherwise prohibited by law, execution of this General Release by Smith operates as a complete bar and defense against any and all past, current, or future claims for damages that may be made by Smith against any person or entity released herein arising on or before the date of Smith's signature to this General Release, including, but not limited to, claims arising out of or in any way related to Smith's employment with Jones and/or the separation of his employment. Nothing herein shall limit or impede Smith's right to participate in any investigation by any local, state, or federal agency, but Smith agrees that, if Smith or anyone acting on his behalf, brings any claim, charge, action, or liability concerning or relating to any claim, charge, action, or liability released in this General Release, Smith waives any right to, and will not accept, any payments, monies, or damages awarded in connection therewith.

(3) Smith covenants and agrees not to disclose to any person, corporation, agency, group, or other organization, other than his immediate family and his personal financial and legal advisors, either directly or indirectly, any information relating to the terms

of this General Release and covenants and agrees that he will keep the terms of this General Release completely confidential. Smith acknowledges that violation of this covenant would constitute a material breach of this General Release.

(4) Smith covenants and agrees that he shall not use or disclose any confidential information of Jones, Jones affiliates, or any person or entity with which Jones does business, including, but not limited to, the following: (a) financial information or data of Jones or its customers; (b) Jones customer lists or customer-related information; (c) Jones business plans, information, and data; (d) confidential personnel information; and (d) any other business plan, trade secret, or other business information. Smith acknowledges that violation of this covenant would constitute a material breach of this General Release.

(5) Smith represents and warrants that he has not transferred or assigned, or purported to transfer or assign, any of the claims and rights herein released or affected.

(6) Smith confirms that he has read this General Release, fully understands its terms and their effect, and signs this General Release voluntarily and with the intention of being legally bound by it. Smith understands that he is waiving legal rights by signing this General Release and that he has been advised by Jones to consult with a lawyer before executing this General Release. The parties agree that this General Release was the product of negotiation such that it shall not be construed against the drafter.

(7) Smith acknowledges that he has been given the opportunity to take at least twenty-one days within which to consider whether to sign this General Release. Smith understands that he may revoke this General Release upon written notice to Jones within seven days after execution of it and that this General Release will become effective on the eighth day after its execution.

(8) It is understood and agreed by Smith that the payment of consideration to which reference is made in this General Release

does not constitute an admission or concession of liability by Jones on account of any claim by Smith, liability for which Jones expressly denies.

(9) This General Release contains all of the terms, promises, representations, and understandings between the parties, and supersedes any other oral or written agreement or understanding between the parties regarding these matters prior to the date hereof. Smith agrees that no promises, representations, or inducements have been made to him that caused him to sign this General Release other than those expressly set forth above.

(10) If any provision of this General Release is held by a court of competent jurisdiction to be invalid, void or unenforceable, the remaining provisions shall, nevertheless, continue in full force and effect without being impaired or invalidated in any way.

(11) This General Release may be executed in one or more counterparts, each of which shall constitute an original, and all of which shall constitute one instrument. It shall not be necessary in making proof of this General Release to account for more than one counterpart. A signature made on a facsimile copy of this General Release or a signature to this General Release transmitted by facsimile shall have the same effect as an original signature.

(12) The provisions of this General Release shall be interpreted at all times to comply with the requirements of Section 409A of the Internal Revenue Code and guidance issued thereunder.

(13) This General Release shall be governed by and construed in accordance with the laws of the State of ________ without reference to its conflict of laws principles.

IN WITNESS WHEREOF, the undersigned have executed this General Release freely and voluntarily with the intention of being legally bound by it.

Dated: ______________________

____

John Smith

Jones Company

By:

Dated: ______________________

____

Mary Lee

Vice President, Human Resources

This form is intended as a sample of a simple release for an individual former employee over forty only and should never be used without careful consideration of the applicable law and the circumstances of the case. If a group of employees is being terminated, the requirements of the Older Workers' Benefit Protection Act must be met.

CHAPTER 12
Ethical Issues Arising Out of Defense of Claims under Employment Practices Liability Policies

Frederick B. Finberg

I. Introduction

As Employment Practices Liability (EPL) policies become more prevalent, labor and employment lawyers will become more and more a part of the "tri-partite relationship" (insurer, insured(s), and lawyer). Labor and employment-law lawyers will, accordingly, confront ethical issues heretofore unfaced, including insurer-directed defenses and defending covered and uncovered claims and settlements within and in excess of

The editor and author would like to thank Ellis B. Murov of Deutsch Kerrigan & Stiles, LLP, for serving as editor for the second edition of the book, and also for his significant contributions to chapter 12 in the second edition of this book.

policy limits, as well as new variations of more familiar matters, such as joint representation of employers and employees. Each of these situations is discussed below.

II. Applicable Model and Disciplinary Rules as Well as Ethical Considerations

There are at least ten Model Rules as well as four Ethical Considerations and one Disciplinary Rule that lawyers must keep in mind when representing insurers and/or insureds. These are set forth in Appendix A.

III. Employment Practices Liability Insurance Policies

A. Introduction

EPL policies first appeared around the time of the Clarence Thomas confirmation hearings and the passage of the Civil Rights Act of 1991. Given the increase in employment-related litigation wherein employers can be held liable for back and front pay, compensatory and punitive damages, plus lawyer fees,[1] such policies have and will become even more prevalent.

B. Typical Provisions[2]

Virtually every EPL policy on the market today has, *inter alia*, the following key characteristics and features in common. First, defense costs are within the limits of liability and subject to the policy's deductible or self-insured retention. Second, insureds under the EPL policy typically include the employer itself and any director, officer, or employee. Third, the EPL insurer typically retains the right to select defense counsel on

1. *See* 42 U.S.C. § 1981(a); 42 U.S.C. § 2000e-5(g). The ADEA affords similar remedies. Liquidated, rather than compensatory and punitive, damages are recoverable. 29 U.S.C. § 626(b). Note: Though front pay is available, reinstatement is the preferred remedy under all statutes. *See, e.g.*, *Weaver v. Amoco Prod. Co.*, 66 F.3d 85, 88 (5th Cir. 1995).

2. *See* Chapters 1 for a more detailed discussion of these and other provisions.

behalf of its insured. Fourth, most policies plainly afford the insurer the right to settle claims. Some policies, however, require the insured's consent. Regardless, the insurer's defense and indemnification obligations may cease where an insured rejects the insurer's recommended settlement.[3]

C. Exclusions[4]

Some policies specifically exclude punitive and liquidated damages. Others cover punitive damages if state law permits reimbursement. Intentional misconduct or intentional violation of a statute is frequently excluded. Many policies apply these exclusions severally (for example, the malicious conduct of an individual insured employee may not necessarily be imputed to the employer if the claim against the employer is premised solely on negligence or *respondeat superior*).[5]

IV. Ethical Issues Arising Out of the Tri-Partite Relationship

A. Counsel Selection (Duty of Competence)

As set forth above, EPL policies typically afford insurers the right to select counsel. Few counsel will acknowledge a lack of competence when asked to represent an insured, and generally for good reason. Moreover, there is explicitly only a duty of competence.[6] Unless, however, competence and expertise are synonymous, given the fact that incurred costs and fees reduce the amount of available coverage under

---

3. ABA Formal Op. 96-403 (Aug. 2, 1996) (stating "the lawyer might remind the insured that the policy gives the insurer the right to control the defense and settle the claim without the consent of the insured or that rejecting the proposed settlement might result in a forfeiture of his rights under the policy. Ultimately, however, . . . the insured retains the power to reject the defense offered by the insurer . . . and to assume the risk and expense of his own defense. Rule 1.16").

4. *See* Chapter 1 for a more detailed discussion of these provisions.

5. Claims *solely* for injunctive relief, job reinstatement, or other equitable remedies are also typically excluded. *See* chapters 1 and 2.

6. Model Rule of Prof'l Conduct 1.1.

EPL policies and that claims can exceed policy limits and/or be uncovered, counsel should recognize the need for expertise.

B. Duty to Defend (Case Direction and Control of Litigation)

1. The General Rule and a Historic Exception Thereto

Besides selection of counsel, "the insurer's duty to defend includes the right to assume control of the litigation."[7] Exceptions, however, have been found where insurers, for example, allegedly had an interest in "providing a less than vigorous defense."[8] There can thus be tension between pressures to reduce costs and the ethical obligations of thoroughness, reasonable preparation, independent judgment, and loyalty.[9]

2. Ethical Obligations for Lawyers Working under Insurer Guidelines

a. Summary

The ABA has issued an opinion addressing "Ethical Obligations of a Lawyer Working Under Insurance Company Guidelines."[10] In short, lawyers "must not permit the [insurer] . . . to require compliance with litigation management guidelines the lawyer reasonably believes will

---

7. *E.g., Nandorf Inc. v. CNA Ins. Cos.*, 479 N.E.2d 988, 991 (Ill. App. Ct. 1985).

8. *Nandorf Inc.*, 479 N.E.2d at 992. The court held that the insured was entitled to reimbursement for fees incurred by counsel it hired to monitor the defense tendered by CNA, where CNA issued a reservation-of-rights letter stating punitive damages were not covered and punitive damages represented the insured's primary exposure. The court added, "[t]he insurer and the insured shared a common interest in a finding of no liability. However, if Nandorf was found liable, their interests diverged. CNA's interests would have been just as well served by an award of minimal compensatory damages and substantial punitive damages. . . . As a result of its reservation of rights, CNA had an interest in providing a less than vigorous defense . . . . Clearly the insurer's fidelity to the insured was hampered by its own interests in this case."

9. *See also* ABA Formal Op. 01-421 (Feb. 2001) ("The interests of [the insurer] . . . and the insureds may diverge when the insurer's paramount interest is cost control and the insured's is to receive the best possible defense.").

10. *Id.*

compromise materially the lawyer's professional judgment or result in his inability to provide competent representation. . . ."[11]

b. Opinion 01-421

Litigation guides normally do not raise ethical concerns for two reasons. First, the employer/insured desires defense and indemnification. Second, because the insurer pays defense costs, settlements, and/or judgments, the insured implicitly delegates control of the case to the insurer.

If, however, the lawyer reasonably believes his or her representation of the insured will be impaired materially by the insurer's guidelines or if the insured objects to the defense provided by a lawyer working under insurance company guidelines, the lawyer must consult with both the insured and the insurer concerning the means by which the objectives of the representation are being pursued. If the lawyer is to proceed with the representation of the insured at the direction of the insurer, the lawyer must make appropriate disclosure sufficient to apprise the insured of the limited nature of his or her representation as well as the insurer's right to control the defense in accordance with the terms of the insurance contract. If the insurer does not withdraw or modify the limitation on the lawyer's representation and the insured refuses to consent to the limited representation, the resulting conflict implicates Rule 1.7(b) and, unless the lawyer is willing to represent the insured without compensation from the insurer, requires the lawyer to terminate the representation of both clients.

In such situations, the lawyer has few alternatives available. The lawyer can try to persuade the insurer to withdraw the limitation. If the lawyer is unable to persuade the insurer-client to withdraw the limitation, the resulting conflict between the insurer's directives and the insured's immediate interests requires the lawyer to withdraw from representing the insurer and to protect the immediate interests of the insured in the litigation. In this unlikely situation, the lawyer must, in

11. *Id.*

contemplation of his or her immediate resignation from representation of the insured, protect the immediate interests of the insured in order to assure that his or her withdrawal can be accomplished without material adverse effect on the insured's interests, as contemplated by 1.16(b). Thereafter, if the lawyer is unable satisfactorily to resolve the conflict implicated by the insurer's guidelines, the lawyer may seek to withdraw pursuant to Rule 1.7 or 1.16(b).[12]

C. Duty to Defend (Disclosures to Auditors)

1. Introduction

Opinion 01-421 cautions against disclosure of confidential information to a third-party auditor absent the insured's informed consent. Opinion 01-421, however, recognizes the propriety of submission of detailed bills and other confidential information to the client's insurer unless disclosure will adversely affect "a material interest of the insured."

2. Opinion 01-421

Some insurers have required defense counsel to submit to audits. Such audits are generally viewed with distrust or as undesirable by lawyers, even though they theoretically have the potential to improve quality and efficiency. That is, audits frequently focus on improper charges and errors in billing rates, expenses, and so on. Moreover, audits sometimes involve interviews, records reviews, and review of billing system and time sheets.[13]

Time sheets and "[b]illing records may, however, reveal the motive of the client in seeking representation, litigation strategy, or the specific nature of the services provided to the insured. This information generally is protected by the confidentiality rule or the attorney-client privilege or both."[14]

---

12. *Id.*

13. *Id.* (citing John Toothman, *Surviving a Legal Bill Audit*, 15 COMPLEAT LAWYER 45 (Winter 1998).)

14. ABA Formal Op. 01-421 (Feb. 2001).

Rule 1.6 prohibits counsel from revealing confidential and privileged information:

> [I]n the absence of the client's informed consent, except for disclosures that are impliedly authorized in order to carry out the representation. Informing the insurer about the litigation through periodic status reports, detailed billing statements and the submission of other information usually is required, explicitly or implicitly, by the contract between the insurer and the insured and also is appropriate in those jurisdictions where the insurer is regarded as a client and there is no conflict between the insurer and insured. . . . In those relatively rare situations when the lawyer reasonably believes that disclosure of confidential information to the insurer will affect a material interest of the client-insured adversely, the lawyer may not disclose such confidential information without first obtaining the informed consent of the client-insured.[15]

Nor may the lawyer disclose the insured's confidential information to a third-party auditor designated by the insurer without the insured's informed consent. Unlike the disclosure of the insured's confidential information to secretaries and interpreters, the disclosure of such information to a third-party auditor, a vendor with whom the lawyer has no employment or direct contractual relationship, may not be deemed essential to the representation and may, therefore, result in a waiver—albeit unintended—of the privilege.[16]

---

15. *Id.*

16. *Id.* (citing Office of the General Counsel of the Alabama State Bar, Op. RO-98-02 (Nov. 9, 2998); Alaska State Bar Ass'n Ethics Committee, Op. No. 99-1 1999, 1999 WL 1494993 (Oct. 22, 1999); Arizona State Bar, Formal Op. 99-08 (Sept. 1999); Cincinnati, Ohio Bar Association, Op. 98-99-02 (Feb. 1999); Colorado Bar Association Ethics Committee, Formal Op. 107 (Sept. 18, 1999); Connecticut Bar Association Committee on Professional Ethics, Informal Op. 00-20 (Sept. 26, 2000); District of Columbia Legal Ethics Committee, Op. No. 290 (Apr. 20, 1999); Florida Bar Professional Ethics

Thus, lawyers must inform and consult with their clients in two situations, that is, when disclosures to the insurer could materially affect coverage and when disclosure is to an auditor. The first situation is easier for most lawyers to handle than is the second.

That is, sensitive defense counsel know that they cannot divulge information that is adverse to their client's interests. After a discussion

---

Committee Proposed Advisory, Op. 99-2 (Mar. 31, 1999); Florida Bar Staff, Op. 20762 (Mar. 9, 1998); Florida Bar Staff, Op. 20591 (Dec. 31, 1997); Georgia State Bar, Proposed Advisory Op. No. 99-2 (Jan. 2000); Hawaii Bar Office of Disciplinary Conduct, Op. 36 (Mar. 25, 1999); Idaho State Bar Association, Formal Op. 136 (Jan. 2000); Indiana State Bar Association, Op. 98-4 (1998); Iowa Supreme Court Board of Professional Ethics and Conduct, Op. 99-01 (Sept. 8, 1999); Kentucky Bar Association, Op. E-404 (June 1998); Louisiana State Bar Association Ethics Advisory Service Committee, Op. 45, as *reported in* LOUISANA BAR JOURNAL 438 (Feb. 1998); Maine Professional Ethics Commission of the Board of Overseers, Op. 164 (Dec. 2, 1998); Maryland State Bar Association Committee on Ethics, Op. No. 99-7 (Jan. 1999); Massachusetts Bar Association Committee on Professional Ethics, Op. 2000-4 (Sept. 13, 2000); Mississippi State Bar Association, Ethics Op. 246 (Apr. 8, 1999); Chief Disciplinary Counsel of the Supreme Court of Missouri, Informal Advisory Op. 980188 (Sept. 9, 1998); New Mexico State Bar, Formal Advisory Op. 2000-02 (June 20, 2000); New York State Bar Association Committee on Professional Ethics, Op. 716 (Mar. 3, 1999); North Carolina State Bar Proposed Formal Ethics, Op. 10, 1998 WL 609887 (Oct. 16, 1998); Oklahoma Bar Association Board of Governors Legal Ethics, Advisory Op. No. 309 (Mar. 27, 1998) (representation of insureds by lawyers who are employees of a liability insurer); Oregon State Bar Association, Ethics Op. 1999-157, 1999 WL 521543 (June 1999); Pennsylvania Bar Association Committee on Legal Ethics and Professional Responsibility, Informal Op. No. 97-119, 1997 WL 816708 (Oct. 7, 1997); Rhode Island Ethics Advisory Panel, Op. 99-17 (Oct. 27, 1999); South Carolina Bar Ethics Advisory Committee, Op. 97-22, 1997 WL 861963 (Dec. 1997); State Bar of South Dakota Ethics, Op. 99-2 (Apr. 16, 1998); Board of Professional Responsibility of the Supreme Court of Tennessee, Ethics Op. 99-F-143, 1999 WL 406886 (June 14, 1999); Utah State Bar Ethics, Advisory Op. No. 98-03 (Apr. 17, 1998); Vermont Bar Association, Ethics Op. 98-7 (Oct. 1998); Virginia Bar Legal Ethics, Op. 1723 (Nov. 23, 1998); Washington State Bar Association, Formal Op. 195 (1999); West Virginia Lawyer Disciplinary Board, Op. LEI 99-02 (Apr. 30, 1999); Wisconsin State Bar, Ethics Op. E-99-1 (Oct. 1999). In ABA Formal Opinion 95-398, this committee recognized that "in this era of rapidly developing technology," lawyers frequently use outside agencies for numerous functions, such as accounting, data processing, photocopying, computer servicing, storage, and paper disposal and that lawyers retaining such outside service providers are required to make reasonable efforts to prevent unauthorized disclosures of client information (Formal and Informal Ethics Opinions 1983–1998 at 367) (ABA 2000). The present inquiry is clearly distinguishable because the lawyer has neither a contract with nor any right to control the conduct of the third-party auditor retained by the insurer.).

and consultation, if necessary, the lawyer and client should generally be able to reach common ground and a decision because the tension is between the lawyer/insured and the insurer.

On the other hand, disclosures to auditors can create tension between the insurer and its insured with defense counsel. Stated differently, whereas preservation of privileges creates a natural alliance between lawyers and clients, preservation of policy proceeds potentially aligns the insured and insurer against defense counsel. After all, most lawyers do not welcome with open arms someone whose role could result in a monetary loss.

Yet, defense counsel must obtain informed consent. Lawyers, therefore,

> . . . must inform the client of the adverse effects that may result, including communicating with the client about the consequences of not consenting to disclosure where the insurance contract requires the insured to cooperate in the defense of the claim and where failure to agree to disclosure could risk loss of insurance coverage. The client also should be informed that the insurance company may interpret the "duty to cooperate" clause in its contract with the insured as meaning that it has the right to give an independent contractor access to the client's confidential information to aid it in representing clients.
>
> The lawyer should inform the client of the risk that the information to be disclosed to the auditor could be obtained by others directly or indirectly as a result of the disclosure, the risk that a disclosure could involve a waiver of the lawyer-client privilege, and that the disclosure could be used to the client's disadvantage.[17]

17. *Id.*

ABA Formal Opinion 01-421 is carefully crafted not to suggest answers to specific fact situations. Yet, one could construe the ABA as generally supporting disclosure to auditors based on the following:

> Such occasions may arise when the information to be disclosed jeopardizes the insured's coverage under the insurance policy; reveals extremely sensitive or personal, irrelevant information about the insured; or otherwise implicates a conflict between the insurer and insured. In these *relatively infrequent* situations, it is essential that the lawyer obtain the informed consent of the client-insured before disclosing the confidential information in question.[18]

That is, Formal Opinion 01-421 could be interpreted to mean that disclosure to auditors is appropriate except in the rare situation quoted above. Yet the same formal opinion concludes with the following:

> A lawyer may disclose the insured's confidential information, including detailed work descriptions and legal bills, to the insurer if the lawyer reasonably believes that doing so will advance the interests of the insured. However, the lawyer may not disclose the insured's confidential information to a third-party auditor without the informed consent of the insured. It is also the opinion of the Committee that unless the lawyer reasonably believes that disclosure of the insured's confidential information to the insurer will not affect a material interest of the insured adversely, the lawyer must not disclose such information without the informed consent of the insured.[19]

---

18. *Id.* (emphasis added).
19. *Id.*

Thus, ABA Formal Opinion 01-421 is anything other than a model of clarity on disclosure of data to auditors.

Counsel, however, are answerable to their state bar associations and the pronouncements of their state supreme courts, and not the ABA. Thus, counsel must carefully examine their obligations as interpreted by their licensing body.

D. Multiple-Party Representation

1. Identification of the Client and Persons to Whom Duties Are Owed

Just as there is a fine distinction between the concepts of competence and expertise, the identity of the client and a lawyer's corresponding ethical duties are not always clear. For example, some courts have held that only the insured is the client,[20] whereas a number of courts hold that absent a conflict of interest both insurer and insured can be co-clients of the law firm.[21] Though courts have properly referred to the insured as a client, an either/or distinction obscures the identity of those

20. *E.g.*, *Atlanta Int'l Ins. Co. v. Bell*, 475 N.W.2d 294, 297 (Mich. 1991) (though even in this case, the court held that the doctrine of equitable subrogation permits the insurer to bring a malpractice action against the counsel that the insurer hired to defend the insured).

21. *Hartford Ins. Co. of the Midwest v. Koeppel*, 629 F. Supp. 2d 1293, 1299 (M.D. Fla. 2009). Very few jurisdictions preclude a direct legal malpractice claim by an insurer against the lawyer retained to represent an insured.

to whom fiduciary duties are owed,[22] as well as economic reality,[23] and is sometimes plainly inaccurate.[24]

This tension has occasionally spawned litigation (see, for example, *Travelers Ins. Co. v. Lesher*[25] and *Harvey v. Allstate Ins. Co.*).[26]

Like *Lesher*, the *Harvey v. Allstate* court dealt with bad-faith allegations. More specifically, Harvey alleged that she had been sexually harassed and defamed by her employer and its president. The president counterclaimed, alleging defamation. Harvey defended herself for eight months, because Allstate's agent represented the nonexistence of coverage. Eventually, however, Allstate retained counsel with whom it had a long relationship to represent her, rather than, for example, the lawyer who had been representing Harvey or someone else with expertise in defamation and sexual harassment cases. In finding bad faith, the court stated:

---

22. *See Tews Funeral Home, Inc. v. Ohio Cas. Ins. Co.*, 832 F.2d 1037, 1045 (7th Cir. 1987) (stating "an insurer normally controls its insured's defense. Attorneys appointed by the insurer to represent the insured owe fiduciary duties to both the insurer and the insured."). *Tews* was overruled on an unrelated issue in *Nat'l Cycle Co. v. Savoy Reinsurance Co.*, 938 F.2d 61, 64 (7th Cir. 1991).

23. *Purdy v. Pac. Auto. Ins. Co.*, 203 Cal. Rptr. 524, 534 (Cal. Ct. App. 1984) (stating "in reality, the insurer's attorneys may have closer ties with the insurer and more compelling interest in protecting the insurer's position, whether or not it coincides with what is best for the insured."); *USF&G v. Louis A. Rosen Co.*, 585 F.2d 932, 938 n.5 (8th Cir. 1978) ("Even the most optimistic view of human nature requires us to realize that an attorney employed by an insurance company will slant his efforts, perhaps unconsciously, in the interests of his real client—the one who is paying his fee and from whom he hopes to receive future business—the insurance company.").

24. Insurers, for example, can retain the same counsel to represent both the insured and the company. Silver & Syverud, *The Professional Responsibilities of Insurance Defense Lawyers*, 45 DUKE L.J. 255, 273–80 (1995) (insurers can contractually retain counsel to represent insureds and themselves); ABA Formal Op. 96-403 n.2 (Aug. 1996) ("Today, absent a contrary agreement as to the identity of the client, the prevailing view appears to be that the lawyer represents both the insured and the insurer, at least for some purposes.").

25. 231 Cal. Rptr. 791 (Cal. Ct. App. 1986) (finding insurer in bad faith for hiring counsel lacking medical malpractice expertise).

26. 13 F.2d 405 (10th Cir. 1993) (Table). The text of the *Harvey* decision is available at Nos. 92-331, 92-3320, 1993 WL 525695, at *1–5 (10th Cir. Dec. 21, 1993).

> There was ample evidence to support a finding that Allstate acted in bad faith in defending Harvey after April, 1985. Evidence presented at trial showed that Allstate hired an attorney who had no intention of jeopardizing his continuing employment with Allstate. . . . The jury could well have concluded, on the basis of this evidence, that Allstate acted in bad faith in hiring a lawyer who would help them avoid liability rather than a lawyer who would provide an adequate defense, and breached its fiduciary duty to defend Harvey by enlisting this lawyer's help in contesting coverage.[27]

As set forth above, EPL policies cover both the employer and employees. Suits naming the employer and one or more employees, therefore, may be referred to one lawyer for handling. Lawyers could also conceivably be asked to represent the insurer,[28] the employer, and the employee. Counsel, therefore, must always determine whether a joint representation is ethically permissible.[29] This, in turn, requires conscious recognition of the ethical obligations owed to the client(s), which include competent representation,[30] avoidance of conflicts,[31] exercise of independent judgment,[32] and unfettered communication.[33]

2. *EPL Policies and Situations in Which Conflicts Are Not Likely*

"Joint representation of the employer and the employee presents little possibility of future conflict if the nature of the case is such that it is unlikely that the clients will take positions adverse to each other. Such

---

27. *Harvey*, 1993 WL 525695 at *4.

28. This is somewhat more likely in direct-action states such as Louisiana (LA. REV. STAT. § 22:655) and Wisconsin (WIS. ST. § 632.24). It, however, also occurs elsewhere. *See* Silver & Syverud, *supra* note 24.

29. *See supra* notes 3–19 and accompanying text.

30. MODEL RULE OF PROF'L CONDUCT 1.1.

31. MODEL RULE OF PROF'L CONDUCT 1.7.

32. MODEL RULE OF PROF'L CONDUCT 2.1.

33. MODEL RULES OF PROF'L CONDUCT 1.4 and 1.6; *see also* MODEL RULE Ethical Considerations 5-14.

occasions may exist in sex, race, age, disability, religion, or national origin discrimination cases where both parties claim that the action forming the basis for the alleged discrimination was based upon legitimate, non-discriminatory reasons."[34]

The unlikelihood of the existence of conflicts is increased by virtue of jurisprudence holding officers, managers, and supervisors not personally liable for damages.[35] Though in some jurisdictions, whether managerial employees may be held personally liable under the state's antidiscrimination law remains an open question.[36] Labor and employment counsel, nevertheless, should "still explain will be ethically bound to withdraw from the case."[37]

3. EPL Policies and Situations in Which Conflicts Are Somewhat Likely

Harassment claims, whether racial, sexual, or otherwise, are more likely to produce actual or potential conflicts, regardless of jurisprudential developments immunizing officers, managers, and supervisors[38] from personal liability, for three reasons. First, state courts have not fully weighed in on whether they will follow federal jurisprudence on this point.[39] Second, there is no such immunity for claims such as assault, battery, and intentional infliction of emotional distress.[40]

---

34. Doyle & Blumenthal, *The Defendants Perspective: Ethical Considerations in Representing and Counseling Multiple Parties in Employment Litigation*, 10 LAB. LAW. 19, 30 (1994) [hereinafter Doyle & Blumenthal].

35. *See, e.g.*, *Stults v. Conoco*, 76 F.3d 651 (5th Cir. 1996); *EEOC v. AIC Sec. Investigations, Ltd.*, 55 F.3d 1276 (7th Cir. 1995); *Birkbeck v. Marvel Lighting Corp.*, 30 F.3d 507 (4th Cir. 1994); *Grant v. Lone Star Steel*, 21 F.3d 649 (5th Cir. 1994); *Miller v. Maxwell's Int'l*, 991 F.2d 583 (9th Cir. 1993).

36. As of this writing, the issue of supervisory liability under the Maine Human Rights Act is before the Maine Supreme Judicial Court as part of an appeal in *Jamie Fuhrman v. Staples, Inc. et al.*, No. Yor-11-551.

37. Doyle & Blumenthal, *supra* note 34, at 30.

38. *See supra* note 35.

39. Some courts have found supervisors personally liable. *See, e.g.*, *Reno v. Baird*, 67 Cal. Rptr. 671 (Cal. Ct. App. 1997).

40. *E.g.*, *White v. Monsanto* Co., 575 So.2d 381 (La. Ct. App. 1991), *rev'd on other*

Third, assertion of defenses available to employers can conflict with the interests of employees. For example, employers can avoid liability in racially and sexually hostile work environment cases by taking prompt remedial action where the harasser is a co-employee.[41] Counsel representing the employer, therefore, should assert same as a defense if the facts permit. Counsel, however, cannot simultaneously represent both the employer and the accused employee when the accused denies misconduct and believes his or her career has been jeopardized, because the accused employee's interests require counsel to assert that remedial action was unnecessary because of the absence of misconduct.[42]

Similarly, employers sometimes defend sexually hostile work environment cases,[43] arguing that they should not be held liable because

---

grounds, 585 So.2d 1205 (1991). There, a jury cast both the company and a supervisor for $60,000 for intentional infliction of emotional distress. *See also Engrum v. Boise S. Co.*, 527 So.2d 362 (La. Ct. App. 1988) (holding that employee stated a claim for intentional infliction of emotional distress against employer, supervisor, plant manager and co-employees); *Morehouse v. Berkshire Gas Co.*, 989 F. Supp. 54 (D. Mass. 1997) (declining to dismiss plaintiff's IIED claim against co-employee on summary judgment); *Poole v. Copland, Inc.*, 498 S.E.2d 602 (N.C. 1998).

41. *See, e.g., Robinson v. Valmont Indus.*, 238 F.3d 1045 (8th Cir. 2001); *Skidmore v. Precision Printing and Packaging, Inc.*, 188 F.3d 606, 615–16 (5th Cir. 1999); *Indest v. Freeman Decorating, Inc.*, 164 F.3d 258, 263 (5th Cir. 1999).

42. Model Rules of Prof'l Conduct R. 1.7, 1.13, and 2.1; *see also* Model Code of Prof'l Responsibility DC-105 and EC 5-14; Pyburn & Mallery, *Ethical Considerations in the Joint Representation of Supervisors and Employers in Sexual Harassment Cases*, 5 Lab. Law. 115, 121 (1989) ("If at any time it becomes apparent that the supervisor's actions could have in any way been interpreted to create a 'hostile environment,' then the employer should consider disciplining the supervisor to strengthen its defense. An attorney representing both the employer and the supervisor cannot freely and independently advise the employer whether to discipline the supervisor. This conflict may force the attorney to withdraw from the case entirely. In view of this pervasive possibility, there may not be many cases in which an attorney can recommend joint representation in light of the requirements of ABA Model Rule 1.7.").

43. In order to establish a sexually hostile work environment case, plaintiff must show:

a. She (he) belongs to a protected group.
b. She (he) was subject to unwelcome sexual harassment.
c. The harassment was based upon sex.
d. The harassment affected a term, condition, or privilege of employment.
e. The employer knew or should have known of the harassment in question

the employee's alleged misconduct was outside of the course and scope of his or her employment.[44] Given the potential personal liability faced

---

and failed to take proper remedial action.

See, e.g., *Meritor Sav. Bank v. Vinson*, 477 U.S. 57, 66–72 (1986); *Skidmore v. Precision Printing & Packaging, Inc.*, 188 F.3d at 615; *Watts v. Kroger Co.*, 170 F.3d 505, 509 (5th Cir. 1999); *Hall v. Gus Constr. Co., Inc.*, 842 F.2d 1010, 1013 (8th Cir. 1988); *Yates v. Avco Corp.*, 819 F.2d 630, 633 (6th Cir. 1987).

44. At first blush, this seems irrelevant after the decisions in *Burlington Indus. v. Ellerth*, 524 U.S. 742 (1998), and, in particular, *Faragher v. City of Boca Raton*, 524 U.S. 775 (1998). The Eleventh Circuit in *Faragher v. City of Boca Raton*, 111 F.3d 1530 (11th Cir. 1997) (en banc), reversed a judgment in favor of plaintiffs and against the city because, *inter alia*, the lifeguards were not acting within the course and scope of their employment when they sexually harassed Ms. Faragher.

The Supreme Court in *Faragher*, however, reversed and remanded the case to the district court to enter judgment in favor of Ms. Faragher. In so doing, it summarized decisions by courts where employers were not held vicariously liable for sexual harassment by supervisors using agency principles such as whether the conduct occurred within the course and scope of employment. Then, the *Faragher* court added the following:

> An assignment to reconcile the run of the Title VII cases with those just cited would be a taxing one. Here it is enough to recognize that their disparate results do not necessarily reflect wildly varying terms of the particular employment contracts involved, but represent differing judgments about the desirability of holding an employer liable for his subordinates' wayward behavior. In the instances in which there is a genuine question about the employer's responsibility for harmful conduct he did not in fact authorize, a holding that the conduct falls within the scope of employment ultimately expresses a conclusion not of fact but of law. As one eminent authority has observed, the "highly indefinite phrase" is "devoid of meaning in itself" and is "obviously no more than a bare formula to cover the unordered and unauthorized acts of the servant for which it is found to be expedient to charge the master with liability, as well as to exclude other acts for which it is not." . . .
>
> The proper analysis here, then, calls not for a mechanical application of indefinite and malleable factors set forth in the Restate, *see, e.g.*, §§ 219, 228, 229, but rather an inquiry into the reasons that would support a conclusion that harassing behavior ought to be held within the scope of a supervisor's employment, and the reasons for the opposite view. The Restatement itself points to such an approach, as in the commentary that the "ultimate question" in determining the scope of employment is "whether or not it is just that the loss resulting from the servant's acts should be considered as one of the normal risks to be borne by the business in which the servant is employed." *Id.* § 229, Comment a. *See generally Taber v. Maine*, 67 F.3d 1029, 1037 (2d Cir. 1995) ("As the leading Torts treatise has put it, 'the integrating principle' of *respondeat superior is* 'that the employer should be liable for those faults that may be fairly

by the accused employee in such a situation, his or her interests require denial of misdeeds or, alternatively, assertion of the employer's condoning/awareness. Counsel representing the employer cannot advance either argument, thereby necessitating separate representation.[45]

4. Multiple Representation Consent Agreements

Joint representation is still possible even when the clients have potentially differing interests, provided the lawyer has conducted a proper investigation, reached a conclusion that representation is not prohibited under the applicable rules, provides full disclosure to all of the parties, and preferably obtains an execution of an agreement.[46] Multiple representation consent agreements, however, are not a panacea.[47] Rather, full disclosure and consent do not alleviate or lessen counsel's duties

---

> regarded as risks of his business, whether they are committed in furthering it or not'")....

Faragher, 524 U.S. at 796–97.

45. Model Rules of Prof'l Conduct R. 1.1, 1.7, and 2.1.

46. *See Smith v. Daggett Cnty. Bd. of Educ.*, 650 F. Supp. 44 (D. Utah 1986). There, in permitting multiple representation, the court stated:

> There are few situations wherein it is appropriate for a lawyer to represent multiple clients who have potentially differing interests. However, the mere assertion that differing interests may arise is not sufficient to require disqualification of counsel. Where such claims of conflict are made, a lawyer who conducts a full good faith investigation of the basis of the apparent claims and finds such to be implausible, or obtains from each client informed consent after full disclosure, may proceed to represent multiple clients....
>
> In this case it appears that a full investigation was undertaken by counsel regarding the claimed conflict, that a full disclosure was made, wherein all defendants were fully informed, and that all defendants freely consented to be represented by the same counsel. It therefore appears that ... [the law firm] ... properly can represent all the defendants in this litigation. This court is persuaded that the defendants' interests are adequately protected by having been informed of the potential and claimed conflict. Under these circumstances, defendants should be allowed to determine the question of joint representation for themselves.... Accordingly, plaintiff's Motion to Disqualify is denied. (Footnotes omitted) (Citations omitted).

Id. at 47.

47. Doyle & Blumenthal, *supra* note 34, at 29–33. Doyle and Blumenthal's sample Multiple Representation Agreement appears at Appendix B.

to his or her *clients*,[48] thereby emphasizing the need for an errorless investigation and twenty-twenty foreseeability or general avoidance of joint representations.

5. Maintaining Confidences and Informing Clients

Opinion 08-450[49]

Maintenance of a client's confidence is a clear obligation.[50] Keeping a client reasonably informed is also a clear ethical duty.[51] Joint representations can bring these principles into conflict and require rejection of joint representation *ab initio.*

Because the scope of the "implied authority" granted in rule 1.6(a) to reveal confidential information "to carry out a representation" applies separately and exclusively to each representation the lawyer has undertaken, a conflict of interest arises when the lawyer recognizes the necessity of revealing confidential information relating to one client in order effectively to carry out the representation of another. In such a circumstance, the lawyer would be required to withdraw from representing one or both of his or her clients.[52]

Formal Opinion 08-450 identifies two points at which the potential problem of confidential information involving multiple clients must be addressed. The first of course is when the joint representation is undertaken.[53] Insureds may not understand the coverage issues that can arise when a lawyer represents both the insurer and the insured. In order to obtain informed consent regarding the potential for a conflict of interest, the lawyer should address as part of informed consent both clients'

---

48. *E.g.*, Cal. St. Bar. Comm. Prof. Resp., Ethics Op. 1995-139, 1995 WL 25539.

49. ABA Formal Op. 08-450 (Apr. 2008), *Confidentiality When Lawyer Represents Multiple Clients in the Same or Related Matters.*

50. Model Rules of Prof'l Conduct R. 1.6.

51. Model Rules of Prof'l Conduct R. 1.4.

52. ABA Formal Op. 08-450 (Apr. 2008) (citing Rule 1.6(a)).

53. *Id.* (resolving whether both the client and insurer are represented by the lawyer need not be resolved to determine the lawyer's duty with regard to the confidential information of the insured).

expectations relating to confidentiality.[54] The second point in time at which the lawyer must address issues of confidentiality arises when the lawyer learns that disclosure to one client will be harmful to the other client's interest. As an example, the insured may disclose information that if shared with the insurer might result in the declination of insurance coverage. Rule 1.6 prohibits disclosure of the confidential information to the insurer. However, the lawyer's withholding the information from the insurer may violate Rule 1.4.[55] Whether the lawyer has an obligation to disclose this information to the insurer must be resolved prior to moving forward. If such disclosure is required, then the lawyer must withdraw from representation of both clients.[56]

E. Conflicts Between Insurers and Insureds Arising Out of Different Interests

1. An Introduction

An insurer's duty to defend is broader than its duty to indemnify.[57] Thus, coverage disputes under EPL policies can arise where there are allegedly covered and noncovered claim(s) and/or where plaintiff asserts

54. *Id.*

55. *Id.*

56. *Id.*; *see also* ABA Comm. on Ethics & Prof'l Responsibility, Informal Op. 1476 (1981). There, a lawyer represented both the employer and an employee. The employee confided that he was acting outside of the course and scope of his employment at the time of the accident, and counsel sought the ABA's advice. The ABA committee counseled nondisclosure and withdrawal from representing both clients. *See also* Ethics Op. 1995-139, 1995 WL 255397 (Cal. St. Bar Comm. Prof. Resp.) ("Where counsel learns that the intentional wrongful acts of insured have damaged insurer, such as where insurer has accepted coverage based on insured's fraudulent assertions, or where the insured has concealed material facts from the insurer, not only does a conflict of interest exist, but the member has learned that the insured/client has acted in a manner injurious to the insurer. When these circumstances are viewed together, withdrawal is required. . . . Moreover, in such circumstances, failure to withdraw would involve the lawyer, who is billing the insurer, in the perpetuation of insured's fraudulent efforts to have insurer pay defense costs."). Breach of client confidences has also given rise to professional liability actions in such situations. *Tante v. Herring*, 453 S.E.2d 686, 687–88 (Ga. 1994); *Owen v. Pringle*, 621 So.2d 668, 671 (Miss. 1993).

57. *E.g.*, *Sanders v. Wysocki*, 631 So.2d 1330, 1335 (La. Ct. App. 1994). *See also* chapters 2 and 3.

entitlement to punitive and/or liquidated damages and state law and/or the policy language prohibits or excludes coverage.[58] Likewise, coverage disputes can arise out of settlement of, as well as failure to settle, claims within policy limits. Defense counsel may confront several ethical issues arising out of these scenarios, as one can see below.

2. *Defense Dilemmas Arising Out of the Existence of Covered and Noncovered Claims*

Assume plaintiffs are a fifty-year-old married male and his wife. He is hired by John Doe of ABC Company. Within several months, Doe decides the husband is a poor employee and discharges him. Around the same time, Doe is upset with the decision of the wife, who works for another company. Doe complains. Doe's comments allegedly result in the wife's termination.

Both file suit. He alleges an ADEA violation. She alleges tortious interference with a contract. The husband's claim is covered by the EPL policy; the wife's is not, because she was not an employee of the insured. The insurer, nevertheless, has a duty to defend the entire suit.

Defense counsel can immediately seek dismissal of the covered claim based on the "same actor inference."[59] If counsel does, however, the insured's coverage ceases and the insured must assume defense costs. If counsel does not, he or she potentially jeopardizes his or her long-term relationship with the insurer and subjects the client to a potential and adverse ADEA judgment (unless, of course, the insurer successfully files an action making the same argument and seeking a declaration of noncoverage).[60]

---

58. *See supra* note 3.

59. *E.g., Brown v.* CSC *Logic, Inc.*, 82 F.3d 651, 657–58 (5th Cir. 1996); *see also Burmaster v. Overnite Transp. Co.*, 61 F.3d 461, 463–64 (6th Cir. 1995), *cert. denied*, 116 S. Ct. 785 (1996); *Proud v. Stone*, 945 F.2d 796, 797 (4th Cir. 1991); *Lowe v. J. B. Hunt Transp. Inc.*, 963 F.2d 173, 174 (8th Cir. 1992).

60. *Cf. Nandorf Inc. v. CNA Ins. Cos.*, 479 N.E.2d 988, 993 (Ill. App. Ct. 1985) (stating "CNA also failed to pursue the preferable course of filing a declaratory judgment action as soon as the coverage issue arose. . . .").

Similarly, for example, assume that plaintiff sues DEF Company for failure to pay wages and intentional infliction of emotional distress (IIED) two years after his termination. The wage claim is arguably not covered,[61] whereas the IIED claim is. The IIED claim, however, is subject to a one-year statute of limitations,[62] whereas the wage claim prescribes in three years.[63]

Defense counsel can seek dismissal of the untimely *but covered* claim. Again, however, if counsel does, the insured's coverage ceases and the insured must assume all defense costs. Again, if he or she does not, counsel potentially jeopardizes his or her long-term relationship with the insurer and subjects his or her clients to a potential judgment on an untimely claim.

These scenarios raise very difficult issues, because there are no bright lines to guide counsel, even though insurers would probably issue a "reservation of rights" letter, thereby reducing the number of clients.[64] Compare Model Rule 1.1 (requiring "competent representation. . . .") with Model Rule 2.1 (requiring exercise of "independent professional judgment").

The Florida State Bar Association offered an opinion on a close set of facts. More specifically, Ethics Opinion 97-1[65] addressed a situation in which the insurer instructed defense counsel to seek partial summary judgment on a negligence claim that was covered. Counsel, realizing the remaining breach of contract claim was not covered, concluded that the value of the "defense" exceeded the reduction of potential damages that would result from the granting of the proposed motion.

---

61. It is not a wrongful act. It may also be expressly excluded.

62. IIED is a tort. Delictual claims prescribe in Louisiana after one year. LA. CIV. CODE art. 3492.

63. LA. CIV. CODE art. 3494.

64. Counsel, otherwise, should reject joint representation. *Storm Drilling Co. v. Atl. Richfield Co.*, 386 F. Supp. 830, 832 (E.D. La. 1974) (stating "the same attorney may not represent both the insured and the insurer where the insurer denies coverage or reserves its right to do subsequently").

65. 1997 WL 461086 (Fla. St. Bar. Assn.).

The bar, therefore, told him to withdraw unless the insurer retracted its instruction.[66]

3. Failure to Settle Within Authorized Limits

Defense counsel have extended but, on occasion, not used their full settlement authority. Failure to exhaust settlement authority is arguably unethical[67] and has triggered professional liability claims.[68]

4. Issues Arising Out of Settlements Within Policy Limits

At first blush, it is seemingly inconceivable that disputes could arise out of a settlement within policy limits. But they have.

For example, assume the insured does not want to settle because it wants to vindicate a policy or reputation, and the plaintiff offers to settle well within policy limits and for a reasonable price. Likewise, assume plaintiff offers to settle for a reasonable sum *and* reinstatement but the employer does not want to reinstate plaintiff. EPL policy language, jurisprudence, and ethical guidelines place defense counsel between a rock and a hard place.

More specifically, policies and jurisprudence afford insurers the right to settle without the consent of the insured, even within the self-insured retention and/or deductible.[69] Given same, one would think that counsel could, at the insurer's direction, settle. Not necessarily.

Suppose the client does not want to settle. Defense counsel then must (1) abide by his or her client's (clients') decisions concerning the objectives of representation,"[70] (2) "explain a matter to the extent

---

66. *Id.*

67. *See* Model Rules of Prof'l Conduct R. 1.2 (requiring counsel "to abide by a client's decision concerning the objectives of representation . . . ."), 1.4 (requiring counsel to keep client informed and to permit client to make informed decision), and 1.1 (requiring competent representation).

68. *Lysick v. Walcom*, 65 Cal. Rptr. 406 (Cal. Ct. App. 1968).

69. *See Am. Home Assurance Co. v. Hermann's Warehouse Corp.*, 563 A.2d 444 (N.J. 1989); *Cas. Ins. Co. v. Town & Country Pre-School Nursery, Inc.*, 498 N.E.2d 1177 (Ill. App. Ct. 1986).

70. Model Rules of Prof'l Conduct R. 1.2(a).

necessary to permit the client to make informed decision . . . ,"[71] and (3) avoid conflicts.[72]

ABA Formal Opinion 96-403 directly addresses counsel's ethical obligations in this situation. According to the ABA,

> [i]f a lawyer for an insured knows that the insured objects to a settlement the lawyer may not settle the claim against the insured at the direction of the insurer, without giving the insured an opportunity to reject the defense offered by the insurer and to assume responsibility for his own defense at his own expense.[73]

Given the ethical opinion described above, it is not surprising that lawyers have been held liable when they participate in settlement against the wishes of their client(s).[74]

The difficulties faced by defense counsel are bad enough in this situation, even though there are jurisprudential and ethical rules. However, they offer little guidance about whether the insurer can achieve a settlement that includes reinstatement when the insured resists reinstatement, because cases affording the insurer an unequivocal right to settle do not require the insured to do anything, much less reinstate an employee. Here, it is not so clear that the insurer has the right to settle or that the defense counsel must withdraw.[75] In fact, despite the preference

71. Model Rules of Prof'l Conduct R. 1.4(b).

72. Model Rules of Prof'l Conduct R. 1.7.

73. ABA Formal Op. 96-403 (Aug. 1996).

74. *Rogers v. Robison, Masters, Ryan, Brummund & Belom*, 392 N.E.2d 1365 (Ill. App. Ct. 1979), *aff'd*, 407 N.E.2d 47 (1980); *Lieberman v. Emp'rs Ins. of Wausau*, 419 A.2d 417, 425 (N.J. 1980).

75. *Cf.* ABA Formal Op. 96-403 (Aug. 1996) (stating "the lawyer might remind the insured that the policy gives the insurer the right to control the defense and settle the claim without the consent of the insured or that rejecting the proposed settlement might result in a forfeiture of his rights under the policy. Ultimately, however, . . . the insured retains the power to reject the defense offered by the insurer . . . and to assume the risk and expense of his own defense. Rule 1.16"); *Caplan v. Fellheimer*, 68 F.3d 828, 838–40 (3d Cir. 1995) (stating insured unlikely to incur damages from exercise of settlement rights).

for reinstatement,[76] it seems unlikely to this author that courts would favor the insured, given the absence of specific policy language[77] and the principle that ambiguities are construed against the insurer.[78]

5. Bad Faith: Refusals to Settle Within Policy Limits

a. Typical Scenarios

Many claims facially seek damages in excess of policy limits, even when punitive damages are not sought or are sought and recoverable. Other claims may seek liquidated and/or punitive damages where neither is covered.

Insurers typically send reservation of rights letters in the scenarios described above, thereby informing insureds of potential coverage gaps.[79] Insurers cannot retain the same counsel to represent both the insurer and the insured in this situation, thereby clearly defining the client. Even this delineation of duties and loyalty, however, does not define or describe defense counsel's duties, given the potential litigation in the future between insurer and insured(s).

b. Bad-Faith Claims: A Simplified Introduction[80]

Punitive damages were initially disfavored.[81] Courts, however, then recognized tort claims for breach of contract in addition to the contractual action in some cases.[82] Next, courts slowly began to read a covenant of good faith and fair dealing into contracts so that one party could not unreasonably deny the benefit of the contract to the other

---

76. *Weaver*, 66 F.3d at 88.

77. *But cf. supra* note 72. Exclusions cover claims *solely* seeking reinstatement.

78. *See, e.g.*, *Pinckney Cmmty. Sch. v. Cont'l Cas. Co.*, 540 N.W.2d 748, 751 (Mich. Ct. App. 1995); *see also Phillips Home Builders, Inc. v. Travelers Ins. Co.*, 700 A.2d 127, 129 (Del. 1997); *Am. Stakes Ins. Co. v. Kiger*, 662 N.E.2d 945, 947 (Ind. 1996); *N. Sec. Ins. Co. v. Hatch*, 683 A.2d 392, 394 (Vt. 1997).

79. *E.g.*, *Nandorf Inc. v. CNA Ins. Cos.*, 479 N.E.2d 988 (Ill. App. Ct. 1985).

80. Bad-faith jurisprudence is a complex practice area, and one cannot do it much justice in this context. The following represents a simplistic summary to facilitate the labor and employment counsel's understanding of the area.

81. *Hadley v. Baxendale*, 156 Eng. Rep. 145 (Exch. 1854).

82. *E.g.*, *Welborn v. Dixon*, 49 S.E. 232, 234 (S.C. 1904) (punitive damages available in breach of contract action where a fraudulent act accompanied the breach).

party.[83] Subsequently, courts and legislatures combined the contractual principle of an implied obligation of good faith and fair dealing with tort principles.[84] Next, courts and legislatures recognized bad-faith claims in first-party cases.[85] Finally, unfair settlement practices claims were recognized.[86]

c. Theoretical Basis (Justification for) Third-Party Bad-Faith Actions[87]

The insured naturally desires the insurer to settle a case in which he, she, or, it faces a judgment in an amount exceeding policy limits. The insurer, however, has nothing to lose by rejecting a policy limits settlement offer and trying the case, because if it loses, its liability is policy limits *in absence of some other basis of liability.*[88]

---

83. *See, e.g.*, LA. CIV. CODE art. 1983; S. WILLSTON, A TREATISE ON THE LAW OF CONTRACTS § 670 (3d Ed. 1961); RESTATEMENT (SECOND) OF CONTRACTS § 205 (1981).

84. LA. REV. STAT. § 22:658; *G. A. Stowers Furniture Co. v. Am. Indem. Co.*, 15 S.W.2d 544, 547 (Tex. App. 1929) (insurer "ought to be held to that degree of care and diligence which an ordinary prudent person would exercise in the management of his own business; and if an ordinary prudent person . . . as viewed from the standpoint of the assured, would have settled the case, and [the insurer] failed or refused to do so, then the agent, which in this case is the indemnity company, should respond in damages"); *see also Home Indem. Co. v. Snowden*, 264 S.W.2d 642 (Ark. 1954).

85. *E.g.*, LA. REV. STAT. § 22:656–58; *Gruenberg v. Aetna Ins. Co.*, 510 P.2d 1032 (Cal. 1973) (tort claim by the insured against the insurer for breach of the implied obligation of good faith and fair dealing recognized where the insurer conspired to deprive plaintiff of benefits provided in several fire insurance policies); *see also Aetna Cas. & Sur. Co. v. Broadway Arms Corp.*, 664 S.W.2d 463 (Ark. 1984).

86. *E.g.*, LA. REV. STAT. § 22:1220; TEX. INS. CODE art. 21.21-2.

87. Again, the following is a simplistic summary to facilitate labor and employment counsel's understanding of the area.

88. *Rova Farms Resort, Inc. v. Investors Ins.* Co., 323 A.2d 495, 508 (N.J. 1974). Specifically, the court stated:

> Since an insurer serves only its own interests by declining to compromise within the insurance coverage, a decision not to settle is perforce a selfish one. In attempting to save some of its own money on the policy, the company necessarily and automatically exposes the insured to the risk of an excess judgment.
>
> Moreover the rule which permits a carrier to escape liability for excess unless its decision to go to trial is marred by dishonesty, bad faith or negligence creates an anomalous situation for insureds. Where a settlement opportunity exists, the more faultless the client seems to have been the

d. Theoretical Basis (Justification for) First-Party Bad-Faith Claims
Courts have perceived that insurers have, can, and/or will resist payment of legitimate claims, because there is an incentive to resist in the absence of a penalty for resisting legitimate claims.[89] Courts, therefore, have authorized the basis of first-party bad-faith claims to

(1) Redress an imbalance of relative bargaining power;[90]
(2) Protect the insured's reasonable expectations;[91]
(3) Create a counterweight to existing incentives for insurers to delay or deny payment of claims.[92]

---

more feasibly he may be subjected by the company to a trial of the case and all the dangers it entails. In the case of an obviously blameworthy client, the carrier would normally take advantage of a settlement opportunity within policy limits since any other disposition would be unduly optimistic. The least blameworthy insured, however, may more readily be delivered to face the risk of excess judgment, since a refusal to compromise a case thought to be a "no liability" case would not be regarded as unreasonable. Thus, in those cases where a compromise may be effected within policy limits the more innocent an insured appears to be, the worse position he is in and the more he is exposed to loss.

Additionally, even the rule requiring the carrier to form its judgment as though it alone were liable for the entire risk may be polluted by institutional considerations which ignore the interests of the specific insured involved.... These considerations may extend to a purpose to keep future settlement costs down, to numb the public's claim-consciousness, to create a conservative image for the discouragement of future claimants or to establish favorable precedents, none of which purposes has anything to do with the protection of the particular insured at hand. Such efforts, it might be hoped, would result in overall savings to the company by discouraging the pressing of marginal claims or by creating a body of low-verdict cases which could be used as a bargaining tool in settling subsequent claims.... Institutional interests of this nature might be pursued by carriers whether or not they were liable for the entire amount of a specific adverse verdict; yet it is generally the insured in the particular case who has had to bear the burden of any excess loss stemming from such an "institutional" decision not to settle.

89. *Standard Life Ins. Co. v. Veal*, 354 So.2d 239, 248 (Miss. 1977).

90. *Hiatt v. Schreiber*, 599 F. Supp. 1142, 1146 (D. Colo. 1984). *But see* Bankers Blanket Bond jurisprudence such as *First Nat'l Bank of Louisville v. Lustig*, No. 87-5488, c/w 88-1682 and 89-202 at p. 3 (E.D. La. 1989); *Bradley Bank v. Hartford Accident & Indem. Co.*, 562 F. Supp. 241, 243 (W.D. Wis. 1983); *State Bank v. Capital Indem. Corp.*, 214 N.W.2d 42 (Wis. 1974).

91. *Noble v. Nat'l Am. Life Ins. Co.*, 624 P.2d 866, 867–68 (Ariz. 1981).

92. *DiSalvatore v. Aetna Cas. & Sur. Co.*, 624 F. Supp. 541, 543 (D.N.J. 1986); *see*

e. The Insurer Is Not the Client

Insurers will issue a reservation of rights letter and retain separate counsel. Defense counsel will be assigned to defend the claim on the merits and will not be paid to contest coverage issues.

f. Defense Counsel's Duties to the Insured: Do They Require or Include Preservation and/or Preparation of a Bad-Faith Claim, and Reporting Requirements?

The insurer will not pay counsel to contest coverage. It is, however, in the insured's interest to have the insurer fund a settlement and otherwise be in a position to pay in excess of policy limits should such a judgment be issued. How far can counsel go in his or her role and still meet his or her ethical and contractual obligations?

Defense counsel cannot relate *facts* harmful to his or her client.[93] Insurers, however, and particularly given their bad-faith exposure, have a duty to investigate[94] and, accordingly, generally request defense counsel's assessment of liability and damages.[95]

Defense counsel, in fact, has a fiduciary duty here to both the carrier and the insured to evaluate the case.[96] Evaluations, of course, are not facts, but they entail relation of facts that collectively could convince an insurer that a judgment in excess of policy limits is unlikely/unjustified or likely/justified. Stated differently, a conservative evaluation may subject the client to a trial and a judgment perhaps in excess of policy

---

also Arnold v. Nat'l Cnty. Mut. Fire Ins. Co., 725 S.W.2d 165, 167 (Tex. 1987).

93. *Parsons v. Cont'l Nat'l. Am. Grp.*, 550 P.2d 94 (Ariz. 1976); *see also* MODEL RULES OF PROF'L CONDUCT 1.6 and Ethical Considerations 5-14.

94. *Betts v. Allstate Ins. Co.*, 201 Cal. Rptr. 528, 539 (Cal. Ct. App. 1984) ("an insurer may breach the covenant of good faith and fair dealing by failing to properly investigate its insured's claim").

95. *Betts*, 201 Cal. Reptr. at 540 (in context of affirming a judgment holding insurer in bad faith for rejecting settlement within policy limits and defense counsel liable for negligence, court characterized as "highly questionable" Allstate's practice of "not putting adverse facts in writing").

96. *Emp'rs Ins. of Wausau v. Albert D. Seeno Const. Co.*, 692 F. Supp. 1150, 1158 (N.D. Cal. 1988).

limits, whereas a generous evaluation, which is in the client's interest, may impair his or her relationship with the insured.[97]

Given the fiduciary duties owed the insurer and the insured, defense counsel should, to the best of his or her ability, call it straight and suggest if appropriate in strong terms that the insured retain independent coverage counsel, that is, counsel to construct a potential bad-faith claim. Nothing, moreover, prohibits defense counsel from conveying facts and legal issues to the insured's coverage counsel so that coverage counsel can understand the case and represent the insured.

V. Conclusion

Labor and employment lawyers will have to become accustomed to working within the tri-partite relationship and the sometimes very tricky ethical issues accompanying the relationship between counsel, insureds, and carriers. Knowledge and understanding of ethical rules regarding (1) permissible and impermissible disclosures, (2) the existence of potential conflicts between employers and individuals, and (3) bad-faith law and the duties of loyalty in the context of bad-faith claims will be crucial.

97. In fact, a prior relationship with the insurer may have resulted in opinion letters and/or other communications conflicting with a position that counsel needs to advance in order to protect the interests of the client.

CHAPTER 12 APPENDIX A

Rule 1.1 Competence

A lawyer shall provide competent representation to a client. Competent representation requires the legal knowledge, skill, thoroughness, and preparation reasonably necessary for the representation.

Rule 1.2 Scope of Representation

(a). Subject to paragraphs (c) and (d), a lawyer shall abide by a client's decisions concerning the objectives of representation and, as required by Rule 1.4, shall consult with the client as to the means by which they are to be pursued. A lawyer may take such action on behalf of the client as is impliedly authorized to carry out the representation. A lawyer shall abide by a client's decision whether to settle a matter. . . .

Rule 1.4 Communication

(a) A lawyer shall:

(1) promptly inform the client of any decision or circumstance with respect to which the client's informed consent, as defined in Rule 1.0(e), is required by these Rules;

(2) reasonably consult with the client about the means by which the client's objectives are to be accomplished;

(3) keep the client reasonably informed about the status of the matter;

(4) promptly comply with reasonable requests for information;

* * *

(b) A lawyer shall explain a matter to the extent reasonably necessary to permit the client to make informed decisions regarding the representation.

Rule 1.6 Confidentiality of Information

(a) A lawyer shall not reveal information relating to the representation of a client unless the client gives informed consent, the disclosure is impliedly authorized in order to carry out the representation or the disclosure is permitted by paragraph (b).

* * *

Rule 1.7 Conflict of Interest: Current Clients

(a) Except as provided in paragraph (b), a lawyer shall not represent a client if the representation involves a concurrent conflict of interest. A concurrent conflict of interest exists if:

(1) the representation of one client will be directly adverse to another client; or

(2) there is a significant risk that the representation of one or more clients will be materially limited by the lawyer's responsibilities to another client, a former client or a third person or by a personal interest of the lawyer.

(b) Notwithstanding the existence of a concurrent conflict of interest under paragraph (a), a lawyer may represent a client if:

(1) the lawyer reasonably believes that the lawyer will be able to provide competent and diligent representation to each affected client;

(2) the representation is not prohibited by law;

(3) the representation does not involve the assertion of a claim by one client against another client represented by the lawyer in the same litigation or other proceeding before a tribunal; and

(4) each affected client gives informed consent, confirmed in writing.

Rule 1.8 Conflict of Interest: Prohibited Transactions

* * *

(b) A lawyer shall not use information relating to representation of a client to the disadvantage of the client unless the client gives informed consent, except as permitted or required by these Rules.

* * *

(f) A lawyer shall not accept compensation for representing a client from one other than the client unless:

(1) the client gives informed consent;

(2) there is no interference with the lawyer's independence of professional judgment or with the client-lawyer relationship;[1] and

1. "A lawyer may be paid from a source other than the client, if the client is informed of the fact and consents and the arrangement does not compromise the lawyer's duty of loyalty to the client. See Rule 1.8(f). For example, when an insurer and its insured have conflicting interests in a matter arising from a liability insurance agreement, and the insurer is required to provide a special counsel for the insured, the arrangement

(3) information relating to representation of a client is protected as required by Rule 1.6.

Rule 1.13 Organization as Client

(a) A lawyer employed or retained by an organization represents the organization acting through its duly authorized constituents.

***

(f) In dealing with an organization's directors, officers, employees, members, shareholders, or other constituents, a lawyer shall explain the identity of the client when it is apparent that the organization's interests are adverse to those of the constituents with whom the lawyer is dealing.

(g) A lawyer representing an organization may also represent any of its directors, officers, employees, members, shareholders, or other constituents, subject to the provisions of Rule 1.7. If the organization's consent to the dual representation is required by Rule 1.7, the consent shall be given by an appropriate official of the organization other than the individual who is to be represented, or by the shareholders.

Rule 1.16 Declining or Terminating Representation

(a) Except as stated in paragraph (c), a lawyer shall not represent a client or, where representation has commenced, shall withdraw from the representation of a client if:

(1) the representation will result in violation of the rules of professional conduct or other law; . . .

---

should assure the special counsel's professional independence." *See* Comment to MODEL RULE OF PROF'L CONDUCT 1.7, "Interest of Person Paying for a Lawyer's Service."

***

(b) Except as stated in paragraph (c), a lawyer may withdraw from representing a client if:

. . .

(7) other good cause for withdrawal exists.

Rule 2.1 Advisor

In representing a client, a lawyer shall exercise independent professional judgment and render candid advice. In rendering advice, a lawyer may refer not only to law but to other considerations such as moral, economic, social, and political factors that may be relevant to the client's situation.

Rule 3.2 Expediting Litigation

A lawyer shall make reasonable efforts to expedite litigation consistent with the interests of the client.

Model Code EC 5-14

Maintaining the independence of professional judgment required of a lawyer precludes his acceptance or continuation of employment that will adversely affect his judgment on behalf of or dilute his loyalty to a client. This problem arises whenever a lawyer is asked to represent two or more clients who may have differing interests, whether such interests be conflicting, inconsistent, diverse, or otherwise discordant.

Model Code EC 5-15

If a lawyer is requested to undertake or to continue representation of multiple clients having potentially differing interests, he must weigh carefully the possibility that his judgment may be impaired or his loyalty divided if he accepts or continues the employment. He should resolve all doubts against the propriety of the representation. A lawyer should never represent in litigation multiple clients with differing interests; and there are few situations in which he would be justified in representing in litigation multiple clients with potentially differing interests. If a lawyer accepted such employment and the interests did become actually differing, he would have to withdraw from employment with likelihood of resulting hardship on the clients; and for this reason it is preferable that he refuse the employment initially. On the other hand, there are many instances in which a lawyer may properly serve multiple clients having potentially differing interests in matters not involving litigation. If the interests vary only slightly, it is generally likely that the lawyer will not be subjected to an adverse influence and that he can retain his independent judgment on behalf of each client; and if the interests become differing, withdrawal is less likely to have a disruptive effect upon the causes of his clients.

Model Code EC 5-16

In those instances in which a lawyer is justified in representing two or more clients having differing interests, it is nevertheless essential that each client be given the opportunity to evaluate his need for representation free of any potential conflict and to obtain other counsel if he so desires. Thus before a lawyer may represent multiple clients, he should explain fully to each client the implications of the common representation and should accept or continue employment only if the clients consent. If there are present other circumstances that might cause any of the multiple clients to question the undivided loyalty of the lawyer, he should also advise all of the clients of those circumstances.

Model Code EC 5-17

Typically recurring situations involving potentially differing interests are those in which a lawyer is asked to represent co-defendants in a criminal case, co-plaintiffs in a personal injury case, an insured and his insurer, and beneficiaries of the estate of a decedent. Whether a lawyer can fairly and adequately protect the interests of multiple clients in these similar situations depends upon an analysis of each case. In certain circumstances, there may exist little chance of the judgment of the lawyer being adversely affected by the slight possibility that the interests will become actually differing; in other circumstances, the chance of adverse effect upon his judgment is not unlikely.

Model Code DR 5-105

* * *

> (b) A lawyer shall not continue multiple employment if the exercise of his independent professional judgment in behalf of a client will be or is likely to be adversely affected by his representation of another client, . . . except to the extent permitted under DR 5-105(C).

APPENDIX 12B
Sample Multiple Representation Agreement

Based upon the agreement between LAWYER and EMPLOYER-CLIENT 1, EMPLOYEE-CLIENT 2, and EMPLOYEE-CLIENT 3, the terms of the agreement regarding the multiple representation of EMPLOYER-CLIENT 1, EMPLOYEE-CLIENT 2, and EMPLOYEE-CLIENT 3 by LAWYER and LAW FIRM are reflected herein:

(1). EMPLOYER-CLIENT 1, EMPLOYEE-CLIENT 2, and EMPLOYEE-CLIENT 3 hereby consent and agree to each of the others being represented by LAWYER and LAW FIRM in defense of the action styled, Civil Action No.

United States District Court, District of
Division.

(2). EMPLOYER-CLIENT 1, EMPLOYEE-CLIENT 2, and EMPLOYEE-CLIENT 3 acknowledge and agree that any communications between either EMPLOYER-CLIENT 1, EMPLOYEE-CLIENT 2, and EMPLOYEE-CLIENT 3 and LAWYER and LAW FIRM will be treated as strictly confidential under the attorney-client privilege, and may not be disclosed to third parties without consent. EMPLOYER-CLIENT 1, EMPLOYEE-CLIENT 2, and EMPLOYEE-CLIENT 3 acknowledge and agree that communications between either EMPLOYER-CLIENT 1, EMPLOYEE-CLIENT 2, or EMPLOYEE-CLIENT 3 and LAWYER and LAW FIRM may be disclosed to either EMPLOYER-CLIENT 1, EMPLOYEE-CLIENT 2, or EMPLOYEE-CLIENT 3 to the extent such information is germane to the defense. EMPLOYER-CLIENT 1, EMPLOYEE-CLIENT 2, and EMPLOYEE-CLIENT 3 acknowledge and agree that while all communications between EMPLOYER-CLIENT 1, EMPLOYEE-CLIENT 2, or EMPLOYEE-CLIENT 3 and LAWYER or LAW FIRM remain privileged during the course of the multiple representation, such communications may lose their privileged character if offered in a subsequent legal proceeding in which any of EMPLOYER-CLIENT 1, EMPLOYEE-CLIENT 2, or EMPLOYEE-CLIENT 3 are adversaries.

(3). EMPLOYER-CLIENT 1, EMPLOYEE-CLIENT 2, and EMPLOYEE-CLIENT 3 acknowledge and agree that there exists the possibility that a conflict of interest may arise in the course of the multiple representation by LAWYER and LAW FIRM. EMPLOYER-CLIENT 1, EMPLOYEE-CLIENT 2, and EMPLOYEE-CLIENT 3 acknowledge and agree that in the event a conflict of interest arises regarding their multiple representation by LAWYER and LAW FIRM, then LAWYER and LAW FIRM will withdraw from the representation of EMPLOYER-CLIENT 1, EMPLOYEE-CLIENT 2, and/or EMPLOYEE-CLIENT 3.

(4). EMPLOYEE-CLIENT 2 and EMPLOYEE-CLIENT 3 acknowledge and agree that if LAWYER and LAW FIRM withdraw as either or both of their lawyers, that LAWYER and LAW FIRM may continue to represent EMPLOYER-CLIENT 1 even if such representation is contrary to either EMPLOYEE-CLIENT 2's or EMPLOYEE-CLIENT 3's interests.

(5). EMPLOYER-CLIENT 1, EMPLOYEE-CLIENT 2, and EMPLOYEE-CLIENT 3 acknowledge and agree that in the event a conflict of interest arises regarding the multiple representation by LAWYER and LAW FIRM, that a court may nevertheless disqualify LAWYER and LAW FIRM from continuing its representation of either EMPLOYER-CLIENT 1, EMPLOYEE-CLIENT 2, or EMPLOYEE-CLIENT 3, notwithstanding the terms of this agreement.

(6). EMPLOYER-CLIENT 1, EMPLOYEE-CLIENT 2, and EMPLOYEE-CLIENT 3 acknowledge and agree that, prior to entering this agreement, they have had an opportunity to seek the advice of independent counsel (not LAWYER or LAW FIRM) regarding the propriety of entering this agreement.

THE UNDERSIGNED HAVE CAREFULLY READ THE CONTENTS OF THE FOREGOING AGREEMENT, WAIVE ANY POTENTIAL CONFLICTS, UNDERSTAND THAT THEY EACH HAVE THE OPPORTUNITY TO SEEK INDEPENDENT COUNSEL REGARDING THE PROPRIETY OF ENTERING THIS AGREEMENT, AND AGREE UNCONDITIONALLY TO THE TERMS AND CONDITIONS SET FORTH HEREIN.

EMPLOYER-CLIENT 1____________ Date By:____________
EMPLOYEE-CLIENT 2____________ Date ____________
EMPLOYEE-CLIENT 3____________ Date____________
LAW FIRM____________Date By:____________ Lawyer

Table of Cases

Case names are alphabetized letter-by-letter (e.g., "Newcomb" precedes "New Hampshire").

A

B

C

D

E

F

G

H

I

J

K

L

Lineberry v. State Farm Fire & Cas. Co., 885 F. Supp. 1095 (M.D. Tenn. 1995) . . . 79n35

Lockard v. Pizza Hut, Inc., 162 F.3d 1062 (10th Cir. 1998) . . . 278n70

Logan v. Kautex Textron N. Am., 259 F.3d 635 (7th Cir. 2001) . . . 231n28

Lore v. City of Syracuse, 670 F.3d 127 (2d Cir. 2012) . . . 232–233, 232n32

Lowe v. J. B. Hunt Transp. Inc., 963 F.2d 173 (8th Cir. 1992) . . . 442n59

Lowry v. Standard Oil Co., 146 P.2d 57 (Cal. Ct. App. 1944) . . . 258n167

Loyola Marymount Univ. v. Hartford Accident and Indem. Co., 271 Cal. Rptr. 528 (Cal. Ct. App. 1990) . . . 86, 86nn57–58

Luciano v. Olsten Corp., 110 F.3d 210 (2d Cir. 1997) . . . 295n156, 296n159, 296n161

Luri v. Republic Servs., Inc., 953 N.E.2d 859 (Ohio Ct. App. 2011) . . . 178n119

Lurie v. Mid-Atl. Permanente Med. Group, P.C., 589 F. Supp. 2d 21 (D.D.C. 2008) . . . 160n38

Lysick v. Walcom, 65 Cal. Rptr. 406 (Cal. Ct. App. 1968) . . . 444n68

M

Mace v. Charleston Area Med. Ctr. Found., 422 S.E.2d 624 (W. Va. 1992) . . . 252n131

Mack v. Nationwide Mut. Fire Ins. Co., 517 S.E.2d 839 (Ga. Ct. App. 1999) . . . 80n37

Madison v. IBP, Inc., 330 F.3d 1051 (8th Cir. 2003) . . . 289n128

Maiden v. APA Transp. Corp., No. C-1-00-883, 2002 U.S. Dist. LEXIS 8076 (S.D. Ohio May 6, 2002) . . . 196–197n220

Makar v. Health Care Corp. of Mid-Atlantic, 872 F.2d 80 (4th Cir. 1989) . . . 171n85

N

O

P

Q

R

S

T

U

V

W

Y

Z

Index

B

E

J

K

L

M

O

P

Q

R

S

T